12416

CYNICISM AND CHRISTIANITY IN ANTIQUITY

Cynicism and Christianity in Antiquity

Marie-Odile Goulet-Cazé

Translated by Christopher R. Smith

WILLIAM B. EERDMANS PUBLISHING COMPANY
GRAND RAPIDS, MICHIGAN

Wm. B. Eerdmans Publishing Co.
4035 Park East Court SE, Grand Rapids, Michigan 49546
www.eerdmans.com

Originally published as *Cynisme et christianisme dans l'Antiquité*
© Librairie Philosophique J. Vrin, Paris, 2015.
http://ww.vrin.fr

25 24 23 22 21 20 19   1 2 3 4 5 6 7

ISBN 978-0-8028-7555-6

Library of Congress Cataloging-in-Publication Data

A catalog record for this book is available from the Library of Congress.

CONTENTS

FOREWORD

In tracing the genealogy of the Valentinian heresy, Tertullian offered a tour of Greek philosophers—Plato, Zeno, Epicurus, Heraclitus, and Aristotle—at the end of which he posed his famous question, *quid ergo Athenis et Hierosolymis? quid academiae et ecclesiae?* What then does Athens have to do with Jerusalem, or the Academy with the Church?[1]

Although Tertullian passed over Diogenes in silence, his verdict on the famous Cynic would doubtless not have been any different. Yet as Marie-Odile Goulet-Cazé shows, the intersection of Christian thinking and Cynicism has had a very long and complex history. Tertullian would not have approved. Lucian of Samosata's Perigrinus of Parium, a would-be Cynic philosopher, had been welcomed by a group of Christians in Palestine, had composed commentaries on their writings, and was elected as their president. And some later Christians even considered themselves to be Cynics.

The engagement of the Jesus movement with Cynicism, or at least evidence of cynic-like thinking and practices, might have been even earlier. Gerd Theissen's celebrated model of itinerant radicalism as the earliest form of the Jesus movement, even if it did not claim a genealogical relationship with Greco-Roman Cynicism, had obvious affinities with the kinds of social practices represented by Cynicism.[2] Gerald Downing, an indefatigable advocate of the utility of comparison of the discourse of the Jesus movement with that of the likes of Diogenes of Sinope, Crates, Bion, and the later Roman Cynics, was able to adduce numerous possible contacts between Christ-

1. Tertullian, *De praescriptione haereticorum* 7.
2. Gerd Theissen, *Sociology of Early Palestinian Christianity*, trans. John Bowden (Philadelphia: Fortress Press, 1978).

followers and Cynics.[3] From a methodological point of view, Downing's work was important, since it moved well beyond the then-customary habit of locating early Christian thought almost exclusively in relation to Second Temple Judaism. Although Downing was sometimes tempted to make genealogical claims about influence, the more important advance was to think of the discursive field of the early Jesus movement as including not only Palestinian Judaism, viewed as an isolated island, but the entire intellectual heritage of the Eastern Mediterranean.

The developments that attracted the most attention, however, were the claims of Burton L. Mack and Leif E. Vaage, that Q, one of the earliest literary artifacts of the Jesus movement, could be viewed meaningfully as cynic-like,[4] and the even more provocative thesis of John Dominic Crossan that Jesus might be treated as a "peasant Jewish Cynic."[5] At least two dimensions of these hypotheses attracted criticism as well as praise. On the one hand, the advocates sometimes claimed that the Q folk and indeed Jesus himself lived in sufficiently close proximity to sites where Cynic philosophers were active— Tyre and Gadara—to know of such figures and to be influenced by them. On the other hand, even apart from the issue of genealogy and influence, one might nevertheless consider Jesus's social posture as cynic-like insofar as he engaged in vocal criticism and burlesque of prevailing social practices.

The reaction to the "Cynic hypothesis" is itself an interesting chapter of scholarship on Christian origins, since the vehemence with which the hypothesis was attacked verged on exorcism.[6] It seems that a very deep nerve had been touched by the allegation that Jesus (or the Q folk) might have been up to something a little more countercultural than many in the guild were willing to countenance. Jesus might be a prophet, but he surely was not comparable to a Cynic! Or so the argument went.

It is now almost twenty years since the height of the controversy over a Cynic Q or a Cynic Jesus, and perhaps it is time for a less fraught assessment

3. F. Gerald Downing, *Christ and the Cynics: Jesus and Other Radical Preachers in First-Century Tradition*, JSOT Manuals 4 (Sheffield: JSOT Press, 1988).

4. Burton L. Mack, *The Lost Gospel: The Book of Q & Christian Origins* (San Francisco: HarperSanFrancisco, 1993); Leif E. Vaage, *Galilean Upstarts: Jesus' First Followers according to Q* (Valley Forge, PA: Trinity Press International, 1994).

5. John Dominic Crossan, *The Historical Jesus: The Life of a Mediterranean Jewish Peasant* (San Francisco: Harper & Row, 1991).

6. See John S. Kloppenborg, "A Dog among the Pigeons: The 'Cynic Hypothesis' as a Theological Problem," in *From Quest to Quelle: Festschrift James M. Robinson*, ed. Jon Asgeirsson, Kristin de Troyer, and Marvin W. Meyer, BETL 146 (Leuven: Peeters, 1999), 73–117.

of the hypothesis. The signal importance of *Cynicism and Christianity in Antiquity* is to bring to bear on the discussion of Cynicism and its possible impact on the early Jesus movement the expertise of Marie-Odile Goulet-Cazé, who has been a major contributor to scholarship on Cynicism in its various forms since the early 1980s. She is not only the author of an important commentary on Diogenes Laertius Book 6 and many articles on Cynicism, but she is also the coeditor of two authoritative anthologies of works on Cynicism, *Le Cynisme ancien et ses prolongements*, edited with Richard Goulet (Paris: Presses universitaires de France, 1993), and *The Cynics: The Cynic Movement in Antiquity and Its Legacy*, edited with R. Bracht (Berkeley and Los Angeles: University of California Press, 1996). The translation of her 2014 *Cynisme et christianisme dans l'antiquité* (Paris: Libraire philosophique J. Vrin) now offers to English-speaking audiences not only a crisp and nuanced survey of Cynicism from its origins to its forms in the Roman Empire, but also a remarkably well-informed and critical engagement with scholarship on Q and the "Cynic hypothesis."

JOHN S. KLOPPENBORG
Department for the
Study of Religion
University of Toronto

ABBREVIATIONS

AC	*L'Antiquité classique*
ADPV	Abhandlungen des Deutschen Palästina-Vereins
ANRW	*Aufstieg und Niedergang der römischen Welt: Geschichte und Kultur Roms im Spiegel der neueren Forschung.* Part 2, *Principat.* Edited by Hildegard Temporini and Wolfgang Haase. Berlin: de Gruyter, 1972–
AR	*Archiv für Religionswissenschaft*
BETL	Bibliotheca Ephemeridum Theologicarum Lovaniensium
Bib	*Biblica*
BZ	*Biblische Zeitschrift*
CAG	Commentaria in Aristotelem Graeca
CCSL	Corpus Christianorum: Series Latina
CCTC	Cambridge Classical Texts and Commentaries
CErc	*Cronache Ercolanesi*
CJA	Christianity and Judaism in Antiquity
CSEL	Corpus Scriptorum Ecclesiasticorum Latinorum
CUF	Collection des Universités de France
CW	*Classical Weekly*
DPhA	*Dictionnaire des philosophes antiques.* Vols. 1–7 and supplement. Edited by Richard Goulet. Paris: CNRS Éditions, 1989–2018
FRLANT	Forschungen zur Religion und Literatur des Alten und Neuen Testaments
GCS	Die griechischen christlichen Schriftsteller der ersten (drei) Jahrhunderte
GFA	*Göttinger Forum für Altertumswissenschaft*
GRBS	*Greek, Roman, and Byzantine Studies*
HCS	Hellenistic Culture and Society

HTR	*Harvard Theological Review*
HTS	Harvard Theological Studies
ID	*Inscriptions de Délos*
IG	*Inscriptiones Graecae*
IGR	*Inscriptiones Graecae ad res Romanas pertinentes*
IosPE	*Inscriptiones antiquae orae septentrionalis Ponti Euxini graecae et latinae*
IScM	*Inscriptiones Daciae et Scythiae minoris antiquae*
JBL	*Journal of Biblical Literature*
JHS	*Journal of Hellenic Studies*
JQR	*Jewish Quarterly Review*
JR	*Journal of Religion*
JS	*Journal des savants*
JSJ	*Journal for the Study of Judaism*
JSJSup	Supplements to the Journal for the Study of Judaism
JSNT	*Journal for the Study of the New Testament*
JSNTSup	Journal for the Study of the New Testament Supplement Series
LCL	Loeb Classical Library
LEC	*Les Études Classiques*
MdB	*Le Monde de la Bible*
MUSJ	*Mélanges de l'Université Saint-Joseph* (Beirut)
NovT	*Novum Testamentum*
NovTSup	Supplements to Novum Testamentum
NPNF	Nicene and Post-Nicene Fathers
NTAbh	Neutestamentliche Abhandlungen
NTS	*New Testament Studies*
OEANE	*The Oxford Encyclopedia of Archaeology in the Near East*. Edited by Eric M. Meyers. 5 vols. New York: Oxford University Press, 1997
OGIS	*Orientis Graeci Inscriptiones Selectae*. Edited by Wilhelm Dittenberger. 2 vols. Leipzig: Herzel, 1903–1905
PG	Patrologia Graeca
PhA	Philosophia Antiqua
PW	*Paulys Real-Encyclopädie der classischen Altertumswissenschaft*. New edition by Georg Wissowa and Wilhelm Kroll. 50 vols. in 84 parts. Stuttgart: Metzler and Druckenmüller, 1894–1980
RAC	*Reallexikon für Antike und Christentum*. Edited by Theodor Klauser et al. Stuttgart: Hiersemann, 1950–
RB	*Revue biblique*

RhM	*Rheinisches Museum*
RHR	*Revue de l'histoire des religions*
RSPT	*Revue des sciences philosophiques et théologiques*
RSR	*Recherches de science religieuse*
SAC	Studies in Antiquity and Christianity
SBLDS	Society of Biblical Literature Dissertation Series
SBLSBS	Society of Biblical Literature Sources for Biblical Study
SBLTT	Society of Biblical Literature Texts and Translations
SBS	Stuttgarter Bibelstudien
SC	Sources chrétiennes
SEG	*Supplementum epigraphicum graecum*
SJ	Studia Judaica
SVF	*Stoicorum Veterum Fragmenta.* Hans Friedrich August von Arnim. 4 vols. Leipzig: Teubner, 1903–1924
TAPA	*Transactions of the American Philological Association*
TSK	*Theologische Studien und Kritiken*
VC	*Vigiliae Christianae*
VCSup	Supplements to Vigiliae Christianae
WUNT	Wissenschaftliche Untersuchungen zum Neuen Testament
ZÄSA	*Zeitschrift für ägyptische Sprache und Altertumskunde*
ZTK	*Zeitschrift für Theologie und Kirche*

INTRODUCTION

Many reasons warrant a study of the connection between Cynic philosophy and Christianity at its outset. Cynicism and Christianity promote similar ways of life founded on moral principles that appear, at first glance, to be identical in many respects, such as a concern for authenticity and for consistency between word and deed, and an indifference toward following social norms. Both movements promoted a form of asceticism based on poverty. Each in its own way sought to bring about a moral, rather than a political, revolution. And both claimed to have a universal message for everyone, regardless of race, gender, or social class. In the second century CE, Peregrinus Proteus claimed to be both a Cynic and a Christian at a certain point in his life. In the fourth century, Maximus Hero of Alexandria, though a Christian, similarly also identified himself as a Cynic. Since both held important positions in the ecclesiastical hierarchy, in different periods, we may conclude that the early church had no objection to Christians practicing a certain form of Cynicism. Several of the church fathers express a genuine admiration for Diogenes, including Clement of Alexandria, Origen, Basil of Caesarea, and Jerome. So it should come as no surprise that a link between Cynicism and Christianity has long been envisioned, primarily on the basis of the witness of the church fathers. But this desire to connect the two movements took a giant step forward in the 1980s when the Jesus Seminar (founded by Robert W. Funk and John D. Crossan in California in 1985) formulated what is known today as the "Cynic Hypothesis," according to which Jesus himself was a Cynic, in a somewhat simplified sense of the term. For some, the connection progressively became so evident that Bernhard Lang, in 2010, published in Munich a book titled *Jesus der Hund: Leben und Lehre eines jüdischen Kynikers* (Jesus the Dog: The Life and Teaching of a Jewish Cynic).[1]

The hypothesis of a Cynical or at least Cynic-like Jesus, like any interpretive hypothesis, deserves to be examined carefully and impartially. But in order to appreciate whether the characterization of Jesus as a Cynic is legitimate, we must recall how Cynic philosophy defined and presented itself, according to its own followers. This is not a simple task, given that various philosophers identified themselves as Cynics over the course of nearly ten centuries. And so we need to take into account the sociohistorical changes that occurred over that period, most notably at the turning point from the Hellenistic era to the Roman Empire. We must find a way to discern what these Cynics, who came from very diverse backgrounds and had varying degrees of education, had in common that allowed all of them to consider themselves disciples of the "Dog." Why would a Cynic never agree to be called a Stoic, and vice versa? But why, at the same time, was it possible under the Roman Empire to confuse Stoics with Cynics, and Christians with Cynics? Before we try to connect Jesus and his movement, as well as the church fathers, with Cynicism, we have to have an accurate understanding of this philosophy that is overall quite complex, even if its theoretical foundations are somewhat basic. The extent of its legacy is astonishing, suggesting that Cynicism does indeed contain some universal element that speaks to everybody. Diogenes was one of Montaigne's favorite models. The Enlightenment philosophers, from Pierre Bayle to d'Alembert, from Wieland to Rousseau, from Voltaire to Diderot, were fascinated by this "Socrates gone mad" whom Plato spoke of. For his part, Nietzsche must have been strongly influenced by Diogenes, the "shameless buffoon," the "scientific satyr," from whom he borrowed his *Umwertung aller Werthe*, his "transvaluation of all values." Cynicism also left traces within Christianity well after the monasticism of the early centuries. Its spirit reemerged especially in the mendicant orders such as the Franciscans, Capuchins, and Dominicans. In our own day, Emil Cioran, Michel Foucault, Heinrich Niehues-Pröbsting, and Peter Sloterdijk have all heard the call of Cynicism. But this universality can also lead to some confusion. That is why we must begin by defining and describing the Cynicism of Diogenes and the one of the imperial period as accurately as as possible.

---

1. Bernhard Lang, *Jesus der Hund: Leben und Lehre eines jüdischen Kynikers* (Munich: Beck, 2010).

In a second part, this study will undertake to catalog all the witnesses found in the ancient literary tradition that suggest specific historical contacts between Cynicism and Judaism. Such a study is necessary not just because Cynicism exerted a real influence on writers such as Philo of Alexandria but also because its discrete presence can be detected within Judaism from the Septuagint to the Talmud. This study is equally indispensable for establishing whether it is imaginable that a young Galilean Jew like Jesus could have come into contact with Cynicism in one way or another.[2]

However, the key element of this investigation will be a study of any possible relationship between Cynicism and the Jesus movement, and then of the historically well-attested relationships between Cynicism and Christianity. Why do contemporary researchers, despite the absence of any historical testimony proving that Jesus might have ever even met any Cynics, want to turn him into a Cynic or assimilate him to Cynicism? How are we to evaluate the arguments that the adherents of this "Cynic Hypothesis" have developed? Finally, how are we to make sense of the astonishing diversity of attitudes among Christians, ranging from the bitterest criticism of Cynic behavior to sincere admiration of it, and of the way that some people belonged to both communities? Christian monks did not hesitate to wear the coarse garment (τρίβων) of the Cynics, and they practiced a radical asceticism themselves.

2. I have already sketched out the broad lines of this research in the article "Kynismus" in *RAC* 22:631–87, esp. 641–49.

1. Cynicism in the Hellenistic Era and under the Roman Empire

Anyone trying to understand Cynicism faces an acute problem of sources. Nothing, or practically nothing, of ancient Cynic literature survives today. The very nature of Cynic philosophy, which was founded more on practice than on theory, partially explains why texts with doctrinal content are rare.[1] Representatives of the movement are known to us primarily through chreias and anecdotes, transmitted through Greek and Latin literature, whose historical accuracy is impossible to verify.[2] Diogenes Laertius preserves a large number of chreias in book 6 of his *Lives of Philosophers*, which is dedicated to Cynic philosophers.[3] Among the documents inspired by Cynicism that have come down to us, special mention should be made of the fragments by

1. Fragments from and testimonies about Cynic philosophers have been collected by Gabriele Giannantoni, *Socratis et Socraticorum Reliquiae*, Elenchos 18 (Naples: Bibliopolis, 1990), 2:137–589, 4:195–583 (notes). Many Cynical texts are translated in Léonce Paquet, *Les cyniques grecs: Fragments et témoignages*, 2nd ed., Philosophica 35 (Ottawa: Presses de l'Université d'Ottawa, 1988), and an abridged version in the series Le Livre de Poche (Paris: Librairie générale française, 1992); in Georg Luck, *Die Weisheit der Hunde: Texte der antiken Kyniker in deutscher Übersetzung* (Stuttgart: Alfred Kröner, 1997); and in Robert Dobbin, *The Cynic Philosophers from Diogenes to Julian* (London: Penguin Classics, 2013).

2. There is also an entire tradition of sayings by Diogenes in the Arabic-language *gnomologia*. Cf. Oliver Overwien, *Die Sprüche des Kynikers Diogenes in der griechischen und arabischen Überlieferung*, Hermes Einzelschriften 92 (Stuttgart: Franz Steiner Verlag, 2005).

3. See the recent critical edition *Diogenes Laertius: Lives of Eminent Philosophers*, ed. Tiziano Dorandi, CCTC 50 (Cambridge: Cambridge University Press, 2013). English translations are adapted from Robert D. Hicks, *Diogenes Laertius*, 2 vols., LCL (Cambridge, MA: Harvard University Press, 1925). I gave a French translation of book 6 in "Diogène Laërce, Livre VI: Introduction, traduction et notes," in *Diogène Laërce, Vies et doctrines des philosophes illustres*, ed. Marie-Odile Goulet-Cazé, 2nd ed. (Paris: Le Livre de Poche, 1999), 655–772.

the poet Cercidas of Megalopolis (ca. 290–after 217) and the extracts from the *Diatribes* of Teles, a Cynic teacher from the middle of the third century BCE who transmitted a number of fragments from Bion of Borysthenes, who had been at one time a Cynic philosopher. From the imperial period, long extracts from *Charlatans Exposed* by Oenomaus of Gadara, written in the second century, have been preserved by Eusebius of Caesarea.[4] These are especially significant because of their length. Other texts that deal with Cynicism come from its opponents, such as Philodemus the Epicurean, Lucian of Samosata (though in his case the relationship with Cynicism is more complicated), and some church fathers who were hostile to such a philosophy. But we may also encounter writings by authors who conceived of Cynicism in idealized terms, in light of their own personal convictions. This next category would include Epictetus and his Περὶ Κυνισμοῦ; Dio Chrysostom, who was a Cynic himself for a while and who presents a Diogenes transformed into an acceptable moral model for his audience;[5] Maximus of Tyre, who considers in his *Dissertation* 36 whether it is right to prefer the Cynic way of life; and the emperor Julian, who sets forth his personal vision of Cynicism in two of his *Discourses*. Finally, a distinct collection has also come down to us, the body of pseudepigraphal letters inspired by Cynicism and attributed to Diogenes and Crates as well as to Socrates and the Socratics. These sources must be used with caution, even when they are not inspired by a hostile or idealizing point of view. It is necessary to recognize, for example, that the doctrinal account given in the doxographies in book 6 of Diogenes Laertius has been contaminated by a Stoic viewpoint that has distorted some theoretical aspects of original Cynicism.[6]

It is also fair to ask whether, over the course of so many centuries, Cynicism actually remained coherent, or whether, rather than speaking of *Cynicism*, it would not be more appropriate to speak of the *Cynicisms* embodied by various philosophers who claimed that label. A philosophy based on scant

4. Eusebius, *Preparation for the Gospel* 5.18.6–36.5 and 6.7.1–42.

5. Dio Chrysostom, *Discourses 4* (*Kingship 4*), *6* (*Diogenes*), *8* (*Virtue*), *9* (*Isthmian Discourse*), and *10* (*Servants*). Cf. Francis Jouan, "Le Diogène de Dion Chrysostome," in *Le cynisme ancien et ses prolongements*, ed. Marie-Odile Goulet-Cazé and Richard Goulet (Paris: Presses Universitaires de France, 1993), 381–97.

6. Cf. Marie-Odile Goulet-Cazé, "Un syllogisme stoïcien sur la loi dans la doxographie de Diogène le Cynique: A propos de Diogène Laërce VI 72," *RhM* 125 (1982): 214–40; Goulet-Cazé, *L'ascèse cynique: Un commentaire de Diogène Laërce VI 70–71* [1986], 2nd ed., Histoire des doctrines de l'antiquité classique 10 (Paris: Librarie Philosophique J. Vrin, 2001), 210–20.

doctrinal sources, which basically boils down to sayings and anecdotes, and which expresses itself through slogans such as "falsifying the currency" or taking the "short path to virtue," could be lived out in various ways by strong personalities. However, even though Cynicism doesn't offer a systematic framework of thought, it must be acknowledged that over the centuries, behind its anecdotes, sayings, and slogans, a coherent moral inspiration can be perceived, one based on an ascetic practice and expressed through a distinct manner of living, the βίος κυνικός.

The History of the Movement

The Context of Its Birth

Cynicism was born in Greece during the fourth century BCE with Diogenes of Sinope, nicknamed "The Dog," and his disciples. The movement continued down to the end of the fifth century CE. The last known Cynic philosopher, Salustius, was connected in Athens with the circle of the Neoplatonist Proclus. We cannot paint the whole picture of the historical context in which Cynicism first appeared, but we can appreciate the radical historical change that took place then by noting two significant dates—the death of Socrates in 399 and that of Diogenes in 323 (on the same day as Alexander, according to legend)—and some historical milestones. In 405 the Spartan victory at Aigos Potamos put an end to Athenian hegemony. In 360 Philip II ascended to the throne of Macedonia, and at Chaeronea in 338 he inflicted a crushing defeat on Thebes and Athens that effectively completed the decline of the Greek polis. Then, from 334 to 323, came the extraordinary campaign under Alexander that brought the Macedonians to the banks of the Hyphasis, a tributary of the Indus. Alexander's expedition turned the Greeks' traditional perception of themselves as citizens of a given city upside down. Once the benchmark of the city as a political community had been weakened or even destroyed, the need for self-affirmation through a heightened individualism became greater and greater. At the same time, on a collective scale, the idea that the traditional distinction between Greeks and Barbarians was no longer meaningful provided an occasion to rethink the traditional value system. Of course, we must not be so naive as to think that the reappraisal of the Greek polis system sufficiently explains the appearance of the Cynical protest movement. But it cannot be denied that the sociopolitical context played a significant role in its appearance.

During the time of Diogenes, Greek society displayed all the opulence of wealth, as is evident from the sayings and anecdotes that portray Diogenes lashing out at the luxurious tables of his contemporaries, their banqueting excesses and their gluttony.[7] Diogenes himself was the son of a banker in Sinope, a city in Pontus that was very active commercially and quite open to the outside world. There he likely engaged in serious studies, which would explain his prolific (but unfortunately lost) literary production, illustrated by the large number of titles reported by Diogenes Laertius. He would not have felt like a total stranger when he arrived in Athens. But Greece in the fourth century, as we can tell from the sayings and anecdotes in book 6 of Diogenes Laertius, was a society of contrasts. The gap continued to increase between a brilliant and refined civilization that benefited only a few and a world of the disinherited whose number kept growing. Poor citizens mingled with slaves—many of whom being former victims of piracy—and exiles. This social and political context explains, in part, the universal scope of ancient Cynicism's morality, its cosmopolitanism, its portrayal of law in opposition to nature, and its conception of equality among all people. Diogenes focuses on the individual rather than the citizen and addresses everyone he encounters: rich and poor, citizens and slaves, men and women.

The First Generations of Cynics

Colorful figures exemplify Cynicism at its origins.[8] But a difficulty arises right from the start: Who was the founder of the movement? Was it Antisthenes (ca. 445–after 366), who, after studying with the rhetorician Gorgias, became one of the best-known disciples of Socrates and was given the surname "True Dog" (Ἁπλοκύων)?[9] Or was it Diogenes of Sinope, who lived in

---

7. Cf., e.g., Diogenes Laertius, *Lives* 6.44, 51, 53; Stobaeus, *Anthology* 3.6.37 (Hense 3:294.10–12) and 3.6.40 (Hense 3:295.4–5); Pseudo-Diogenes, *Letter 28*, 5–6.

8. Cf. "Répertoire des philosophes cyniques connus," in Goulet-Cazé, *L'ascèse cynique*, 231–49, reprinted in R. Bracht Branham and Marie-Odile Goulet-Cazé, eds., *The Cynics: The Cynic Movement in Antiquity and Its Legacy*, HCS 23 (Berkeley: University of California Press, 1996), 389–413. In addition, all Cynic philosophers have an entry in *DPhA*. Some Cynic philosophers are sketched by Klaus Döring, "Sokrates, die Sokratiker und die von ihnen begründeten Traditionen," in *Die Philosophie der Antike*, vol. 2.1, *Sophistik, Sokrates, Sokratik, Mathematik, Medizin*, ed. Hellmut Flashar, Grundriß der Geschichte der Philosophie (Basle: Schwabe, 1998), 267–321; Döring, *Die Kyniker*, Faszination Philosophie (Bamberg: Buchner, 2006).

9. The exact meaning of this surname, cited in Diogenes Laertius, *Lives* 6.13, is difficult

a large jar,[10] who searched with a lantern in broad daylight for a (real) man,[11] and who, according to legend, one day told a flabbergasted young Alexander to step aside and stop blocking the sunlight when he was sunning himself at the gymnasium of Craneion in Corinth?[12] Ancient tradition, which is illustrated by later authors such as Epictetus, Dio Chrysostom, Aelian, Diogenes Laertius, Stobaeus, and the *Suda*, leans toward Antisthenes, whose disciple Diogenes was. But some ancient authors suggest that the role Antisthenes actually played in the birth of the Cynic movement was overemphasized by certain Stoics who wanted to trace their pedigree back to Socrates[13] and so declared that Zeno was a disciple of Crates, Crates of Diogenes, and Diogenes of Antisthenes, creating out of thin air a lineage that ran from Socrates directly to Zenon via Antisthenes, Diogenes, and Crates. The authors of the *Successions of Philosophers*, who were devotees of pedigrees,[14] and the biographers, who were highly interested in master-disciple relationships,[15] would have hastened to pick up this lineage, since it made their task of reconstructing the history of the Socratic schools that much easier. However,

---

to determine. It could mean "Outspoken Dog," an allusion to Cynic frankness, or "Natural Dog," meaning one whose manners were based on the demands of nature rather than on social conventions, and eventually "Dog with a Simple Cloak," because of the famous τρίβων.

10. Cf. Diogenes Laertius, *Lives* 6.23.

11. Cf. Diogenes Laertius, *Lives* 6.41.

12. Cf. Diogenes Laertius, *Lives* 6.38.

13. Cf. Philodemus, *On the Stoics* 3, col. 13.1–9 (Tiziano Dorandi, "Filodemo, Gli Stoici [PHerc. 155 e 339]," *CErc* 12 [1982]: 91–133, here 101).

14. Thus, the Peripatetic Sotion (second century BCE) seems to have placed the Cynics in book 7 of his *Diadochai* (cf. Diogenes Laertius, *Lives* 6.80; Fritz Wehrli, *Sotion, Die Schule des Aristoteles: Texte und Kommentar*, Supplementband 2 [Basle: Schwabe, 1978], fr. 19) and the Stoics in book 8 (cf. Diogenes Laertius, *Lives* 7.183; Wehrli, *Sotion*, fr. 22), which can be harmonized reasonably well with the hypothesis of a link between the two movements. The same succession but with different book numbers is in books 6–7 in Diogenes Laertius.

15. See, for instance, Diocles of Magnesia (first century BCE), who wrote a work titled *On the Lives of Philosophers* as well as an *Overview of Philosophers* and who favored the idea of a lineage that ran from Antisthenes to Diogenes and then to Crates. (Cf. Diogenes Laertius, *Lives* 6.13, where Diocles affirms that Antisthenes was the first to fold his cloak double and that he had a walking stick and a knapsack, and Diogenes Laertius, *Lives* 6.87, where he presents Diogenes as the one to whom Crates is indebted for his conversion to philosophy.) It was certainly from Diocles that Diogenes Laertius borrowed such a lineage. See Marie-Odile Goulet-Cazé, "Le livre VI de Diogène Laërce: Analyse de sa structure et réflexions méthodologiques," *ANRW* 2.36.6:3881–4048, esp. 3936–51, where it is suggested that Diocles is dependent on the section devoted to ethics in the work by the Stoic Apollodorus of Seleucia titled *Introductions to Dogmas*.

modern historians, starting with D. R. Dudley,[16] have offered many arguments, especially from chronology and numismatics, challenging the idea that Diogenes, after his exile from Sinope, could have been in Athens at the same time as Antisthenes. They have advanced the idea that the founder of Cynicism was not Antisthenes but Diogenes himself. But in recent years this questioning of the ancient tradition has itself been reconsidered, and the tendency has been to regard Antisthenes once again as the founder of Cynicism.[17] In the absence of absolute certainty, everyone can at least agree on the fact that Antisthenes played a decisive role in the emergence of Cynicism, if only through the influence his writings had on the earliest Cynics, but that the person who actually launched the Cynic movement, who set its direction and became its symbol, was instead Diogenes, who was nicknamed the "Dog." But we shall eventually discover that the task of identifying the founder of Cynicism is in fact more complicated than the simple alternative of Antisthenes versus Diogenes would lead us to believe, and that in antiquity others were also thought deserving of the title.

The lives of several outstanding representatives of Cynicism will be briefly described, not out of anecdotal interest, but because they are in themselves testimonies of the βίος κυνικός, the Cynic way of life. It makes no sense to speak of Cynicism in an abstract manner, apart from the behavior and actions of those who lived according to its precepts, given the nature of this philosophy. Cynicism is unquestionably the philosophical movement that most authentically embodied a way of life in which actions had to be consistent with words.

16. Donald R. Dudley, *A History of Cynicism: From Diogenes to the 6th Century A.D.* (London: Bloomsbury, 1937), 1–16; Giannantoni, *Socratis et Socraticorum Reliquiae*, 4:223–33, 423–33.

17. A recent study by Pedro Pablo Fuentes González, "En defensa del encuentro entre dos Perros, Antístenes y Diógenes: Historia de una tensa amistad," *Cuadernos di filología clásica: Estudios griegos e indoeuropeos* 23 (2013): 225–67, offers solid arguments in favor of the traditional theory according to which Antisthenes was the master of Diogenes and the founder of Cynicism. I have also advanced an argument that supports the theory that Diogenes could have become acquainted with Antisthenes after this one had already become a Cynic, in Branham and Goulet-Cazé, *The Cynics*, appendix B, "Who Was the First Dog?," 414–15: contrary to what was previously believed, it was Antisthenes and not Diogenes whom Aristotle would describe as "The Dog" in *Rhetoric* 3.10 (1411a 24–25). The question is taken up in Marie-Odile Goulet-Cazé, *Le cynisme, une philosophie antique*, Textes et Traditions 29 (Paris: Librairie Philosophique J. Vrin, 2017), 607–30, where I conclude that Antisthenes, the "Real Dog" (Ἁπλοκύων), was the initiator of a way of life but not yet a "cynical" philosopher (Κυνικός).

Diogenes of Sinope

Most of the details of Diogenes's biography are provided in book 6 (20–23 and 74–79) of Diogenes Laertius.

Diogenes was exiled from Sinope to Athens, probably because, as he says himself in his *Pordalos*, he was guilty of debasing the currency in his native city.[18] Once in Athens, according to tradition, he became a disciple of Antisthenes, adopted the clothing that would become emblematic of Cynic philosophy, and set about to practice a life of frugality. He later left Athens, perhaps because Antisthenes had died, and while sailing for Aegina he was captured by pirates, taken to Crete, and sold into slavery. A rich Corinthian, Xeniades, bought him and made him his children's tutor. It's not known whether from then on he lived only in Corinth, or whether he divided his time between Athens and Corinth. In any event, he must have traveled often, because various anecdotes place him in many different cities in Greece and Asia Minor: Megara, Olympia, Myndus, Samothrace, Sparta, Aegina, Rhodes, Miletus, Cyzicus, Salamis, and Eleusis. This is the basis of the image of the Cynic philosopher wandering from city to city, as described in the couplet he liked to recite: "Without city, without home, having no country / Beggar, vagabond, living from day to day." Various stories are in circulation regarding the circumstances and place of his death, which occurred when he was quite old. (Was it in Corinth, in Athens, or even in Olympia during the games?) It's possible that, in his desire to return to nature, he ate a raw octopus that gave him cholera. But according to the meliambic poems of Cercidas the Cynic of Megalopolis, he asphyxiated himself by holding his breath. Other accounts say that he suffered a fatal bite from dogs who were

---

18. Cf. Diogenes Laertius, *Lives* 6.20–21. This episode, which played a decisive role in the birth of the Cynic movement and in the development of Diogenes's philosophical thought, is known in multiple versions. According to Diocles, Diogenes went into exile because his father, who was entrusted with state funds, adulterated the coinage. But according to Eubulides, it was Diogenes himself who was guilty of forgery and he was exiled along with his father. According to another source, anonymous this time, the workers who manufactured the coinage in Sinope persuaded him to commit this deception, as he had become an *epimeletos* or administrator of the mint. Before deciding what to do, Diogenes went to Delphi to consult the oracle of Apollo, which "granted him the public mint." On the strength of this response from the oracle, whose symbolic meaning he failed to grasp, he altered the coinage and was caught. Finally, another source claims it was his father who gave him the coinage but that it was Diogenes who debased it. His father died in prison and Diogenes went to question the oracle to ask what he needed to do to become famous, and the oracle told him to "debase the currency."

fighting over an octopus, or that he was taken with fever when he went to watch the Olympic Games. The accounts of his burial are also varied, and disturbing. Was he buried in Corinth, beside the gate that led to the Isthmus? Or was he, supposedly according to his final wishes, left unburied so that the wild beasts could eat him, or covered only with a bit of dust, or thrown into the Ilissus River (in Athens) as food for the fish?

Tradition attributes a number of works to Diogenes whose authenticity is sometimes questioned, primarily dialogues (including a notorious *Republic*), seven tragedies, and some letters.[19]

Diogenes had disciples;[20] the best known are Crates of Thebes, Monimus of Syracuse, and Stilpo (who is best known for later directing the school at Megara). But Cynicism itself never functioned as a "school" that was situated in a particular place and taught within an institutional setting. The movement intentionally placed itself outside the traditional context of scholarly life: there was no fixed location for teaching, no succession of scholars, no courses or conferences, only disruptive "barkings" hurled at the open sky in the most-visited public places by strong personalities who knew how to give their words extra weight through the testimony of their actions and way of life.

Crates of Thebes

The best-known disciple of Diogenes was unquestionably Crates of Thebes (ca. 368/365–288/285 BCE), a figure who was just as exceptional as his master, but who had a very different style.[21] Diogenes was uncompromising both with himself and with others; he led a life that was heroic in many respects, based on poverty and asceticism. His difficult character, caustic language, and deliberately aggressive behavior won him many enemies. Crates, by contrast, though he had just as much moral conviction and practiced just as severe an asceticism, had a more humane manner and was closer to his fellow citizens. While people admired Diogenes, the "heavenly dog," they nevertheless feared him; by contrast, those who admired Crates, the "dear hunchback," loved him.

---

19. Cf. Diogenes Laertius, *Lives* 6.80, where two lists of works are provided, one anonymous and the other from Sotion. They have only four titles in common.

20. Cf. Diogenes Laertius, *Lives* 6.75–76 and 6.82–85.

21. For the life of Crates, see Diogenes Laertius, *Lives* 6.85–93 and 6.98.

Crates was launched toward Cynic philosophy when he saw Telephus, the son of Heracles, portrayed in a tragedy in a miserable plight.²² The son of a wealthy family in Thebes, he gave away all his possessions in order to consecrate himself to Cynicism, either by converting his property and goods into money and distributing it to his fellow citizens, or else by abandoning his fields to become sheep pastures and throwing his money into the sea. He then spoke this famous phrase: "Crates sets free Crates of Thebes." His disability—he was a hunchback—drew mockery when he exercised at the gymnasium, but he was indifferent to δόξα and he didn't bother about it. He married Hipparchia of Maroneia in Thrace, who went so far as to threaten to kill herself if her parents wouldn't let her marry him. He led a true "dog's life" with her, including a "dog's marriage" (ἡ κυνογαμία) consummated in public.²³ They had a son whom Crates brought to a brothel, telling him that this was the wedding he was offering him, and a daughter whom he gave in marriage for a trial period of thirty days. Crates died at an old age, and he was buried in Boeotia. He was given an evocative nickname, the "Door-opener,"²⁴ because he would go into people's homes to admonish them with the Cynic message. But he was able to show great compassion, and he was revered as a *lar familiaris*, an arbiter of family quarrels.²⁵

Like Diogenes, Crates wrote literary works. His writings are described by Diogenes Laertius and Julian as light poetry (παίγνια);²⁶ he has to his credit particularly tragedies, elegies, parodies of Homer, a poem titled "Knapsack," a hymn to frugality, a daybook, letters, and a eulogy to the lentil. His writings, whose surviving fragments indicate the talents of their author, must have been in a style characteristic of Cynic literature, because Pseudo-Demetrius of Phalerum considered Crates's way of writing an illustration of the κυνικὸς τρόπος in literary matters.²⁷

22. Cf. Diogenes Laertius, *Lives* 6.87. Cynicism saw itself in continuity with Heracles (i.e., Hercules) and his twelve labors. It regarded Telephus, the son of Heracles, as an embodiment of the Cynic way of life (see Pseudo-Diogenes, *Letter 34* [*To Olympias*]; Eike Müseler, ed., *Die Kynikerbriefe: Kritische Ausgabe mit deutscher Übersetzung*, Studien zur Geschichte und Kultur des Altertums 1.7 [Paderborn: F. Schöningh, 1994], 48–51).

23. *Suda*, s.v. Κράτης, K 2341 (Ada Adler, ed., *Suidae Lexicon* [Leipzig: Teubner, 1928–1938], 3:182.14–15); Clement of Alexandria, *Miscellanies* 4.19.122.1; Theodoret, *Therapeutic for Hellenic Maladies* 12.49.

24. Diogenes Laertius, *Lives* 6.86; Plutarch, *Table Talk* 2.1.6 (632e).

25. Apuleius, *Florida* 22.1–4.

26. Diogenes Laertius, *Lives* 6.85; Julian, *Discourse 9* (*To the Uneducated Cynics*), 17 (199c).

27. Pseudo-Demetrius of Phalerum, *On Style* 170.259.

Crates had disciples of his own: his brother Pasicles, known primarily afterward as a Megarian philosopher; Monimus of Syracuse, who was formerly the slave of a banker in Corinth and had been a disciple of Diogenes; Metrocles of Maroneia, the brother of Hipparchia, who studied under Theophrastus before following Crates; Hipparchia herself; and also two future Stoics, Zeno of Citium and his successor Cleanthes.[28] We should probably add to these names Theombrotus, Cleomenes, and the celebrated Menippus of Gadara, who had also been a slave, and who had a decisive literary influence on writers including Varro, Seneca, Petronius, Apuleius, and many others.[29] The case of Hipparchia (fl. 336/333), the only known female Cynic philosopher—apart from the courtesan Nicion, nicknamed the "Dog-Fly," a character in the *Banquet of the Cynics* by Parmeniscus, cited by Athenaeus— deserves specific attention.

Hipparchia of Maroneia

Hipparchia was introduced to Crates by her brother Metrocles, and she became his wife.[30] From then on, she went everywhere with him. The two Cynic philosophers consummated their marriage in public, causing great embarrassment to Zeno, who, completely mortified, tried to hide them with his cloak.[31] Renouncing the traditional role of Greek women, who were usually confined to female apartments and required to keep silent, she went unhesitatingly to banquets with her husband. It was at a banquet in the home of Lysimachus, one of Alexander's generals, that she met Theodorus the Atheist and was able to confound him with a sophism. Apparently caught off guard, Theodorus found no way to reply but tried to remove Hipparchia's cloak. She didn't let this inappropriate action bother her; instead, when Theodorus asked, alluding to a verse from Euripides's *Bacchantes* (v. 1236), "Is this she who quit woof and warp and comb and loom?" She replied, "It is I, Theodorus—but do you suppose that I have been ill-advised about myself, if instead of wasting further time upon the loom I spent it in education?"[32]

---

28. See Marie-Odile Goulet-Cazé, "Cratès de Thèbes," *DPhA* 2: esp. 498.

29. Cf. Marie-Odile Goulet-Cazé, "Une liste de disciples de Cratès le Cynique en Diogène Laërce 6, 95," *Hermes* 114 (1986): 247–52.

30. Cf. Diogenes Laertius, *Lives* 6.96.

31. Apuleius, *Florida* 14.

32. Diogenes Laertius, *Lives* 6.97.

In addition to practicing philosophy, Hipparchia wrote treatises. The *Suda* lists the following titles: *Philosophical Hypotheses, Epicheiremes,* and *Questions,* addressed to Theodore the Atheist.[33] Eight pseudepigraphal letters are addressed to her, seven from Crates and one from Diogenes (*Letter* 3). Several of these insist on the equality of men and women and encourage women to devote themselves to philosophy.

Menippus of Gadara

Menippus (late fourth century to mid-third century BCE) was born in Gadara,[34] a city to the south of Lake Tiberias, and was a Phoenician according to Diogenes Laertius, *Lives* 6.99. He played a unique role in the Cynic movement because of his extraordinary literary influence.[35]

Menippus was the slave of a man named Baton who lived in Pontus. He later won his freedom, and by "begging in an unwholesome way, out of the love of money," he acquired the means to become a citizen of Thebes. There he probably met Crates. He was a money lender, and this, if the Peripatetic philosopher Hermippus is to be believed, enabled him to amass a colossal fortune and also earned him the nickname "Lender by the Day." But he fell victim to a scam, lost everything, and in despair hanged himself. These biographical details, however, reported in Diogenes Laertius, *Lives* 6.99–100, are doubtful. They don't correspond with the picture that Varro gives of the man—*[Menippus], ille, nobilis quondam canis*[36]—nor with the figure whom Lucian, in *The Fugitives* 11, sets alongside the greatest Cynics, Antisthenes, Diogenes, and Crates.

A prolific author, Menippus produced veritable best sellers, including *Necromancy, Letters Artificially Composed as If by the Gods,* and *The Sale of Diogenes.* Described by Strabo as a σπουδογέλοιος,[37] "one who uses humor seriously," Menippus employed both the dialogue and letter genres for comic purposes. It is often believed that he wrote satires that inspired Varro's *Menippean Satires.* However, satire as a literary genre

---

33. *Suda,* s.v. Ἱππαρχία, I 517 (Adler 2:657.15–17).
34. Cf. Strabo, *Geography* 16.2.29.
35. See Marie-Odile Goulet-Cazé, "Ménippe de Gadara," *DPhA* 4:467–75.
36. Varro, *The Tomb of Menippus,* in Nonius Marcellus, *De compendiosa doctrina* 4, Mercier, p. 333.33 (Lindsay 1.525 = Bücheler frag. 516).
37. Strabo, *Geography* 16.2.29.

probably originated with Varro himself.[38] Nevertheless, *prosimetrum*, the mixture of prose and verse that characterizes the genre, can already be found in Menippus.[39] This author, whom Marcus Aurelius included among the "arrogant mockers of the perishable and ephemeral life of man,"[40] intended to point out the farcical side of the human comedy and to ridicule traditional values in a spirit that was both satirical and joking at the same time.

Bion, Cercidas, Teles

In the third century, two atypical figures, both with clearly strong personalities, appear within the Cynic movement. One of them, Bion of Borysthenes (ca. 335–245 BCE), the son of a courtesan and a freedman who sold salted fish, had a thoroughly eclectic philosophical training that led him successively from the Academy to the Cynics, then to the Cyrenaics and finally to the Peripatetics.[41] The other, Cercidas of Megalopolis (ca. 290–after 217 BCE), a friend of Aratos of Sicyon, was at once a statesman, a general, a legislator, and a poet.[42] Thanks to Stobaeus, we also know of a humble professor of philosophy, Teles, who lived in the third century in Athens and Megara and taught a group of young people. His *Diatribes* are the earliest vestiges we have of what would become for modern philosophy the celebrated "Cynico-Stoic diatribe." They preserve for us the sayings of several philosophers from the first generations of Cynicism,

38. The only ancient testimony to satires by Menippus comes from the first-century grammarian M. Valerius Probus, commenting on Virgil, *Bucolics* 6.31, and alluding to Varro (Hermann Hagen, "Appendix Serviana," in *Servii Grammatici qui feruntur in Vergilii carmina commentarii* 3 [Leipzig: Teubner, 1902], 336.24). It's possible that the characterization of Menippus's writings as "satires" was suggested to Probus by the title of Varro's work *Saturae Menippae*.

39. Cf. Lucian, *Double Indictment* 33.

40. Marcus Aurelius, *Meditations* 6.47 (trans. George Long).

41. Cf. Jan Fredrik Kindstrand, *Bion of Borysthenes: A Collection of the Fragments with Introduction and Commentary*, Acta Universitatis Upsaliensis, Studia Graeca Upsaliensia 11 (Uppsala: Almqvist & Wiksell, 1976).

42. Cf. Enrico Livrea, *Studi Cercidei (P. Oxy. 1082)*, Papyrologische Texte und Abhandlungen 37 (Bonn: R. Habelt, 1986); Liana Lomiento, *Cercidas*, Lyricorum Graecorum quae exstant 10 (Rome: Gruppo Editoriale Internazionale, 1993); Juan L. López Cruces, *Les Méliambes de Cercidas de Mégalopolis: Politique et tradition littéraire*, Classical and Byzantine Monographs 32 (Amsterdam: A. M. Hakkert, 1995).

including Diogenes, Crates, Metrocles, and especially Bion, who was Teles's favorite model.[43]

An Eclipse?

The Cynic tradition seems to have undergone a sort of eclipse during the last two centuries BCE. Some scholars, such as E. Zeller and J. Bernays, consider this to have been a total eclipse. Others, such as D. R. Dudley, explain that Cynicism actually lived on in obscurity throughout this period.[44] Were there no strong personalities capable of an asceticism like that of Diogenes? Was there an incompatibility between Rome, which was steadily becoming the Mistress of the World, and the Cynical spirit, an explosive mix of seriousness and mockery that called all established values into question? Whatever the case, we actually can detect the movement's survival in the works of Meleager of Gadara (fl. 96 BCE), author of the famous *Garland* of epigrams, which made him one of the poets best represented in the *Palatine Anthology*.

Thanks to three autobiographical poems in the *Garland*,[45] we know that Meleager was born in Gadara, that he lived in Tyre, and that he died at an old age in Cos. Athenaeus classifies him as a Cynic.[46] During his youth, Meleager came under the literary influence of Menippus, who was from Gadara himself, and so it is believed that his work *The Graces*, which Athenaeus cites,[47] is Menippean in its inspiration. He also wrote a *Banquet*[48] and a work whose tone is typically Cynical: "A comparison of pureed lentils with whole lentils" (Λεκίθου καὶ Φακῆς Σύγκρισις).[49] Moreover, he displays a cosmopolitanism that's consistent with Cynicism.[50] However, it appears that under the influence of his lover Myiscos, he renounced that philosophy.[51]

---

43. Cf. Pedro Pablo Fuentes González, *Les diatribes de Télès*, Histoire des doctrines de l'Antiquité classique 23 (Paris: Librairie Philosophique J. Vrin, 1998).

44. On these divergences in points of view, see Margarethe Billerbeck, *Der Kyniker Demetrius: Ein Beitrag zur Geschichte der frühkaiserzeitlichen Popularphilosophie*, PhA 36 (Leiden: Brill, 1979), 3–5.

45. *Palatine Anthology* 7.417–19.

46. Athenaeus, *The Dinner Sophists* 11.502c.

47. Athenaeus, *The Dinner Sophists* 4.157b.

48. Athenaeus, *The Dinner Sophists* 11.502c.

49. Athenaeus, *The Dinner Sophists* 4.157b.

50. *Palatine Anthology* 7.417.5.

51. *Palatine Anthology* 12.23, 101, 117.

The survival of Cynicism may also be seen in the pseudepigraphal *Letters*, some of which may date from this same period.[52] Beyond this, in the middle of the first century BCE, a prominent political leader with a brusque and violent temperament, the senator Marcus Favonius, in his infatuation with Cato the Younger (ἐραστὴς γεγονὼς Κάτωνος) made statements that Plutarch portrayed as Cynical in their bluntness.[53] Brutus, whom he's pestering in Plutarch's narrative, doesn't hesitate to treat him as a ἁπλοκύων, a "true dog" (the same nickname that Antisthenes was given), and a ψευδοκύων, "fake Cynic."[54] Cato's supporters would hardly be pleased that a Roman senator had behaved like a Cynic! This is further proof that Cynicism was present, at least theoretically, in the first century BCE. We may say "theoretically" because this is actually the point of view of a historian of philosophy. When Varro, in his *De philosophia*,[55] distinguishes between 288 possible schools of philosophy, the Cynic way of life is one of the criteria that he uses, in combination with others, to arrive at this figure. To this end he contrasts the Cynics' way of life with that of other philosophers, and this at least shows that the Cynic way of life was still a meaningful concept to his readers. Cicero himself, in his treatise *On Duties*, doesn't hesitate to castigate Cynic amorality vigorously because it shows no respect for modesty.[56] If this amorality had actually presented no danger at the time, it's unlikely that Cicero would have opposed it so strenuously.

Under the Roman Empire

If we recognize that Cynicism was not totally eclipsed but was instead maintaining itself discreetly, we can appreciate how, under the Roman Empire, in a setting much like that of Hellenistic Greece in the age of Alexander, it found new vigor and experienced an extraordinary revival. We find Cynics

52. For a recent edition with a German translation, see Müseler, *Die Kynikerbriefe*. On the dating of the various corpora of these letters (Anacharsis, Crates, Diogenes, Heraclitus, Socrates, Socratics), see Abraham J. Malherbe, *The Cynic Epistles*, SBLSBS 12 (Missoula, MT: Scholars Press, 1977), 1–34, which includes Greek text and English translation.

53. Plutarch, *Brutus* 34.4–5. Cf. Plutarch, *Caesar* 41.3. Favonius's bluntness may even have gone beyond Cynic παρρησία and constituted αὐθάδεια (smugness) and ὕβρις (arrogance), *Pompey* 60.7.

54. Plutarch, *Brutus* 34.7.

55. Varro, *On Philosophy*, in Augustine, *City of God* 19.1.2–3.

56. Cicero, *On Duties* 1.35.128 and 1.41.148.

in all the great cities of the Roman Empire, not just in Athens, Corinth, and Rome, but also in the cities of Asia Minor, in Gadara in the Decapolis, in Alexandria, on Cyprus, and in Constantinople, the capital of the emperor Julian. Such an expansion is not surprising, since under the Roman Empire the limits of the civilized world were extended to new areas: wealth and luxury were being flaunted shamelessly, while the gap between the rich and the poor kept widening. Even though philosophers like Demonax and Salustius came from the leisure classes, imperial Cynicism—and this is one of its characteristics—drew its followers especially from the disadvantaged classes, who, if Lucian may be believed, saw in Cynicism a way of escape from hard work and their desperate situation.[57] Attracted by Cynic frankness and the reverence in which the philosophers were held, poor citizens who pursued small trades in the great cities of the Roman Empire, and slaves as well, began to leave their workplaces in order to become followers of a philosophy that enabled them to escape their hopeless social condition and the hunger that was stalking them. It wouldn't be an exaggeration to say that the philosophy of Diogenes became, under the Roman Empire, the popular philosophy par excellence. Bands of Cynics could be encountered wandering the streets of Rome or Alexandria, begging at street corners or at temple gates, setting up wherever crowds gathered, in places teeming with people, around stadiums, and in harbors. Cynicism, to accomplish its pedagogical mission, had to become an urban philosophy.

If we want to recover the names of some of these Cynics who came from the masses of the Roman Empire, we need to depend on epigrammatic poetry, even though we have no guarantee that the names cited are those of actual people:[58] Menestratos and Hermodotos in Lucilius;[59] Gorgias in an anonymous epigram;[60] Sochares in Leonidas of Alexandria (to be distinguished from Leonidas of Tarentum).[61] Others are mentioned but not named, like the

---

57. Lucian, *Fugitives* 13.17; *Philosophies for Sale* 11.

58. Cf. Simone Follet, "Les cyniques dans la poésie épigrammatique à l'époque impériale," in Goulet-Cazé and Goulet, *Le cynisme ancien et ses prolongements*, 359–80.

59. For Menestratos, see Lucilius, *Palatine Anthology* 11.153, and for Hermodotos, see *Palatine Anthology* 11.154: "If anyone is an illiterate beggar, no longer of any use for grinding grain or carrying heavy loads for a meager salary, he lets his beard grow and raises his baton at the street corner, claiming to be the chief dog of virtue. This is the highly wise view of Hermodotos. If anyone is penniless, all he has to do is take off his small tunic and that's the end of hunger!"

60. *Palatine Anthology* 7.134.

61. Cf. Follet, "Les cyniques dans la poésie épigrammatique," 372–74.

old Cynic whom Martial describes, with long and dirty hair and beard, wearing a filthy robe, carrying a knapsack and staff, and often standing in Minerva's temple or at the threshold of the temple of Augustus,[62] or the unfortunate man whom Antipater of Thessalonica finds a fine way to insult by contrasting him, a "dog lying in ashes," with Diogenes, the "heavenly dog."[63] But alongside these filthy, impudent bearded men, often parasites, who dished out insults and injury, who led difficult lives, and whom the authors of epigrams jab with savage pleasure, ancient literature has also preserved the memories of some exceptional personalities, who came from the most prosperous levels of imperial society and who often made their way into the circles of power.

Demetrius

The first person who stands out is Demetrius, a friend of Seneca and of Thrasea Paetus. He settled in Rome, probably during the reign of Tiberius. He was banished from the city successively by Nero and Vespasian, and he didn't spare either of them his criticism.[64] He belonged to the aristocratic circle of the Stoic Thrasea Paetus. Seneca clearly tries to make him an idealized model of the sage and so we need to exercise some prudence in interpreting his portrayal, but there's nevertheless no doubt that Demetrius was "though he might deny it, a man of superb wisdom, with an unbending consistency in carrying out his intentions."[65] His way of life was faithful to the harsh asceticism of Diogenes: he went about half-naked or even naked[66] and slept on a straw "mattress" that hardly deserved the name. Adopting the "shortcut" of Cynicism, Demetrius scorned riches, but he took this rejection to the limit: unlike other Cynics who simply forbade ownership, he forbade even begging, and so he was poorer than the rest.[67] But this philosopher was at the same time a man of culture who spoke with a natural eloquence, stripped of all the traditional ornaments,[68] and who believed it sufficient to have at his disposal and for his use (*in promptu et in usu*) a small number of

---

62. Martial, *Epigrams* 4.53.
63. Antipater of Thessalonica, *Palatine Anthology* 11.158.
64. Cf. Epictetus, *Discourses* 1.25.22; Suetonius, *Vespasian* 13.4.
65. Seneca, *On Benefits* 7.8.2 (*On Benefits*, trans. Miriam Griffin and Brad Inwood, The Complete Works of Lucius Annaeus Seneca [Chicago: University of Chicago Press, 2010]).
66. Seneca, *Letters to Lucilius* 62.3 and 20.9.
67. Seneca, *Letter to Lucilius 20*, 9.
68. Seneca, *On the Happy Life* 18.3.

precepts whose coherence with Cynic philosophy is evident—for example, leave aside what is useless to know; fear neither the gods nor men; don't regard death as an evil; behave in all circumstances as if you were in public.[69] According to Demetrius, meditating daily on these precepts allowed one to live *in solido ac sereno*, "on solid ground and under a serene sky."[70] We owe to Seneca a formula that captures the extraordinary moral stature of this figure: *Non praeceptor veri, sed testis est*, "He does not teach the truth, he witnesses to it."[71]

In the second century CE, two unusual personalities arose within the movement, Demonax of Cyprus (ca. 70–170) and Peregrinus Proteus (ca. 100–165). They were each the object of a treatise by Lucian, along the lines of a eulogy in the former case (Lucian was his student), but in the form of scathing, malicious criticism in the latter. While Lucian admired the one, he couldn't stand the other, and as a result, he presented Demonax as an outstanding figure but portrayed Peregrinus as a charlatan.

Demonax

Born into a prosperous and influential family, the Cypriot Demonax, after studying poetry and rhetoric, took up philosophy and spent the rest of his life in Athens. He was the student of a famous Cynic who appears to have been a sort of "rock star" that everybody wanted to meet: Agathobulus, who taught asceticism in Alexandria and was among the *philosophi insignes* (notable philosophers) of the year 119 according to the *Chronicle* of Jerome.[72] He was also acquainted with Demetrius, Epictetus, and Timocrates of Heraclea (*Life of Demonax* 3). Demonax left no written works, but he so impressed his contem-

---

69. Seneca, *On the Happy Life* 7.1.3–7.

70. Seneca, *On the Happy Life* 7.1.7.

71. Seneca, *Letter 20*, 9. The only blemish on Demetrius's life is the stance he took at the trial of the Stoic Publius Egnatius Celer, who was accused by Musonius Rufus of committing the perjury that caused Barea Soranus to be condemned to death. Demetrius astonishingly tried to defend Celer, while Musonius was attacking him. Tacitus, as he relates these events in *Histories* 4.40.6–8, passes sharp judgment on Demetrius, saying that anyone who could defend the crime of Celer had to be *ambitiosius quam honestius* ("showing more selfish interest than honorable purpose"). Cf. John L. Moles, who, in "'Honestius quam ambitiosius'? An Exploration of the Cynic's Attitude to Moral Corruption in His Fellow Men," *JHS* 103 (1983): 103–23, attempts to justify Demetrius's behavior, which he considers honorable and profoundly Cynical.

72. Jerome, *Chronicle of Eusebius* (Rudolf Helm, *Die Chronik des Hieronymus*, GCS 47 [Berlin: Akademie-Verlag, 1956], 198.1–3).

poraries that when he stopped at a house to eat and sleep, they considered him a "divine epiphany" or a "good daemon" (63).[73] His mere appearance in the Assembly was enough to silence the dissensions there (64), and he was able to reconcile disagreements between brothers and between husbands and wives (9). His discourses were filled with Attic grace (6). His "mild, civilized and joyful" Cynicism (9) appears to have been compatible with a certain eclecticism (5) that led him to "revere Socrates, admire Diogenes and love Aristippus" (62). In fact, the portrait that Lucian paints of him presents him more as a disciple of Socrates than as a Cynic, though he resembled the Cynics particularly by the way he disciplined himself physically to endure hardship (4) and through his external appearance: "He seemed most similar to Socrates, even if, in his external appearance and simple way of life, he appeared to imitate the man of Sinope" (5). But Lucian, torn between his limitless admiration for his teacher, who was in his eyes the greatest of philosophers, and the necessity of admitting that he had indeed been a disciple of Diogenes the Dog, couldn't allow himself to present just a parody, nor could he alter the Cynical traits of Demonax. And so he had to credit him with a resolute spirit, self-sufficiency (4), freedom from all arrogance (5), disregard for *ponoi*—the sufferings of poverty, exile, old age, and sickness (8)—criticism of religious beliefs (32) and practices such as divination (37), and an aspiration to a happiness based on the suppression of both hope and fear (20). When he was nearly a hundred years old, Demonax, realizing that he could no longer provide for his own needs, chose to die by abstaining from eating. Like Diogenes, he wanted his body to provide food for the birds and dogs (65–66). But Athens, in appreciation, gave him a magnificent funeral (67)! One thing to highlight, which is reminiscent of the love for neighbor practiced in Christianity: he considered friendship the greatest good among humanity, and for that reason he befriended everyone, and there was no one who was not dear to him, even if he preferred to be with some people more than others.

Peregrinus Proteus

Lucian adopts an entirely different tone in his work *The Passing of Peregrinus*. Lucian had the opportunity to meet Peregrinus personally while sailing home from Troas, just as he had met Demonax, but more briefly (*The Pass-*

73. See Pedro Pablo Fuentes González, "Le *Démonax* de Lucien entre réalité et fiction," *Prometheus* 35 (2009): 139–58.

ing of Peregrinus 43). He was also present on the day when the philosopher climbed onto the pyre at Olympia (35–42).

This complex personality, surnamed Proteus and Phoenix, claimed to be a Christian, a Cynic, and a follower of the Brahmins. According to his hostile biographer, he acted throughout his life as if he were performing tragedy for an audience, including when he spectacularly threw himself into the flames of the Olympic pyre "for the love of glory" (δόξης ἕνεκα). By saddling him with salacious anecdotes of doubtful authenticity (9–10), suggesting that he was a Christian for profit (13) and presenting him as a champion of Cynic "indifference" (ἀδιαφορία) (17), all the better to ridicule him, Lucian gives his readers a portrait of Peregrinus that doesn't square with the testimony of Gellius, who had the opportunity to meet the philosopher several times in Athens.[74] According to that author, Peregrinus was actually a man *gravis atque constans*, dignified and firm, who lived in a hut outside the city and spoke with anyone who came to see him. The elevated moral character of his sayings shows that he was a serious philosopher and nothing like the charlatan Lucian tries to portray. Lucian explains that Peregrinus was, at least for a time, an active and committed member of the Christian community in Palestine, where he explained and wrote Christian books (11). We may conclude that Peregrinus certainly had a role in the relationship that Cynicism maintained with Christianity during the second century. The life of Peregrinus is that of a great traveler, as is the case for other Cynics under the Roman Empire. In that sense, his name was aptonymic. Born in Parium in Mysia, in northwest Asia Minor (14), he moved to Palestine, where he was imprisoned because he was a Christian (12). When freed, he returned to Parium wearing Cynic attire (15), then left for Egypt to be trained in Cynic asceticism by Agathobulus (17). From there he sailed for Italy, where he was banished by the prefect of Rome because he spoke with excessive frankness, especially about the emperor (18). So he left for Greece, staying mostly in Athens, though he also went to Elea (19) and four times to Olympia, where the games were a desirable forum for the Cynics because of their connection with Heracles, the progenitor of their philosophy. His suicide by fire, in imitation of the Brahmins, at the games of 165 was intended to demonstrate how to disregard death and endure things that are terrifying (23). After his death, the Eleans and other Greeks erected statues to him and a cult was established in his honor (28, 41).[75]

---

74. Aulus Gellius, *Attic Nights* 12.11.

75. On the figure of Peregrinus and the problems posed by Lucian's presentation of him, see Marie-Odile Goulet-Cazé, "Pérégrinus surnommé Proteus," *DPhA* 5a:199–230.

Oenomaus of Gadara

In the second century, if we rely on Jerome's *Chronicle* for the year 119, or at the start of the third century, if we trust instead the testimony of the entry about him in the *Suda*, there lived a man who expressed such audacious opinions that he later drew violent criticism from the emperor Julian: Oenomaus of Gadara, author of a work that apparently caused quite a stir and which we know under two titles, *Against Oracles*[76] and *Charlatans Exposed*.[77] In it he launches unusually violent attacks against the gods, whom he declares unjust; against soothsayers, whom he treats as ignorant and charlatans; and especially against oracles, whose fraudulent character he takes great delight in exposing.[78] It's possible that this is the same person as Abnimos of Gadara, who was a friend of the Jewish Rabbi Meir (living in Tiberias under the reign of Hadrian), and was also connected with Rabbi Gamaliel II. So we will meet him again in the chapter on Cynicism and Judaism.

We know nothing of his life except that he came from Gadara in the Decapolis, like Menippus and Meleager, and that he went three times to consult the oracle at Claros, whose ambiguous and obscure responses left him highly dissatisfied.[79] Oenomaus didn't fit the image of the uneducated popular preacher; far from it. He knew the *Phoenissae* of Euripides, he'd read Herodotos, and he was familiar with the Stoic theories of Fate and of knowledge. Several works are attributed to him in the *Suda* Οι 123: *On Cynicism*, a *Republic*, a work titled *On Philosophy according to Homer* and another called *On Crates and Diogenes*.[80] Julian cites these titles himself, along with some others: *The True Voice of the Dog*, which may be the same work as *On Cynicism* (that could be its subtitle); *Against Oracles*, probably identical with

---

For Lucian's perception of Cynicism, see Heinz-Günter Nesselrath, "Lucien et le cynisme," *L'Antiquité classique* 67 (1998): 121–35.

76. Julian, *Discourse 7* (*Against the Cynic Heracleios*), 5 (209a–b).

77. Eusebius, *Preparation for the Gospel* 5.18.6–5.36.5 and 6.7.1–42. The work is sometimes known in English as *Detection of Deceivers*.

78. See Jürgen Hammerstaedt, *Die Orakelkritik des Kynikers Oenomaus*, Beiträge zur klassischen Philologie 188 (Frankfurt am Main: Athenäum, 1988); Marie-Odile Goulet-Cazé, "Oinomaos de Gadara," *DPhA* 4:751–61.

79. Cf. Eusebius, *Preparation for the Gospel* 5.22.1–6.

80. This title is followed by the words καὶ τῶν λοιπῶν, which we interpret not as the end of this title (*On Crates, Diogenes and the Others*), but as including other titles not mentioned, "and on other subjects," just as Aldo Brancacci does, based on a compelling parallel, in "Libertà e fato in Enomao di Gadara," in *La filosofia in età imperiale: Le scuole e le tradizioni filosofiche*, ed. Aldo Brancacci, Elenchos 31 (Naples: Bibliopolis, 2000), 37–67, esp. 42n4.

Charlatans Exposed;[81] and some tragedies.[82] Julian, eager to restore Hellenism and especially its religion, contrasts Oenomaus with an idealized Diogenes who fully respects the gods. Oenomaus may well have devised a fresh conception of Cynicism. In an era when the question of the movement's founder was being posed, he affirmed without hesitation that "Cynicism is neither Antisthenism nor Diogenism,"[83] thus distancing himself from the great Cynics. It appears that he didn't want to reduce the philosophy to a single person's thought and way of life, even if the person was Antisthenes or Diogenes. It's likely that in his work *On Cynicism* he offered a thorough reconsideration of the movement, and that his *Republic* was intended as a counterpoint to the one by Diogenes. Julian, after citing Oenomaus's affirmation about Cynicism, reports that "the better sort of Cynics assert that in addition to the other blessings bestowed on us by mighty Heracles, it was he who bequeathed to mankind the noblest example of this mode of life." Should we conclude that Julian considered Oenomaus one of this "better sort of Cynics" and consequently that Oenomaus regarded Heracles as the founder of the movement? That would be unexpected considering the criticisms that Julian otherwise levels against the philosopher; moreover, we really don't know whom Oenomaus himself would have considered a precursor and model of an authentic Cynicism. In any event, the emphasis Julian places on criticizing his theories proves that in Julian's eyes Oenomaus was the representative embodiment of a renewed Cynicism whose theories he found threatening to his own project of restoring Hellenism.

Among the major figures of imperial Cynicism, there's at least one left who is worth mentioning: Maximus Hero of Alexandria (fl. 380), who wore, apparently without difficulty, the labels of both Christian and Cynic.

•

Maximus Hero of Alexandria

Maximus is known to us primarily through the writings of Gregory of Nazianzus, who was once his friend but who became his bitter enemy after the two competed for the bishopric of Constantinople. Gregory, especially in

81. *The True Voice of the Dog* and *Against Oracles* are cited by Julian in *Discourse 7* (*Against the Cynic Heracleios*), 5 (209b).

82. Julian, *Discourse 7* (*Against the Cynic Heracleios*), 6 (210d).

83. Julian, *Discourse 9* (*To the Uneducated Cynics*), 8 (187c). English translations are by Wilmer Cave Wright (LCL).

his *Oration 26*, left to posterity an unfair and incomplete image of Maximus that needs to be nuanced as much as possible.

Maximus was born in Alexandria to a family of Christian martyrs.[84] During the Arian Controversy, he sided with Athanasius against the Arians; after Athanasius died in 373, he fought so actively against the Arian Lucius that in 374 he was banished to the desert, where he remained for four years. He was therefore closely involved in the quarrels that pitted the orthodox and the Arians against each another, but after his return from the desert, he also became involved in the rivalries over the bishopric of Constantinople that pitted against one another the orthodox of Alexandria and Constantinople. In 379 Gregory of Nazianzus came to Constantinople and became a friend of Maximus. But when Gregory wanted to become bishop of that city, at least as he tells the story, Maximus conspired with the help of Peter, bishop of Alexandria, the brother of Athanasius, to become the bishop instead. This was hastily arranged in the middle of the night.[85] This was the beginning of the "Maximus Affair," which finally ended in defeat for Maximus.[86] In May 381 the ecumenical Council of Constantinople, with Meletius of Antioch presiding, declared his ordination noncanonical and elected Gregory as bishop of the city. Nevertheless, in September of the same year, Maximus got the western council of Aquileia to recognize him as the legitimate bishop of Constantinople, and Ambrose, the bishop of Milan, eagerly intervened in his favor with the emperor Theodosius. But the Council of Rome, held in 382 under the authority of Pope Damasus, and which Ambrose attended, didn't even take up the question of the seat of Constantinople, and after that date nothing more is heard of Maximus.

While their friendship lasted, even though Gregory confirmed, in his *Oration 25*, that the philosopher was indeed a Cynic—recalling, for example, his cosmopolitanism (par. 3.19–20)—he nevertheless clearly portrayed Maximus as innocent of the excesses of Diogenes's philosophy, such as impudence, gluttony, and barking (par. 2.14–18). He identified him clearly as a Christian. He explained that Maximus repudiated the atheism of Cynic philosophy but adopted its frugality, and he refuted the arrogance of those others by wearing the same outfit as they did (par. 6.5–10). Gregory concluded that anything Maximus might have done was still better than "the

84. Cf. Gregory of Nazianzus, *Oration* 25.3.16–17 (Mossay 162).

85. Cf. Gregory of Nazianzus, *Concerning His Own Life*, vv. 887–950; *Oration* 26.3.15–17 (Mossay 230).

86. For the details of this complicated episode, see Marie-Odile Goulet-Cazé, "Maxime Héron d'Alexandrie," *DPhA* 4:348–63, esp. 352–60.

insolence of Antisthenes, Diogenes's consumption of raw food, and the public marriage of Crates" (par. 7.18–20). But after the Maximus Affair, we see a complete change of attitude in Gregory. While he had previously praised his friend, now, in his *Oration 26: Against Maximus* and his *Concerning His Own Life*, he poured out all his bile against him in unrestrained invectives, and at the same time he made the earlier Cynics look better, at Maximus's expense (*Concerning His Own Life*, vv. 1030–33).

This extreme attitude on the part of a churchman who felt unfairly treated and betrayed invites skepticism, particularly since figures such as Athanasius, Peter of Alexandria, Basil, Jerome, and Ambrose trusted the philosopher. Despite what Gregory says about him, there's no question that Maximus was a genuine intellectual. Jerome mentions favorably the book *Against the Arians* that Maximus presented to the western emperor Gratian in Milan,[87] while Basil invited Maximus to come and consult with him about the question of consubstantiality.[88] These details hardly match the portrayal of Maximus as a detestable and grotesque individual that Gregory urges upon his readers. Maximus was probably a victim, caught up in the stakes of ecclesiastical politics, where he was out of his league. Bishop Peter of Alexandria may have used him as a pawn in the rivalry between the churches of Alexandria and Constantinople. We'll return to this quite extraordinary example of a man who belonged both to Cynicism and to Christianity as we try to understand better how a Christian so involved in ecclesiastical affairs could wear the garment of a Cynic and follow that way of life.

Many other names could be mentioned to illustrate the extreme diversity of Cynicism in this period, such as that of the Egyptian boxer Horus, winner of the Olympic Games in Antioch in 364, who later in life turns up unexpectedly as a Cynic philosopher.[89] The last Cynic known in antiquity is Salustius in the fifth century, who came from Syria.

Salustius

In his *Life of Isidore*, Damascius reports that after studying law, Salustius was given a solid foundation in rhetoric by the Sophist Eunoios of Emesa. From

---

87. Jerome, *On Illustrious Men* 127 (Richardson 54).
88. Basil, *Letter 9*, 3.
89. Cf. Libanius, *Letters* 1278 and 1279 (Richard Foerster, ed., *Libanii Opera* [Leipzig: Teubner, 1922], 11:352–53); Macrobius, *Saturnalia* 1.7.3, 14; 1.15.3; 7.7.8; 7.13.10; 7.17.14.

there he went to Athens and then to Alexandria, where he attended schools of rhetoric and studied with Neoplatonic philosophers, but where he ultimately committed himself to Cynicism, adopting a rigorous and austere asceticism. His behavior was in the authentic tradition of Diogenes: he sparred with the crowds, contradicting and ridiculing one and all, in a way that was both humorous and mocking; he tried to endure pain and he loved to joke to try to make others laugh, in both cases excessively.[90] Proclaiming that it was not merely difficult but impossible for men to do philosophy, he succeeded in turning away from philosophy a certain Athenodorus, who belonged to the circle of Proclus in Athens, and he would later quarrel with Proclus himself.[91]

These biographies of exceptional figures demonstrate the extreme diversity of the personalities that might be found under the label "Cynic" and of the contexts in which Cynicism developed. It's therefore important to identify as accurately as possible what, amidst this social and intellectual diversity, determined membership in the movement. To that end, we need to begin with the key ideas of Diogenes, which represent the theoretical and practical foundation of Cynic philosophy.

The Cynicism of Diogenes

The Heritage of Antisthenes

Whether or not Diogenes actually knew Antisthenes, and whether or not Diogenes Laertius is right to present Antisthenes as "the one who first opened the way to Cynicism" (*Lives* 6.2), there's no doubt that Cynic morality finds its roots in the philosophy of Antisthenes, and thus in Socratism, which emphasized the study of the human soul over the study of the cosmos. Antisthenes taught in the gymnasium at Cynosarges (6.13), where in the early fifth century there stood a temple dedicated to Heracles, who would become the Cynic hero par excellence and the incarnation, thanks to his twelve labors, of the struggle against hardships (πόνοι).[92] This gymnasium

---

90. Damascius, *Life of Isidore*, frag. 138 (Zintzen 115.10–119.9) = *Suda*, s.v. Σαλούστιος, Σ 62 (Adler 4:315.12–316.3); s.v. Σαλούστιος, Σ 63 (Adler 4:316.22); see also Photius, *Library*, codex 242, par. 89 (Bekker 342a.27–35) = frag. 89, Zintzen 130.1–3.

91. Damascius, *Life of Isidore*, frags. 144, 145, 147 (Zintzen 125.13–17; 125.18–127.4; 127.11–14) = *Suda*, s.v. ἀπῆγεν, A 3142 (Adler 1:282.9–13); s.v. Ἀθηνόδωρος, A 735 (Adler 1:70.26–31); s.v. Σαλούστιος, Σ 63 (Adler 4:316.4–5).

92. Antisthenes devoted several works to Heracles (Diogenes Laertius, *Lives* 6.16, 18),

was reserved for νόθοι, bastards—that is, during the period we are concerned with, principally those with Athenian fathers and foreign mothers.[93] Antisthenes's father was Athenian, but his mother was from Thrace. This lineage, which denied him Athenian citizenship, may explain at least in part his concern to define nobility not by social criteria but rather by virtue.[94]

Diogenes Laertius cites a catalog in which Antisthenes's works are divided into ten volumes (τόμοι) that contain more than sixty titles on the subjects of rhetoric, ethics, politics, dialectics, and poetry.[95] It's striking to see, in the two doxographies found in book 6 of Diogenes Laertius (one anonymous, the other attributed to Diocles of Magnesia), how the seeds of Cynic philosophy, in its essence, are already present in the thought of Antisthenes: its clarity of vision, its morality based on actions, its radical challenge to presently accepted social norms.

Antisthenes declared that virtue is the same for women as for men (*Lives* 6.12), that this virtue was a matter of actions, and that it had no need of extensive discourses or learning (11). He was the first to introduce a force (ἰσχύς) into the virtuous act similar to the one that Heracles manifested[96] and which Socrates would later personify (11), a force that certainly represents the first appearance of the concept of will in moral philosophy. By identifying the τέλος of life as ἀτυφία[97]—which may be defined as both the absence of pride and the rejection of any illusions about oneself and others[98]—Antisthenes anticipates the importance that the concept of τῦφος will take on within

---

and Diogenes wrote a tragedy that bore the name of this hero (Diogenes Laertius, *Lives* 6.80); cf. Juan L. Lopez Cruces, "Une tragédie perdue: l'*Héraclès* de Diogène le cynique," *LEC* 78 (2010): 3–24. Cf. also Dio Chrysostom, *Discourse 4 (On Kingship)*, 27–32.

93. Cf. Diogenes Laertius, *Lives* 2.31, 6.1.4. In earlier times, the term νόθοι designated those who were born from a common-law relationship between Athenians, from adultery, or from an illegitimate union with a slave or a prostitute.

94. Cf. Diogenes Laertius, *Lives* 6.10.

95. Diogenes Laertius, *Lives* 6.15. For a detailed study of this catalog, its structure, and its titles, see Andreas Patzer, *Antisthenes der Sokratiker: Das literarische Werk und die Philosophie, dargestellt am Katalog der Schriften* (PhD diss., Heidelberg University, 1970; partial printing). See also Aldo Brancacci, *Antisthène: Le discours propre*, Tradition de la pensée classique (Paris: Librairie Philosophique J. Vrin, 2005), esp. 17–39.

96. One of the works Antisthenes wrote about Heracles, according to Diogenes Laertius, *Lives* 6.16, was titled *The Greater Heracles* or *On Strength*.

97. Clement of Alexandria, *Miscellanies* 2.21.130.7.

98. Cf., e.g., Menander, who, in one of his plays, *The Groom*, has the Cynic Monimus of Syracuse express the following thought: "Wholly vain (τῦφος) [are] all man's supposings" (Diogenes Laertius, *Lives* 6.83).

Cynicism. The Cynics also derived another fundamental notion of their philosophy from him, besides those of ἄσκησις (training) and ἀτυφία—namely, the concept of πόνος, which includes not only wrongs and sufferings experienced but also the effort and labor required to overcome them.[99] For it was Antisthenes who insisted, in his works *The Greater Hercules* and *Cyrus*, that "πόνος is a good thing" (2). Moreover, in his eyes, a bad reputation (ἀδοξία) was a good thing in the same way as suffering (11). This attitude of indifference toward others' opinions provided the main justification for the way Cynics treated social conventions—basically by sweeping them off the table. It's connected with the idea that "the most necessary thing to learn is how to unlearn the bad things"[100]—that is, how to rid oneself of the false notions of good and bad that society instills in its citizens through its assorted customs and conventions. Antisthenes furthermore recommends building bulwarks around one's own ideas to make them impregnable (13)—a means of creating within oneself a space of freedom resting on the supremacy of the λόγος, which no other person and no circumstance will ever be able to shake. Antisthenes described the sage as possessing certain qualities that would become emblematic of the Cynical sage, specifically firmness of soul (καρτερία), mastery of self (ἐγκράτεια), and impassivity (ἀπάθεια),[101] all qualities that would lead to victory over πόνοι in daily life.

Diogenes would radicalize this morality of actions based on effort and will by developing the idea of fighting a battle on behalf of nature against civilization through "falsifying the currency" (παραχαράττειν τὸ νόμισμα) and by advocating bodily training (ἄσκησις) for moral purposes. He would turn his life into a shining example of the moral principles that Antisthenes established.

The Name "Dog"

Since Cynics are frequently described by the term "dog," it may be useful to review at this point why the Cynics adopted that particular symbol for them-

99. On this notion, see Goulet-Cazé, *L'ascèse cynique*, 45–48. Two Latin words, *labor*, "effort," and *dolor*, "suffering," translate the two aspects of the Greek term πόνος (cf. Cicero, *Tusculan Disputations* 2.15.35).

100. Stobaeus, *Anthology* 2.31.34 (Wachsmuth 2:207.22–23).

101. Cf. Diogenes Laertius, *Lives* 6.2 ("From Socrates he [Antisthenes] learned his hardihood, emulating his disregard of feeling, and thus he inaugurated the Cynic way of life") and 6.15 ("Antisthenes gave the impulse to the indifference of Diogenes, the continence of Crates, and the hardihood of Zeno").

selves. Already in antiquity there were two explanations for this nickname of Diogenes, which he did not choose voluntarily, we should specify, but which he claimed in the end. Should the name "dog" (κύων) be traced back to the name of the gymnasium at "Cynosarges" (Κυνόσαργες), where Antisthenes taught? The etymology of this term is uncertain today, but the word could mean "dog meat" (κυνὸς σάρκες), or else "white dog" or "shining dog" or "swift dog" (κυνὸς ἀργοῦ), all in reference to the myth of how such a dog snatched some meat that was being offered in sacrifice and carried it off to the spot where the gymnasium was founded.[102] Those who suggest this interpretation understand Antisthenes as the founder of Cynicism. The second explanation is that the term was originally used mockingly to compare Cynics to dogs because of their simple conduct and because of the shamelessness of their way of life, which led them to perform in public any actions they considered natural, including eating, sleeping, and making love.[103] Rather than rejecting a nickname that was meant to be disparaging, Diogenes decided to accept it and adopt it for himself.[104] When he agreed to become known as "The Dog," Diogenes demonstrated that he cared nothing about what others thought of him and that he wasn't a prisoner of false values such as modesty or reputation, just like a dog who defecates wherever he might be and isn't bothered by false constraints. He also wanted to show that he had an accurate perception of people, like the dog who wisely knows when to bite and when to wag his tail.[105]

The allusion to the "dog" was certainly much more than a nickname. That animal embodies a life that is conformed to nature; it possesses nothing. Man, by contrast, renounces his natural life and wrongly fabricates all sorts of conventions that estrange him from nature and push him continually to acquire more and more, preventing him from becoming happy. So the Cynic returns often to the dog as a model. I would suggest that the Cynic philosopher envisioned a Great Chain of Being that was somewhat paradoxical because it was based on the criterion of the absence of needs. Man was at the bottom of the chain, divinity was at the top, and situated between the two was the animal, the best model of natural, self-sufficient conduct to be found among earthly creatures. We must not be mistaken about the gods: they

---

102. Cf. *Suda*, s.v. Κυνόσαργες, K 2721 (Adler 3:215.6–13).

103. Cf. Diogenes Laertius, *Lives* 6.58, 69.

104. Cf. Diogenes Laertius, *Lives* 6.55, 60. On the term "dog," see, e.g., Giannantoni, *Socratis et Socraticorum Reliquiae*, 4:491–97.

105. Cf., e.g., Elias, *In Aristotelis Categorias, Prooemium* (Busse 111.1–32), who offers four interpretations of the origin of the word "Cynic," each one corresponding to some quality of a dog that Cynics were believed to share.

provided a theoretical model for the Cynics, not on account of any religious faith, but because they were beings that by definition had no needs,[106] and who therefore embodied the ideal self-sufficiency that Cynics considered to be the sine qua non of complete happiness.[107] Below the gods, who had no needs, came the animals, who were content to satisfy only their natural needs. And below them came civilized man, who had managed to create for himself, alongside his natural needs such as eating, drinking, urinating, and sleeping, all sorts of useless needs to which he had become prisoner. The Cynic's enterprise is more complex than may first appear. Taking the animal as his model, he seeks to limit his needs as much as possible, in order to be faithful to what nature has bestowed on him. By contrast with the dog, however—and the contrast is enormous—man is both animality and λόγος. And this reason has been perverted by social conventions. He must therefore rid it of all false notions, all bad habits, and all conventions imposed by society so it can allow him to live well—that is, according to nature.

The Basis of the Cynic Movement

Cynicism, like all Hellenistic philosophies, aimed at individual happiness. But the Cynic was aware that this happiness had been compromised because man had enslaved himself to all sorts of bondage that prevented him from experiencing total serenity. And so he needed to be guided by the Cynic message along the road to self-sufficiency, which was also the road to freedom and equanimity. Courage was needed to liberate the individual—beginning with oneself—from this slavery and to show him another way, counter to all the recommendations he'd gotten from society since infancy. Diogenes's fellow citizens were right to inscribe the following verses on the bronze statue they raised in his honor:

Time makes even bronze grow old:
but thy glory, Diogenes, all eternity will never destroy.
Since thou alone didst point out to mortals
the lesson of self-sufficiency and the easiest path of life.[108]

106. Cf. Diogenes Laertius, *Lives* 6.105; Pseudo-Lucian, *The Cynic* 13.
107. See Marie-Odile Goulet-Cazé, "Les premiers cyniques et la religion," in Goulet-Cazé and Goulet, *Le cynisme ancien et ses prolongements*, 117–58.
108. Diogenes Laertius, *Lives* 6.78 (*Palatine Anthology* 16.334).

Diogenes was keenly aware of the bondage into which humanity had plunged. The extent of its slavery could be measured by the magnitude of the needs that were constantly besieging men. Of course they had natural needs, such as eating, for example, but they didn't have to eat to excess; or drinking, but they needed only water, not the wines of Chios and Lesbos. Accordingly Diogenes calls people "triple slaves" who, because they have no self-control, allow themselves to be overcome by food, sex, and sleep.[109] Because he's able to regard himself and others with a cold eye, the philosopher is extremely lucid about human weakness, and this leads him to denounce vigorously all the servitudes to which man falls victim. These include the ones that come from his own bad management of natural needs, and also those that come from society, which imposes social duties on people that push them to participate in political activities, get married, have children, and pursue an occupation.[110] Society also arbitrarily creates out of whole cloth the false values of civilized life: wealth, reputation, power, acquisition of knowledge, respect for law, and social duties.[111] It's precisely because man is enslaved to a good reputation, to wealth that turns him into a veritable "dropsy patient,"[112] and to social duties that he spends his life in feverish activity oriented toward the most pointless goals and wastes his time dealing with completely unnecessary πόνοι. In this regard, Diogenes points to those athletes who train like fanatics by digging ditches and who kick one another to win the victory;[113] those orators who chase after reputation, whom he calls "thrice human," meaning "thrice wretched";[114] those politicians who are prepared to sacrifice anything and make every concession in order to stay in power;[115] and those rich people who are eager to have a good table, and who spend a great deal of energy trying to obtain the most refined luxuries for their dainty palates.[116]

---

109. *Gnomologium Vaticanum*, no. 195 (Sternbach 79).

110. Cf. Diogenes Laertius, *Lives* 6.29; Pseudo-Diogenes, *Letter 47* (*To Zeno*; Müseler, 74–76); Maximus of Tyre, *Dissertation* 32.9 (Trapp 263.160–67), 36.5 (Trapp 292.136–48).

111. See Goulet-Cazé, *L'ascèse cynique*, 53–57.

112. Cf. Stobaeus, *Anthology* 3.10.45 (Hense 3:419.8–12).

113. Cf. Diogenes Laertius, *Lives* 6.27; see also Maximus, *Loci communes, Sermo* 27 (PG 91:876c–d); Stobaeus, *Anthology* 3.5.39 (Hense 3:267.16–268.4), 3.4.111 (Hense 3:246.12–247.2).

114. Diogenes Laertius, *Lives* 6.47.

115. Cf. Pseudo-Diogenes, *Letter 33* (*To Phanomachus*), 3.

116. Cf. Dio Chrysostom, *Discourse 6* (*Diogenes, or On Tyranny*), 12–13.

"Falsifying the Currency" or the Critique of Civilization

In such a cultural context, the Cynics felt that they needed to distinguish themselves from the folly that surrounded them, on the one hand by criticizing the civilization (φύσις vs. νόμος), and on the other hand by living differently, in the form of an asceticism whose parameters Diogenes first established by the way of life he led. The Cynics' critique of civilization sought to reverse traditional social values completely. To this end, as he explains himself in the *Pordalos*, Diogenes adopted the motto "falsify the currency." We should understand this expression in connection with the episode of counterfeiting that tradition attributes to his father and/or to Diogenes himself.[117] The word νόμισμα signifies not only currency but also custom (νόμος). This metaphor of counterfeiting, of "transvaluation," as Nietzsche puts it in *Götzen-Dämmerung* (*Twilight of the Idols*) and in *Ecce Homo* with his famous phrase *Umwertung aller Werthe* (revaluation of all values),[118] implies reversing the currently respected values in every sphere of human activity in order to replace them with new ones that correspond to the Cynic's conception of man and life, which he wants to "ensavage."[119] While a counterfeiter generally alters the weight of currency, reducing the amount of precious metal even while maintaining the currency's nominal value, Diogenes wanted to strike a new currency, stamping onto the νόμος of his time a new imprint,[120] that of φύσις. This new strike that he proposed to his contemporaries subverted all the customs of the time and their whole

117. It might be more accurate to translate the expression as "striking a new currency," but I have retained the traditional translation "falsifying" in light of the counterfeiting episode associated with Diogenes.

118. Cf. Marie-Odile Goulet-Cazé, "La contestation de la loi dans le cynisme ancien," in *Actes du Colloque international: Les doctrines de la loi dans la philosophie de langue arabe et leurs contextes grecs et musulmans, Villejuif, 12–13 Juin 2007*, ed. Maroun Aouad, *MUSJ* 61 (2008): 405–30, esp. 429–30.

119. Cf. Plutarch, *On the Eating of Flesh* 1.6 (995d: ἵνα τὸν βίον ἀποθηριώσῃ). For recent reflections on "falsifying the currency," see, e.g., A. Pizzone, "Solone, Diogene e la *paracharaxis*. Contributo alla storia di un'immagine e della sua fortuna," *Acme* 55 (2002): 91–116; William D. Desmond, *Cynics*, Ancient Philosophies 3 (Berkeley: University of California Press, 2008), 77–131 (chap. 2, "Renunciation of Custom"); Michel Foucault, *Le courage de la vérité: Le gouvernement de soi et des autres II; Cours au Collège de France, 1984*, Hautes études (Paris: Gallimard, 2009), 208–9.

120. Diogenes uses the Greek word χαρακτήρ, which designates this imprint on currency, in a context of moral reflection to indicate the type of life that he leads (Diogenes Laertius, *Lives* 6.71).

manner of living. He was, in a sense, deconstructing civilization in order to impose more effectively the norms of natural law. The Cynics claimed that they were battling to recover—by means of a new method, asceticism—a paradise that humans lost when Prometheus gave them the gift of fire.[121] We recognize that such an endeavor is ultimately unrealistic; it's impossible to escape from νόμος completely, just as it is to rediscover a natural law that civilization has obscured.[122] But even if the objective was somewhat illusory, the campaign that the Cynics fought for it was real enough.

Beginning with the principle that man holds false views of right and wrong because of society's influence,[123] the Cynics sought to replace what was good by convention—commended by the δόξα of society—with what was good by nature, which was of a different order and so seemed scandalous to their contemporaries. Consequently they applied the "falsification of currency" to all types of behavior, and particularly to social behaviors that they wanted to strip of the "modesty" (αἰδώς) that generally accompanied them. Hence the shocking conduct that Diogenes adopted and the odor of scandal that surrounded him personally.[124] This philosopher, who took primitive peoples,[125] animals,[126] and children[127] as his models, broke every taboo and went so far as to allow, in his notorious *Republic* (Πολιτεία), incest and cannibalism, and to extol complete sexual liberty as well as the sharing of wives and children.[128] He once protested that animals practice

121. Cf. Dio Chrysostom, *Discourse 6* (*Diogenes, or On Tyranny*), 25; Plutarch, *Whether Fire or Water Is More Useful* 2 (956b).

122. See the interesting analysis by Suzanne Husson in *La "République" de Diogène: Une cité en quête de la nature*, Histoire des doctrines de l'Antiquité classique 40 (Paris: Librairie Philiosophique J. Vrin, 2011), 181–83.

123. Cf. Diogenes Laertius, *Lives* 6.24: "Diogenes used to say that when he saw physicians, philosophers and pilots at their work, he deemed man the most intelligent of all animals; but when again he saw interpreters of dreams and diviners and those who attended to them, or those who were puffed up with conceit of wealth, he thought no animal more silly. He would continually say that for the conduct of life we need right reason or a halter."

124. See Derek Krueger, "The Bawdy and Society: The Shamelessness of Diogenes in Roman Imperial Culture," in Branham and Goulet-Cazé, *The Cynics*, 222–39.

125. Cf. Diogenes Laertius, *Lives* 6.73.

126. Witnesses refer to the dog, but also to the mouse (Diogenes Laertius, *Lives* 6.22.40), to horses and lions (Pseudo-Lucian, *The Cynic* 15; Diogenes Laertius, *Lives* 6.75), to pasture animals and to fish (Dio Chrysostom, *Discourse 6* ["Diogenes, or On Tyranny"], 13, 18) and even to birds (Dio Chrysostom, *Discourse 10* ["Diogenes, or On Servants"], 16).

127. Cf. Diogenes Laertius, *Lives* 6.37.

128. The most important source for Diogenes's *Republic* is the treatise *On the Stoics* by Philodemus, transmitted in two papyri from Herculaneum and edited by Dorandi, "Filo-

incest without making a fuss about it as Oedipus and Jocasta did.[129] Diogenes himself behaved scandalously, doing with brazenness (ἀναίδεια), in public places, without any hesitation, whatever he wanted, "the works of Demeter and of Aphrodite alike" (i.e., functions related to both eating and sexuality), even to the point of masturbating in public.[130] As he saw it, bashfulness is a sentiment that only civilized man, perverted by society's irrational rules, can feel; animals, barbarian peoples, and children know nothing of it. By contrast, the absence of shame can be a sign of authenticity and truth. Even though the Cynics were indifferent to the judgment of others, they found in disapproving glances proof that their falsification of the currency was truly achieving its goal.

The deconstruction was intended to be radical. Essentially, for Diogenes to be consistent with his principle of life κατὰ φύσιν, he had to be ready to accept all natural acts, including the special cases he raised in his *Republic*, such as incest, necrophagia, and cannibalism,[131] actions that society, concerned for its own survival, required its members to consider reprehensible on the basis of its own categories of right and wrong. Diogenes ate raw meat in full view of everyone, thereby denouncing cooking and, as a result, civilization;[132] he asked that after his death, his body be left unburied as food for wild animals or fish.[133] But Greek society could not, at the risk of self-destruction, accept this way of responding to the requirements of nature, all of nature, that was customarily described by the concept of "indifference" (ἀδιαφορία).[134] So it decried the scandal, brandishing the standard of modesty to try to reduce the work of Diogenes to pure provocation—but the scandal was intentional; it was merely the scandal of nature itself. For Diogenes it was a matter of "dressing life differently" (μεταμφιέννυσθαι

---

demo, Gli Stoici," 91–133. For the contents of this work, see, e.g., Tiziano Dorandi, "La *Politeia* de Diogène de Sinope et quelques remarques sur sa pensée politique," in Goulet-Cazé and Goulet, *Le cynisme ancien et ses prolongements*, 57–68; Marie-Odile Goulet-Cazé, *Les "Kynika" du stoïcisme*, Hermes Einzelschriften 89 (Stuttgart: Steiner, 2003), 11–38; Husson, *La "République" de Diogène*; Robert Bees, *Zenons Politeia*, Studies on the Interaction of Art, Thought and Power 4 (Leiden: Brill, 2011), 261–94.

129. Dio Chrysostom, *Discourse 10* (*Diogenes, or On Servants*), 29–30.

130. Cf. Diogenes Laertius, *Lives* 6.58, 69.

131. Diogenes does not encourage such practices, but because they are natural and therefore beyond societal categories of right and wrong, he refuses to condemn them.

132. Cf. Plutarch, *On the Eating of Flesh* 1.6 (995c–d); Diogenes Laertius, *Lives* 6.34, 76, 77.

133. Cf. Diogenes Laertius, *Lives* 6.79.

134. Cf. Goulet-Cazé, *Les "Kynika" du stoïcisme*, 129–32.

βίον)—the expression is from Philodemus[135]—in order to change one's value system radically.

The Cynics pursued "falsification" and challenged society's preconceived values in every area of human activity.

On the Sociopolitical Level

Diogenes declared himself ἄπολις, without a city; ἄοικος, without a home;[136] and κοσμοπολίτης, a citizen of the world.[137] Even on his journeys in exile he felt at home, because wherever he went, he remained in harmony with the laws of nature. But Diogenes, citizen of the world, also seemed to be a citizen of nowhere,[138] because he advocated abstaining from any political engagement; the very notion of engagement constituted, in his view, an obstacle to individual liberty. He rejected the law of the city and set the law of nature against it. In his *Republic*, knucklebones had to be accepted as legal tender in place of money[139] so there was no longer any need for weapons.[140] By challenging marriage as a social institution in favor of a free union based on the consent of both partners,[141] and by advocating the community of women and children, Diogenes deconstructed the traditional concept of the city. His community of sages appears, however, more like an aggregate of individuals preoccupied with their own happiness, even though some of its characteristics anticipate Stoic cosmopolitanism. Gone are the barriers of race and

135. Philodemus, *On the Stoics* 7 (col. 18.6–7); Dorandi, "Filodemo, Gli Stoici," 102.

136. Diogenes Laertius, *Lives* 6.38.

137. Diogenes Laertius, *Lives* 6.63. Crates declared similarly, "Not one tower hath my country nor one roof, but wide as the whole earth its citadel and home prepared for us to dwell therein" (Diogenes Laertius, *Lives* 6.98).

138. In my view, Diogenes's cosmopolitanism had a negative character. For a different conception, see John L. Moles, "Le cosmopolitisme cynique," in Goulet-Cazé and Goulet, *Le cynisme ancien et ses prolongements*, 259–80 (English translation in Branham and Goulet-Cazé, *The Cynics*, 105–20).

139. Athenaeus, *The Dinner Sophists* 4 (159c), and Chrysippus in Philodemus, *On the Stoics* 6 (col. 16.7–9); Dorandi, "Filodemo, Gli Stoici," 102. Was this simple derision on the part of Diogenes, or a new conception of economic exchange in a society of sages where everyone agreed to recognize knucklebones, though they were guaranteed by nothing, as having a determined value?

140. Chrysippus in Philodemus, *On the Stoics* 6 (col. 16.1–4); Dorandi, "Filodemo, Gli Stoici," 102. Cf. Crates in Diogenes Laertius, *Lives* 6.85.

141. Cf. Diogenes Laertius, *Lives* 6.72.

nationality, and there's no longer any reason to fight wars; distinctions are abolished between male and female, master and slave, and rich and poor; the idea of an elite based on wealth or intelligence has lost all validity.[142]

On the Religious Level

Falsification did not spare the religious domain, in which the Cynics, displaying an attitude of agnosticism, broke deliberately with traditional beliefs. For them the gods served only as a theoretical model and, as they were addressing their contemporaries, as a benchmark to the extent that they symbolized the absence of needs.[143] The Cynics' confrontation encompassed the rejection of all anthropomorphism; the critique of religious institutions and traditional forms of worship, especially the Mysteries;[144] and challenges to prayer, the interpretation of dreams, rituals of purification, oracles, and superstition. The Cynics could not tolerate human happiness being made dependent on practices that had nothing to do with the moral disposition of the individual. They didn't hold a rationalist image of the world or a providentialist conception of Nature; that's why they refused to experience any fear of the gods, and particularly any fear of death or of infernal torments, because such fear would be an obstacle to their impassivity. In the Hellenistic era, which witnessed a great resurgence of religiosity through the cults of many gods imported from the Orient, such as Cybele from Anatolia and the Egyptian god Serapis, and especially through the Mysteries, which were observed here and there—Orphic Mysteries, Eleusinian Mysteries, mysteries of Dionysius, of the Cabeiri in Greece, of Isis and Osiris in Egypt, of Attis in Phrygia and Adonis in Syria—the Cynics raised a discordant and disturbing voice, preventing their contemporaries from practicing their religion quietly and without questions. The Cynics' realism, their rejection of all illusions, led them to submit to the laws of nature and not pronounce on matters that went beyond their comprehension. This is why, in my view, the best definition of ancient Cynicism's religious attitude appears to be agnosticism.[145]

142. Cf. Goulet-Cazé, "La contestation," 421–25.

143. Cf. Diogenes Laertius, *Lives* 6.105.

144. Cf. Diogenes Laertius, *Lives* 6.39: "The Athenians urged him to become initiated, and told him that in the other world those who have been initiated enjoy a special privilege. 'It would be ludicrous,' quoth he, 'if Agesilaus and Epaminondas are to dwell in the mire, while certain folk of no account will live in the Isles of the Blest because they have been initiated.'"

145. We have not addressed the monotheism of Antisthenes here because it is not

On the Literary Level

In the literary domain there was confrontation as well. At first it seems strange that these philosophers who rejected every form of erudition would, all told, have produced such an extensive body of literature. But they were actually practicing subversion at the very core of writing. While they borrowed the framework of traditional genres (dialogues, letters, tragedies), they stamped them with their own imprint by using a new style so characteristic that it became known as the "Cynic turn" (κυνικὸς τρόπος), "resembling a dog that wagged its tail and bit at the same time."[146] A new term was coined, σπουδογέλοιος, to express the mixture of humor and seriousness displayed in the light poetry of Monimus of Syracuse and the works of Menippus of Gadara.[147] But the Cynics also invented new literary genres that would be widely used in the future, such as the "diatribe" (Bion of Borysthenes);[148] satire, or at least *prosimetrum* (see p. 15, nn. 38–39),[149] a mixture of prose and verse that Varro would later use in his Menippean satires; and the chreia, a philosopher's saying, typically brief, a genre that had unprecedented success in the Hellenistic era and under the Roman Empire.

It's worthwhile to spend a bit more time on the chreia because this literary genre played, without a doubt, a decisive role in the relationship between Cynicism and Judaism, and just as surely between Cynicism and Christianity. The chreia, tied to the ideal of the sage, is a vital genre in Cynic literature and may have first appeared within the Cynic milieu. This genre

---

characteristic of ancient Cynicism, but we will treat it below. On the religious attitude of Cynicism, see Marie-Odile Goulet-Cazé, "Les cyniques et la religion," in Goulet-Cazé and Goulet, *Le cynisme ancien et ses prolongements*, 116–58 (English translation in Branham and Goulet-Cazé, *The Cynics*, 46–80).

146. Pseudo-Demetrius of Phalerum, *On Style* 259–61, who cites, to illustrate this "turn" that mixed seriousness and farce, a verse of Crates and two anecdotes that each report a saying of Diogenes.

147. Regarding Monimus, we read in Diogenes Laertius, *Lives* 6.83, that "Monimus has left us . . . some trifles blended with covert earnestness" (παίγνια σπουδῇ λεληθυίᾳ μεμιγμένα), and in Strabo, *Geography* 16.2.29, the adjective σπουδογέλοιος describes Menippus of Gadara. Cf. Klaus Döring, "'Spielereien mit verdecktem Ernst vermischt': Unterhaltsame Formen literarischer Wissensvermittlung bei Diogenes von Sinope und den frühen Kynikern," in *Vermittlung und Tradierung von Wissen in der griechischen Kultur*, ed. Wolfgang Kullmann and Jochen Althoff (Tübingen: Narr, 1993), 337–52.

148. Diogenes Laertius, *Lives* 6.77. On the question of the diatribe in general, see Fuentes González, *Les diatribes de Télès*, esp. 44–78.

149. See section "Menippus of Gadara" on pp. 14–15.

comprises simple sayings, often in the form of an answer to a question, featuring a witty remark (this is the strict definition of a chreia); apothegms (this term describes either short moral maxims, often associated with the Seven Sages, or, more often, sayings attributed to specific individuals, along with an indication of the situation that contextualizes the barb of the chreia); and anecdotes that consist of a genuine narrative, built around the sayings of famous persons. A chreia will often combine a witty remark, a polemical aspect, and an ethical recommendation.[150] Various steps led to the creation and diffusion of a chreia. First there was an oral stage, the transmission by word of mouth, especially by their disciples, of sayings by Cynic philosophers and of anecdotes about them. Then there was a preliminary written stage, that of Cynic and Stoic authors such as Metrocles, Zeno, and Persaeus who wrote down these sayings as they put together collections or composed works centered on a given philosopher, from which apothegms were later drawn (one thinks, for example, of *The Sale of Diogenes* by Menippus). And finally there were subsequent written stages: that of biographers, such as Diogenes Laertius and Lucian in his *Life of Demonax*, who both include chreias in the biographies they compose; that of the authors of literary works (for example, Plutarch in his *Banquet of the Seven Sages*); and that of compilers who gathered collections of chreias from a given philosopher, or from a given group (Plutarch provides an example once again, with his *Apothegms of the Lacedaemonians* and his *Apothegms of Kings and Generals*).

At the start of the whole process, a notable person directly composes chreias that will then circulate under his name. Thus we encounter, in the list of the works by Aristippus, "A Chreia to Dionysius; another, On the Statue; another, On the Daughter of Dionysius."[151] In the same way, the list of Diogenes's works transmitted by Sotion includes chreias, which were most likely spoken publicly by Diogenes and later gathered by someone else into

---

150. See Jan Fredrik Kindstrand, "Diogenes Laertius and the Chreia tradition," *Elenchos* 7 (1986): 217–43; Ronald F. Hock and Edward N. O'Neil, *The Progymnasmata*, vol. 1 of *The Chreia in Ancient Rhetoric*, SBLTT 27 (Atlanta: Scholars Press, 1986); Goulet-Cazé, "Le livre VI de Diogène Laërce," 3880–4048, esp. 3978–4039; Oliver Overwien, "Das Gnomologium, das Gnomologium Vaticanum und die Tradition," *GFA* 4 (2001): 99–131; Overwien, *Die Sprüche des Kynikers Diogenes*; Teresa Morgan, *Popular Morality in the Early Roman Empire* (Cambridge: Cambridge University Press, 2007), 122–29.

151. Diogenes Laertius, *Lives* 2.84. The way these three *chreiai* appear quite individually in the list of works by Aristippus leads us to think that they were *chreiai* that Aristippus himself composed, not ones drawn from a collection that Aristippus assembled. Nevertheless, it remains curious that a chreia would appear as an independent work in a list of writings.

a collection.[152] We know for a fact, thanks to the following anecdote, that Diogenes was accustomed to creating chreias orally, and that philosophers such as Aristotle were apparently afraid of their barbs: "When Diogenes offered him a dried fig, Aristotle saw that he had prepared a chreia if he did not take it; so he took it and said Diogenes had lost his fig and his chreia in the bargain. And on another occasion, when Diogenes made the same offer, he took it, lifted it up aloft, as you do babies, and returned it with the exclamation, 'Great is Diogenes!'"[153] These genuine chreias would have circulated and been amplified, while others may have been fabricated out of whole cloth. Eventually the disciples and friends of a philosopher would gather them into collections. It is to such collections that the *Lives* of Diogenes Laertius are indebted, in one way or another, for their sections that present the collected sayings of philosophers.

The earliest attested work of this type, titled *Chreias—In a Book*, may be found in the list of the works of the Peripatetic Demetrius of Phalerum, transmitted by Diogenes Laertius.[154] Now chreias are indeed attributed to Demetrius by Diogenes Laertius and by the *Gnomologium Vaticanum*.[155] Nevertheless, we must ask ourselves whether these chreias are strictly to be identified with the *Chreias—In a Book*. That is, were the "chreias in a book" composed by Demetrius himself, and do they express his own thought, as is the case for those of Aristippus and Diogenes mentioned above? Or is this a collection of chreias for which Demetrius gathered the sayings of other philosophers? The chreias attributed to him by Diogenes Laertius and the *Gnomologium Vaticanum* could have been drawn from his discourses or other publications,

---

152. Diogenes Laertius, *Lives* 6.80. On the *chreiai* of Diogenes, see Giannantoni, *Socratis et Socraticorum Reliquiae*, 4:466–74, who mentions specifically that several papyri, for which he gives the references, contain the *chreiai* of this philosopher.

153. Diogenes Laertius, *Lives* 5.18 (trans. Hicks, LCL, modified). Stobaeus attributes some *chreiai* to Aristotle, but they all report the sayings of others, e.g., Demosthenes, Zeno the Stoic (which is chronologically impossible!), the comic poet Alexis, and the rhetor Gorgias (*Anthology* 3.5.42; 3.7.29; 3.29.70; 3.29.90; 4.1.144; 4.15b.31; 4.31c.91; 4.50b.83; 4.51.28).

154. Diogenes Laertius, *Lives* 5.81 (Fritz Wehrli, *Demetrios von Phaleron*, vol. 4 of *Die Schule des Aristoteles, Texte und Kommentar*, 2nd ed. [Basle: Schwabe, 1968], frag. 113 = William W. Fortenbaugh and Eckhart Schütrumpf, eds., *Demetrius of Phalerum: Text, Translation and Discussion*, Rutgers University Studies in Classical Humanities 9 [New Brunswick: Transaction, 2000], frag. 1.109).

155. References to thirty-four *chreiai* of Demetrius of Phalerum, with indications of the corresponding fragments, may be found in Fortenbaugh and Schütrumpf, eds., *Demetrius of Phalerum*, 132–35. See also frags. 113, 115–22, and 198 in Wehrli, *Demetrios von Phaleron*, 26–27, 42, and commentary at 68–70.

and they could have been collected by somebody else along with the thoughts of other authors, while the "chreias in a book" could be the sayings of other figures that Demetrius himself collected.[156] Around the same time, Metrocles of Maroneia, a disciple of Crates of Thebes, is himself presented as the author of a work of chreias, but in this case Diogenes Laertius quotes a sample, and the chreia that he cites belongs to Diogenes the Cynic.[157] The oldest known collection of Greek chreias attributed to philosophers could therefore well be that of Metrocles (possibly along with the *Chreias—In a Book* of Demetrius of Phalerum). This collection must have had a considerable influence, since it was the first work to transmit the many sayings of Diogenes.

The Stoics also made use of the genre. Zeno had a stock of chreias he told that featured Crates, among others;[158] the list of Persaeus's works includes four books of chreias,[159] while the works of Ariston of Chios include eleven such volumes.[160] Furthermore, the Stoic Hecato of Rhodes, a disciple of Panaetius, is credited with a collection of chreias that comprised at least two books and is known to have featured both Cynic and Stoic philosophers.[161] Under the Roman Empire, Dio Chrysostom continued the dissemination of Diogenes's sayings through his own chreias.[162] These sources explain why chreias are generally believed to have originated within the Cynic milieu and why the Stoics are considered to have continued that tradition. We may also imagine that the *Recollections of Crates* by Zeno (Diogenes Laertius, *Lives* 7.4), the *Recollections* of Persaeus (7.36), those of Ariston of Chios in three books (7.163), and later those of Favorinus of Arles, which, in book 2, also feature Crates the Cynic,[163] contained chreias and that they contributed significantly to their spread.

These chreias were able to engage ethical and practical questions in a way that was never off-putting because of the witty spirit they embodied. Often the same chreia is known in several different revisions; it may be ex-

---

156. Wehrli, *Demetrios von Phaleron*, 54 and 68, references a saying of Crates in response to a gift of bread and wine from Demetrius, which could be considered a chreia of Crates (Diogenes Laertius, *Lives* 6.90, and Athenaeus, *The Dinner Sophists* 10 [422c] = Wehrli, frags. 58a and 58b).

157. Cf. Diogenes Laertius, *Lives* 6.33.

158. Cf. Diogenes Laertius, *Lives* 6.91.

159. Cf. Diogenes Laertius, *Lives* 7.36.

160. Diogenes Laertius, *Lives* 7.163. On the other hand, it's not known whether the title Περὶ χρειῶν attributed to Cleanthes in *Lives* 7.175 signifies "On Chreiai" or "On Needs."

161. Cf. Diogenes Laertius, *Lives* 6.4, 32, 95; 7.26, 172.

162. Cf. Stobaeus, *Anthology* 3.13.42, 3.34.16.

163. Cf. Diogenes Laertius, *Lives* 6.89 (Mensching frag. 12 = Barigazzi frag. 42 = Amato frag. 50).

panded into an anecdote, or an anecdote may be abridged into a simple saying. Collections of chreias circulated widely in the Hellenistic era and under the Roman Empire. They served especially to characterize well-known figures, such as Socrates, Aristippus, Antisthenes, Diogenes, and Crates. It's significant that in the first century or in the first half of the second century,[164] when Aelius Theon wants to illustrate in his *Progymnasmata* the different types of chreias, he relies on several by Diogenes, as well as on some from Antisthenes and Bion.[165] This shows to what an extent the collection of Cynic chreias would be the preferred source for someone who, under the Roman Empire, wanted to explain the literary genre of chreia to teachers and students of rhetoric.[166] This was done in support of the preparatory exercises assigned during the study of rhetoric. As its name indicates, the chreia was designed to be useful, showing how a given philosophical position would apply in a particular situation. On the literary level, then, the Cynic chreia played a role of its own in the "falsification of the currency": by its size—it was usually short; by its wittiness—it provides the best illustration of Cynic humor; and by its moral force and impact—it accosted the reader and fostered moral discourse in an unprecedented way.

From Cynic chreias, a fairly accurate portrait of a philosopher emerges, a sort of composite sketch that illustrates the way of life of this person whose outspokenness uncovered the false evidence and stripped off, one at a time, the masks that humans love to hide behind. The nature of Cynicism as a philosophy accounts for the decisive role that the chreia played in it: Cynicism was a philosophy of actions and of concrete, lived-out examples; it was hortatory; and it was popular. Thanks to the chreia, episodes in the life of Diogenes (for example, when he was captured by pirates and sold as a slave) came to have great symbolic value. *The Sale of Diogenes* by Menippus, which was the source of many of the chreias that fed the legend of Diogenes, was written to illustrate, in terms of the master-slave relationship, how Diogenes had brought about a reversal of values: though he had been reduced to slavery, he was still able to command others; even his master had to obey him.[167]

164. These are the dates proposed for the treatise by Michel Patillon, ed., *Aelius Theon: Progymnasmata*, CUF (Paris: Les Belles Lettres, 1997), 16.

165. According to Diogenes Laertius, *Lives* 4.47, Bion "left . . . sayings of useful application" (ἀποφθέγματα χρειώδη πραγματείαν ἔχοντα).

166. Aelius Theon, *Progymnasmata*, dedicates an entire chapter (chap. 3 = Patillon 18–30) to the chreia and its different forms; similarly Pseudo-Hermogenes, *Progymnasmata* 3 (Patillon 185–87), and Aphthonius, *Progymnasmata* 3 (Patillon 114–17).

167. Cf. Goulet-Cazé, "Le livre VI de Diogène Laërce," 4006–25.

The Cynics, it must be admitted, were particularly inventive writers who knew how to use words in original ways, employing humor, cutting jabs, and plays on words with multiple resonances. It's not one of the least paradoxes of Cynicism that these philosophers themselves benefited from a solid education and put it to good use in their writings, even as they castigated book knowledge.

On the Philosophical Level

But it was certainly with regard to philosophy itself that the Cynics were the most combative. They denounced other philosophers for their intellectualism, dogmatism, and incompetence,[168] but at the same time they did more than denounce; they proposed a new kind of philosophy, a "shortcut," the only one (as they saw it) that could assure human happiness and be accessible to everyone, even the uneducated.[169] The elite were defined no longer by social milieu or intellectual aptitude (the very notion of an "intellectual elite" had no meaning among the Cynics anyway) but by the strength of the will, the ἰσχύς, the force that Antisthenes spoke about. Their "falsification" of philosophy encompassed a rejection of knowledge and a mistrust of studying, traditional education (παιδεία), reasoning, and discourse.[170] Content to have only a few unquenchable convictions as their doctrinal store in trade, the Cynics broke deliberately with the intellectual component of philosophy and privileged its existential component instead. Cynic existentialism was accompanied by a revaluation of bodily things; the body and the gesture took on the force of argument. To someone who claimed

168. Thus this remark of Diogenes concerning Plato: "What use to us is a man [i.e., Plato] who, even though he has already practiced philosophy for a long time, still hasn't upset anybody?" (Themistius, *On the Soul*, in Stobaeus, *Anthology* 3.13.68 [Hense 3:468.6–8]).

169. For Antisthenes, virtue had no need of learning (Diogenes Laertius, *Lives* 6.11), and Diogenes considered music, geometry, astronomy, and similar sciences to be useless and unnecessary (Diogenes Laertius, *Lives* 6.73; see also Diogenes Laertius, *Lives* 6.103–4, which describes the Cynics' rejection of logic and physics, of the ordinary subjects of instruction [τὰ ἐγκύκλια μαθήματα], and of geometry and music). Diogenes passed severe judgment on grammarians, musicians, mathematicians, and orators (Diogenes Laertius, *Lives* 6.27–28).

170. Traditional παιδεία actually diverts us from what should be our primary concern—namely, ourselves—and offers no help in guiding our lives. Diogenes contrasts it with being educated by πόνοι. On the two types of education, see Dio Chrysostom, *Discourse 4 (On Kingship)*, 29–35.

that movement didn't exist, Diogenes gave a definitive response by getting up and walking.[171] He testified to his philosophy simply through his life and actions, without wasting time in long proofs or extended discussions.[172] In the process, reality was rehabilitated and its presence incontestably underscored. Diogenes did not envision the *idea* of a table, or of a cup, but emphasized the real table itself, the real cup.[173] This novel concept of a philosophy outside the traditional παιδεία must have profoundly shocked other philosophers. During the imperial period, Philosophy, one of the characters in Lucian's *The Fugitives*, complains that contemporary Cynicism, built as it was on audacity, ignorance, impudence, and wantonness, is merely a counterfeit of true philosophy.

When one strikes a currency anew, when one changes its "character," showing that the most common opinions need to be revised because they're mostly false, one can only scandalize, and that's exactly what occurred. Cynicism was indeed a scandal. "Diogenes used to say that he followed the example of the trainers of choruses; for they too set the note a little high, to ensure that the rest should hit the right note."[174] This setting of a higher note, this surpassing of the proper social limits, accounts for why scandal became so viscerally attached to Cynic philosophy and why Diogenes saw himself as a lonely sage among fools. The Cynics legitimated behaviors that they considered natural but which were intolerable to their contemporaries; they comprehensively pushed back and even abolished taboos that the society of their time had painstakingly established in order to maintain its own cohesion. They invited their contemporaries to reflect on the scandal of nature and to admit that what's really shameful isn't what's natural but the effects of irrationality: injustice, greed, and the love of vainglory.

---

171. Cf. Diogenes Laertius, *Lives* 6.39.

172. Cf. Diogenes Laertius, *Lives* 6.48: "Hegesias having asked him to lend him one of his writings, he [Diogenes] said, 'You are a simpleton, Hegesias; you do not choose painted figs, but real ones; and yet you pass over the true training and would apply yourself to what's written in books about the subject.'"

173. Cf. Diogenes Laertius, *Lives* 6.53.

174. Diogenes Laertius, *Lives* 6.35. Cynics didn't hesitate to adopt extreme and scandalous attitudes in order to liberate other men from their own failings (cf. in 6.94 the episode that led to the conversion of Metrocles).

Cynic Asceticism, a "Shortcut to Virtue"

But it wasn't enough for the Cynics to critique social morality; they had to present an alternative. For them the good was to be achieved not in the inaccessible realm of ideas, nor in the complexity of discourse, but in specific, concrete acts of individuals knowing how to live well and to bring their actions into harmony with their words. In effect, all that matters is the individual, in all of his uniqueness, and it's up to him to become, through each of the actions he performs, the artisan of his own happiness. Diogenes insisted deliberately on the contrast. "He was going into a theatre, in the opposite direction of those who were coming out, and being asked why, 'This,' he said, 'is what I practise doing all my life.'"[175] When people laughed at him because he was walking backward on the portico, Diogenes shot back this scathing response: "Aren't you ashamed, you who walk backward along the whole path of existence, but who blame me for walking backward along the path of the promenade?"[176] But leading this other kind of life required a strenuous effort of the will, because people needed to strip off their social shells in order to be rid of the various desires and anxieties that society stirred up in them and rediscover, thanks to the λόγος, a life according to nature. To do this, one needed a conversion, which was made possible by a specific method based on a concept the Cynics derived from the vocabulary of athletics: asceticism, as conceived by Diogenes.[177] "Nothing in life, he maintained, has any chance of succeeding without strenuous practice; and, in contrast, this is capable of overcoming anything."[178] Within the conceptual landscape of Cynicism, asceticism is at the center of several opposing pairs that recur constantly in Cynic chreias and anecdotes: nature versus society; reason versus folly; truth and freedom versus lies; liberty versus slavery. This Cynic asceticism has a specific focus: even though it's bodily, it doesn't have the same goal at all as athletic asceticism; nor does it have anything to do with the spiritual exercises the Stoics would pursue. It's a physical asceticism with a moral goal—the only effective method, as the Cynics saw it, of leading a life according to nature.

The definition of Cynicism as a "shortcut to virtue" goes back directly to asceticism. This lapidary formula is known from the Stoic Apollodorus

175. Diogenes Laertius, *Lives* 6.64.
176. Stobaeus, *Anthology* 3.4.83 (Hense 3:238.7–11).
177. Cf. Goulet-Cazé, *L'ascèse cynique*, esp. 53–71.
178. Diogenes Laertius, *Lives* 6.71.

of Seleucia (second century BCE), in the ethical part of his *Introductions to Dogmas*: "The sage will act like a dog, Cynicism being a shortcut to virtue."[179] Though we don't know whether the formula ultimately goes back to the Cynics themselves, we can at least say that the idea it expresses is theirs. This simple, efficient shortcut, which they identified with a very precise form of asceticism, contrasted first of all with the long route traditionally adopted by philosophical schools that led through study, the acquisition of knowledge, and theoretical speculation. The Cynics considered all the other disciplines—logic, music, geometry, physics, and metaphysics—"useless and unnecessary" because they diverted people from what should have been their principal preoccupation—namely, themselves—and because they offered them no help in guiding their lives.[180] As heirs of Socrates in this regard, the Cynics identified philosophy with morality. But their shortcut also contrasted with the long route of civilization, which encouraged man to make lengthy and fruitless efforts, to endure vain πόνοι, in order to acquire various manual, technical, or intellectual abilities, or simply to get rich, rather than to aim at becoming wise. Diogenes realized that if civilization seduced man by promising him comfort, a good reputation, power, and riches, this was so it could subjugate him and strip him of his liberty. Anyone who wanted to take the shortcut would have to be satisfied with poverty, because "poverty is an instinctive aid to philosophy, for the things that philosophy attempts to teach by reasoning, poverty forces us to practice."[181] Where ordinary philosophers were content to prepare themselves for the possibility of losing all their goods, Diogenes embraced actual poverty. This, he believed, was the price a man had to pay in order to preserve his freedom; these were the authentic but paradoxical riches that Diogenes offered his contemporaries. He was rich himself, though he didn't have a mite to his name,[182] because true wealth doesn't consist of possessions; rather, it consists in self-sufficiency (αὐτάρκεια).[183] When Crates was asked what profit he'd gained from philosophy, he replied, "A pint of lupines, and no worries."[184] Truly it's impossible

179. Diogenes Laertius, *Lives* 7.121. On this formula and on the decisive role that Apollodorus played in the transmission of Cynic and Stoic doxographies, see Goulet-Cazé, *Les "Kynika" du stoïcisme*, 137–81.

180. Cf. Diogenes Laertius, *Lives* 6.73.

181. Stobaeus, *Anthology* 4.32.11 (Hense 5:782.17–20); cf. also Stobaeus, *Anthology* 4.32.19 (Hense 5:784.19–20).

182. *Gnomologium Vaticanum*, no. 182 (Sternbach 74).

183. *Gnomologium Vaticanum*, no. 180 (Sternbach 74).

184. Diogenes Laertius, *Lives* 6.86.

to take anything from someone who has no possessions. Accordingly, to make use of asceticism as a shortcut, a person had to be willing to live in poverty.

Asceticism was a battle, and the first adversaries to conquer were those passions of the soul that had not yet been tamed—for example, pride, which "like a shepherd leads most people wherever it wants";[185] fear, which is the "mark of a slave";[186] and sorrow, which ruined the lives of men such as Xerxes, Cresus, and Alexander.[187] Asceticism also had to overcome the false values of civilization that society presented to people as criteria of happiness, such as riches or fame, as well as the social duties it demanded they fulfill. But that wasn't all. People also had to face unexpected blows that came from the whims of Fortune; illness; and, inevitably, death, dealt by Nature when it took the form of Fate. Cynics knew well that all these adversaries kept people from being happy. They therefore offered a preventive method that, by providing daily training for the body, strengthened the soul so it didn't feel any burden under the trials sent by Fortune and Fate.

The important thing was to choose to fight the right battle. Some πόνοι were useless, such as the daily exertions of the athlete trying to win a victory in the stadium, the musician straining to acquire artistic virtuosity just to win a musical competition, the careerist seeking glory, or simply the person trying to conform to social norms. But there were also useful πόνοι. These were πόνοι κατὰ φύσιν—that is, the efforts required to live according to nature by meeting only needs that were natural and strictly necessary: drinking water; eating as frugally as possible; sleeping on a hard surface; enduring the cold of winter and the heat of summer; dressing in a very simple way. All this was done to tame the body, through a life of extreme frugality, so it would never pose an obstacle to what a person wanted to do.

Those who practiced this preventive asceticism acquired not just good health but also strength of character, which enabled them to remain indifferent to the hazards of existence, whatever Fortune might send. This is how we should understand the formula "Suffer in order not to suffer."[188] In fact, if one day, through the whims of Fortune, a Cynic began to be beleaguered by poverty, or exile, or a bad reputation, he'd be able to endure these misfortunes, thanks to the way asceticism had already equipped him. Beyond this,

---

185. Cf. *Gnomologium Parisinum*, no. 207 (Sternbach 22).

186. Cf. Diogenes Laertius, *Lives* 6.75.

187. Cf. Maximus of Tyre, *Dissertation* 32.9.

188. Stobaeus, *Anthology* 4.36.10 (Hense 5:868.16–19). Cf. Pseudo-Crates, *Letter 33* (*To Hipparchia*), 1; *Letter 4* (*To Hermaiscus*).

he'd have acquired the strength of character to recognize that these tests sent by Fortune were not actually anything negative, as civilized life would have him believe. It was through daily training in a life κατὰ φύσιν that in the end people acquired their independence from the outside world, the celebrated αὐτάρκεια. Antisthenes said that on a voyage one should bring provisions that would float, in case of shipwreck.[189] When Diogenes was asked what profit he'd gotten from philosophy, he replied, "If nothing else, at least I've become ready for any eventuality."[190] From the Cynic perspective, taming the body through useful πόνοι enabled people to govern their lives rationally and prove themselves stronger than the vagaries of existence. This was the moral challenge that the Cynics held out. It had to be faced constantly, and it was just as difficult as the one their hero Heracles had accepted. But once he had completed his twelve labors, he was able to remain free, even when his cousin Eurystheus kept him under his domination.[191]

The outfit that the Cynics adopted symbolized their asceticism and the social nonconformity it embodied: a knapsack that contained all the philosopher's goods and enabled him to live day to day; the τρίβων, a small, thin coat, folded in two, generally filthy, which served as a garment in both winter and summer, and also as a blanket at night; a walking stick for a staff, indispensible to the cosmopolitan mendicant and missionary who strode barefoot along city streets and distant highways. A long beard, and hair that was often long and dirty, completed the outfit of the Cynic, which was designed to reflect an authentic asceticism.[192]

However, even if, thanks to being trained by useful πόνοι, someone succeeded in living according to nature, there is another major component of Cynic asceticism that must be taken into account. Even if people managed to get free from the bonds of civilization, they still wouldn't be perfectly happy, because, like every living creature, they'd still be subject to Nature, which rules the cosmos and which takes on the role of Fate when it condemns everyone inevitably to experience sickness and death—not to mention hunger, thirst, heat, and cold, phenomena that, if they're excessive and surpass the human threshold of resistance, can threaten people's very lives.[193] In con-

---

189. Diogenes Laertius, *Lives* 6.6.

190. Diogenes Laertius, *Lives* 6.63.

191. Cf., e.g., Dio Chrysostom, *Discourse 8* (*Diogenes, or On Virtue*), 29–30, and Pseudo-Lucian, *The Cynic* 13.

192. Numerous testimonies about the Cynic outfit are listed in Goulet-Cazé, *L'ascèse cynique*, 60–61n140.

193. Cf. Maximus, *Loci communes, Sermo* 67 (PG 91:1008d), which cites these verses

trast with the beneficent nature, offering every living thing, whatever lot Fortune might have in store for it, water from her springs and fruits from the ground, we have now to do with Nature as a hostile force, which, as everyone knows only too well, will have the last word. In this context the Cynic holds a very different attitude from that of the Stoic. While the latter freely accepts Fate and follows its orders voluntarily, the Cynic resigns himself because he hasn't got a choice, and this brings no joy to his heart. While the Stoic lives in an ordered and reassuring world where all things, even the caprices of Fortune, are ultimately integrated into the plan that Fate/Providence has foreseen,[194] the Cynic, for his part, confronts absurdity. He's well aware that the first level of asceticism, which consists of braving πόνοι κατὰ φύσιν to become capable of enduring the attacks of Fortune, is not sufficient in the face of sickness and death. And so Diogenes resorted to a second level of asceticism, of a more rigorous type. The idea that he envisioned two levels of asceticism makes good sense of certain examples of extreme asceticism that tradition describes him engaging in—for example, hugging statues that were covered in snow, or rolling about in the burning sand.[195] Nothing in life according to nature, which only implies renouncing civilization's artifices and taking advantage of what nature has to offer, requires a person voluntarily to endure ordeals such as burning sand or freezing snow. If Diogenes went above and beyond the efforts required to live κατὰ φύσιν, this was to overcome the limits that Nature had set for human beings, to show that he could dispassionately endure even the blows of Fate. Cynic asceticism thus had two foundations, with different inspirations. One permitted man, thanks to his efforts to live according to nature, to break the chains of civilization and dispassionately endure the assaults of Fortune; the other enabled him, thanks to a much more rigorous training, just as dispassionately to contemplate his situation as a mortal being within the cosmos.

---

from Diogenes, probably taken from one of his tragedies: "O human race, mortal and miserable, / We are nothing but reflections of shadow / Who go astray, useless weight upon the earth"; and Dio Chrysostom, *Discourse 4* (*On Kingship*), 82, which portrays Diogenes citing to Alexander the three first verses that Electra delivers at the beginning of Euripides's *Orestes*: "There is naught so terrible to describe, be it physical pain or heaven-sent affliction, that man's nature may not have to bear the burden of it" (trans. Edward Philip Coleridge).

194. The *Hymn to Zeus* by Cleanthes (Stobaeus, *Anthology* 1.1.12 [Wachsmuth 1:25.4–27.4 = *SVF* 1:537]) illustrates the harmony of the world directed by Zeus, the first cause of Nature, who governs all things according to his law.

195. Cf. Diogenes Laertius, *Lives* 6.23.

Cynic Happiness

"Like any other philosophy, the goal and end that Cynic philosophy proposes is happiness," the emperor Julian affirmed. "And this happiness consists of living in conformity with nature, not according to the opinions of
the crowd."[196] The life that Diogenes led actually combined the three conditions required by Cynicism for an individual to be happy: self-sufficiency,
liberty, and impassivity. Cynic virtue goes no farther than this state of total
independence. The Cynic sage has no need of civilization, or riches, or
the favors of Fortune. Since he holds on to nothing outside himself, no
one can compromise his happiness by taking anything from him.[197] This
happiness consists of serenity, tranquility of soul, inner peace. But can it
still be called happiness if it's actually the elimination of all pleasures, one
by one? It must be admitted that "falsification" is also at work with regard
to pleasures and happiness. The harsh asceticism that the Cynics practiced
actually gave rise to genuine pleasures, though these had nothing to do
with what is usually understood by "pleasures." "The pleasures to pursue
are the ones that follow suffering," Antisthenes said, "not the ones that pre-
cede it."[198] However, if what Diogenes says about this can be believed, joy
and gladness can accompany such pleasures. "Diogenes affirmed that true
pleasure was for one's soul to be in tranquility and gladness."[199] In all circumstances he appeared free, serene, and profoundly happy,[200] while his
disciple Crates, "with his knapsack and thin coat, spent his life joking and
laughing as if he were at a party."[201] In this way the Cynics accomplished
the impressive feat of transforming into sources of pleasure things that
were anything but that for the ordinary person. Others might find pleasure in drinking a wine from Lesbos; Diogenes would find it in drinking
water. Hence this remark by Maximus of Tyre: "You call his (Diogenes')
pleasures labours, because you are assessing Diogenes' life by the defec-
tive measure of your own nature. You would feel pain if you behaved like

196. Julian, *Discourse 9* (*To the Uneducated Cynics*), 13 (193d).

197. Cf. Diogenes Laertius, *Lives* 6.46: the choice of masturbation, for example, illustrates Diogenes's aspiration to self-sufficiency in the sexual domain; he similarly refused the
bonds of marriage (cf. Diogenes Laertius, *Lives* 6.29).

198. Stobaeus, *Anthology* 3.29.65 (Hense 3:640.5–7).

199. *Gnomologium Vaticanum*, no. 181 (Sternbach 74).

200. Cf. Dio Chrysostom, *Discourse 6* (*Diogenes, or On Tyranny*), 60–62; Stobaeus,
Anthology 4.39.20 (Hense 5:906.10–13), 4.39.21 (Hense 5:906.14–17).

201. Plutarch, *On Tranquility of Mind* 4 (466e).

that, but Diogenes felt pleasure."[202] One must imagine Diogenes happy, in all circumstances, even when he was undergoing rigorous training. As he said himself, "Does not a good man consider every day a festival?"[203] Paradoxically, Cynicism saw itself as both hedonism and eudaemonism.

Relationship with Others

In the ancient world, where the figures of the slave and the beggar were considered to occupy the most humiliating of all situations and were tarred with a bad reputation (ἀδοξία), Diogenes dared to challenge this opinion. He stood alone against social folly, embracing the humiliation of slavery, when he was captured by pirates, and of beggary,[204] all the while insisting that he was the only true king,[205] the only physician of souls capable of showing all of humanity that it was deceived in its definitions of right and wrong.[206] Not only did he force his contemporaries to reflect on the scandal of nature; he also made them face the scandal of the truth. He testified to the truth by his manner of living, by his dress, through the actions he dared to perform in front of everyone else, and by his rejection of all pretense. At the same time, he spoke the truth to others—to the rulers of this world and its intellectuals as well as to the man on the street.

To accomplish this, he had several weapons at his disposal. First and foremost was the famous Cynic παρρησία,[207] unlimited freedom of speech, unrestrained frankness that allowed him to speak biting reprimands. Diogenes presented himself as "an interpreter of truth and free speech"[208] who,

202. Maximus of Tyre, *Dissertation* 32.9 (Trapp 263.156–59; trans. Michael B. Trapp [1997]).

203. Plutarch, *On Tranquility of Mind* 20 (477c).

204. Cf. Diogenes Laertius, *Lives* 6.67. Diogenes justified the practice of begging through a syllogism: everything belongs to the gods; sages are friends of the gods; therefore, everything belongs to the sages (Diogenes Laertius, *Lives* 6.72). He thus drew a distinction between αἰτεῖν (begging) and ἀπαιτεῖν (reclaiming, i.e., what in reality belongs to us) (Diogenes Laertius, *Lives* 6.46).

205. Cf. Julian, *Discourse 9* (*To the Uneducated Cynics*), 14 (194d–195b). On the royalty of Diogenes, besides the discourses that Dio devotes to that theme, see the very beautiful passage in Maximus of Tyre, *Dissertation* 36.5 (Trapp 292.148–293 [175]).

206. Cf. Dio Chrysostom, *Discourse 9* (*Diogenes, or the Isthmian Discourse*), 1–2.

207. Cf. Diogenes Laertius, *Lives* 6.69: "Being asked what was the most beautiful thing in the world, Diogenes replied, 'Freedom of speech.'"

208. Lucian, *Philosophies for Sale* 8. This frankness was exhibited toward, among others,

out of love for humanity and concern for others, explained to his contemporaries that what seemed to be self-evident actually was not. He wandered the streets in broad daylight with his lantern lit, crying, "I am looking for a [real] man."[209] Or he would shout, "Attention! Men!" and when some onlookers were imprudent enough to assemble, he struck them with his staff and told them, "I called for men, not scoundrels!"[210] His second weapon was comedy, specifically sarcastic joking, which took the form of mockery, satire, and clowning, which disconcerted others and made them feel sheepish. The term σπουδογέλοιον, "serious humor," has been applied to this type of comedy, which was stinging in its effects and whose extreme sarcasm veiled its desperate motivation. If Diogenes played the fool, it was because he recognized that human folly needed to be cured urgently.[211] Diogenes's final weapon was provocation, which jolted others out of their conformist lethargy and made them question established practices[212] and previously unchallenged opinions[213] and finally get rid of all misplaced shame.[214] The Cynic had only the power of his words and example, but those enabled him at the very least to serve as the troubled conscience of his era. Despite appearances, the weapons he bore were not those of the misanthrope; rather, they were pedagogical tools designed to reprimand, to convey a message, and, if possible, to heal.

The Cynicism of Diogenes was not a philosophical "system," because, as we have seen, it limited itself to being a way of life; but it had genuine coherence, and the Cynics of the earliest generations, equipped with the body of simple but radical doctrine bequeathed by Diogenes, as well as by the example of the way of life he led, had the clear sense of belonging to a movement. This heritage was transmitted to Cynicism under the Roman Empire, but its character, which we will address next, became more complex and indistinct. This was basically for two reasons. The first is because Stoicism developed alongside Cynicism. The relationship between the two movements is amazingly complex because they were at once so similar and

---

powerful leaders such as Alexander (Diogenes Laertius, *Lives* 6.38.60.68) and his father, Philip of Macedon (Diogenes Laertius, *Lives* 6.43). For Crates and Alexander, see Diogenes Laertius, *Lives* 6.93.

209. Diogenes Laertius, *Lives* 6.41.

210. Diogenes Laertius, *Lives* 6.32.

211. Cf. Diogenes Laertius, *Lives* 6.42, for Diogenes's critique of someone who thought this could be accomplished through rites of religious purification.

212. E.g., the votive offerings in Samothrace (Diogenes Laertius, *Lives* 6.59).

213. E.g., attitudes toward exile (Diogenes Laertius, *Lives* 6.49).

214. Cf. Diogenes Laertius, *Lives* 6.35.

so different, to such an extent that some Stoics (Musonius, for example) praised Cynicism, while others such as Epictetus cast opprobrium on the Cynicism of their day while idealizing the Cynicism of Diogenes. It must also be noted that, at least when regarded by outsiders, Cynics and Stoics could easily be confused, since they both wore the τρίβων and the beard of a philosopher. The second reason is tied to the emergence of a new religion that was in a sense just as revolutionary as Cynicism: Christianity, whose morality was compatible in many regards with that of Cynicism, to such an extent that, in this case as well, strong ties were woven between the two movements. Thus figures emerge who call themselves both Christians and Cynics, though at times the relationship between Christians and Cynics also became strained, and even hostile. As in the case of the Stoics, when seen from the outside by pagans, Cynics and Christians could be confused with one another. A more indistinct portrait of the Cynic began to displace the clear one drawn by the movement's first generations. The situation is complicated further by the fact that, somewhat incredibly, a distinction emerged between a good Cynicism, which was respectable and partly idealized, and a popular Cynicism that went hungry, begged, barked, and bothered. It's this complexity that we wish to emphasize, because in order to avoid serious misconceptions, it's imperative to understand as precisely as possible what imperial Cynicism actually was, before attempting to recognize what connections might eventually have been established between Cynicism on the one hand and Jesus and the earliest Christian communities on the other hand, and later with the church fathers and monasticism.

Cynicism in the Imperial Era

A number of questions emerge as we move forward from the first generations of Cynicism to address the Cynicism of the imperial era. How was Diogenes's Cynicism effectively transmitted to the Roman Empire? In such a changed context, to what extent did Cynicism under the Roman Empire remain true to its origins, and to what extent did it become something different? How do we explain the extraordinary fascination it held for its detractors and defenders alike? In a complex philosophical landscape, where Middle- and then Neoplatonists, Peripatetics, Stoics, and Sextians all defended their vision of the world with arguments and treatises, what location did Cynicism occupy on the philosophical grid? Who could call himself a Cynic? What do we know of any historic ties that connected Cynicism concretely with

Stoicism, and of the attitude, often highly ambiguous, that Stoics held of their relationship with Cynics? These are the many questions that we will now attempt to answer.[215]

Transmission and Reception

There are so few witnesses to Cynicism in the last two centuries BCE that it's tempting to believe that Cynicism practically disappeared before the start of the Christian era. However, as we explained earlier,[216] certain evidence contradicts the theory of such a disappearance in the first century BCE. Athenaeus describes the poet Meleager of Gadara unambiguously as a Cynic; Plutarch appeals to the frankness of Cynics in order to characterize the behavior of the senator Marcus Favonius;[217] Cicero vigorously attacks Cynic amorality in his discussion of *decorum*;[218] and this is the period in which the first pseudepigraphal *Letters* attributed to Cynics appear. Furthermore, if Cynicism had been nothing but a vague memory, an abstraction, in this same first century BCE, how do we explain the way that the mimist Decimus Laberius was able to make a crude reference to the *Cynica haeresis* in one of his mimes?[219] And, as we've already mentioned, even if the classification of philosophical schools that Varro proposes in his *De philosophia*[220] is offered out of theoretical concerns, as he enumerates 288 possible philosophical schools, he uses the Cynic way of life as a criterion of classification that allows him to move from forty-eight schools to ninety-six. How could such a classification have been meaningful if the Cynic way of life had no longer any meaning for Varro's readers in the first century BCE?

215. Comprehensive studies: Margarethe Billerbeck, "Greek Cynicism in Imperial Rome?," *AC* 51 (1982): 151–73, reprinted in Margarethe Billerbeck, ed., *Die Kyniker in der modernen Forschung: Aufsätze mit Einführung und Bibliographie*, Bochumer Studien zur Philosophie 15 (Amsterdam: Grüner, 1991), 147–66; Marie-Odile Goulet-Cazé, "Le cynisme à l'époque impériale," *ANRW* 2.36.4:2720–833; M. T. Griffin, "Le mouvement cynique et les Romains: attraction et répulsion," in Goulet-Cazé and Goulet, *Le cynisme ancien et ses prolongements*, 241–58.

216. See "An Eclipse?" on p. 16.

217. Plutarch, *Brutus* 34.5.

218. Cicero, *On Duties* 1.35.128 and 1.41.148.

219. Laberius, *Compitalia*, Ribbeck frag. 3 = Panayotakis frag. 22: *sequere <me> in latrinum, ut aliquid gustes ex Cynica haeresi*, "If you want to taste something from the Cynic school, come with me to the latrines."

220. Varro, *On Philosophy*, in Augustine, *The City of God* 19.1.2–3.

So Cynicism must still have had adherents who were maintaining it as a living tradition. At the same time, it had a literary tradition that was faithfully transmitting the memory of its great founders and the principles of their philosophy. Consider some evidence. The fact that Dionysius of Halicarnassus, Epictetus, Longinus, and Julian, and later Photius, all knew the works of Antisthenes is one indication that these continued to be read throughout the period of the Roman Empire. For its part, Diogenes's *Republic* is cited extensively by the Epicurean Philodemus in the first century BCE, and Diogenes's writings were also known by Theophilus of Antioch and Clement of Alexandria in the second century CE. His tragedies drew the ire of Julian, who also said that he possessed numerous texts by Crates.[221] The work of Menippus had a considerable impact because it influenced not only Varro but also Petronius, Lucian, Apuleius, and later Martianus Capella and Boethius. Along with the direct transmission of original works, a whole literature of philosophers' *Lives* developed, together with works of biographical character such as *The Sale of Diogenes* by Menippus,[222] the work of the same title by Eubulus,[223] and *The Pedagogue* by Cleomenes.[224] These played a decisive role in the diffusion of Cynicism, in the sense that they helped make known the exemplary character of Diogenes. A *Life of Crates* by Plutarch, which Julian tells us he owned,[225] also circulated, along with *Lives* by Satyrus[226] and by Diocles of Magnesia[227] that include Cynics. To these must be added the literature of *Recollections*, along with the collections of chreias already described, which had been popularizing the sayings of the movement's great figures ever since the first days of Cynicism. In this way, educated people in the early centuries of the Roman Empire continued to be familiar with the message of Diogenes, and his asceticism must still have been practiced.

But it's not until the first century CE that an actual Cynic philosopher is attested in Rome—namely, Demetrius, a friend of Seneca. However, from then on the Cynic tradition continues uninterrupted right through

---

221. Julian, *Discourse 9* (*To the Uneducated Cynics*), 17 (200b).

222. Diogenes Laertius, *Lives* 6.29.

223. Diogenes Laertius, *Lives* 6.30–32.

224. Diogenes Laertius, *Lives* 6.75.

225. Julian, *Discourse 9* (*To the Uneducated Cynics*), 17 (200b) and Lamprias Catalogue no. 37.

226. Satyrus was a Peripatetic of the late third century BCE (cf. Diogenes Laertius, *Lives* 6.80).

227. Diocles was an author of the first century BCE on whom Diogenes Laertius depends heavily for his book 6 (in 12, 13, 20, 36, 87, 88, 91, 99, 103).

Salustius in the fifth century. One suspects that Cynic philosophers, with their rebellious streak, their challenge to all established values, their rejection of παιδεία, their agnosticism in religious matters, and their ascetic and provocative way of life, could only have shocked the gravitas of the Roman people.[228] Comedians and satirists had a field day letting loose on the Cynics, their outfit and their asceticism, setting them front and center in the gallery of figures they mocked. Horace drew a distinction between the excessive and sordid way of life (*sordidus victus*) of an Avidienus, who bore the well-deserved cognomen *Canis*, and the frugal way of life (*tenuis victus*) that would ensure health;[229] in one of his *Epistles*, he offers a dialogue between Aristippus, who's able to adapt to all circumstances by playing the courtier, and Diogenes, who, even as he claims not to need anyone's help, begs for things of little value, which makes him that much more inferior to those who give them.[230] Persius mentions a shameless prostitute pulling the beard of a Cynic,[231] and Martial, in one of his *Epigrams*, draws a comparison to a "withered old Cynic" in order to mock the courtesan Vetustilla, whom he considers completely decrepit, for her dreams of marriage: "You have the rump of a lean duck and your bony cunt would defeat an aged Cynic."[232] The number of Cynics who invaded the streets of Athens, Rome, and Alexandria is striking, showing that Cynicism had become the Roman Empire's popular philosophy par excellence.

The testimony of Dio Chrysostom, in his *Discourse 32: To the Alexandrians*, written after the period when he lived as a Cynic, provides a precise and highly interesting typology of the philosophical landscape of his time, from which it emerges that the Cynics occupied, at least by their number, a major place in Alexandria.[233] Dio distinguishes six categories of philosophers; the Cynics belong to at least one of them, and possibly two.[234] (1) Those who don't go out in public (εἰς πλῆθος) because they don't want to take risks, probably, according to Dio, because they have no hope of improving the

---

228. Cf. Griffin, "Le mouvement cynique et les Romains," 243, 249, 253.

229. Horace, *Satires* 2.2.53–69.

230. Horace, *Epistles* 1.17.15–32.

231. Persius, *Satires* 1.133.

232. Martial, *Epigrams* 3.93.12–13 (trans. David R. Shackleton Bailey, LCL).

233. Dio Chrysostom, *Discourse 32* (*To the Alexandrians*), 8–12.

234. Abraham J. Malherbe, *Paul and the Popular Philosophers* (Minneapolis: Fortress, 1986), 37–47, appears to believe that these categories all correspond to different categories of Cynics, while it is more likely that they cover the whole range of philosophers (cf. in 32.8: παρὰ τοὺς καλουμένους φιλοσόφους and at the start of 32.9: τῶν δὲ Κυνικῶν λεγομένων).

common people. Later, in 32.20, he becomes harshly critical of philosophers in this category and concludes that they are useless. (2) Those who speak in auditoriums to listeners who are bound to them by contract. This is certainly a description of professional philosophers who taught in public. (3) The Cynics of the streets, whom he describes in lively detail as follows:

> As for the Cynics, as they are called, it is true that the city contains no small number [πλῆθος οὐκ ὀλίγον] of that sect, and that, like any other thing, this too has had its crop—persons whose tenets, to be sure, comprise practically nothing spurious or ignoble, yet who must make a living—still these Cynics, posting themselves at street-corners, in alley-ways, and at temple-gates, pass round the hat and play upon the credulity of lads and sailors and crowds of that sort, stringing together rough jokes and much tittle-tattle and that low badinage that smacks of the marketplace. Accordingly they achieve no good at all, but rather the worst possible harm, for they accustom thoughtless people to deride philosophers in general, just as one might accustom lads to scorn their teachers, and, when they ought to knock the insolence out of their hearers, these Cynics merely increase it.[235]

Dio clearly condemns these philosophers who have to beg in order to eat and who exert a nefarious influence through their unrestrained speech, thereby discrediting the very profession of philosopher. (4) Educated people who deliver stupid epideictic orations or who sing their own amateur lyric poetry. Dio has no problem with this if these people present themselves as orators or poets, but if they adopt the role of philosophers because they want money and glory, rather than because they want to benefit their hearers, he finds their attitude scandalous. (5) A small number of people who speak with frankness (παρρησίαν ἀγηόχασι) but don't say much at all, only one or two phrases. They berate (λοιδορήσαντες) rather than teach, and as soon as they're done speaking, they hurry off for fear of being chased away. In light of their παρρησία and the insults they hurled, we may think that this is another category of Cynic philosophers employing Diogenes's rough liberty of speech. But the fact that "they hurry off for fear of being chased away" should lead us to conclude instead that they are actually charlatans. (6) The philosopher who "speaks his mind with frankness, in plain terms and without guile," who is ambitious for neither glory nor money, "but out of good

---

235. Dio Chrysostom, *Discourse 32*, 9 (trans. James Wilfried Cohoon, LCL).

will and concern for his fellow-men stands ready, if need be, to submit to ridicule and to the disorder and the uproar of the mob." Dio recognizes that such an (ideal) philosopher is not easy to find, but he believes that he, driven by the will of some deity, has chosen this role for himself.

This typology is all the more interesting because while Dio lived as a Cynic during the time of his exile, and while he praised Diogenes warmly in several of his earlier discourses, here he regards Cynicism completely from the outside, without any sympathy for the Cynics who were then overrunning the cities. They annoyed him, and he considered them a menace to the profession of philosophy. Were there two different Cynicisms? Suffice it to say at this point that the Cynics were making their presence felt in the philosophical landscape of Alexandria at the start of the second century, either begging on the street corners or forcing people to endure their speeches—which appear not to have been to Dio's liking.

Other authors confirm how ubiquitous the Cynics became at this time, among them Lucian, who refers in *The Fugitives* to a "tribe of sophists"[236] and complains that "every city is filled with such upstarts, particularly with those who enter the names of Diogenes, Antisthenes, and Crates as their patrons and enlist in the army of the dog."[237] He echoes the same theme in *The Double Indictment*, in which Zeus, comparing the time of Socrates, when few people practiced philosophy, to the present day, asks Justice:

> Do not you see how many short cloaks and staves and knapsacks there are? On all sides there are long beards, and books in the left hand, and everybody preaches in favor of you; the public walks are full of people assembling in companies and in battalions, and there is nobody who does not want to be thought a scion of Virtue. In fact, many, giving up the trades that they had before, rush after the knapsack and the cloak, tan their bodies in the sun to Ethiopian hue, make themselves extemporaneous philosophers out of cobblers or carpenters, and go about praising you and your virtue.[238]

Clearly the "Cynic profession" was attractive to many. Other philosophers, however, and the people of the cities generally, who encountered Cynics everywhere—at the entrances to temples, at crossroads, in the forum—and

---

236. Lucian, *The Fugitives* 10.
237. Lucian, *The Fugitives* 16 (trans. Austin M. Harmon, LCL).
238. Lucian, *The Double Indictment* 6 (trans. Austin M. Harmon, LCL).

who were confronted constantly with their invective and their begging, eventually became exasperated with them.

The great novelty of Cynicism in the imperial period was its extreme diversity; in its first generations, the movement had been relatively homogeneous. This diversity was actually due to different understandings of what Cynicism was. To explore this diversity within imperial Cynicism, and particularly so as not to leave the false impression of a basic homogeneity, we will now consider some contrasts. The first is one that some modern researchers have drawn and applied to the entire history of Cynicism, though I would argue that its validity has yet to be established. Another contrast, attested by Diogenes Laertius, probably comes originally from Apollodorus of Seleucia, a Stoic philosopher of the second century BCE; it was still influencing understandings of Cynicism as late as Augustine. The third contrast arises from the discrepancy that ancient authors themselves described under the Roman Empire between respectable, literate Cynicism and popular Cynicism, which they openly criticized and mocked.

An Austere, Rigorous, Spartan Cynicism versus a Soft, Hedonistic, Aristippean Cynicism?

During the first half of the twentieth century, the idea developed that two tendencies could be distinguished within the heart of Cynicism itself: on the one hand, an austere Cynicism, which was characterized by rigorous asceticism, rough behavior toward others, and an audacious attitude toward the onslaughts of Fortune; and on the other hand, a soft Cynicism, which was more relaxed about asceticism, given to philanthropy, and adaptable to circumstances.[239] This idea is constantly encountered in studies of Cynicism; Ronald F. Hock and Abraham J. Malherbe have most recently taken it up.[240] This idea of two tendencies deserves a deeper investigation whose broad

239. See Gustav Adolf Gerhard, "Zur Legende vom Kyniker Diogenes," *AR* 15 (1912): 388–408; Kurt von Fritz, *Quellen-Untersuchungen zu Leben und Philosophie des Diogenes von Sinope*, Philologus: Supplementband 18.2 (Leipzig: Dieterich, 1926), 42–46; Karl Praechter, *Die Philosophie des Altertums*, 12th ed. (Berlin, 1926 = Friedrich Überweg, *Grundriß der Geschichte der Philosophie*, 1:452); Ragnar Höistad, *Cynic Hero and Cynic King: Studies in the Cynic Conception of Man* (PhD diss., University of Uppsala, 1948), 118–23, 131–38.

240. Ronald F. Hock, "Simon the Shoemaker as an Ideal Cynic," *GRBS* 17 (1976): 41–53, repr. in Billerbeck, *Die Kyniker in der modernen Forschung*, 259–71; and Malherbe, *Paul and the Popular Philosophers*, 12–24 (the chapter "Self-Definition among the Cynics").

outlines we can only indicate here. First of all, we must not confuse the presence of a duality within Diogenes—who, according to some, presents an incoherent figure across the various literary strata of the tradition, appearing sometimes as a strict ascetic and other times as a hedonist[241]—with the presence of two opposing tendencies that manifest themselves throughout the history of the Cynic movement. On this last point, which interests us specifically here, I do not agree with A. J. Malherbe, who sees two such tendencies at work within Cynicism.

At the Beginning, Diogenes and Crates: Two Temperaments

The distinction between these two tendencies has been traced back to the earliest days of Cynicism, specifically to a contrast between the personalities of Crates and Diogenes. The latter was intransigent and heroic, fanatical about an asceticism that aimed at virtue. He confronted πόνοι daily and met only his most basic needs in order to take the "shortcut to virtue." He went so far as to throw away his cup after he saw a child drinking out of his hands;[242] he refused to please the crowds, even displaying some hardness in his teaching, when he urged them to face the effort and suffering that his way of life required. As we saw earlier, he called for "men" but then denounced those who gathered as "scoundrels."[243] By contrast, Crates, his disciple, nicknamed the "Door Opener," was a *lar familiaris* who entered homes in order to resolve family quarrels;[244] he was respected by everyone for his humanity and philanthropy. Even when he had to criticize someone, he did so graciously.[245] Everyone agrees about these significant differences between the characters of the two philosophers.

But do these differences really require the conclusion that Crates embodied a "soft" Cynicism and Diogenes an "austere" Cynicism, and that a dichotomy between these two tendencies persisted throughout the whole history of the Cynic movement? It seems excessive to draw conclusions

241. See, e.g., Praechter, *Die Philosophie des Altertums*, 434. For an interpretation of this incoherence as the reflection of two levels within Diogenes's asceticism, see Goulet-Cazé, *L'ascèse cynique*, 77–84, and above 48–49.

242. Cf. Diogenes Laertius, *Lives* 6.37.

243. Cf. Diogenes Laertius, *Lives* 6.32 (see "Relationship with Others" on p. 51).

244. Diogenes Laertius, *Lives* 6.86; Apuleius, *Florida* 22.1–4.

245. Cf. Plutarch, *Table-Talk* 2.1.7 (632e): ποιεῖ δ᾽ εὔχαρι σκῶμμα καὶ μέμψις ἐμφαίνουσα χάριν.

about the kind of asceticism these philosophers practiced based on their character and personalities. In fact, there's every indication that Crates, despite the mildness of his character, practiced a strict asceticism in the purest tradition of Diogenes. The playwright Philemon, a contemporary of his, testifies eloquently to this: "In summer-time a thick cloak he would wear, to achieve mastery of himself, and in winter, rags."[246] We also know that even though Crates was a hunchback, he exercised at the gymnasium and ran daily for fitness, without worrying about what others thought,[247] and he didn't hesitate to give up all of his possessions.[248] Crates said he wanted to "erect a trophy to the victory over poverty,"[249] and he wrote a hymn to Frugality.[250] When his disciple Metrocles left Theophrastus to follow him, the new way of life he adopted, of which Teles paints a very evocative portrait, could not have been more faithful to the asceticism of Diogenes.[251] We may also note that the image of Crates conveyed through the collection of his pseudepigraphal *Letters*, which many believe date to the early imperial period, conforms to this portrait of asceticism and rigor.[252] So in Diogenes and Crates we are facing not two Cynicisms but two men with different temperaments who adapted the same kind of asceticism to their respective personalities. The same holds true for their behavior toward others. Even if they went about it with a difference in tone, they both saw themselves as physicians of the soul, and they both corrected their hearers.

Bion of Borysthenes and Adaptation to Circumstances

Those who argue for the existence of a "soft" Cynicism generally offer as examples, besides Crates, Bion of Borysthenes in the third century BCE and, under the Roman Empire, Demonax and Dio. They emphasize particularly how these philosophers adapted themselves to the circumstances. This ar-

---

246. Diogenes Laertius, *Lives* 6.87 (reading ἵν' ἐγκρατὴς ᾖ).

247. Cf. Themistius, *On Virtue*, folio 36a of the Syriac version (Mach 59); Diogenes Laertius, *Lives* 6.91.

248. Diogenes Laertius, *Lives* 6.87.

249. Teles, *Diatribe* 2 (Hense 15.1–2; Fuentes González, *Les diatribes de Télès*, 140).

250. Cf. *Palatine Anthology* 10.104; Julian, *Discourse* 9 (*To the Uneducated Cynics*), 16 (199a).

251. Cf. Teles, *Diatribe* 4a (Hense 40.4–41.13; Fuentes González, *Les diatribes de Télès*, 368).

252. Cf. Pseudo-Crates, *Letters* 11, 14, 15, 18.

gument is not necessarily valid, however. Bion first enrolled at the Academy, where he was a student of Crates of Athens, but after that he moved in Cynic circles and, for a time at least, was an itinerant Cynic philosopher.[253] But he then left Cynicism and joined Theodorus the Atheist and the Cyrenaic school before finally following the Peripatetic Theophrastus. Diogenes Laertius includes him among the philosophers of the Academy, while Favorinus and the *Gnomologium Vaticanum* describe him as a Peripatetic.[254] Thanks to Teles, who had access to Bion's *Diatribes*, we have an idea of his moral philosophy.

The passage that's most significant for our purposes comes in the diatribe "On Self-Sufficiency,"[255] as Bion develops a comparison between a good actor, who will properly play whatever role the dramatist assigns, and the person of valor who will properly play whatever role Fortune assigns. Bion advises becoming able to adapt to whatever role Fortune entrusts to us, whether that of a king or a vagabond. A bit later, to illustrate the idea that it's not things in themselves that cause our distress, but the way we understand them in light of our character and ideas, he presents an original analogy:

The bite of a wild animal depends on how you try to capture it. If you grab a serpent by the middle, you'll be bitten. But if you pick it up by its neck, you'll suffer no harm. In the same way, how much distress things create depends on how you take them. If you take them like Socrates, you'll experience no distress. But if you take them otherwise, you'll be afflicted, not because of the situations themselves, but because of your own character and wrong ideas. That's why you must try not to change things, but prepare yourself to face them as they occur, as sailors do.[256]

This adaptation to circumstances has been interpreted as a softening of the attitude that Diogenes took toward Fortune. Two arguments, however, suggest that this interpretation may not be well grounded. First of all,

253. Favorinius, Barigazzi frag. 115 = Amato frag. 50 (Bion, Kindstrand frag. 39a).

254. Favorinus, Barigazzi frag. 115 = Kindstrand frag. 39a = Amato frag. 125; *Gnomologium Vaticanum*, no. 161 (Sternbach 67 = Kindstrand frag. 39c).

255. Teles, *Diatribe* 2 (Hense 5–20; Fuentes González, *Les diatribes de Télès*, 134–43, commentary at 144–272). The passage we are interested in here comes at the beginning of the diatribe (Hense 5–6) and it must be completed by the quotation from Bion (Hense 9).

256. Teles, *Diatribe* 2 (Hense 9.2–20; Fuentes González, *Les diatribes de Télès*, 136). It's not easy to say exactly where the quotation from Bion ends. It's possible that after the reference to Socrates, it's actually Teles who is speaking.

there's no guarantee that Bion is expressing a Cynic point of view on this question. As we've already noted, he was a follower of Theodorus the Atheist, and hence of the Cyrenaic school, which took Aristippus and his way of life as its model.[257] And as Diogenes Laertius informs us, adaptation to circumstances was characteristic of Aristippus: "He was capable of adapting himself to place, time and person, and of playing his part appropriately under whatever circumstances. Hence he found more favor than anybody else with Dionysius, because he could always turn the situation to good account. He derived pleasure from what was present, and did not toil to procure the enjoyment of something not present. Hence Diogenes called him a 'royal dog.'"[258]

Consequently, we could conclude that Bion is actually expressing an attitude toward circumstances characteristic of the Cyrenaic school. However—and this is our second argument—not only does the admiration that Diogenes expresses here indicate that Aristippus's attitude was not opposed to his own, but tradition actually attributes to Diogenes this same kind of adaptation to circumstances: "On being asked what he had gained from philosophy, he replied, 'This at least, if nothing else—to be prepared for any eventuality.'"[259] Similarly, when someone asked Crates, "What will it benefit me if I become a philosopher?" he responded,

> You'll be able to untie your bag easily, pull out some money with your own hand, and give it away with detachment, not like now, in inner torment, hesitating and trembling, like someone whose hands are paralyzed. On the contrary, when your bag is full, that's how you'll see it, and if you see that it's empty, you won't complain; if you've decided to make use of it, you can do so easily, and if you have nothing, you'll have no regrets; instead, you'll content yourself with what you presently have, without wanting anything you haven't got and without complaining about anything that happens to you.[260]

The attitude of both Cynics and Cyrenaics was to try to adapt to their situations and to be content with what they had. Therefore, adaptation to

257. Cf. Diogenes Laertius, *Lives* 4.52 (Kindstrand T 19).

258. Cf. Diogenes Laertius, *Lives* 2.66; Horace, *Letters* 1.17.15–32.

259. Diogenes Laertius, *Lives* 6.63.

260. Teles, *Diatribe* 4a (Hense 38.5–39.1; Fuentes González, *Les diatribes de Télès*, 366–68).

circumstances cannot, in itself, serve as a distinguishing factor between supposed "soft" and "austere" forms of Cynicism. If there is a distinction, at most it's between the spirit in which Cynics and Cyrenaics understood this adaptation. Bion envisioned that one might be either a king or a vagabond; in other words, he serenely pictured all the roles that Fortune might assign and advised facing them by being content with what one had, whatever one's lot. Diogenes, on the other hand, dealt with the blows of Fortune in a different spirit. When it struck him, he fought back vigorously: "Diogenes claimed that to Fortune he could oppose courage, to convention nature, to passion reason."[261] He treated it with superior disdain: "When Diogenes fell once more into misfortune, he said, 'Really, Fortune, you do well to stand up to me in as virile a way as possible'; in such a situation he was able to go off humming to himself."[262] Through this defiant response, Diogenes was actually throwing down the gauntlet to Fortune: "Diogenes used to say that he thought he saw Fortune hurling herself at him and saying" (in the words of the *Iliad* 8.299), "I cannot reach this mad dog with my darts."[263] Julian admired the way Diogenes continued to joke even when he was captured by pirates, and the way Crates, faced with the deformity of his own body, made fun of his own crippled leg and stooped shoulders.[264] Beyond this, while Bion submitted to Fortune and agreed to play whatever role it assigned, Diogenes would not let a role be imposed on him; rather, he decided for himself, by falsifying the currency, what role he wanted to play. When, through the caprice of Fortune, he was captured by pirates and put up for sale, he demanded that the auctioneer cry out, "Who would like to buy a master?"[265] While Bion tried to find the best way to deal with the blows of Fortune, Diogenes attacked, provoked, and audaciously defied Fortune, never letting it succeed in defeating him, because he managed to turn to his own advantage things that would have plunged anyone else into despair.

Finally, both men prepared themselves to face the blows of Fortune, but the methods they used were not identical. For Bion (or perhaps Teles), the technique to adopt was that of sailors, who know how to adapt to the

---

261. Diogenes Laertius, *Lives* 6.38.

262. Stobaeus, *Anthology* 4.44.71 (Hense 5:976.3–6; trans. Helena Caine-Suarez from Goulet-Cazé, "Religion and the Early Cynics," in Branham and Goulet-Cazé, *The Cynics*, 56).

263. Stobaeus, *Anthology* 2.8.21 (Wachsmuth 2:157.7–9; trans. Helena Caine-Suarez from Goulet-Cazé, "Religion and the Early Cynics," in Branham and Goulet-Cazé, *The Cynics*, 56).

264. Julian, *Discourse 9 (To the Uneducated Cynics)*, 18 (201b).

265. Diogenes Laertius, *Lives* 6.29.

wind: if the wind was favorable, they hoisted the sails, but if the wind was contrary, they furled the sails. In the same way, a weaker person shouldn't seek to do things that call for greater strength, nor should an older person try to do what's appropriate for someone younger. The moment Fortune strikes, we adapt. For Diogenes, the technique was to practice a preventive asceticism by fighting against πόνοι, to have all the strength necessary to face the blows of Fortune when they came. Bion strategically submitted to Fortune in order to preserve his independence; Diogenes was forced to submit, but still resisted with rage and determination. For Bion, Fortune was something of an abstract concept that embodied all the insecurity of the human condition; for Diogenes, Fortune was a real adversary that had to be opposed with a vital energy.[266] In the end, the attitude taken toward circumstances led to the same result in both cases: the philosophers didn't let themselves be bothered by the vicissitudes of life, and they knew how to be content with what they had. The difference lays rather in their characters. Diogenes never gave up, never submitted; he fought back against the caprice of Fortune with an unfailing pugnacity and a rage for victory. He practically stepped into Fortune's blows. Crates and Bion never showed such rage. But once we take into account the complexity of Bion's philosophical associations, the related views that the Cyrenaic and Cynic schools held of the proper attitude toward circumstances, and the diverse temperaments of these philosophers, it becomes clear that adaptation to circumstances cannot provide decisive support for the idea that there were two divergent tendencies within Cynicism in the fourth and third centuries BCE.

The "Softness" of Demonax and Dio Chrysostom

Under the Roman Empire, a similar situation arises in the case of Demonax ("the best philosopher I know," as Lucian described him): he's frequently cited as an example of "soft" Cynicism. Even though Lucian doesn't make a point of it, since he didn't look favorably on the asceticism of the Cynics, he does testify that Demonax indeed practiced an asceticism like that of Diogenes: "He exercised his body and trained it for endurance" (πρὸς καρτερίαν διεπεπόνητο) (*Life of Demonax* 4).[267] Otherwise, the similari-

266. Cf. Kindstrand, *Bion of Borysthenes*, 207.

267. English translations of the *Demonax* are based on *The Works of Lucian of Samosata*, trans. H. W. Fowler and F. G. Fowler (Oxford: Clarendon, 1905).

ties to Crates are incontestable. In his relationships, Demonax knew how to offer correction without being severe (6). He never raised his voice, and he didn't get agitated or lose his temper, taking as his example those doctors who never get angry with the patients they're treating (7). Just like Crates, he was able to reconcile feuding brothers, as well as husbands and wives (8). Lucian defines his style of philosophy as "gentle" (πρᾶος), "civilized" (ἥμερος), and "joyful" (φαιδρός) (9), even though he also notes those occasions when Demonax spoke to the Athenians frankly and independently, particularly when they criticized him for not offering sacrifices and not being initiated into the Eleusinian Mysteries (11). Demonax served his friends faithfully and had no enemies. In his older years, he would enter people's homes uninvited and eat and sleep there, being regarded as "a divine epiphany" and "a good daemon" (63). Lucian's treatise about him is filled with laughter; it's clear that Demonax loved to laugh wholeheartedly (8, 13, 15, 21, 44). But while he seems to have been so similar in personality to Crates, he also practiced an eclecticism reminiscent of Bion's multiple connections: "Instead of confining himself to a single school of philosophy, he made a mixture of several, without showing clearly which of them he preferred; he appeared to be nearest akin to Socrates, although as regards externals and plain living, he seemed to imitate Diogenes" (5). One day Demonax was asked which philosophers he appreciated, and he replied, "I admire them all; Socrates I revere, Diogenes I admire, Aristippus I love" (62). Since antiquity the practice has been to classify philosophers into schools, but a case like this shows how too strict a classification can be an oversimplification. Through his asceticism, dress, frankness, and independence, Demonax was faithful to Diogenes; but through the mildness of his character, he followed instead in the line of Socrates and Aristippus—and, I should add, Crates.

Dio is also called on sometimes to support the idea of a "soft" Cynicism. His presentation of Diogenes in the discourses he devotes to him (4, 6, 8, 9, 10) fully respects that philosopher's asceticism.[268] As for Dio himself, though he came from a rich family in Prusa and was well known as a sophist, there's no doubt that during his time in exile he genuinely practiced an ascetic Cynicism, even if only for that time. Since the people he met on the roads took him to be a philosopher, he decided to become one, and so he reflected on

---

268. See, e.g., Dio Chrysostom, *Discourse 6* (*Diogenes, or On Tyranny*), 8–10, 14–15, 21–22; *Discourse 8* (*Diogenes, or On Virtue*), 21–26; *Discourse 9* (*Diogenes, or the Isthmian Discourse*), 12.

the questions that people asked him.[269] This led him to decide on an itinerant life, and by his own choice he went from city to city for fourteen years. Still, he was closer in character to Crates than to Diogenes: even when he reprimanded cities that had fallen into excesses, he didn't insult them and he didn't get unpleasant.[270] To define the ethos of Dio's philosophy, Philostratus explains that despite the severity of his attacks, they were moderated by a "seasoning," his gentleness (τῇ πραότητι).[271] Like Crates and Demonax, Dio practiced a severe asceticism in his daily life, but he was able to transmit the message of Cynicism in a way suited to the mildness of his character.

Witnesses to an Austere Asceticism under the Roman Empire

Various examples may be offered of figures who practiced an austere asceticism under the Roman Empire. Demetrius, who went about naked or half-naked, illustrates this radical asceticism, faithful to the tradition of Diogenes. Unlike other Cynics who simply forbade ownership, he forbade even begging, and so he was poorer than the rest, according to Seneca.[272] He spoke freely, just like Diogenes, disregarding the risks he might run, as the statement he made to the emperor Nero testifies: "You may condemn me to death, but it's Nature itself that condemns you."[273] Peregrinus provides another illustration of asceticism. He went to Alexandria to study under a great master of Cynicism, Agathobulus, who was also master to Demonax (*Life of Demonax* 3), and specifically to be trained in "the remarkable asceticism" (*The Passing of Peregrinus* 17). With half of his head shaved and his face daubed with mud, he demonstrated "what is known as the act of indifference" (τὸ ἀδιάφορον δὴ τοῦτο καλούμενον ἐπιδεικνύμενος) by masturbating in public and by being beaten on the buttocks with a baton (*The Passing of Peregrinus* 17). Lucian describes this asceticism exaggeratedly to show that he disapproves, but we may imagine that Peregrinus became a disciple of Agathobulus for a time because, like Demonax, he wanted to be initiated into the authentic tradition of Diogenes's asceticism. Oenomaus is sometimes mentioned in this connection as well. We know very little about

269. Cf. Dio Chrysostom, *Discourse 13* (*To the Athenians, On Exile*), 11–12.
270. Philostratus, *Lives of the Sophists* 1.7 (Olearius 487 = Kayser 7.5–8).
271. Philostratus, *Lives of the Sophists* 1.7 (Olearius 487 = Kayser 11–14).
272. Seneca, *On the Happy Life* 18.3.
273. Epictetus, *Discourses* 1.25.22.

him, and nothing suggests that he led the Cynic way of life, but Eusebius, who preserves some extracts from his work *Charlatans Exposed*, indicates that he spoke with much frankness (παρρησία) and with the bitter acerbity of the Cynics (κυνικὴ πικρία) (*Preparation for the Gospel* 5.21.6). This, along with the highly virulent tone of the passages transmitted by Eusebius, makes us recognize that Oenomaus was not gentle like Crates or Demonax. But the most outstanding example of asceticism under the Roman Empire is without a doubt Salustius, who put a burning coal on his thigh and blew on it to see how long he could stand it.[274]

All the philosophers I have examined, without exception, unquestionably practiced an austere, rough, and demanding Cynic asceticism. In my view, it is actually the difference in their characters—some were hard, others more gentle—along with the influence on some of them of other philosophies, that has given modern researchers the idea of two opposing Cynicisms.

The Pseudepigraphal Letters

Before leaving this issue, we must also take into consideration some documents already mentioned, the pseudepigraphal *Letters*. These were written, for the most part, in the first century CE. Their authors probably had two goals in mind: first, the letters are literary efforts (rather mediocre ones, truth be told), and second, they are instruments of propaganda to promote Cynicism. They're attributed to Diogenes, Crates, Heraclitus, Socrates, and to the Socratics. A. J. Malherbe, for one, makes great use of them to justify the contrast he draws between two Cynicisms. For him the letters of Diogenes testify to an austere Cynicism and those of Crates to a softened version. The austere form is recognizable in Diogenes's *Letter 29*, when the philosopher informs Dionysius that he's going to send him a pedagogue armed with a painful whip; this pedagogue resembles neither Aristippus nor Plato, but by inspiring Dionysius with courage, he cures him of softness (μαλακία) and love for gourmet meals. In paragraph 5, using vivid imagery, Diogenes contrasts the medical expedients of amputation, cauterization, and drugs, which he says are far preferable, with grandparents or nurses pleading gently with a child to get it to swallow its medicine.

---

274. Simplicius, *On the Handbook of Epictetus* 14.299–302 (*Simplicius, Commentaire sur le Manuel d'Épictète*, ed. Ilsetraut Hadot, CUF 411 [Paris: Les Belles Lettres, 2001], 89).

But the same kind of rigor is evident in the *Letters* of Crates, when he tells his companions to flee pleasures, which are sources of injustice and intemperance, and to pursue πόνοι, the sources of temperance and strength of soul.[275] Similarly, in *Letter 19* he refuses to consider Ulysses the "father of Cynicism" because he was more effeminate than his companions, he put pleasure above everything, and he praised the easy life. Crates confers this title on Diogenes instead, who was above both pleasure and suffering, and who showed great courage by training himself for virtue. *Letter 29*, addressed to Hipparchia, may also be cited in this regard: Crates tells her, "It is not because we are indifferent to everything that others have called our philosophy Cynic, but because we robustly endure those things that are unbearable to them because they are effeminate or subject to false opinion."[276] Even if these letters may occasionally contain exaggeration and even caricature, like *Letter 29* of Diogenes, they're still consistent with the communal vision of Cynic asceticism.

But what happens when we get to the *Socratic Letters*, probably written after the start of the second century CE? According to Malherbe, "The author of the Socratic letters . . . has a striking conciliatory tendency. . . . The letters thus provide valuable evidence for an attempt to bring rigoristic and hedonistic Cynicism into harmony, and are thus a major source for the history of Cynicism."[277] The letters that interest us specifically are the ones that offer a debate on the opportunity that philosophers have to associate with tyrants. They're sent to and from Aristippus, who is at the court of Dionysius of Syracuse. The question—and I do not agree with Malherbe on this point—is whether Aristippus represents a "hedonistic cynicism" to which the author of the letters would be sympathetic. What Aristippus says in these letters is in fact consistent with what we otherwise know of that philosopher's views: he doesn't want to suffer hunger or thirst, or have a bad reputation, or wear a long beard (*Letter 9*, 3). On the other hand, when Antisthenes speaks, he reproaches Aristippus for wishing that sages could make a lot of money and have powerful people for their friends (*Letter 8*). Simon the shoemaker, who doesn't appreciate the way Aristippus has been belittling his way of life, which is also Antisthenes's one, encourages him not to forsake hunger and thirst, because they can do much for those who want to develop self-control (*Letter 12*). Aristippus does send him a rather

---

275. Cf. Pseudo-Crates, *Letter 15* (*To His Companions*).
276. English translation of Cynic Epistles by Abraham J. Malherbe.
277. Malherbe, *Cynic Epistles*, 29.

conciliatory response, expressing admiration and even praise for him. He mentions those who are accustomed to come and speak with him, sitting alongside him as he works—Socrates and the young people who surround him, as well as those responsible for public affairs, including Pericles himself, when he's not occupied by his duties as a general—and then Aristippus notes that Antisthenes himself also visits Simon. This gives him the opportunity to contrast Antisthenes, who goes barefoot and advises the Athenians to do the same, denying Simon of work and income, with himself, Aristippus, who wears shoes. He invites Simon to come and practice philosophy at Syracuse (that is, in the court of Dionysius), where he would also have work as a shoemaker. Accordingly, Simon should admire Aristippus for accommodating leisure and pleasure, and he should also be led to belittle the boastfulness of those who wear long beards and carry staffs, who are dirty and louse-ridden and whose fingernails are like those of wild animals, meaning Cynics (*Letter 13*).

Should we conclude that Aristippus embodies a soft Cynicism, with which the author of these letters sympathizes, as opposed to a more rigorous Cynicism, represented by Antisthenes and Simon? Should the debate in these *Letters* be interpreted in terms of an internal debate within Cynicism, between Cynics who were strict and those who were less so, as Hock believes, and Malherbe after him? I would argue instead that these *Socratic Letters* are first of all literary efforts that seek to present the philosophers consistently with their traditional portraits. Accordingly, Antisthenes goes barefoot, Aristippus wears shoes, and Simon philosophizes even while trimming leather. The *Socratic Letters* bring back to life the diverse points of view that were held among the disciples of Socrates, depicting each according to the characteristics that tradition has preserved. But we do not see any concern on the part of the author to resolve a difference between two tendencies within Cynicism. As a result, we must conclude that a distinction between a "soft" Cynicism and an "austere" Cynicism cannot be supported by appeal to these letters.

Indeed, we have not spoken in terms of a supposed opposition between hedonistic Cynicism and rigorist Cynicism at all to this point for the simple reason that Diogenes and Crates themselves affirmed, as noted earlier, that the "shortcut" they were taking brought them pleasure and happiness, a happiness that consisted of tranquility, serenity, and gladness.[278] Precisely

---

278. Stobaeus, *Anthology* 4.39.21 (Hense 5:906.14–17); *Gnomologium Vaticanum*, no. 181 (Sternbach 74).

because Cynicism saw itself as both hedonism and eudaemonism, it would be inappropriate to believe that it existed in two separate forms, one hedonistic and the other rigorist.

Some also speak of an Aristippean Cynicism and offer a simple contrast between it and a Spartan Cynicism,[279] on the grounds that some Cynics expressed their admiration for Spartan values.[280] But this opposition, which is not documented in ancient literature, is based on the same presuppositions as the one between a soft Cynicism and an austere Cynicism, without any further justification.

Cynicism as a School of Thought and as a Way of Life

The second of the three contrasts we wish to explore is much different. It has to do with a debate between two conceptions of Cynicism that Diogenes Laertius describes in detail, though it dates back to long before him. The fact that he brings it up out of his own concerns proves that these two conceptions were still held in opposition to one other in the early centuries CE. They're related to the theoretical discussion of what constitutes a αἵρεσις. Is Cynicism a αἵρεσις—that is, a school of thought with a theoretical foundation, based on δόγματα?[281] Or, on the contrary, is Cynicism only an ἔνστασις βίου, a way of life? Diogenes chooses the first position and defends it personally with some emphasis:[282] "We believe that Cynicism is really a philosophy, and not, as some maintain, just a way of life."[283] This is why book 6 of *Lives* offers two doxographies of Antisthenes (10–13), one doxography of Diogenes (70–73), and a general doxography of Cynicism (103–5). These allow certain great dogmas of the school to be enunciated: in the doxography of Diogenes, for example, notably the conception of asceticism and πόνοι;

279. Cf., e.g., Bernhard Lang, *Jesus der Hund: Leben und Lehre eines jüdischen Kynikers* (Munich: Beck, 2010), 160–61.

280. See Stobaeus, *Anthology* 3.13.43 (Hense 3:462.11–15); Diogenes Laertius, *Lives* 6.27, 59.

281. Diogenes Laertius, *Lives* 1.20, explains why one might not consider the Skeptic school a αἵρεσις: "If we are to understand by 'sect' a bias in favor of coherent positive doctrines, they could no longer be called a sect, for they have no positive doctrines." Cf. Sextus Empiricus, *Outlines of Pyrrhonism* 1.16–17.

282. Diogenes Laertius rarely comments within his own work, so this statement of a personal position is therefore significant.

283. Cf. Diogenes Laertius, *Lives* 6.103.

falsification of currency; the need for consistency between words and actions; the model of Heracles; community of goods among friends; and even community of women and children.

The difference between these two conceptions is not unimportant. What's at stake is nothing less than the status of Cynicism as a philosophical school at all.[284] The difference also bears directly on the identity of the movement's founder, and moreover it affects an analysis of the connections between Cynicism and Stoicism. In effect, those who see Cynicism as a αἵρεσις based on dogmas, and who believe that a kinship exists between Cynicism and Stoicism, trace Cynicism back to Antisthenes and derive Stoicism from Cynicism. This allows them to make the Stoics heirs of Socrates through this lineage: Socratism (through Antisthenes) → Cynicism (Diogenes and his disciples) → Stoicism (through Crates, disciple of Diogenes and master of Zeno). This is just what Diogenes Laertius does[285] when he attributes the same τέλος[286] to the Cynics and Stoics: "The Cynics hold that 'life according to virtue' is the End to be sought, as Antisthenes says in his *Heracles*: exactly like the Stoics. For indeed there is a certain close relationship between the two schools. Hence it has been said that Cynicism is a shortcut to virtue; and after the same pattern did Zeno of Citium live his life."[287]

Definitions of the Cynic τέλος, which all come from the period after the earliest Cynicism, are varied. Diogenes Laertius's doxographic definition, "living according to virtue," is clearly influenced by Stoicism.[288] According to Clement of Alexandria,[289] Antisthenes advocated ἀτυφία as the end, meaning the refusal of illusions to which man might be tempted to succumb; this definition is reasonably consistent with Cynic views. Julian, for his part, says that the end the Cynics pursued was ἀπάθεια, "which is equivalent to

---

284. Cf. Marie-Odile Goulet-Cazé, "Le cynisme est-il une philosophie?," in *L'anti-platonisme dévoilé*, vol. 1 of *Contre Platon*, ed. Monique Dixsaut, Tradition de la pensée classique (Paris: Librairie Philosophique J. Vrin, 1993), 273-313.

285. Cf. Diogenes Laertius, *Lives* 6.2 and 6.14-15.

286. The problem of τέλος certainly postdates Antisthenes and Diogenes. It's essentially after Aristotle and his *Nicomachean Ethics* that each school was led to specify its τέλος and people began to define philosophical schools by their τέλος and arrange them in relation to one another according to this criterion. Epicurus, Cleanthes, and Chrysippus each wrote a Περὶ τέλους.

287. Diogenes Laertius, *Lives* 6.104. In Diogenes Laertius, *Lives* 7.121, the definition of Cynicism as a shortcut to virtue is notably attributed to the Stoic Apollodorus (of Seleucia).

288. In Diogenes Laertius, *Lives* 7.87, Zeno is credited with designating the end of philosophy as "life in agreement with nature . . . which is the same as a virtuous life."

289. Clement of Alexandria, *Miscellanies* 2.21.130.7.

becoming God,"[290] though a little later in the same discourse he says that "the end and aim of the Cynic philosophy, as indeed of every philosophy, is happiness."[291]

I have demonstrated elsewhere that Diogenes Laertius could be indebted for his position on the kinship between Cynicism and Stoicism to the *Compendium of Philosophers* (Ἐπιδρομὴ τῶν φιλοσόφων) by Diocles of Magnesia, who in turn was inspired by the *Introduction to Dogmas* (Αἱ εἰς τὰ δόγματα εἰσαγωγαί) by Apollodorus of Seleucia (second century BCE), for whom Cynicism was "a shortcut to virtue."[292]

On the other hand, the alternative position, the one that Diogenes Laertius opposed, denied Cynicism the status of a αἵρεσις. It must have been supported by Hippobotus, author of a work *On the Sects* (Περὶ αἱρέσεων) and a *Register of Philosophers* (Τῶν φιλοσόφων ἀναγραφή),[293] because, according to Diogenes Laertius, in his list of ethical schools this Hippobotus did not include the "Cynic, Elian and Dialectical schools."[294] As a result, Hippobotus doesn't credit Antisthenes with playing any role in the formation of the Stoic school; for him, the true founder is Zeno. The Epicurean Philodemus notes this disagreement between Hippobotus and "Socratic" Stoics: "[They (i.e., Stoics who advocate the lineage Socrates → Diogenes → Crates) say that it was by Socrates,] Antisthenes and Diogenes that the school (i.e., Stoicism) was constituted in the beginning, because they also want to be called Socratics. But the largest group of Stoics saw considerable growth thanks to Zeno, and all the Stoics, so to speak, give him first place in the school, as do Hippobotus and the chronographer Apollodorus."[295]

In keeping with his position, Hippobotus makes Crates of Thebes the disciple of Bryson of Achaia, and not of Diogenes,[296] thus denying any credibility to those who would relate Stoicism to Socrates through Zeno, Crates, Diogenes, and Antisthenes. Moreover, probably in order to deny, or

---

290. Julian, *Discourse 9* (*To the Uneducated Cynics*), 12 (192a).

291. Julian, *Discourse 9* (*To the Uneducated Cynics*), 13 (193d).

292. Diogenes Laertius, *Lives* 7.121. Apollodorus of Seleucia was a disciple of Diogenes the Babylonian, who was at that same time the master of Panaetius of Rhodes and of Boethius of Sidon. Cf. Goulet-Cazé, "Le Livre VI de Diogène Laërce," 3880–4048, esp. 3937–51.

293. Various dates are assigned to Hippobotus (Hans von Arnim: end of the third century/beginning of second; John Glucker: end of first century; Marcello Gigante: flourished during the first half of the second century); see Goulet-Cazé, "Le Livre VI de Diogène Laërce," 3923n106.

294. Cf. Diogenes Laertius, *Lives* 1.19.

295. Philodemus, *On the Stoics* 3, col. 13.1–12 (Dorandi, "Filodemo, Gli Stoici," 101).

296. Cf. Diogenes Laertius, *Lives* 6.85.

at least minimize, a Cynic influence on Stoicism through Crates, he presents Zeno as a Dialectician of the school of Megara, being a disciple of Diodorus Cronus.[297]

This debate on the status of Cynicism is clearly still taking place under the Roman Empire. It is worth noting how Julian is careful to define Cynicism: "Since it is a fact that Cynicism is a branch of philosophy, and by no means the most insignificant or least honorable, but rivaling the noblest, I must first say a few words about philosophy itself."[298] And now compare this telling remark from Eunapius: "Among the Cynics, Carneades [first or second century CE] was well known, if we must consider Cynicism at all."[299] Why are these two conceptions of Cynicism—as either a school of thought (a validating perspective) or as a simple way of life (a perspective that tended to discredit Cynicism as a philosophy)—so important? If Cynicism was not a school of thought, if it had no dogmas and it could be reduced to a way of life, then it would no longer have a place among the other philosophical schools and it would become a vague notion, susceptible to being claimed by anybody who adopted the Cynic way of life. Varro seems to have envisioned this as a genuine possibility, as evidenced by the passage from his *De philosophia* transmitted by Augustine to which we have already referred.[300] He uses the Cynics' way of life, especially their dress, as one of the criteria for his classification. By doing this, he proves that for him Cynicism is not a school with a distinct τέλος, and he suggests indirectly that it's just a way of life that can be adopted by philosophers with various doctrinal orientations: "Again in the case of that variable which derives from the manners and customs of the Cynics, the question is not about the supreme good, but whether he who pursues that which seems to him to be the true good, no matter what, and to be the proper object of pursuit, should live according to the manners and customs of the Cynics. There were, in fact, men who pursued different final goods, some virtue, others pleasure, yet who held to the same manners and customs, from which they were called "Cynics."[301]

---

297. Diogenes Laertius, *Lives* 7.25.

298. Julian, *Discourse 9 (To the Uneducated Cynics)*, 2 (182c). Julian may have been taught about Cynicism in the course of his philosophical studies, perhaps by Maximus of Ephesus (see Jean Bouffartigue, "Le cynisme dans le cursus philosophique au IVᵉ siècle," in Goulet-Cazé and Goulet, *Le cynisme ancien et ses prolongements*, 339–58).

299. Eunapius, *Lives of the Philosophers and Sophists* 2.5 (Goulet 3.9–11).

300. See "An Eclipse?" on p. 16 and "Transmission and Reception" on p. 54.

301. Varro, *On Philosophy*, in Augustine, *The City of God* 19.1.2–3 (trans. William Chase Greene, LCL).

Augustine takes up Varro's idea and applies it in his case to philosophers who want to be Christians. While Varro may have been talking theoretically about somebody adopting the Cynic way of life, Augustine envisions Christians actually doing this: "It matters not to the heavenly city whether one who follows the faith that leads to God follows it in one dress or manner of life or in another, so long as these are not contrary to the divine precepts; wherefore when even philosophers become Christians, they are not compelled to change their dress or customary fare, which are no hindrance to religion, but only their false doctrines. So the peculiarity of the Cynics that Varro alleged is a matter of indifference, provided that nothing indecent or uncontrolled is done."[302]

Thus a Cynic philosopher who became a Christian could continue to follow the Cynic way of life, so long as (if Augustine's teaching were followed) he gave up the shamelessness that otherwise characterized adherents of Cynicism. It must be recognized that under the Roman Empire, in the background to the practice of Cynic philosophy, there was an extensive theoretical reflection that envisioned at least three specific cases in which people could claim to be Cynics. For some, Cynicism was a full-fledged philosophy, and they had the sense of belonging to a Cynic philosophical school (αἵρεσις), even if it didn't have an institutional framework; they recognized a certain number of dogmas and pursued a specific τελός. We may suppose that someone like Demetrius illustrates this first case. Others didn't bother with dogmas but still claimed to belong unambiguously to Cynicism on the sole basis that they dressed the same as Diogenes had and led the same way of life (ἔνστασις βίου). The many philosophers who could be found on the streets, who traveled from city to city, and who were not highly instructed belonged to this category. Finally, some others claimed that they adhered to other philosophical schools, or even were Christians, and as a result they had a different τέλος from Cynicism, but they still led a Cynic way of life and wore the τρίβων. We shall see that this was the case for Peregrinus during his Christian phase, and notably for Maximus Hero. We may also think in this connection of a Pythagorean such as Secundus (beginning of the second century), who, at the end of his studies, "put himself forward as a follower of the Cynic discipline,"[303] or a Neoplatonist such as Maximus of Ephesus,

---

302. Varro, *On Philosophy*, in Augustine, *The City of God* 19.19.

303. See Ben Edwin Perry, ed., *Secundus, the Silent Philosopher: The Greek Life of Secundus*, Philological Monographs 22 (New York: American Philological Association, 1964), 69.

whom Julian thought he recognized near Besançon "looking like a Cynic with his τρίβων and staff."[304]

This debate about the nature of Cynicism went hand in hand with a debate about the movement's founder, whose identity continued to be a matter of controversy under the Roman Empire. Julian admits, "Now the founder of this philosophy, to whom we are to attribute it in the first instance, is not easy to discover, even though some think that the title belongs to Antisthenes and Diogenes."[305] Julian cites Oenomaus, who declared that "the Cynic philosophy is neither Antisthenism nor Diogenism,"[306] and he mentions that a certain Cynic he knows even disparages Diogenes, the Dog par excellence, by claiming that he "paid a sufficient penalty for his folly and vanity" when he died from eating a raw octopus.[307] This shows that, under the Roman Empire, some Cynics were prepared to challenge the figure of Diogenes, though he was steadily growing into a legend. Julian alludes to a different theory about the movement's founder, advanced by some Cynics themselves: "The better sort of Cynics assert that in addition to the other blessings bestowed on us by mighty Heracles, it was he who bequeathed to mankind the noblest example of this mode of life."[308] But Julian doesn't leave things at that; he suggests a further explanation of his own. Because he sees in Cynicism a universal philosophy, he considers that the founder of Cynicism, and indeed of philosophy in general, is the god of Delphi, Pythian Apollo, who gave Diogenes two great counsels, "Know thyself" and "Falsify the currency."[309] In Julian's view, Antisthenes, Diogenes, and Crates were the *coryphaei* of this philosophy.[310] His strategy is clear: wanting to deny any significance or credibility to the Cynics of his era, such as Heracleios and the anonymous one he addresses in his discourse *To the Uneducated Cynics*, Julian, by his own hand, transforms the Cynicism of Diogenes into a natural, universal philosophy, respectful of the gods and especially of Apollo its founder, and not given to immodesty. Finally, if we wish to leave no stone unturned, we should mention that besides Antisthenes, Diogenes, Heracles, and Apollo, some appeared to have envisioned a fifth possibility: Ulysses. We

---

304. Julian, *Letter 26* (*To Maximus the Philosopher*), 414d.

305. Julian, *Discourse 9* (*To the Uneducated Cynics*), 8 (187b).

306. Julian, *Discourse 9* (*To the Uneducated Cynics*), 8 (187c).

307. This is an anonymous Cynic who addresses Julian in his *Discourse 9* (*To the Uneducated Cynics*), 1 (181a).

308. Julian, *Discourse 9* (*To the Uneducated Cynics*), 8 (187c).

309. Julian, *Discourse 9* (*To the Uneducated Cynics*), 8 (188a–b).

310. Julian, *Discourse 9* (*To the Uneducated Cynics*), 8 (188b).

deduce this from the fact that the author of a pseudepigraphal letter of Crates refuses to regard Ulysses as the founder of the movement. He explains that the clothes don't make the Cynic: he would rather consider Diogenes, who lived above both suffering and pleasure, as the true founder of the philosophy than Ulysses, because, even if he sometimes wore the garb of a Cynic, he was effeminate and he venerated pleasure.[311]

The three theoretical definitions of Cynicism we have just described (school of thought; way of life identifying itself as Cynicism; way of life compatible with a different philosophical school or with Christianity), which corresponded to actual situations under the Roman Empire, made it complicated enough to answer the question "Who can call himself a Cynic?" But beyond this, a cultural and sociological factor intruded within Cynicism, creating a new kind of contrast based on a criterion that didn't apply to other philosophies, specifically the contrast between literate Cynicism and popular Cynicism.

A Literate Cynicism and a Popular Cynicism

The historian of Cynicism is struck by the way witnesses speak not only of a literate Cynicism, originating in the leisure classes, exemplified by great men, and often judged positively, but also of a popular Cynicism, promulgated by street preachers, described as rude and uncouth, and often judged negatively. The contrast is so striking that it may legitimately be asked whether these witnesses are all speaking about the same philosophical movement. Is the Cynicism of Demetrius and Demonax the same Cynicism that Philosophy castigates in Lucian's *The Fugitives*? Are the "uneducated Cynics" whom Julian targets truly Cynics?

Literate Cynicism

Of course, it is the proponents of a literate Cynicism who are best known to us. This is either because, like Oenomaus, they left literary works themselves or because they belonged to a prominent social milieu and had friends who paid tribute to them in their own writings, as Seneca did for Demetrius, or

311. Pseudo-Crates, *Letter 19* (*To Patrocles*) (or *To Metrocles*, if we adopt Wilamowitz's correction).

Lucian for Demonax. In these privileged circles, young people benefited from all the resources of παιδεία. The example of Demonax is eloquent. As Lucian explains, though he had wealth and rank, he aspired to philosophy, and "certainly he did not rush into this with unwashed feet, as they say." In fact, he had already studied the poets so thoroughly that he knew practically all of them by heart, and he'd been trained in rhetoric. Only then did he study with several teachers: the Cynics Demetrius and Agathobulus, the Stoic Epictetus, and the philosopher Timocrates of Heraclea.[312] Peregrinus provides another example. He came from a family in Mysia that appears to have been quite wealthy since his father left him a large inheritance (*The Passing of Peregrinus* 14), and he was clearly well educated because he composed two Olympic discourses (19–20), he commented on certain Christian books and wrote himself some others (11), and before his death he addressed open letters to all the major cities (41). Demetrius, for his part, belonged to the aristocratic circle of the Stoic Thrasea Paetus. While this milieu was typically frequented by *conchyliati*, "wearers of purple," he chose deliberately to go naked or half-naked and to sleep on a straw "mattress" that hardly deserved the name, because he had handed all his goods over for others to possess.[313] The last known Cynic, Salustius, according to the testimony of Damascius, studied law and rhetoric with the Sophist Eunoios of Emesa and then attended schools of rhetoric in Alexandria.[314] Such privileged backgrounds take nothing away from the genuineness of the asceticism that these "haves" of Cynicism embraced—far from it. Nevertheless, it must be appreciated that those who chose poverty voluntarily had a different experience from those who chose it out of necessity. The significance of the difference in circumstances between literate Cynics and uneducated Cynics must not be underestimated.

The Cynicism of the Disadvantaged Classes

Along with these Cynics who came from wealthy families, the movement gathered followers from the most disadvantaged classes of society, from disreputable professions, and from among the slaves. But it's difficult for the historian of philosophy to get a fair appreciation for this popular Cynicism

312. Lucian, *Demonax* 3–4.
313. Seneca, *Letters to Lucilius* 62.3.
314. See references in n. 90 on p. 27.

because the available documents that speak about it come almost entirely from its detractors. And so one has to read between the lines. The disadvantaged classes may actually have been practicing a genuine Cynicism, but their detractors could have transformed it into a caricature and imposture, believing that real Cynicism could only be cultivated, moderate, and socially respectable. Some of them appear to be trying to discredit popular Cynicism by playing up its scandalous element, stripping it of its theoretical justification within the framework of Cynic asceticism (as Lucian does in *The Fugitives*, for example). Other detractors of the popular version, however, such as Epictetus and Julian, argue that true Cynicism cannot contain any such scandalous elements; they idealize the philosophy in order to rehabilitate it. Except for the few educated figures just mentioned, Cynicism in the imperial period was a Cynicism of the popular classes. If Lucian can be believed—and there's no reason to doubt what he says on this point—people who called themselves Cynics were either slaves or *thetes*—that is, poor citizens who worked at small trades such as shoemaker, carpenter, fuller, or wool carder. Lucian says that they saw Cynicism as a sinecure that would enable them to escape from their sordid lives: instead of working hard all day at their trades to get enough to eat, they would rather put on the Cynic outfit, go around begging,[315] and make money without effort.[316] Lucian claims mercilessly—and here he is probably exaggerating—that once they have "stocked themselves up to their heart's content," they "throw off that ill-conditioned philosopher's cloak" (τρίβων) and act as if they were rich: "They buy farms . . . and luxurious clothing, and long-haired pages, and whole apartment houses, bidding a long farewell to the knapsack of Crates, the mantle of Antisthenes, and the jar of Diogenes."[317] He depicts their Cynicism as a transformation of the "shortcut to virtue" into a "shortcut to fame" and portrays it advertising itself this way: "Even if you are an unlettered man—a tanner or a fishmonger or a carpenter or a money-changer—nothing will hinder you from being wondered at, if only you have impudence and boldness, and you learn how to abuse people properly."[318] Dio Chrysostom, in his discourse *To the Alexandrians* (mentioned earlier for its typology of philosophies),

---

315. There are numerous witnesses in the imperial period to Cynics begging, among others Martial, *Epigrams* 4.53; *Palatine Anthology* 11.153 and 11.410; Lucian, *The Fugitives* 14.

316. Lucian, *The Fugitives* 17 (trans. Austin M. Harmon, LCL). Future references to this work are from the Harmon translation.

317. Lucian, *The Fugitives* 20.

318. Lucian, *Philosophies for Sale* 11 (trans. Austin M. Harmon, LCL). Future references to this work are from the Harmon translation.

is a bit more charitable than Lucian toward the Cynics. He recognizes that they're begging in the streets because they're hungry; still, at the same time he readily accuses them of having a bad influence on the people they meet.[319]

The social behavior of these ragged, hairy Cynics shocked their contemporaries. Ammianus, in one of his epigrams, insists that a beard produces not intelligence but lice.[320] Lucian speaks of them as people who "shout" or rather "bray, or howl, and slang everyone,"[321] and Julian challenges Heracleios the Cynic with these words: "Do you really think it so great an achievement to carry a staff and let your hair grow, and haunt cities and camps uttering calumnies against the noblest men, and flattering the vilest?"[322] These Cynics wore out their contemporaries with their practice of begging. Epictetus describes them with an expression borrowed from the *Iliad*: "dogs of the table that guard the doors."[323] And Lucian says deliciously that they go from house to house "shearing the sheep."[324] Beyond this, with a severity toward them unequaled in other writers, he rebukes their penchant for gluttony, which makes them discontent to have just salt fish and thyme with their bread; now they want meat of all sorts and the sweetest wine.[325]

Another complaint against these disruptive beggars, by no means the least, was their lack of modesty, which was due to their total disregard for public opinion. Cicero, echoing Panaetius, criticized Cynicism as hostile to *verecundia* (the sense of shame), saying loud and clear that "the entire system of the Cynics is to be shunned; for it is opposed to modesty, without which there can be neither right nor honor."[326] The philosopher Porphyry attacked the "indifference" of these Cynics, which he considered responsible for their errors and which led them to believe that they could get away with anything.[327] Just as indecency was one of the principal charges leveled against Diogenes for masturbating in public, and against Crates for consummating his marriage in public with his wife Hipparchia, Lucian similarly mocks Peregrinus, who (if Lucian can be believed), when he was with Agathobulus in Egypt, demonstrated "what they call 'indifference' by erecting his yard amid

319. Dio Chrysostom, *Discourse 32* (*To the Alexandrians*), 9.
320. Ammianus in *Palatine Anthology* 11.156.
321. Lucian, *The Fugitives* 14.
322. Julian, *Discourse 7* (*Against the Cynic Heracleios*), 18 (223c–d).
323. *Iliad* 22.69, cited by Epictetus in *Discourses* 3.22.80.
324. Lucian, *The Fugitives* 14.
325. Lucian, *The Fugitives* 14.
326. Cicero, *On Duties* 1.41.148 (trans. Andrew P. Peabody).
327. Porphyry, *On Abstinence* 1.42.5.

a thronging mob of bystanders."[328] The concept of "indifference," which is connected to the pursuit of what is good by nature and scorn for δόξα, is used in an audacious sense within the framework of Cynicism to express the absence of shame for an act that would ordinarily produce shame. This concept is not original to Cynicism, even if the Cynics may later have made use of it; it appears not to have been applied to Cynic behavior until the second century CE, and it almost certainly comes from the Stoic Aristo of Chios and his theory of indifferents.[329] Justin, who was hostile to Cynicism, even claimed that indifference was the good that Cynics pursued.[330] It became customary to group together under this concept all of the indecent acts that Cynics committed. They were reproached for all sorts of shameful things, which they themselves embraced as faithful to nature, but which, in the eyes of their contemporaries, they were wrong to perform intentionally in public. In *Philosophies for Sale*, Lucian has his Cynic offer the following counsel: "Do boldly in full view of all what another would not do in secret."[331]

The presence of women among the Cynics only enhanced their wide reputation for indecency. In the account that Athenaeus gives of the *Cynics' Banquet* by Parmeniscus, two "notorious courtesans" appear: Melissa, presented as a "stage-thumper," and Nicion the "dog-fly," who cites a passage from the *Graces* by Meleager of Gadara and mentions another work by the same author that "contains the comparison of pease-porridge with lentil-soup." Nicion's nickname, her knowledge of Cynic literature, and the fact that she quotes "the words of the Socratic Antisthenes" prove that she belongs to the group of Cynics present at this banquet.[332]

Charlatan Cynics

Seeing these attacks gushing up from everywhere leads us to two conclusions. First, there were certainly some charlatans among those who claimed to be Cynics; they took advantage of the philosophy in order to escape from their desperate social situation. But second, even so, the generalized attacks directed against the Cynics of the streets are probably exaggerated; they're

---

328. Lucian, *The Passing of Peregrinus* 17 (trans. Austin M. Harmon, LCL).
329. Cf. Goulet-Cazé, *Les "Kynika" du stoïcisme*, 112–29.
330. Justin, *Second Apology* 3.7.
331. Lucian, *Philosophies for Sale* 10.
332. Athenaeus, *The Dinner Sophists* 4.157a–b.

actually more the leisure classes' reactions of disdain and distrust against the poor for daring to pretend to philosophy, and the resentment of established philosophers against the uneducated who didn't have the benefit of παιδεία. A Demetrius or a Demonax might be admitted to the circle of philosophers, but the generosity that a shoemaker like Simon was shown in the time of Socrates was no longer in evidence (except in the *Socratic Letters*!). The Cynics of the streets were lumped together with ordinary beggars and treated ungraciously by other philosophers, even by those such as Epictetus and Dio.

If there were charlatans—and certainly there were some—their outfit, characteristic of a traveler, certainly helped with the imposture. The components of this outfit had remained the same since ancient Cynicism: staff, τρίβων, knapsack, long beard, long and dirty hair, and bare feet or perhaps sandals. But originally, even as this outfit symbolized a deliberate choice of social nonconformity and an ardent desire to return to nature through asceticism, above all it was actual equipment for the practice of asceticism. When the outfit reappeared on certain pseudo-philosophers who had nothing to do with asceticism, however, it was nothing but imposture, deception, and inauthenticity. Ironically, those who thought they could become philosophers simply by putting on Diogenes's outfit were turning him into a synonym for conformity, even though he had originally embodied a nonconformity par excellence. Hence the protests that are continually heard throughout the imperial period. In the first century, Antipater of Thessalonica, in one of his *Epigrams*, challenges the right of a Cynic of his day even to carry the knapsack and staff and wear the τρίβων of Diogenes: "Truly I take Diogenes himself to be the dog of heaven, but you are the dog that lies in the ashes. Put off, put off the arms that are not yours! The work of lions is one thing; that of bearded goats is another!"[333]

Seneca, appealing to common sense, warns Lucilius against those who try to attract attention by their "repellent attire, unkempt hair, slovenly beard, open scorn of silver dishes, a couch on the bare earth." If they act this way, he says, it's only because they want to show off. Seneca also expresses his disgust for their excesses of all sorts, explaining that "it is quite contrary to nature to torture the body, to hate basic cleanliness, to be dirty on purpose, to eat food that is disgusting and forbidding."[334] In the next century, Apuleius expresses a wish that reveals his vexation: "If only . . . uncouth, grubby, uneducated people should not play the philosopher as far as wearing

---

333. *Palatine Anthology* 11.158.5–8 (trans. William Roger Paton).
334. Seneca, *Letters to Lucilius* 5.2, 4 (trans. Richard Mott Gummere, LCL).

the cloak, and debase the queen of disciplines, which was invented for the art of good speaking and good living, by evil speech and a life to match."[335] In *The Fugitives* by Lucian, Philosophy complains that people who leave their trades and take up Cynicism "very plausibly transform themselves in looks [σχηματίζουσιν] and apparel to counterfeit Philosophy, doing the same sort of thing that Aesop says the jackass in Cyme did, who put on a lion skin and began to bray harshly, claiming to be a lion himself; and probably there were actually some who believed him!"[336] For his part, Epictetus insists to one of his students who has a penchant for Cynicism that the clothes don't make the Cynic,[337] and later Julian would also insist that an outfit has no value in itself; the attributes of a genuine philosopher are different: "Therefore let him who wishes to be a Cynic philosopher not adopt merely their long cloak or knapsack or staff or their way of wearing the hair, as though he were like a man walking unshaved and illiterate in a village that lacked barbers' shops and schools, but let him consider that the marks of the Cynic philosophy are reason rather than a staff, and a certain plan of life rather than a knapsack."[338]

Julian was very severe toward some Cynics who came uninvited to his headquarters, whose names he records for us in his seventh *Discourse*: Heracleios, Asclepiades, Serenianus, and Chytron.[339] It should be noted, however, that those who thus opposed both forms of the Cynicism they encountered were either people who were hostile to Cynicism itself, like Lucian, or else people like Epictetus and Julian who idealized the Cynicism of the past in order better to reject the Cynicism of their own day. Prudence must therefore be exercised in evaluating all these testimonies, which may have some basis in truth, but which should not be taken at face value. Diogenes practiced a radical asceticism, which Cynicism's detractors rejected as excessive. If Seneca could praise Demetrius despite his asceticism, this was because Demetrius was a friend whose moral caliber drew forth his admiration; when lesser people who claimed to be Cynics practiced this same asceticism, he wouldn't stand for it. When Epictetus and Julian violently criticize the Cynics they encounter, but they idealize Diogenes to the point of making him virtually unrecognizable, isn't it legitimate to be a bit suspicious of their testimony?

335. Apuleius, *Florida* 7.9–10 (trans. Christopher P. Jones, LCL).
336. Lucian, *The Fugitives* 13.
337. Epictetus, *Discourses* 3.22.10; cf. 4.8.12, 15–16, 20.
338. Julian, *Discourse 9 (To the Uneducated Cynics)*, 18 (200d–201a).
339. Julian, *Discourse 7 (Against the Cynic Heracleios)*, 18 (224d).

The Literary Works of Literate Cynicism
and Popular Cynicism

To speak of a literate Cynicism is to refer not only to a body of doctrine but also to the practice of literature. A brief survey of Cynic literary productions from the imperial era reveals that these reflect the dichotomy between the two forms of Cynicism. The most original literary work of imperial Cynicism is certainly *Charlatans Exposed* by Oenomaus of Gadara, which is probably the same work Julian attributes to him under the title *Against Oracles*.[340] Unfortunately we have no further traces of this important author's other writings, although Julian transmits some of their names: *The True Voice of the Dog*; *On Cynicism* (in which Oenomaus apparently develops his renewed conception of Cynicism); a *Republic*; *On Philosophy According to Homer*; and *On Crates and Diogenes*,[341] along with some tragedies whose content infuriated Julian. But if Oenomaus's writings drew such violent attacks from the emperor, this was because he recognized their significance and feared the threat they posed to his personal project of restoring Hellenism, especially its religion. Oenomaus effectively refuted prophecies made by the Delphic oracle, criticized the credulity of the people, treated Apollo as a "sophist," and protested the shameless use of oracles by the guardians of the temples. The influence that this Cynic writer had on Christian authors particularly, who drew on his work to fight paganism, attests to his literary stature. Besides Eusebius, who transmits some extracts from *Charlatans Exposed*, it appears that Clement of Alexandria, Origen, John Chrysostom, Theodoret (probably via Eusebius), and Cyril of Alexandria all read this work. Oenomaus embodied a fresh conception of Cynicism, less radical perhaps in the way of life it recommended (though the extracts that survive are unclear about this) than in the attack it launched against the values of the surrounding society, especially its religious values. It's deeply disappointing to historians of Cynicism that other works by Oenomaus such as *On Cynicism* and his *Republic* have disappeared completely. Had they survived, we would be able to understand precisely the new conception of Cynicism that he was advocating, which he said was "neither Antisthenism nor Diogenism."

Other Cynics under the Roman Empire were also authors, but their works, which might not actually have been genuinely Cynical in character, have not come down to us. It's not impossible that Demetrius, the friend of

---

340. Julian, *Discourse 7* (*Against the Cynic Heracleios*), 5 (209b).
341. See n. 80 on p. 23.

Socrates, may have written some diatribes.[342] We know from Lucian that Peregrinus was not just an exegete of Christian works, but that he also wrote such works himself,[343] and we know from Jerome that Maximus Hero wrote a work against the Arians that he presented to the western emperor Gratian in Milan.[344] Gregory of Nazianzus was outraged and attacked Maximus for showing such literary presumption, and he tells us that Maximus responded further to him in writing.[345]

Along with these works of literate Cynicism, there are two documents that I believe must be attributed to popular Cynicism, not because I am so naive as to believe they originate with uneducated people, but because in my view they express popular Cynicism's state of mind, which, contrary to what its detractors would have us think, appears to have been faithful to Diogenes—charlatans excepted. There is, first of all, the collection of pseudepigraphal *Letters* by Diogenes and Crates, most of which were composed under the Roman Empire. They are the work of several different authors, who all had a good understanding of Cynic themes. They are based on anecdotal material that was circulating to promote the legends of Diogenes and Crates. They testify to a Cynicism that is popular but not illiterate, and they repeatedly emphasize the characteristic means and objectives of Cynicism, which they don't promote as mere crying out on the street corners. From a strictly literary point of view, these letters, which are often quite brief, are not masterpieces. They were probably written, without any speculative pretentions, for simple people, for whom it was appropriate simply to share some of the main ideas of Cynicism. But they have the advantage of offering us an accurate picture of what popular Cynic morality was like under the Roman Empire. They contain, in effect, a sort of catechism that delivers the credo of popular Cynicism through a certain number of τόποι, through popular sayings and catchy slogans such as these: "To be a Cynic (τὸ δὲ κυνίζειν) is to take a short cut in doing philosophy"; "Be a dog; that's the shortcut to becoming a philosopher";[346] "The way that leads to happiness through

---

342. Cf. Billerbeck, *Der Kyniker Demetrius*, 57–60, who freely attributes to Demetrius the Cynic a dialogue between Courage and Cowardice, an extract from which is preserved in Stobaeus, *Anthology* 3.8.20; however, this could be, as is the case with Musonius and Epictetus, an oral teaching of Demetrius that one of his hearers wrote down.

343. Lucian, *The Passing of Peregrinus*, 11.

344. Jerome, *On Illustrious Men*, 127.

345. Gregory of Nazianzus, *Against Maximus* (PG 37:1339–44, esp. 1343).

346. Pseudo-Crates, *Letter 16* (*To His Companions*) (trans. Abraham J. Malherbe). Future references to *Letters* of Pseudo-Crates are from this translation.

words is long, but that which leads through daily deeds is a shortened regimen"; "Long is the way that leads to happiness through words; the way that goes through daily actions is a shortcut";[347] "Cynicism is an investigation of nature."[348] One must flee the worst evils (injustice, self-indulgence) and their causes (that is, pleasures); and one must pursue the greatest goods (self-control, determination) and their causes (that is, πόνοι).[349]

These *Letters* emphasize the major principles of asceticism, especially the need for a frugal life. The Crates of the *Letters* exhorts the young people he's addressing as follows: "Accustom yourselves to wash with cold water, to drink only water, to eat nothing that has not been earned by toil, to wear a cloak, and to make it a habit to sleep on the ground."[350] These *Letters*, especially those of Crates, constitute a sort of memento, a manual for the Cynic way of life, and they have twin objectives: both to advance Cynic propaganda[351] and to defend the philosophy of Diogenes against attacks, which we've heard in the words of Lucian, Epictetus, and Julian. Even though the collection was heterogeneous, it rallied the Cynics around a common tradition whose great figures were Heracles, the mythical hero who had proved "mightier than every turn of fortune,"[352] and Diogenes and Crates, the founders. Pseudo-Crates describes the τρίβων and the knapsack as "the weapons of Diogenes" and "the weapons of the gods,"[353] but at the same time he stresses that the coat doesn't make the Cynic but it's the Cynic who must make the coat.[354] This shows an awareness of the damage that could be done by those who were content to wear the coat without truly practicing asceticism. Begging, so violently criticized by Cynicism's detractors, was justified by the following explanation, said to be passed down from Socrates: "The gods are masters of all; the property of friends is held in common; the sage is a friend of god; therefore, you will be begging for what is your own."[355] These literary efforts, though of poor quality, show that Cynicism had taken

---

347. Pseudo-Crates, *Letter 21* (*To Metrocles the Dog*).
348. Pseudo-Diogenes, *Letter 42* (*To Melesippe the Prostitute*).
349. Pseudo-Crates, *Letter 15* (*To His Companions*).
350. Pseudo-Crates, *Letter 18* (*To Young People*).
351. Cf. Malherbe, *Cynic Epistles*, 2–3.
352. Cf. Pseudo-Diogenes, *Letter 26* (*To Crates*).
353. Pseudo-Crates, *Letters 16* (*To His Companions*) and *23* (*To Ganymede*).
354. Pseudo-Crates, *Letter 19* (*To Patrocles*).
355. Pseudo-Diogenes, *Letter 10* (*To Metrocles*); cf. also Pseudo-Crates, *Letters 2, 26*, and *27*; Diogenes Laertius, *Lives* 6.37: "All things belong to the gods. The wise are friends of the gods, and friends hold things in common. Therefore all things belong to the wise." See also 6.72.

root among simple folk, and that it was useful to remind them of the broad lines of asceticism and of the example that Cynicism's greatest figures had set, along with Heraclitus, Socrates, and the Socratics.

The second document mentioned above is also pseudepigraphal, attributed this time to Lucian; it's titled *The Cynic*. Unfortunately we don't know when it was written. Much more carefully composed than the *Letters*, this text draws on analogies and appeals to mythological figures such as Heracles, Theseus, and Chiron. Nevertheless, the ideas it develops are still quite simple; they're much like those found in the *Letters*—for example, that there's no value in facing useless πόνοι, and that wealth is the source of many evils. Lycinus asks his Cynic interlocutor to explain why he wears such an outfit and why he leads a nomadic, antisocial life. Claiming to be in the genuine tradition of Heracles,[356] the Cynic offers a spirited defense of his outfit and his way of life, explaining how these are responsible for his happiness and contrasting them with those of his contemporaries. All the τόποι of Cynicism are pulled together here. These writings, the *Letters* and *The Cynic*, constitute something of a bridge between literate Cynicism and the Cynicism of the street preachers, in the sense that they are writings (even though their literary value is limited) and also moral preaching based on the principles that all Cynics of every sort had to embrace.

Opponents, however, had a grand time dismissing the discourse of popular Cynicism as little more than barking,[357] insults,[358] and jokes and endless babblings,[359] and mercilessly mocking these uneducated beggars who'd decided to become Cynics. But I am inclined to believe that an authentic practice of Diogenean asceticism lay behind the catechism of the *Letters* and *The Cynic* by Pseudo-Lucian, and it was this that threatened philosophers from the other schools. Hence the desire to denigrate street Cynicism and substitute an idealized version that someone like Epictetus or Julian could use to promote their own values.

By now it should be clear that there were several ways of conceiving of Cynicism: (1) as a school of thought that had characteristic δόγματα and a τέλος of its own; (2) as a way of life pursued apart from δόγματα; (3) as that same way of life, but with a different τέλος from Cynicism and with an allegiance to a different philosophical school or even to Christianity. These

---

356. Pseudo-Lucian, *The Cynic*, 13.
357. Lucian, *The Fugitives* 14.
358. Lucian, *Philosophies for Sale* 11; Epigram of Lucilius in *Palatine Anthology* 11.155.
359. Dio Chrysostom, *Discourse* 32 (*To the Alexandrians*), 9.

definitions corresponded to actual situations under the Roman Empire, un-like a fourth conception that should be noted along with them—namely, the idealized Cynicism of Epictetus and Julian. These distinctions are explained in part by the sociological background: a literate Cynicism, arising within the upper classes, was in conflict with a popular, uncultivated Cynicism. The diverse character of Cynicism under the Roman Empire is real enough and well attested; there's also no doubt that a certain number of charlatans were in the picture. Unfortunately, we have to depend for our understanding of popular Cynicism, whose adherents had no voice of their own, on the works of literate Cynics and philosophers of other schools who all condemned the impudence and ignorance of those who dared, like Diogenes in his own time, to go all the way in their return to nature. But I am convinced that, not counting the charlatans who put on the outfit just to get a free ride, for the most part popular Cynics were authentic, faithful to the asceticism of Dio-genes and to the requirements of his way of life. There was genuine Cynicism under the Roman Empire from the moment that a bodily asceticism began to be practiced, with a moral goal that involved rejecting all the δόξαι imposed by society, and human naturalness began to display itself to the eyes of all, in truth, without pretending. There was genuine Cynicism from the moment that the individual joined in pitched battle against pleasure and all the πόνοι, including humiliation and a bad reputation, which became springboards to self-mastery. There was genuine Cynicism from the moment that a radical and unlimited poverty was actively embraced.

Cynicism and Pagan Religion under the Roman Empire

Antisthenes was the only ancient Cynic who was clearly a monotheist.[360] This belief is attested by two statements he makes in his Φυσικός: "By cus-tom there are many gods, but by nature one"[361] and "God cannot be known through an image; he's not visible to the eye, he resembles no one [or "noth-ing"], and that's precisely why no one can grasp him through an image."[362]

---

360. Cf. Aldo Brancacci, "La théologie d'Antisthène," *Philosophia* 15–16 (1985–1986): 218–30.

361. Philodemus, *On Piety* 7a.3–8 (Theodor Gomperz, *Philodem, Über Frömmigkeit*, Herkulanische Studien 2 [Leipzig: Teubner, 1866], 72): trans. by Susan Prince, *Antisthenes of Athens. Texts, translations and commentary*, Ann Arbor: University of Michigan Press, 2014, fr. 179A.

362. Theodoret, *Therapeutic for Hellenic Maladies* 1.75 = fr. 181D Prince; see also Clem-

Validating φύσις and criticizing νόμος, Antisthenes situates the true God on the level of unity and of nature, and the gods of polytheism on the level of multiplicity, tradition, and opinion. It's possible that he combined this monotheistic tendency with a genuine piety.[363] But the earliest Cynicism, which cared little about the question of religion anyway, didn't follow his example of monotheism; it appears generally to have been rather agnostic. However, it rarely missed a chance to criticize traditional religion.

Under the Roman Empire, this rationalist critique of the incoherence of traditional beliefs, superstitions, and religious practices continued. Among the pseudepigraphal *Letters* of Heraclitus, which date from the first century and are Cynical in spirit, *Letter 4: To Hermodorus* vividly criticizes religious practices in Ephesus.[364] Its author, a worshiper of Heracles who became a god by virtue of his labors, denounced the practice of locking the gods up in temples and fabricating their images, because as far as he's concerned, what testifies to divinity is not stone altars but the changing seasons, the earth bearing fruit, and the orb of the moon. Others speak rather flippantly about the Mysteries. Demonax, a famous Cynic, was never initiated into the Eleusinian Mysteries—as was the case with Diogenes earlier—and he takes full responsibility for this decision (*Life of Demonax* 11), among other things delighting in exposing an inconsistency: the Athenians exclude barbarians from their Mysteries, but the founder of the rite, Eumolpus, was Thracian (34). When Demonax sees the faithful going into the temple of Asclepius in order to pray to him there, he has a grand time asking whether this is because the god is hard of hearing and so can't make out their prayers if they're offered outside the temple (27). He doesn't spare those who practice divination for a fee either (37).

But the most radical critiques were directed against the gods themselves and the value of their oracles. In the first century, the Cynic Didymus Planetiades complained that "those maladies and emotions of the soul which it would be good to disclaim and conceal," people "bring naked and exposed before the god," until "the tripod is constantly occupied with shameful and impious questions which people propound to the god."[365] The most vir-

---

ent of Alexandria, *Exhortation to the Greeks* 6.71.2 (= Prince fr. 181A); *Miscellanies* 5.14.108.4 (= Prince fr. 181B).

363. Cf. Diogenes Laertius, *Lives* 6.5: Antisthenes said that "those who would fain be immortal must live piously [εὐσεβῶς] and justly."

364. Cf. Harold W. Attridge, *First-Century Cynicism in the Epistles of Heraclitus*, HTS 29 (Missoula, MT: Scholars Press 1976), 58–61.

365. Cf. Plutarch, *On the Decline of Oracles* 7 (413a–b) (trans. Frank Cole Babbitt).

ulent on the question of oracles is unquestionably Oenomaus in *Charlatans Exposed*. According to Eusebius, he denies that the oracles have any divine character, describing them as "frauds and tricks of human impostors" and denouncing their deceptive nature.[366] Apollo of Delphi, "the Pythian prophet, in his folly" is his favorite target; he terms his oracles "sophistic responses."[367] His extreme views prompted the emperor Julian to become so irritated, not to say angry, that he warned others who might want to imitate him, "Let not the Cynic be like Oenomaus, shameless and impudent, a scorner of everything human and divine."[368] Julian's fears were not unwarranted; he'd personally attended a lecture by the Cynic Heracleios and heard him speak of Helios in terms that he considered irreverent.[369]

But we must not let these violent critiques of traditional religion overshadow some evidence of respect for the gods and even of piety. The example of Peregrinus after his Christian phase comes to mind immediately, even though Lucian's portrayal of him doesn't give us a completely accurate view of his religious attitude. Apart from Lucian's hostility, it doesn't appear that Peregrinus's religious character can be called into question. As he was delivering his own funeral oration, he situated his suicide by fire on a pyre near Olympus firmly in the tradition of Heracles, insisting that "one who had lived as Heracles should die like Heracles and be commingled with the ether" (*The Passing of Peregrinus* 33). His disciple Theagenes freely compared him with Heracles, Asclepius, Dionysus, and Empedocles (4), and Peregrinus himself claimed he would become a "guardian spirit of the night" (27). Lucian is careful to specify that he witnessed these events and that they took place without any portents, but in relating them afterward, he decided to "thicken the plot a bit . . . for the benefit of the dullards," and so he embellished his account with an earthquake and a vulture flying up out of the pyre and soaring toward Olympus; he also reports an apparition of Peregrinus dressed in white and wearing a garland of wild olive sprigs (39–40). It's not clear exactly what to make of all these details. It appears, however, that a cult of Peregrinus with an oracular shrine was established at the site of the pyre (28) and that statues were erected in his honor (41). The testimony of Gellius leads us to believe that Peregrinus was a man of great moral stature

---

366. Eusebius, *Preparation for the Gospel* 5.21.6 (trans. David Hamilton Gifford).

367. Eusebius, *Preparation for the Gospel* 5.27.1 (Hammerstaedt frag. 9); 5.20.7 (Hammerstaedt frag. 4).

368. Julian, *Discourse 9* (*To the Uneducated Cynics*), 17 (199a).

369. Julian, *Discourse 7* (*Against the Cynic Heracleios*), 1 (205a); 4 (208b).

and that he was recognized as such by all his contemporaries—except for Lucian, who couldn't stand him.[370]

Further testimonies to Cynics practicing religion are found in the later tradition. (We will consider them further when we examine the relationship between Cynicism and Christianity.) In 359, under the Christian emperor Constantius II, the philosopher Demetrius Cythras (who may have been a Cynic, if he's the same person as the Chytron that Julian mentions)[371] was tortured for his piety. He had offered sacrifice to a popular god of the Greeks, Besa, whose oracle was at Abydum in Thebaid, and was, for this reason, suspected by the emperor to be among those who were "inquiring about gaining imperial power."[372] Under Julian, in 362, another Cynic, Asclepiades, went into the temple at Daphne and placed at the feet of the statue of Apollo a little silver image of Venus Urania, which he carried with him wherever he went, and lit some wax tapers. Some sparks from these set the temple's ancient woodwork on fire, accidently burning down the building.[373] But should we also see hints of piety in the assertion by the authors of the pseudepigraphal *Letters* of Diogenes and Crates that the sage is friend of the gods,[374] and in the portrayal of Diogenes as wandering freely over the whole earth under the direction of his father Zeus?[375] The first statement was a commonplace and we probably shouldn't draw any conclusions from it, but we may recognize in the second statement, at least, an affinity with the tradition of a "pious Diogenes," consistent with the idealized image of him that we find in Epictetus, Dio, and Julian.

It would be a mistake, however, to take into account only historical attestations such as these when exploring the Cynic religious attitude. We must also consider a counterpoint: some of those who were pious themselves insisted at all costs that the earliest Cynics had themselves been pious people with a strong religious faith. This perspective, which is diametrically opposed to the one held by Cynics on the street, is certainly an idealized vision of what ancient Cynicism was, but it had considerable influence, especially on Christian authors, and for that reason it's significant. Epictetus insisted to a student who wanted to become a Cynic that this would be impossible without the help of God: it was Zeus who had sent the Cynic to humankind as his mes-

---

370. Cf. Gellius, *Attic Nights* 12.11.

371. Julian, *Discourse 7* (*Against the Cynic Heracleios*), 18 (224d).

372. Cf. Ammianus Marcellinus, *History* 19.12.12.

373. Ammianus Marcellinus, *History* 22.13.2–3.

374. Pseudo-Crates, *Letters 26* and *27* (*To the Same*, i.e., to the Athenians).

375. Pseudo-Diogenes, *Letter 34* (*To Olympias*), 3.

senger to enlighten them and show them that they were wrong about good and evil; if the Cynics had to endure πόνοι, this was because Zeus was testing them. From this perspective, the true Cynic, who renounced marriage, children, and familial and social duties, would be entirely at God's disposal.[376] Dio, whom we know to have been pious,[377] also refers to Zeus. He explains, through the character of Diogenes, that the offspring of Zeus bear a mark in their souls that allows them to be recognized;[378] this mark is the education they receive that shapes them in the model of the noble Heracles, building in them the virtues known as "true manhood" and "high-mindedness."[379] We might anticipate that the emperor Julian would also want to see the Cynics as pious, since he said of the gods, "I love, I revere, I venerate them, and have the same feelings towards them as one would have towards kind masters or teachers or fathers or guardians."[380] And in fact Diogenes is portrayed in Julian's *Discourses* as pious in word and deed,[381] as is Crates, whose "Hymn to the Muses of Pieria" is happily cited as proof of his piety.[382] Julian says it was the god of Delphi who gave Diogenes the means to falsify the currency and who led him to disregard public opinion by telling him, "Know thyself."[383] Under the pen of Julian, Cynicism becomes a universal philosophy, with none other than Pythian Apollo as its founder, a philosophy whose goal is godlikeness and whose grand principle is self-knowledge.[384] If Diogenes declined to be initiated, Julian explains, he did this out of respect for the gods; the Pythian god had commanded that "the candidate for initiation must first be registered as an Athenian citizen," and this was not the case for him.[385] The vision of Cynicism infused with religion that we get from these authors is one thing; the convictions that inspired Cynics on the streets were no doubt something very different. What they wished Cynicism to have been was as far removed from what it actually was as the ideal is from the real. We must bear this in mind when we look into parallels with Christianity.

376. Epictetus, *Discourses* 3.22.23–25, 57, 67–76.

377. See, e.g., the beautiful passage in *Discourse 32* (*To the Alexandrians*), 14–16, where Dio credits God for every good thing that happens to the earth.

378. Cf. Dio Chrysostom, *Discourse 4* (*On Kingship*), 23.

379. Dio Chrysostom, *Discourse 4* (*On Kingship*), 30–31 (trans. James Wilfried Cohoon, LCL).

380. Julian, *Discourse 7* (*Against Heracleios the Cynic*), 8 (212b–c).

381. Julian, *Discourse 7* (*Against Heracleios the Cynic*), 8 (212d).

382. Julian, *Discourse 7* (*Against Heracleios the Cynic*), 9 (213b).

383. Julian, *Discourse 7* (*Against Heracleios the Cynic*), 7 (211c).

384. Julian, *Discourse 7* (*Against Heracleios the Cynic*), 19 (225d).

385. Julian, *Discourse 7* (*Against Heracleios the Cynic*), 25 (238a–239c).

The Cynic Relationship to Power

Cynicism, in whatever forms it took and in whatever era it appeared, was always disruptive. There were constant efforts to silence it, but right from the start, Cynics never feared men of power: Diogenes himself spoke flippantly to Philip of Macedonia and Alexander.[386] Still, their critique took the form of quips, or it was expressed in writings that didn't incite rebellion. Diogenes wrote a *Republic* and Crates wrote a utopian poem titled "Knapsack,"[387] but no Cynic ever thought of getting involved in a political struggle. As a result, those in power decided simply to put up with their sarcasm.

But things changed under the Roman Empire. The very lives of Cynics, as well as Stoics, were threatened in the first century CE. Nero "would not allow anyone to be a philosopher."[388] Cynics then had to do more than write; they joined in practical battle. And so we find them caught up in Nero's persecutions, alongside other philosophers, especially Stoics. At the start of his reign, Nero limited himself to exiling from Rome and Italy figures such as Isidorus, who publicly taunted him "because he was a good singer of the ills of Nauplius, but made ill use of his own goods."[389] But later he didn't hesitate to condemn the Stoic Thrasea Paetus to death, to force Barea Soranus and his daughter Servilia to commit suicide, and to banish from Italy Helvidius Priscus (Barea's son-in-law) and Paconius.[390] The Cynic Demetrius, who belonged to the aristocratic circle of Thrasea and Helvidius, was also banished by Nero. He took refuge in Greece, but he returned, probably under Galba, and we know that when he met Vespasian in public, he insulted him.[391] In 71 he was forced once again into exile, this time on an island. But in 75 some Cynics started to come back to Rome, even though the expulsion decree against them had not been lifted, and two of them, Diogenes and Heras, protested, in front of a full

---

386. For Alexander, see Diogenes Laertius, *Lives* 6.38, 44, 60; for Philip, see Diogenes Laertius, *Lives* 6.43.

387. Cf. Diogenes Laertius, *Lives* 6.85 (*Supplementum Hellenisticum* 351): "There is a city called / Knapsack in the midst of wine-dark vapour, / Fair, fruitful, passing squalid, owning nought, / Into which sails nor fool nor parasite / Nor glutton, slave of sensual appetite, / But thyme it bears, garlic, and figs and loaves, / For which things' sake men fight not each with other, / Nor stand to arms for money or for fame."

388. Philostratus, *Life of Apollonius of Tyana* 4.35.

389. Suetonius, *Life of Nero* 39.5–6 (trans. John C. Rolfe, LCL).

390. Cf. Tacitus, *Annals* 16.30–33.

391. Cf. Suetonius, *Life of Vespasian* 13.4.

theater, against the relationship of Vespasian's son Titus to Berenice. The Cynics weren't just creating unrest among the proletariat in the cities; they were now confronting monarchy and tyranny. If the emperor received his power from God, then the monarchy couldn't be hereditary. But Vespasian wanted his sons to succeed him.[392] Diogenes was flogged for his persistent criticisms of the couple, while Heras, "expecting no harsher punishment, gave vent to many senseless yelpings in true Cynic fashion, and for this was beheaded."[393] Under Domitian, groups of philosophers were exiled twice, in 89 and 94. Two Stoics were among them, Artemidorus, the son-in-law of Musonius Rufus, and Epictetus, but apparently no Cynics.

Liberty returned to Rome with the Antonines: Trajan embodied the Cynic and Stoic idea of the good king, the opposite of the tyrant that Domitian had been, and the empress Plotina was interested in philosophy. Even though the Cynic Peregrinus was imprisoned during the reign of Trajan, this wasn't because of his status as a philosopher; rather, he was accused of being the leader of the Christian community in Palestine.[394] Later this same Peregrinus was banished from Italy by the prefect of Rome for speaking with characteristic Cynic frankness.[395] Arriving in Greece, he instigated a revolt there against Rome,[396] and once he got to Athens, he persistently harassed Herodes Atticus.[397] In Egypt, it's possible that the Cynics who wandered the streets of Alexandria played a role in the troubles that city went through under the reign of Commodus, at the end of the second century.[398] Under Julian, philosophers once again came into direct conflict with power. As emperor, he attacked the Cynics he encountered in Constantinople because they represented, in his eyes, a threat to his project of restoring Hellenism. He was particularly critical of Heracleios, who was so bold as to blaspheme the gods.

It's inspiring to see that throughout their troubled relationship with the emperors, the Cynics never spared the authorities. What was new under the Roman Empire was that they, along with the Stoics, had to pay dearly for their opposition: many among them were exiled, and one was put to

392. Cf. Michael Rostovtseff, *The Social and Economic History of the Roman Empire*, 2nd ed. (Oxford: Clarendon, 1957), 115–16.

393. Cf. Cassius Dio, *Roman History* 65.15.5.

394. Lucian, *The Passing of Peregrinus* 12.

395. Lucian, *The Passing of Peregrinus* 18.

396. Lucian, *The Passing of Peregrinus* 19.

397. Philostratus, *Lives of the Sophists* 2.1 (Olearius 563 = Kayser 2.71.11–20).

398. Cf. Rostovtseff, *Social and Economic History*, 395.

death. Nevertheless, while the emperors would have loved to silence them, apparently they never succeeded.

The Complicated Relationship between Cynicism and Stoicism

Before we conclude our discussion of Cynicism itself, it will be valuable to analyze precisely the particularly complex relationship that Cynicism had with Stoicism. Full-blown theories are in circulation that hold, for example, that there were characteristic common Cynico-Stoic themes, or that some popular preachers were Cynico-Stoics, as if there were a well-defined group that embraced these themes and expressed them through a vaguely defined genre that moderns have taken to calling the "Cynico-Stoic diatribe," an exposition that was either delivered orally by a popular preacher or cast in literary form. To add to the confusion, when Pohlenz, for example, wants to situate Cynicism in relation to Stoicism, he treats it as little more than a crude Stoicism, "ein vergröberter Stoizismus."[399] If such stereotypes were true, then we should wonder why, under the Roman Empire, no Cynic ever claimed to be a Stoic, and vice versa. This calls for more careful analysis.

An Embarrassing Heritage

The first Stoics were directly connected to the Cynics. Zeno of Citium (and likely Cleanthes as well)[400] was a student of Crates of Thebes,[401] and Zeno's *Republic*, "written on the dog's tail,"[402] was strongly influenced by a similarly titled work by Diogenes of Sinope.[403] Zeno and Cleanthes practiced an asceticism quite similar to that of the Cynics: poverty, sobriety, frugality, effort. As he developed his own ethical system, Zeno borrowed from the Cynics the fundamental idea that morality must be freed from anything that doesn't depend on the individual, so that morality cannot be made subject to an actual external law dictated by the society in which one lives, nor to a

---

399. Max Pohlenz, *Die Stoa: Geschichte einer geistigen Bewegung*, 3rd ed. (Göttingen: Vandenhoeck & Ruprecht, 1964), 1:279–80.

400. Cf. *Suda*, s.v. Κλεάνθης, K 1711 (Adler 3:126.16–17).

401. Cf. Diogenes Laertius, *Lives* 6.105; 7.2.

402. Diogenes Laertius, *Lives* 7.4.

403. For a different interpretation of the phrase ἐπὶ τῆς τοῦ Κυνὸς οὐρᾶς, see Bees, *Zenons Politeia*, 7–26.

particular social condition, nor to a metaphysic beyond one's control. Hence his theory of goods, evils, and indifferents (τὰ ἀδιάφορα) that become vices or virtues depending on a person's inner attitude. It's also possible that the spiritual exercises of the Stoics were based on the concept of asceticism pursued by the Cynics, and that Antisthenes's description of the "strength" (ἰσχύς) necessary for virtue was the source of a concept that's absolutely fundamental to Stoicism, that of "tension" (τόνος).[404]

Another Stoic, Aristo of Chios, was also closely related to Cynicism. We can detect an influence of Antisthenes on him; like Antisthenes, he taught in the gymnasium at Cynosarges.[405] Aristo differed with Zeno on the doctrine of preferables (προηγμένα). While Zeno distinguished three types of indifferents—preferables, nonpreferables, and fully undifferentiated indifferents—Aristo disagreed, rejecting all natural preferability and admitting only fully undifferentiated indifferents. He even made "indifference"—a concept that would be readily linked to Cynicism starting in the second century of our era—the τέλος of his morality and the emblem of his philosophy.[406] Stoicism, with Chrysippus at its head, thanks to his theory of indifferents and of "appropriate actions" (καθήκοντα), particularly of "actions appropriate under the circumstances" (καθήκοντα περιστατικά), which provided enough flexibility to accommodate all the scandalous aspects of Cynicism, succeeded in integrating the Cynico-Zenonian heritage of the two *Republics* of Diogenes and Zeno.[407] Cleanthes praised Diogenes's *Republic* in his treatise *On Clothing*,[408] and Chrysippus not only praised both *Republics* but actually took over many of Diogenes's and Zeno's ideas as his own, as several of his works testify.[409]

However, the two *Republics* eventually triggered a lively controversy within the Stoic movement, as we learn from Philodemus in *On the Stoics*.[410] Divided between admiration and embarrassment over the Dogs'

---

404. Cf. Goulet-Cazé, *L'ascèse cynique*, 165–72.

405. Diogenes Laertius, *Lives* 7.161.

406. Cf. Clement of Alexandria, *Miscellanies* 2.21.129.6 (*SVF* 1:360). On Aristo's position regarding indifferents, see Goulet-Cazé, *Les "Kynika" du stoïcisme*, 97–98, 119–29.

407. Cf. Goulet-Cazé, *Les "Kynika" du stoïcisme*, 98–108.

408. Philodemus, *On the Stoics* 6, col. 15.21–24 (Dorandi, "Filodemo, Gli Stoici," 102).

409. Cf. Diogenes Laertius, *Lives* 7.188 (*On the Republic, On Things for Their Own Sake Not Desirable, On Justice,* and *On the Means of Livelihood*); Philodemus, *On the Stoics* 6, col. 15.26–16.27 (Dorandi, "Filodemo, Gli Stoici," 102) (*On Life According to Nature* and *On the Good and On Pleasure* 4); Plutarch, *The Contradictions of the Stoics* (*Protrepticus*) 22 (1044f). See also Sextus Empiricus, *Outlines of Pyrrhonism* 3.205, 247, 248.

410. Miriam T. Griffin aptly observes that "it is not an accident that the disowning by

way of life and their excesses, the Stoics never came close to reaching a consensus about the *kynika*, and the legacy of the *Republics* was at the center of the debate. Some Stoics, who probably belonged to the circle of Panaetius, couldn't accept the excesses of Diogenes's *Republic*. The fact that the list of Diogenes's writings in Diogenes Laertius 6.80, which comes from Sotion, doesn't include his *Republic* or his tragedies testifies to the activity of these Stoics who were hostile to Cynic excesses, as does the presence of a syllogism on the law in 6.72 and the distinction between two asceticisms, one mental and the other bodily, in 6.70, which expresses a Stoic point of view in the midst of a Cynic doxography.[411] We know that certain Stoics expressed doubts about the authenticity of Diogenes's *Republic* (*On the Stoics*, col. 15), while others formulated the hypothesis of a malicious forgery (col. 17). The same held for Zeno's *Republic*, which prompted various negative reactions within Stoicism itself. Some, trying to make excuses for the philosopher, regarded his *Republic* as a youthful indiscretion, the product of a foolish immaturity. Others judged the work faulty and condemned it on that basis, while still others denied that Zeno had even written it. There were also those who argued that there was no basis for accusing Zeno of error if the same was not done for the earliest writings of Epicurus, and those who felt the *Republic* should be regarded as a utopia (even though Philodemus specifies that Zeno was writing intentionally for the people of his time). Another group wanted to minimize the role that Zeno had played in Stoicism and deny that he was its founder, and they held that he'd lost his way in writing the work, but that fortunately the Stoics hadn't had to suffer any consequences because their school had actually been constituted by Socrates, Antisthenes, and Diogenes (which explains why they wanted to be known as Socratics). On the other hand, some further Stoics continued to admire Zeno, on the grounds that he had discovered the τέλος of their school and as a result was its founder; they were willing to disregard anything he'd said that was shameful or shocking. And while yet others, finally, felt that the salacious διαμηρίζειν passage (col. 15.8) disqualified the work, according to Philodemus it's the *Republic* as a whole that's scandalous (cols. 9–15).[412] It certainly appears that the

---

the Stoa of Zeno's *Republic* is first attested for Philodemus's time," when the Romans were obsessed with gravitas and decorum ("Cynicism and the Romans: Attraction and Repulsion," in Branham and Goulet-Cazé, *The Cynics*, 196).

411. See the references in n. 2 on p. 4.

412. Cf. Goulet-Cazé, *Les "Kynika" du stoïcisme*, 13–19.

question of the *kynika* posed a serious problem for the later Stoics,[413] who tried to minimize, or even eliminate, the influence of Zeno's work, either by calling it a youthful indiscretion or by regarding it as full of errors and so as inauthentic. The librarian at Pergamum, Athenodorus Cordylion of Tarsus, himself a Stoic, went so far as to excise passages from Stoic works (Diogenes Laertius, *Lives* 7.34). Did Stoics have to embrace the heritage of the *kynika*, and if so, did they have to admit that Zeno had "played the dog" (κυνιεῖν)?

The Stoic Apollodorus of Seleucia, to whom we owe the definition of Cynicism as a "shortcut to virtue," tentatively resolved this question in the second century of our era in his *Introductions to Dogma*, by proposing something of a compromise: the sage will act as a dog; that is to say, he continues in the Cynic way of life instead of adopting this philosophy after becoming a sage, cynicism being a shortcut to virtue, as Apollodorus says in his *Ethics*. This is how Zeno of Citium lived.[414] Apollodorus's reasoning imagines two paths leading to virtue, one of them short, the Cynic way of life, appropriate for those who, before converting to Stoicism, already practiced this way of life; and the other long, passing through study and an acceptance of social life—the path of Stoicism. The Stoic who came to wisdom thanks to the Cynic way of life, based on asceticism, should continue to live according to that way of life, now seen as a shortcut to virtue; on the other hand, the Stoic who attained wisdom by following Stoic philosophy didn't have to choose to follow Cynic asceticism. In neither case was Apollodorus thinking of replacing Stoicism with Cynicism; rather, he succeeded in the tour de force of harmonizing them rather than putting them in conflict with one another. In his eyes, the two philosophies constituted different paths that both led to virtue. As we indicated earlier, it's also apparently to Apollodorus that we owe the definition of Cynicism as a αἵρεσις, a school of thought with its own dogmas, and not a mere way of life, ἔνστασις βίου. This is consistent, since the Cynic option that Apollodorus proposes, even if it's a shortcut, is a genuine philosophical choice, parallel to the one made within Stoicism. Finally, and also consistently, Apollodorus is among those for whom Sto-

413. The dispute may actually have begun in the time of Zenon, if Philodemus, *History of the Stoics*, col. 4.1–12 (Dorandi, 54), is correctly citing the testimony of two men who were close to Zeno, Persaeus and Philonides.

414. I have reconstituted this reasoning from three passages that furnish its elements: Diogenes Laertius, *Lives* 7.121; *Suda* K 2711; and Arius Didymus in Stobaeus, *Anthology* 2.7.11. See Goulet-Cazé, *L'ascèse cynique*, 22n22.

icism goes back to Socrates via Antisthenes.[415] The *Introductions to Dogma* by Apollodorus played an absolutely decisive background role to book 6 of Diogenes Laertius, especially to the doxographies: for Diogenes Laertius as for Apollodorus, Cynicism and Stoicism are two Socratic schools, and Cynicism is a school of thought; Antisthenes, who dedicated several of his writings to Heracles, stands at the head of each school; one of the options for a Stoic was therefore to take the Cynic shortcut.

Later, Cicero addressed this same question, which he may have learned about from Panaetius, who studied with Apollodorus under Diogenes the Babylonian: "Regarding the principles and life of the Cynics, there are some Stoics who say that they are suited to a wise man, if indeed any chance should befall him that might compel him to act in such a manner; but others wholly deny this."[416] It is clear that Apollodorus's conciliatory position was not unanimously accepted. Cicero also speaks of "those Stoics who are almost Cynics, who make it a matter of reproach and ridicule that we deem things that are not shameful in fact unfit to be called by their right names, while we apply their proper names to things that are really shameful. . . . To perpetuate one's family is right in fact, yet obscene in name. On this notion those same philosophers hold prolix arguments at the expense of modesty."[417] Here Cicero signals the key word in this whole discussion: modesty.[418] Even though everything is taking place on the level of language, it's the failure of the Cynics, and of those Stoics who choose to follow the Cynic path, to show modesty that's bothering the other philosophers.

Under the Roman Empire, the question remained far from settled; people kept wondering whether the sage ought to "play the dog." Epictetus recognized that in a city of Stoic sages, no one would be readily inclined to take up the Cynic way of life (τὸ κυνίζειν), and it would be quite conceivable that Cynics would marry and have children. But in the world as it was, he allowed, the Cynic constituted something of a necessary exception: he had to be freed from all social duties so he could give himself fully to the service of God, who had sent him among men to help them live well.[419] We may conclude that as far as Epictetus was concerned, Stoics, even if the choice remained an exceptional one, could decide to "play the dog."

415. Cf. my demonstration in Goulet-Cazé, *Les "Kynika" du stoïcisme*, 154–68.

416. Cicero, *On the Ends of Good and Evil* 3.68 (*SVF* 3:645) (trans. Charles Duke Yonge).

417. Cicero, *On Duties* 1.35.128 (trans. Andrew P. Peabody).

418. Regarding the Cynics' negative conception of *verecundia*, see also Cicero, *On Duties* 1.41.148.

419. Epictetus, *Discourses* 3.22.67–85.

The controversy seems to have spread well beyond the circle of Stoic philosophers, because the second-century orator and Platonic philosopher Maximus of Tyre addressed the question "Is the Cynic life preferable?" in his *Discourse 36*. Not only does he respond positively (in chaps. 5 and 6) by appealing to the example of Diogenes's way of life; he goes so far as to consider him greater than Lycurgus, Solon, Artaxerxes, and Alexander and freer than Socrates! But there were also many poor imitations of the "Cynic shortcut": as we've seen, it attracted charlatans who were ready to usurp the outfit while abandoning the asceticism. Is it any surprise, then, that under the pen of Galen, the Cynic shortcut became "a shortcut to bragging,"[420] and in Lucian's *Philosophies for Sale*, a "shortcut to fame"?[421]

Stoics and Cynics under the Roman Empire

Seneca's attitude was somewhat ambiguous. He was very severe toward the dirty, poorly clad Cynics of his day who spent their time begging in the streets of Rome. The advice he gives to Lucilius is eloquent in this regard: there are no grounds on which to allow oneself to wear rough clothing, or torture the body, or eat repugnant foods.[422] But Seneca can also see Cynicism as a radicalization of Stoicism—a step beyond it, as it were—as his contrasting formulas attest: the role of the Stoics is to overcome human nature (*hominis naturam cum stoicis vincere*), while the role of the Cynics is to surpass it (*cum cynicis excedere*).[423] As a result, while the Stoic may endure the blows of Destiny, he feels them, but the Cynic doesn't even notice them. The difference in attitude is particularly significant for the way Seneca conceives of asceticism. As a good Stoic, he advocates an asceticism of the soul,[424] but this may be supplemented temporarily by physical asceticism with a moral end, limited to three or four days or so, for a prophylactic goal, so that the soul will have the *firmitas animi* necessary to endure adversity should it ever strike.[425]

---

420. Galen, *The Diagnosis and Treatment of the Passions of the Soul* 3.12–13 (De Boer 48.23–49.10).

421. Lucian, *Philosophies for Sale* 11.

422. Seneca, *Letters to Lucilius* 5.1–4. Cf. Lucian, *Hermotimus* 18, where Hermotimus contrasts the Stoics walking with dignity, properly dressed, looking healthy, wearing short hair, with the Cynics and their highly exaggerated indifference.

423. Seneca, *On the Brevity of Life* 14.2.

424. Seneca, *Letters to Lucilius* 15.5.

425. Cf. Seneca, *Letters to Lucilius* 18.5–7.

This is very different from the asceticism of Diogenes, which was practiced continually and was unlimited in its embrace of poverty. Where the Stoic occasionally tried to strengthen his constitution through a real but temporary asceticism, the Cynic entered into a deliberately chosen and genuine poverty and daily lived out a rigorous asceticism. Cynics took things to the limit, and that made all the difference between the two movements.[426]

While Seneca didn't hesitate to express his loathing for most Cynics of his time, he did make one exception, when he offered a heartfelt tribute to his friend Demetrius the Cynic, "the best of men,"[427] and presented him as a model for imitation.[428] The portrait he paints is probably somewhat idealized: it leaves us with an inspiring picture of Demetrius as a man who "does not teach the truth, but witnesses to it."[429] While other Cynics begged, he wouldn't allow himself to do so: "This boldest of heroes, fighting against all the desires of nature, [was] poorer than the rest of the Cynics in that, while they banned possessions, he banned even asking for them."[430] Faithful in his way of life to Cynicism at its origins, Demetrius chose to be poor and free, and thus capable of triumphing over any adversity. His practical philosophy was based on having a small number of precepts "at his disposal and for his use" (*in promptu et in usu*)[431] that enabled him, if he meditated on them daily, to live *in solido ac sereno*, "on solid ground and under a serene sky."[432] For example, "leave aside what is useless to know"; "the soul should fear neither the gods nor men." As for the παρρησία of Demetrius, Seneca need only cite his friend's reaction to Caligula's attempt to corrupt him by offering him two hundred thousand sesterces: "If he meant to tempt me, he ought to have tried to do so by offering his entire kingdom."[433] But we know from other sources that Demetrius could be a troublemaker. Epictetus cites an

---

426. This even made a difference between Cynicism and the way of life practiced by Socrates himself, whom Diogenes reproached for a certain softness: "Diogenes said that even Socrates himself indulged in luxuries, because he took undue care of his modest house, his small couch, and his sandals—which in fact Socrates sometimes wore" (Aelian, *Various Histories* 4.11, trans. Nigel G. Wilson, LCL). Cf. also Maximus of Tyre, *Dissertation* 36.6, where Diogenes is presented as more free and happier than Socrates.

427. Seneca, *Letters to Lucilius* 62.3.

428. Seneca, *On Benefits* 7.8.3.

429. Seneca, *Letters to Lucilius* 20.9.

430. Seneca, *On the Happy Life* 18.3 (trans. John W. Basore, LCL).

431. Seneca, *On Benefits* 7.1.3.

432. Seneca, *On Benefits* 7.1.4–7.

433. Seneca, *On Benefits* 7.11.1.

example of his bluntness toward Nero,[434] and Dio Cassius presents him as a provocateur alongside Helvidius Priscus, as a veritable rebel who refused to withdraw when Vespasian banished him.[435] Seneca, partially out of prudence, probably, but partly also because he didn't like provocation, appears to have intentionally omitted every disturbing trait from the picture of his friend. The touched-up, idealized portrait he does offer is based on a subtle selectivity that leaves room for Cynic radicalism while expurging the disturbing traits, particularly those connected with blunt speech and provocative behavior. But we can tell that Demetrius was also influenced by Stoicism, through its theory of Fate.[436] His attitude toward Fate was consistent with Stoic doctrine: not only did he accept it; he outguessed its demands. Diogenes, on the other hand, wanted to be capable, thanks to his asceticism, of vanquishing the blows of a capricious Fortune that he regarded as an implacable foe. The result was the same: both philosophers endured the onslaught, but their state of mind was very different. Demetrius accepted the blows of Fate/Providence positively, since he believed it guided the world in a rational fashion, while Diogenes daily waged a desperate battle against the whims of Fortune, which he considered anything but rational. Demetrius was therefore a Cynic who was tinged with Stoicism. For Seneca, however, Demetrius was simply a Cynic philosopher, and he would have never classified him as a Stoic.

Musonius provides a different example. He actually was a Stoic, but he was personally quite influenced by Cynicism, to the extent that Eunapius makes a mistake and includes him among the notable representatives of Cynicism, along with Demetrius, Menippus of Lycia, and a certain Carneades.[437] The extracts that survive from Musonius show that he was working with the same theoretical background as the Cynics, though always with one slight exception: he rejected their shamelessness. The titles of several of his diatribes express principles or questions that could just as easily have come from Cynics: "That One Should Disdain Hardships,"[438] "That Women Too

434. Cf. Epictetus, *Discourses* 1.25.22: "You may condemn me to death, but it's Nature itself that condemns you."

435. Dio Cassius, Roman History, 65.13.3: when Demetrius wouldn't comply when he was banished, Vespasian told him, "You are doing everything to force me to kill you, but I do not slay a barking dog" (trans. Earnest Cary, LCL).

436. Cf. Seneca, *On Providence* 5.5.

437. Eunapius, *Lives of the Philosophers and Sophists* 2.5 (Goulet 3.9–13).

438. The perspective is exactly the same as Diogenes's: one must not go to a lot of trouble over useless πόνοι, but rather direct all of one's efforts toward virtue. It's through the discipline of πόνοι that one acquires everything valuable.

Should Study Philosophy," "Should Daughters Receive the Same Education as Sons?," "That Exile Is Not an Evil," and even "Which Is More Effective, Theory or Practice?" In his work "On Training," he explains his concept of an asceticism that's appropriate for the soul and the body, which must be pursued alongside an asceticism specifically for the soul. The examples he gives of this first kind of asceticism are very reminiscent of the Cynic practice of physical asceticism with a moral goal: he says one must accustom oneself "to cold, to heat, to thirst, to hunger; to eating simply, to sleeping on the hard ground, to abstaining from pleasant things and enduring difficult things." And the reflections he offers in "On Food"[439] and "On Clothing"[440] could have been written by Diogenes himself. Musonius, as a good Stoic, was convinced that an asceticism for the soul was unavoidable,[441] but as an heir of Cynicism, he considered suffering and pleasure as major adversaries of the soul, and so was aware of the need for a bodily asceticism with a moral goal. Nevertheless, Musonius is careful to stress the need for modesty, and in that way he distinguishes himself radically from Cynicism. In his view, women who are philosophers should follow the argument, which proves that "modesty is the greatest good,"[442] and he explains that boys and girls "must be inspired with a feeling of shame toward all that is base."[443] By contrast with the Cynics, he condemned sexual relations outside marriage, for example, in the context of adultery, or with courtesans.[444] We don't know specifically how Musonius lived, but we may imagine that he practiced the Cynic way of life, though without its shamelessness. Musonius was one of those Stoics who traced the roots of his philosophy back to Cynicism. He admired Diogenes profoundly, saying that "through his asceticism that aimed at virtue, he came to surpass the philosophers,"[445] but he would never have considered himself a Cynic, if only because of the shamelessness that was intrinsically tied to Cynicism.

The situation is yet different with Epictetus, who was a disciple of Musonius. When one of his own disciples showed a penchant for Cynicism, he gave the movement a frankly idealized interpretation so that he could

---

439. Musonius Rufus, *Oration* 18a–b (Hense 94–105).

440. Musonius Rufus, *Oration* 19 (Hense 105–9).

441. Musonius Rufus, *Oration* 6 (Hense 25.14–26.5).

442. Musonius Rufus, *Oration* 3 (Hense 12.21 = Cora E. Lutz, "Musonius Rufus 'The Roman Socrates,'" *Yale Classical Studies* 10, 1947, 43).

443. Musonius Rufus, *Oration* 4 (Hense 18.5–6 = Cora E. Lutz 49).

444. Musonius Rufus, *Oration* 12 (Hense 64.4–12).

445. Musonius Rufus, *Oration* 9 (Hense 43.18–44.1 = Cora E. Lutz 71 modified).

condemn the popular Cynicism of his era, which, as far as he was concerned, was little more than a wretched knapsack, a staff, strong jaws, an eagerness to devour everything, a facility for insulting others indiscriminately, and a desire to show off one's beautiful shoulders.[446] Making no effort to hide his contempt for these Cynics, Epictetus describes them with an expression borrowed from the *Iliad* (22.69), "dogs of the table that guard the doors," and he says that they "follow the example of the masters in no way at all, except perhaps in farting in public, but in nothing apart from that."[447] His Diogenes is a messenger sent to men by Zeus who no longer has any shocking traits, or, more precisely, whose shocking traits have taken on a positive character. Does Diogenes insult others? "It's as a father that he does so, as a brother, and as a servant of Zeus."[448] Does he reprimand others? Yes, but he does so in a royal manner. What right does he have to speak to others so frankly? Because he's watching over them and going to great troubles for them.[449] The reader no longer recognizes the character of Diogenes, the fringe element who would engage in anything scandalous, shameless, or immodest in order to awaken the conscience of his contemporaries, when Epictetus says that the Cynic must fence himself off with virtuous shame! There's something like a Christian connotation in one trait embodied in this portrait: the Cynic must allow himself to be beaten by others without striking back; he must actually love those who beat him; and like Heracles, his illustrious predecessor, he must not think himself miserable.[450] As we noted earlier, Epictetus's revised, corrected, and highly idealized Diogenes still differs from the Stoic philosopher in that he is entrusted with an exceptional mission, with a divine vocation that leads him temporarily to renounce the social duties that still have a claim on the Stoic sage. Even the physical portrait of the Cynic undergoes some transformation: his body must demonstrate that a regime of simple, frugal living out in the fresh air is good for the health; he must never go about as a beggar, but be clean and attractive.[451] Gone is the filthy,

446. Cf. Epictetus, *Discourses* 3.22.50.

447. Epictetus, *Discourses* 3.22.80 (trans. Robin Hard).

448. Epictetus, *Discourses* 3.22.82 (trans. Robin Hard).

449. Epictetus, *Discourses* 3.22.97.

450. Epictetus, *Discourses* 3.22.54, 57. We can connect this trait with two anecdotes (Diogenes Laertius, *Lives* 6.33, 89) in which Diogenes and Crates don't fight back against those who strike them, but instead make and wear signs bearing the names of their aggressors. This is not done in quite the same spirit, however, because when Diogenes did this, he covered his aggressors with ridicule and brought universal blame and beatings upon them.

451. Epictetus, *Discourses* 3.22.86–89.

repulsive exterior; that would be unworthy of a "messenger and spy and herald of the gods."[452]

This idealized Cynic sage expresses himself in Epictetus's characteristic vocabulary. He believes that his essential task is to make "the correct use of impressions," the famous χρῆσις τῶν φαντασιῶν,[453] and he adopts the Stoic vision of the unity of the cosmos.[454] It would appear that Epictetus interpreted the Cynic message through the lens of his own Stoicism. Though he was a fervent admirer of Diogenes, he nevertheless could not accept his shocking traits, and so he corrected them in light of his own Stoic convictions, and in the process he transferred the Cynic mission into the religious sphere. He considered the Cynics whom he met, who slept on the ground, begged, and insulted passers-by, to be a caricature of Cynicism, and he invited his readers to disabuse themselves of this picture as quickly as possible so that they could appreciate what Cynicism truly was. From Epictetus's perspective, authentic Cynicism and Stoicism complemented one another. But once a city of Stoic sages came into being, there would be no further need for the exceptional role of the Cynic sage.[455]

It should be clear by now that Stoic and Cynic attitudes were fundamentally different. Behind the similarities in speech, behind the partial similarities in their respective asceticisms, it may be discerned how the Cynic "shortcut" preserved all its originality. A Cynic wouldn't practice the spiritual exercises of the Stoics, and a Stoic wouldn't practice, at least on an ongoing basis, the Cynics' physical asceticism with a moral goal. Beyond this, the Stoics rejected the lack of modesty in Diogenean Cynicism, and they wouldn't accept the Cynic choice of what is good by nature, which mocked what is good by convention and flouted the judgment of society. Christians would later have the same reaction. If we also consider that Stoicism had a theoretical edifice of logic, physics, and ethics that Cynicism lacked, we can understand why no Stoic ever claimed to be a Cynic, and vice versa.

The diversity of attitudes that Stoics under the Roman Empire took toward Cynicism is striking. Some recognized the value of the Cynic "shortcut," but they considered it only one path, alongside Stoicism, that led to wisdom, and they remained Stoics themselves. While Musonius had room

---

452. Epictetus, *Discourses* 3.22.69.

453. Epictetus, *Discourses* 3.22.21; see also 3.22.103–4 where other Stoic terminology is also found: προαίρεσις, συγκατάθεσις, ὁρμή, ὄρεξις, ἔκκλισις.

454. Epictetus, *Discourses* 4.1.155.

455. Epictetus, *Discourses* 3.22.67–69.

for a body-and-soul asceticism within his overall concept of asceticism, he still considered himself to be a Stoic. Others, such as Epictetus, idealized the past and reinterpreted the Cynic path along Stoic lines. But his Diogenes, revised to meet Stoic standards, looks much more like a Stoic sage than the figure we know from the Cynic chreias. Epictetus took for granted that the final phase of philosophy would be the Stoic phase and that Cynicism was only a temporary, exceptional phenomenon. Still others, even though they disapproved generally of the Cynics they encountered, admitted that some might follow this philosophy in an exemplary way. This was the case with Seneca and his friend Demetrius. Stoicism developed the perspective that Cynicism was a way of taking things to the limit and that this should be attempted only by people of exceptional character who could manage the extreme conduct required to defy νόμος and δόξα and who were called to live according to nature. But Cynic "indifference" never appealed to Stoics, and the problems that Philodemus described regarding the *Republics* continued to haunt the minds of Stoics under the Roman Empire.

Conclusion

The goal of this chapter on imperial Cynicism has been to show that the label "Cynic" cannot be used as if the definition of Cynicism were obvious. In the Hellenistic era, the word had a clear sense, because Diogenes, inspired by the heritage of Antisthenes, outlined the major ideas of his philosophy, thereby giving Cynicism a theoretical framework that, if limited, was a theoretical framework just the same, and which was readily available to everyone. Beyond this, through his very way of life, he bore striking witness to the value of bodily asceticism with a moral goal. In other words, in the Hellenistic era, when one spoke of Cynicism, the reference was clear and unambiguous. Under the Roman Empire, the situation became much more complex. Cynicism could be confused with Stoicism, whose origins were within Cynicism but which had quickly become autonomous. And there were two opposing conceptions at the heart of Cynicism itself: Was Cynicism a school of thought, just like the other philosophical schools, or was it simply a way of life? Finally, the idea spread, particularly among Christians, that it was possible to embrace any philosophy, whatever its τέλος might be, and still follow the Cynic way of life.

Despite this complexity, those who considered themselves Cynics and followed the principles of Diogenes claimed that this brought them into a specific spiritual condition that could not be reached by pursuing the objectives of any of the other schools. As the saying goes in the pseudepigraphal *Letters* of the Cynics, and as Epictetus and Julian also stress, the outfit alone doesn't make the Cynic; it's also necessary to practice Diogenean asceticism, directed toward a τέλος (probably ἀτυφία) and to respect a certain number of precepts first expressed by Antisthenes and then by Diogenes and Crates. We will encounter this problem again as we consider the relationship between Cynicism and Christianity, which was even more complex than the relationship between Cynicism and Stoicism. But first we will explore all the witnesses that demonstrate that historical contacts took place, before and after Jesus, between Cynicism and Judaism. This will ultimately allow us to ask whether it's legitimate to speak of a "Jewish Cynicism," as Bernhard Lang does, who finds the first trace of such a Cynicism in the book of Ecclesiastes![456]

456. Lang, *Jesus der Hund*, 63–69. See "The Problems with Bernhard Lang's Position" on pp. 184–89.

2. Contacts between Cynicism and Judaism from the Septuagint to the Talmud

How Strongly Hellenized Was the Jewish World in the Hellenistic and Roman Eras?

In order to study the relationship between Cynicism and Judaism in antiquity, it's necessary first to inquire into the relationship between Judaism and Hellenism. Several major studies have been conducted into this question and their conclusions often differ.[1] While the Jews of the Diaspora were more clearly Hellenized, it's difficult to determine the extent of the knowledge that Jews in Palestine had of Greek language and culture.

According to the testimony of his disciple Clearchus of Soli, who relates the anecdote in the first book of his treatise *On Sleep*, when Aristotle was traveling in Mysia around 345 BCE, he met a Jew from Coele-Syria whom

---

1. We will cite only a few examples here: Saul Lieberman, *Greek in Jewish Palestine: Studies in the Life and Manners of Jewish Palestine in the II–IV Centuries CE* (New York: Jewish Theological Seminary of America, 1942) and *Hellenism in Jewish Palestine* (New York: Jewish Theological Seminary of America, 1950), both reprinted in Lieberman, *Greek in Jewish Palestine; Hellenism in Jewish Palestine*, with a new introduction by Dov Zlotnick (New York: Jewish Theological Seminary of America, 1994), as well as Lieberman, "How Much Greek in Jewish Palestine?," in *Biblical and Other Studies*, ed. Alexander Altmann (Cambridge, MA: Harvard University Press, 1963), 123–41; B. Lifshitz, "L'hellénisation des Juifs de Palestine: A propos des inscriptions de Besara (Beth-Shearim)," *RB* 72 (1965): 520–38; Martin Hengel, *Judentum und Hellenismus*, WUNT 10 (Tübingen: Mohr Siebeck, 1969), 191–95 and 565–70 (English translation: Martin Hengel, *Judaism and Hellenism: Studies in Their Encounter in Palestine during the Early Hellenistic Period*, trans. John Bowden [Philadelphia: Fortress, 1974]); John J. Collins and Gregory E. Sterling, eds., *Hellenism in the Land of Israel*, CJA 13 (Notre Dame, IN: University of Notre Dame Press, 2001); Louis H. Feldman, "How Much Hellenism in the Land of Israel?," *JSJ* 33 (2002): 290–313 (this is a book review of the contributions gathered by Collins and Sterling).

he said "was Greek not only in his language, but in his soul also" and whose learning he greatly admired.[2] But does this testimony, assuming that it's historically genuine, represent a notable exception, or does it illustrate a real phenomenon, the progressive Hellenization of the Jewish population? And if that is the case, then how far did this Hellenization go, in Palestine as well as in the Diaspora? A contrasting testimony comes from several centuries later. In *Against Celsus*, Origen, after mentioning that Celsus's Jew . . . is described as being acquainted with a remark of Bacchus in Euripides (*Bacchae*, v. 498), adds that "Jews are not at all well read in Greek literature," thereby expressing his skepticism about the knowledge a Jew might have of Greek literature.[3] Drawing on the information provided by several major studies, let us now offer a sketch, necessarily quite brief, of this partial Hellenization of the Jewish world, in order to account for how connections could have formed between Cynicism and Judaism. We will always have to keep in mind clearly the distinction between Palestine and the Diaspora, and between information drawn from witnesses prior to the destruction of the temple in 70 CE and information drawn from rabbinic literature.

Martin Hengel believes the evidence shows clearly that from the middle of the third century BCE, all of Judaism, both in Palestine and in the Diaspora, should be regarded as "Hellenistic Judaism" in the strict sense, and that the eventual triumph of Christianity is explained precisely by the fact that Hellenistic Judaism prepared the way for Christianity. Starting in the third century BCE, many Greek names or dual Greco-Semitic names appear in the area of Phoenicia. In the Phoenician colony of Marisa, which was the principal city of Idumea, founded in the middle of the third century BCE and situated only about twenty-five miles south of Jerusalem, one encounters a mixture of Phoenician, Idumean, Jewish, and Greek names in a cultural milieu that was already fully Hellenized.[4] Greek names can be found even among the conservative Jews of Palestine. The second son of the high priest Simon the Just, who wanted to transform Jerusalem into a Greek *polis* in 175 BCE under Antiochus Epiphanes, took the name Jason, even though he

2. The testimony of Clearchus is transmitted by Josephus, *Against Apion* 1.22.179–81 (Wehrli frag. 6). Cf. Eusebius, *Preparation for the Gospel* 9.5. See P.-M. Schuhl, "Sur un témoignage de Cléarque: A propos des rapports entre savants grecs et juifs," in *Études platoniciennes* (Paris: Presses Universitaires de France, 1960), 132–37.

3. Origen, *Against Celsus* 2.34 (trans. Henry Chadwick).

4. Cf. Hengel, *Judentum und Hellenismus*, 115, who cites many other examples on the following pages (116–20); Martin Hengel, *Juden, Griechen und Barbaren: Aspekte der Hellenisierung des Judentums in vorchristlicher Zeit*, SBS 76 (Stuttgart: Katholisches Bibelwerk, 1976), 157.

was originally called Jesus. This Jason advocated an extreme Hellenization and even built a gymnasium at the foot of the Acropolis that dominated the temple esplanade in Jerusalem, and the priests themselves, "despising the sanctuary and neglecting the sacrifices, hurried to take part in the training in the wrestling arena."[5] The author of Second Maccabees says that Jason "shifted his compatriots over to the Greek way of life" (πρὸς τὸν Ἑλληνικὸν χαρακτῆρα).[6] It's hard to imagine that this could have taken place unless the philhellenes among the Jews already had a good understanding of the Greek language. This same author also cites the names of two of Judas Maccabeus's generals who both had Greek names: Dositheus and Sosipater.[7] Another detail: the *Letter of Aristeas*, a pseudepigraphy that may date to the beginning of the second century BCE, contains a list of the seventy-two inhabitants of Jerusalem, descended from the twelve tribes, who were chosen by Demetrius of Phalerum to translate the Septuagint, and many among them have Greek names—for example, Theodosius, Jason, Theodotus, Theophilus, and Dositheus. Moreovoer, they're all described as thoroughly familiar not only with Jewish writings but also with Hellenistic culture.[8] Rabbinic literature, for its part, shall offer later on indications that lead to the conclusion that there were mixed marriages in Palestine.[9]

In the Diaspora, where knowledge of Aramaic was rapidly lost, Hellenization was strong—quite strong, in some locations. This was particularly true of Egypt. In the time of Philo, who was a contemporary of Jesus, the city of Alexandria, which was very Hellenized, played a decisive role in the connections that formed between the Greek and Jewish communities. In the year 37 of our era, no fewer than a million Jews lived in Egypt,[10] and it's estimated that the city of Alexandria at that time would have contained some 180,000 of them.[11] For the rabbis who often visited Greek-speaking communities outside Palestine and held erudite conversations there, Alexandria was

---

5. See 2 Macc. 4:7–15; 1 Macc. 1:10–15. Cf. Hengel, *Judentum und Hellenismus*, 135–43; Hengel, *Juden, Griechen und Barbaren*, 158.

6. 2 Macc. 4:10 (NRSV). It is believed that the Maccabean revolt was a reaction to Jason's decision to promote a Greek-style life in Jerusalem.

7. See 2 Macc. 12:19.

8. *Letter of Aristeas* 47–50 and 121 (cf. Hengel, *Judentum und Hellenismus*, 120).

9. Cf. t. Sukkah 4:28; y. Sukkah 55d; b. Sukkah 56b.

10. Cf. Philo, *Against Flaccus* 6.43.

11. See Diana Delia, "The Population of Roman Alexandria," *TAPA* 118 (1988): 275–92, esp. 286–87, who relies on the reconstitutions and interpretations of a fragment of the *Acta Alexandrinorum* by A. von Premerstein and by L. Koenen; Feldman relies on this estimate in his article "How Much Hellenism in the Land of Israel?," 309.

a major source of information about Greek wisdom. The Jews of the Diaspora in Egypt, in Asia Minor, and in the countries around the Aegean Sea spoke Greek, and when they went to Jerusalem on pilgrimage, they brought this Greek language with them. Hengel discerns the influences of Greek thought first on Qohelet (Ecclesiastes was probably written in the third century BCE) and an influence of Stoicism on Ben Sira, the author of Ecclesiasticus, which was translated into Greek in 132 BCE.[12] He notes also that in the list of musical instruments presented in the book of Daniel, written under Antiochus Epiphanes between 167 and 164, many instruments (σάλπιγξ, σῦριγξ, κιθάρα, σαμβύκη, ψαλτήριον, συμφωνία)[13] are familiar from Greek music. With this objective data, Hengel reaches the following conclusion: "Thus by and large we may term the Judaism of the Hellenistic Roman period, both in the home country and the Diaspora, 'Hellenistic Judaism.'"[14]

For his part, Saul Lieberman had already shown that Greek was introduced irreversibly into Jewish culture in the first four centuries of our era. Jews in Palestine spoke Greek: a good Greek in the case of educated Jews, whom the middle class tried to imitate; and a sort of "Aramaic Greek Jargon," with a limited and vulgar vocabulary, in the case of the common people. The degree of Greek culture depended on one's social standing.[15] Jewish epitaphs in Jaffa, found for the most part in the cemetery, support the thesis of an extension of Greek even into the popular classes: sixty of the epitaphs are in Greek, while only six are in Hebrew. The numerous Greek inscriptions that have been found in the synagogues and cemeteries in cities in the interior of Palestine offer similar support.[16] Greek was spoken by the common people, not just written by the educated classes. In Jerusalem itself, the language made its way into certain synagogues. The Acts of the Apostles alludes to "Hellenists" (that is, Jews who had lived outside Palestine[17] and who had their own synagogues in Jerusalem where the Bible was read in Greek)[18] and to

12. See the pages that Hengel devotes to Qohelet and to Ben Sira in *Judentum und Hellenismus*, 210–75.

13. Dan. 3:5, 7, 10, 15.

14. Martin Hengel, *Jews, Greeks and Barbarians: Aspects of the Hellenization of Judaism in the Pre-Christian Period*, trans. John Bowden (Philadelphia: Fortress, 1980), 125–26.

15. Lieberman, *Greek in Jewish Palestine* (1942), 15–28.

16. Lieberman, *Greek in Jewish Palestine* (1942), 30.

17. Cf. Acts 6:1 (where the Hellenists criticize the Hebrews for neglecting their widows in the daily distribution of food).

18. In the third century CE, at Caesarea in Palestine, there was a synagogue where Rabbi Levi ben Hittah heard the Shema prayer being recited in Greek (y. Sotah 7.1.21b).

"Hebrews" (that is, native Jews, in whose synagogues the Bible was read in Hebrew). We know from rabbinic literature that in the synagogue, the rabbis didn't hesitate to draw on Greek sources in order to explain biblical events, and that in Hellenized cities, even though they were preaching in Aramaic, they cited Greek translations for certain passages of the Bible in order to make sure they were understood by the Jews who lived there.[19] A great number of rabbis, even though they remained convinced of the superiority of Judaism, diligently pursued a good understanding of Greek literature and sought to make use of Greek culture to help Judaism spread among the gentiles.[20]

Actually the rabbis' attitude toward Greek was rather complex. Their preference was definitely for Hebrew, but they had to acknowledge that the majority of Jews used the Aramaic language in their daily lives, not Hebrew. And beyond this, in light of political realities, rabbis in general chose to use Greek rather than Aramaic for speaking and writing. Even though they wanted to resist assimilation, they were aware that the Jews needed to maintain good relationships with their neighbors.

According to the testimony of Rabbi Simon ben Gamaliel II, in the house of his father, the patriarch Rabbi Gamaliel II—and thus in Jewish Palestine in the first century—there were a thousand students, five hundred of whom were studying the Law, and five hundred Greek wisdom. Permission to teach Greek was granted to him because he was closely associated with the Roman government.[21] But the Talmud presents this situation as an exception, which, moreover, caused some dissatisfaction among rabbis.[22] In the following century, Rabbi Judah Hanassi (135–ca. 220), the son of Rabbi Simon ben Gamaliel II, spoke with disdain of "that Syrian language,"

---

19. Cf. Lieberman, *Greek in Jewish Palestine* (1942), 29–67. Michael Avi-Yonah, *Geschichte der Juden im Zeitalter des Talmud in den Tagen von Rom und Byzanz*, SJ 2 (Berlin: de Gruyter, 1962), 73, also notes that in the Midrash there are lists of foreign words that Jews used to translate their names from Hebrew into Greek; these words sometimes translated the sense of the name, and sometimes reproduced its sound. He cites *Leviticus Rabbah* 32.5, where, for example, Isaac is translated as Gelasios, "the one who laughs," and Menahem as Paregorios, "the one who consoles," while Reuben becomes Rufus, Joseph becomes Justus, and Esther becomes Estreia.

20. In the second century, when Aquila presented his Greek translation of the Bible to R. Eliezer and R. Joshua, they appreciated his work for it style and accuracy (cf. b. Megilla 3a), which implies that Eliezer and Joshua knew Greek well enough to be able to judge the stylistic quality of a text translated into Greek.

21. b. Sotah 49b and b. Bava Qamma 83a.

22. b. Sotah 49b and b. Bava Qamma 83a. See Feldman, "How Much Hellenism in the Land of Israel?," 313.

meaning the contemporary Judeo-Aramaic dialect,[23] and opted clearly for Greek, not hesitating to ask, "Why use that jargon in the land of Israel, when either the holy language [Hebrew] or Greek could be used there?"[24] But there must have been some controversy over the matter of teaching Greek to one's children, because when Rabbi Joshua (late first century/early second century) was asked whether a Jew had the right to teach Greek to his son, he answered that this could be done during the hours that were not part of either the day or the night, since it is written (cf. Josh. 1:8) that one should meditate on the Law day and night.[25] Lieberman concludes from this that education in Greek wasn't forbidden in itself, but only to the extent that it interfered with study of the Law. In the third century, Johanan bar Nappaha (also known as John of Tiberias), who taught at Sepphoris and Tiberias, believed that a Jew could teach Greek to his daughter; he believed that this learning would serve as an adornment for her. Relying on this stance, Rabbi Abbahu, who had studied Greek himself, gave his daughters a Greek education.[26] Lieberman emphasizes that it wasn't forbidden to teach Greek to adults, but only to children (which is why the permission given to Gamaliel II was so exceptional). According to Rabbi Hiyya b. Abba, the concern was that this might lead some of them to become *rhetores*, and they might then in turn become *delatores*, since Greek was the language of the government administration.[27] But according to Lieberman, the actual concern was that if people were dissatisfied with the decisions of Jewish courts, and they knew Greek, some might appeal to the Roman government. He notes that Rabbi Hiyya b. Abba, for example, once fell victim to this procedure: a woman was unhappy with a decision he rendered, so she appealed it to the proconsul in Caesarea.[28] But Lieberman insists on the fact that rabbinic literature gives us no indications that would lead us to believe that the personal study of Greek wisdom or the Greek language was forbidden for adults. There were only reservations about teaching Greek to children, for fear that this might lead

23. b. Sotah 49b and b. Bava Qamma 83a.

24. b. Sotah 49b and b. Bava Qamma 83a.

25. y. Pe'ah 1.1.15c 7–12 (Gerd A. Wewers, *Terumot: Priesterhebe* [Tübingen: Mohr Siebeck, 1985], 12). Cf. Lieberman, *Greek in Jewish Palestine* (1942), 16, and Lieberman, *Hellenism in Jewish Palestine* (1950), 101.

26. y. Pe'ah 1.1.15c 12–15 (Wewers, *Terumot*, 12).

27. y. Pe'ah 1.1.15c 7–12 (Wewers, *Terumot*, 12). Cf. Lieberman, *Hellenism in Jewish Palestine* (1950), 101n13.

28. y. Megilla 3.2 (1), 74a 48–53 (Frowald G. Hüttenmeister 119). Cf. Lieberman, *Greek in Jewish Palestine* (1942), 24.

them to become informers. To summarize the divergent attitudes that rabbis held toward Greek, we may say that in the third century there were rabbis who knew Greek very well, along with others who ignored it deliberately. On the one hand, Rabbi Jonathan of Eleutheropolis was very familiar with the respective intricacies of Greek, Latin, Syriac, and Hebrew,[29] and his younger contemporary Rabbi Abbahu, the head of the rabbinic school in Caesarea, loved to play word games in Greek as well as in Aramaic.[30] But Lieberman also cites contrasting examples from the same time period. Rabbi Hiyya b. Abba, mentioned above, and Rabbi Simeon b. Abba were both originally from Babylon and immigrated to Palestine, and they were both opposed to Greek culture and never learned the Greek language.[31]

Some, however, such as Louis H. Feldman, challenge the overall picture of widespread Hellenization that Hengel, for example, supports.[32] Feldman cites the testimonies of John of Tiberias and Origen as support for his confident belief that the predominant language of Palestinian Jews during the Hellenistic era and under the Roman Empire was not in fact Greek but Aramaic, even though Hebrew continued to be spoken during the period of the Mishnah. He offers as evidence the fact that Paul addressed the Jews of Jerusalem "in the Hebrew language" (τῇ Ἑβραΐδι διαλέκτῳ),[33] an expression that probably indicates Aramaic, and that Flavius Josephus, when he was charged by Titus with convincing the Jews to surrender the city of Jerusalem to him, spoke to them "in the language of their fathers" (τῇ πατρίῳ γλώσσῃ),[34] probably meaning Aramaic once again. No one, in fact, actually denies that the language that Jews spoke was Aramaic; nor does anyone deny that Greek had penetrated the Jewish world. The disagreements arise over the question of how widespread Greek was as a spoken language. Some see it as having been quite widespread, others not nearly so much. While we must certainly not imagine that everybody in Palestine spoke Greek, and we should not exaggerate the extent of Hellenization (Hengel may perhaps overemphasize it), it would nevertheless also be a mistake to think that the Jews of Palestine

29. y. Megilla 1.11, 71b, 63–69 (Hüttenmeister 43). Cf. Lieberman, *Greek in Jewish Palestine* (1942), 21n36.

30. b. Eruvin 53b; *Genesis Rabbah* 14.2 (cf. Lieberman, *Greek in Jewish Palestine* (1942), 21n38 and 22n45).

31. See Lieberman, *Greek in Jewish Palestine* (1942), 25–26.

32. See his demonstration in Feldman, "How Much Hellenism in the Land of Israel?" and the conclusion on 313.

33. Acts 21:40; 22:2.

34. Flavius Josephus, *Jewish War* 5.361.

remained impermeable to the influence of Greek. The distinctions that Avi-Yonah suggests, along the lines of Lieberman, seem probable enough: on the one hand, rabbis in Palestine, especially by the fourth century of our era, had a profound knowledge of Greek culture and law; on the other hand, those who came from Babylonia barely knew Greek; in the provinces, the rabbis and the middle class were not very familiar with Greek; as for the common people, especially the peasants, they were ignorant of Greek, or knew just enough to purchase goods in the market; while in the cities the lower-class Jews spoke a simple, popular Greek, a sort of "Greek jargon."[35] There is no doubt that Hellenization was taking place, but it had its limits. At any rate, to whatever extent there was Hellenization in the culture, and there certainly was some, there was none in the cult.[36]

Attested Contacts between Cynicism and Judaism in Antiquity

Let us now document, in chronological order, all of the passages in Greek and Hebrew literature that mention a link, of whatever nature or extent, between Cynicism and Judaism, in Palestine as well as in the Diaspora.

The Septuagint (Third Century BCE)

The first testimony dates to the third century BCE and is found in the Septuagint. A priori, there's no reason to expect that the Hebrew Bible translated into Greek would mention Cynicism. Nevertheless, that's what happens in the first book of Kingdoms,[37] as the author is relating the story of Nabal, a very rich man, who's described as hard (σκληρός), evil in his dealings (πονηρὸς ἐν ἐπιτηδεύμασιν), and cynical (κυνικός), but whose wife Abigail was intelligent and beautiful. Nabal had rebuffed the messengers David had sent him, even though he was obliged to him, and in response David was preparing to attack him with four hundred men. But Abigail saved the day by bringing David many gifts and by persuading him that as the future king of Israel, he should not take the law into his own hands by shedding Nabal's

35. See Avi-Yonah, *Geschichte der Juden*, 73–74.
36. Cf. John J. Collins, *Jewish Cult and Hellenistic Culture: Essays on the Jewish Encounter with Hellenism and Roman Rule* (Leiden: Brill, 2005), 43.
37. 1 Kingdoms (1 Sam.) 25:2–43.

blood. Ten days later, Nabal died. This was how Yahweh punished him for having insulted David, who then asked Abigail to become his own wife. The Septuagint is probably dependent, for the passage that interests us, on a Hebrew text that characterizes Nabal with the word *keleb*, "dog," which is paleographically close to the *qere* of the Masoretic Text, *kālibbî*, "Calebite" (that is, from the tribe of Caleb).[38] The Septuagint translators rendered the word as κυνικός. It's impossible to know whether, for them, the adjective referred to Cynicism, in which case we would have to acknowledge that they were familiar with the philosophy, or whether they simply wanted to indicate that Nabal was behaving like a dog. But either way, the Septuagint's own readers understood the term as a reference to Cynicism. For example, we hear the Jewish historian Flavius Josephus, as he is commenting on this passage at the end of the first century, say that Nabal was "hard, and evil in his dealings, because he conducted his life according to Cynic asceticism" (σκληρὸς καὶ πονηρὸς τοῖς ἐπιτηδεύμασιν ἐκ κυνικῆς ἀσκήσεως πεποιημένος τὸν βίον). This proves that he knew both about Cynicism and about the most significant characteristic of the way of life associated with that philosophy, specifically asceticism. But it also shows that he had an unreservedly negative conception of Cynicism.[39] No firm conclusion can be drawn from the passage about whether the translators had any knowledge of Cynicism, but that should certainly not be ruled out.

Meleager of Gadara (Second/First Century BCE)

The second testimony is more definite. It comes from the poet and epigrammist Meleager, author of the famous *Garland* of epigrams attributed to him.[40] Athenaeus classifies him unambiguously as a Cynic.[41] Meleager, the son of Eucrates, was born in Gadara, but he grew up in the city of Tyre, "which made a man of him," and he retired in his old age to Cos.[42] It's clear that he knew several languages, and it's possible that Aramaic was the one he spoke at home. His funerary epigram, preserved in the *Palatine Anthology*, ends

38. See Gilles Dorival, "L'image des Cyniques chez les Pères grecs," in *Le cynisme ancien et ses prolongements*, ed. Marie-Odile Goulet-Cazé and Richard Goulet (Paris: Presses Universitaires de France, 1993), 419–43, esp. 419–20.

39. Flavius Josephus, *Antiquities of the Jews* 6.296.

40. Cf. *Palatine Anthology* 4.1.3, 12.257.5–6.

41. Athenaeus, *The Dinner Sophists* 11.502c.

42. Cf. *Palatine Anthology* 7.417.1–4, 7.418.1–4.

with a triple interjection addressed to passers-by that invites us to think so: Σαλάμ in Syriac (= Aramaic), Αὐδονίς in Phoenician, and χαῖρε in Greek.[43]

Here is the epigram that proves Meleager had contact with the Jewish community in Gadara or Tyre: "White-cheeked Demo, someone holds you naked next to him and is taking his delight, but my own heart groans within me. If the Sabbath desire has come over you, no great wonder! Love burns hot even on cold Sabbaths."[44] We may imagine that Meleager was rather young at this point, because he later had romantic relationships with men, which led him to abandon Cynicism.[45] Here he is addressing a girl he's in love with, named Demo.[46] He has a rival for her affections who is undoubtedly Jewish. Should we assume that Demo herself is also Jewish, as the expression σαββατικὸς πόθος, the "Sabbath desire," would lead us to believe?[47] We can't rule this out, but the fact that the name Demo also appears in a Greek inscription found at Larissa in Thessaly would suggest otherwise.[48] The allusion to Sabbaths being cold suggests that the scene takes place in winter. This could have been in Gadara, where the poet was born, or in Tyre, where he lived as an adult. The ironic meaning is that on the Sabbath, when all work is forbidden—including lighting fires[49]—people keep warm in bed,[50] and on those days people also have leisure for amorous activities.

43. Cf. *Palatine Anthology* 7.419.7–8.

44. *Palatine Anthology* 5.160 [159], in Pierre Waltz, *Anthologie grecque*, vol. 2, CUF (Paris: Les Belles Lettres, 1928), 75 (English translation by William Roger Paton).

45. He left Cynicism specifically because of the homosexual attraction he felt for a certain Myiscos (*Palatine Anthology* 12.101 and, more discreetly, *Palatine Anthology* 12.23, 117).

46. Demo appears in three places in book 5: *Palatine Anthology* 5.172 [171], 173 [172], 197 [196].

47. It's interesting to note that Meleager is one of the first pagan writers to mention the Sabbath. See Menahem Stern, *From Herodotus to Plutarch*, vol. 1 of *Greek and Latin Authors on Jews and Judaism*, Fontes ad res judaicas spectantes (Jerusalem: The Israel Academy of Sciences and Humanities, 1974), 140n43.

48. See *IG* 9.2, no. 988.

49. Cf. Philo, *On the Special Laws* 2.65.

50. This is the explanation that Hermann Beckby offers in *Anthologia Graeca*, vol. 1, 2nd ed. (Munich: Heimeran, 1965), 676n160. But we may also think of the boredom that characterized this day on which people didn't work (cf. the note by Waltz, *Anthologie grecque*, vol. 2, on 5.137, which cites Henri Ouvré, *Méléagre de Gadara* (Paris: Hachette et cie, 1894), 75: "Among the Hebrews, on sacred days, the meditative faces and silent streets inspired in him [i.e., Meleager] a profound ennui"). The same idea is implicit in *De reditu suo* 1.387–92, by the fifth-century poet Rutilius Namatianus, who was very critical of the Jews, claiming that their hearts were even colder than their religion: "Reddimus obscenae convicia debita genti, quae genitale caput propudiosa metit, radix stultitiae, cui frigida sabbata cordi, sed

This, at least, is the most plausible explanation. What's significant to note is that a Cynic poet of the first century BCE, who grew up in Gadara and Tyre and wrote in the Greek language, could be in love with a girl—also loved by a Jew—and tease her about the Sabbath.

Philo of Alexandria (First Century CE)

About a century and a half later, in the time of Christ, but in an entirely different milieu, that of the Hellenized Jews, Cynicism formed part of the philosophical culture in Alexandria, along with Stoic ethics, Platonic metaphysics, and Aristotelian logic. Philo of Alexandria was educated in this Greek philosophy and displays a sincere admiration for Cynicism in many of his writings. As he tells it, the disciples of Diogenes were numerous: he speaks of the "incalculable number of men" (ἀπερίληπτος ἀριθμός) "who chose to practice the same mode of life as Diogenes."[51] But even more significantly for our purposes, Philo speaks further of an individual named Chaereas, an educated man living in Alexandria, whom he describes as "a zealous [ζηλωτής] imitator of Diogenes's freedom of speech." He illustrates this by citing the reply that Chaereas gave when threatened by King Ptolemy: "Rule your Egyptian slaves; but as for me, I neither care for you, nor fear your wrath and angry threats."[52] We may conclude confidently from this that Chaereas was a Cynic, but unfortunately it's not possible to determine when he lived. Philo uses the aorist (ἐγένετο) when speaking of him, and

---

cor frigidius religione sua, septima quaeque dies turpi damnato veterno, tamquam lassati mollis imago dei" ("We pay him back with all the scorn that's owed a filthy and disgraceful race that circumcises. The root of foolishness! They love their chilly Sabbath, but their hearts are colder than their creed. Every seventh day is damned to lazy sloth, a feeble image of its tired god!" [trans. Martha Malamud]). Étienne Wolff, in his CUF edition of Namatianus (Paris: Les Belles Lettres, 2007), 83n164, explains the term *frigida* this way: "Fires were not lit on the Sabbath day (Exodus 35:3)." A *scholion* on Virgil's *Georgics* 1.336 (Hagen 256.8–10), highlighted by Menahem Stern, *From Tacitus to Simplicius*, 654, no. 537c, also refers to cold on the Sabbath, in connection with astronomy and food: "Satis cognitum est, Saturni stellam frigidam esse et ideo Iudaeos Saturni die frigidos cibos esse" ("It's well known that the star of Saturn is cold, and that's why the Jews have cold meals on the day of Saturn").

51. Philo, *Concerning Noah's Work as a Planter* 151 (English translations for all quotations from Philo by Charles Duke Yonge). Half a century later, Dio Chrysostom would make a similar remark about the number of Cynics in Alexandria, but the tone he adopted would be very critical (*Discourse* 32.9).

52. Cf. Philo, *Every Good Man Is Free* 125 (Chaereas is alluding to the *Iliad* 9.180–81).

this could indicate that he lived either in the remote past or the recent past. Philo also doesn't specify which King Ptolemy was involved.

Philo holds up Antisthenes and Diogenes as examples of moral virtue for his readers, and he doesn't hesitate to draw a strong comparison: Antisthenes and Moses shared a common view about the sage's stability.[53] There is no doubt that Philo was familiar with the collections of Cynic chreias, because he passes along the anecdotes about Diogenes being captured by pirates[54] and searching for a real man in daylight with a lantern.[55] A number of clearly Cynic themes run through his writings.[56] Even if he doesn't say so explicitly, we can recognize that as he understood it, the behavior of the Essenes,[57] who were hostile to luxury and refinement, closely resembled that of Cynic ascetics. He describes their behavior in *Every Good Man Is Free*: they disparaged wealth and sought to live frugally (76–77); they refused to fight in wars or bear arms (78); they rejected slavery (79); they concentrated only on the moral part of philosophy, abandoning the logical and metaphysical parts as useless for the acquisition of virtue (80); they had no private property, but held all goods in common (85–86). We should therefore not be surprised to find typical Cynic virtues such as self-control, endurance, and humility on the list of virtues that Philo attributes to these Essenes. However, he pairs them with virtues that are foreign to Cynicism, such as piety, holiness, love of God, and respect for the Law. We should therefore simply note these similarities between the Essenes, as Philo portrays them, and the asceticism of the Cynics, without assuming that the latter necessarily influenced the former.

How should we interpret the more than favorable attention that Philo pays to Cynicism? Should we conclude that he personally read not only the collections of Cynic chreias but also the works of Antisthenes, Diogenes,

53. Philo, *Every Good Man Is Free* 28–29.

54. Philo, *Every Good Man Is Free* 121.

55. Philo, *On the Giants* 33.

56. See, e.g., *On the Contemplative Life* 37 ("eat only so far as not to be hungry, and . . . drink just enough to escape from thirst"); *On Rewards and Punishments* 99 ("the simple wealth of nature is food and shelter," i.e., just what we need); *Allegorical Interpretation* 3.135 (ἄσκησις and πόνος); *On the Migration of Abraham* 86–88 (δοκεῖν and εἶναι); *On Dreams* 1.120–25 (e.g., πόνος and καρτερία in 120; criticism of luxury, τρυφή, in 123; praise of πόνοι for acquiring virtue in 124); *On the Special Laws* 2.42 (life is a festival), 45 (cosmopolitanism), 46 (indifference toward things that are indifferent).

57. Dio Chrysostom, cited by Synesius, *Dio* 3.1, also praises the Essene community as "a whole happy township in the midst of Palestine, beside the Dead Sea" (trans. Augustine Fitzgerald).

and Crates, and that the message of these philosophers answered, at least in part, to his own aspirations? The way he presents the famous episode of Diogenes being captured by pirates in his *Every Good Man is Free* 121–24 shows that he had firsthand knowledge of *The Sale of Diogenes* by the Cynic philosopher Menippus.[58] Beyond this, Philo shares the idea of "unlearning" with Antisthenes, who is generally considered to have developed it in one of his *Cyrus* compositions, where he describes "unlearning evil" (ἀπομαθεῖν τὰ κακά) as "the most necessary knowledge."[59] This same idea is found often in Philo, for example, when he advises that we should ἀπομαθεῖν ἀμαθίαν, "unlearn ignorance."[60] I. Heinemann holds that Cynicism had a decisive influence on Philo; he believes, for example, that besides the allegorists, the source that Philo depended on for his treatise *On the Special Laws* was a Jewish author who had been won over to Cynicism.[61] And it's certainly true that many of the ideas developed in 2.42–48 of that work—for example, that every day is a festival, that we should be submitted to nature, that we should adopt an attitude of complete indifference toward things that are indifferent, that we shouldn't flinch at the blows of Fortune, because we should know enough to expect its attacks—are classic ideas of Cynicism. It should be particularly emphasized, and this is a strong argument in support of Heinemann's thesis, that the idea of seeing each day as a festival is found nowhere else in Judaism, nor anywhere in the rest of Greek culture, but only in Diogenes and Crates,[62] in the sense that for them life is a festival if one is able to return to nature. Philo thus provides an emblematic example of educated Alexandrian Judaism, suffused in Greek studies and aware of what philosophies such as Cynicism and Stoicism could have in common with Jewish culture.

58. See Marie-Odile Goulet-Cazé, "Le livre VI de Diogène Laërce: Analyse de sa structure et réflexions méthodologiques," *ANRW* 2.36.6:4005–25.

59. Stobaeus, *Anthology* 2.31.34 (Wachsmuth 2:207.22–23). The expression is attributed to Cyrus in the *Violetum* of Arsenius (Walz 502.13–14).

60. Cf. Philo, *On the Migration of Abraham* 149; *On the Virtues* 220; *Every Good Man Is Free* 12. The verb "unlearn" can have other complements in Philo's writings. In *On the Migration of Abraham* 151, τὰ πάθη; in *Allegorical Interpretation* 3.236 and *On the Preliminary Studies* 162, τὸ πάθος.

61. Isaak Heinemann, *Philons griechische und jüdische Bildung: Kulturvergleichende Untersuchungen zu Philons Darstellung der jüdischen Gesetze* (Breslau: M. & H. Marcus, 1932), 106–9.

62. Cf. Plutarch, *On Tranquility of Mind* 4.466e and 20.477c.

Flavius Josephus (First Century CE)

Another Jewish writer, the historian Flavius Josephus, a contemporary of Philo, was born into a priestly family in Judea and trained to become a Jewish priest. He initially took part in the Jewish revolt against Rome that began in 66, but after surrendering and defecting to the Romans, he became a protégé of the Flavians, particularly of Titus and Vespasian. Josephus doesn't speak of Cynicism as such, except, as we saw above, in the case of Nabal, which demonstrates that he at least knew of this philosophical movement. However, in his *Jewish Antiquities*, he does speak of a "fourth philosophy of the Jews,"[63] meaning the party of Zealots that gathered around Judas the Galilean, essentially a rebel sect that took its place alongside the three other parties within Jewish philosophy: the Pharisees, the Sadducees, and the Essenes. It has been observed that the Zealots had certain traits in common with Cynicism.[64] But as in the case of Philo and the Essenes, prudence is well advised here, because in order to appreciate the nature of a parallel, we need to compare the contexts, and we often discover that parallelism is a far cry from dependence.[65] When Josephus says that this sect was characterized by an invincible love for liberty, and that it refused to serve any man as master, we may be tempted to think that the Zealots were inspired by the Cynics. However, Josephus goes on to explain that it was because they regarded God as their sole master that they refused any human domination, and this attitude appears to be completely foreign to the position that the Cynics took toward religion under the Roman Empire (cf. "'Falsifying the Currency' or the Critique of Civilization–On the Religious Level" on p. 37). Moreover, the Cynics would never have agreed to take up arms to defend a homeland of any kind; they were not revolutionaries in any sense, but rather pacifist anarchists for whom the notion of a homeland had no meaning. Consequently, if we can discern intellectual connections between Philo and Cynicism, it would be imprudent to draw any conclusions from what Flavius Josephus says about the group of Zealots that formed around Judas the Galilean.

---

63. Flavius Josephus, *Jewish Antiquities* 18.23. See Martin Hengel, *Die Zeloten: Untersuchungen zur jüdischen Freiheitsbewegung in der Zeit von Herodes I bis 70 n. Chr.* (Leiden: Brill, 1976), 336–49.

64. See, e.g., F. Gerald Downing, *Cynics and Christian Origins* (Edinburgh: T&T Clark, 1992), 153.

65. See Abraham J. Malherbe, "Hellenistic Moralists and the New Testament," *ANRW* 2.26.1:267–333, esp. 277.

Oenomaus of Gadara (Second Century CE)

The research of a number of scholars supports the hypothesis that Oenomaus of Gadara was the inspiration for the character of the philosopher Abnimos ha-gardi (that is, "born in Gader" = Gadara), who appears as a friend of Rabbi Meir in several anecdotes found in rabbinic literature from the third through the sixth century and also in the ninth century.[66] Two different datings are attested for Oenomaus: the second century, based on Jerome's *Chronicle* for the year 119, and the beginning of the third century, based on the *Suda*.[67] We have already met this philosopher, the author of *Charlatans Exposed*, and seen how important a figure he is in the Cynic movement. He offered a renewed conception of the philosophy under the Roman Empire, with less of an emphasis on asceticism and more of a stress on literary activity.[68] The emperor Julian's violent attacks against him confirm how influential he was.

The sages of Tiberias who are associated with the figure known as Abnimos ha-gardi could have become acquainted with Cynicism through the contacts they had with Greeks in Gadara, and specifically with Oenomaus. Several of the texts that associate Oenomaus with Abnimos are found in the Midrash Rabbah.[69] But this hypothesis still requires us to account for the linguistic transposition of the name Oenomaus into Abnimos (with the

---

66. See, e.g., S. J. Bastomsky, "Abnimos and Oenomaus: A Question of Identity," *Apeiron* 8 (1974): 57–61; Menahem Luz, "A Description of the Greek Cynic in the Jerusalem Talmud," *JSJ* 20 (1989): 49–60; Jürgen Hammerstaedt, "Der Kyniker Oenomaus von Gadara," *ANRW* 2.36.4:2834–65, esp. 2836–39; Marie-Odile Goulet-Cazé, "Oinomaos de Gadara," *DPhA* 4:751–61.

67. See Jürgen Hammerstaedt, *Die Orakelkritik des Kynikers Oenomaus*, Beiträge zur klassischen Philologie 188 (Frankfurt am Main: Athenäum, 1988), 11–18; Hammerstaedt, "Der Kyniker Oenomaus von Gadara," 2835–36.

68. Cf. "Oenomaus of Gadara" on p. 23.

69. Here are the references to these texts in the edition of the *Midrash Rabbah* by Harry Freedman and Maurice Simon (London: Soncino, 1939). For convenience of reference, we will assign each one a letter: (a) Genesis Rabbah 65.20 (ca. 425 CE), trans. H. Freedman, 2.596; (b) Exodus Rabbah 13.1 (800–900 CE), trans. S. M. Lehrman, 3.150; (c) Ruth Rabbah 2.13 (ca. 600 CE), trans. L. Rabinowitz, 8.35; (d) Lament. Rabbati praef. 2 (ca. 480 CE), trans. A. Cohen, 7. 3–4. To these texts may be added (e), a variant of (b) and (d), in Pesiqta of Rab Kahana 15.5 (fifth century CE), ed. B. Mandelbaum, 1.254, trans. W. G. Braude and I. J. Kapstein, 1.279; (f) a passage from the Babylonian Talmud, b. Ḥagigah 15b (third to fifth century CE), trans. I. Abrahams, in the edition of I. Epstein, 4.100; and (g) Avot of Rabbi Natan B 24.7 (ca. 200 CE), ed. S. Schechter.

variants Abnomos and Nimos also attested in the texts)[70] as we move from Greek writing into Hebrew. Menahem Luz, who has examined this question in detail, suggests the possibility that the Greek Οἰνόμαος became 'Inomos (or, with apocope, Nimos/Nomos) in the Talmud, and then Abnimos or Abnomos in the Midrash.[71] 'Abnimos (or 'Abnomos or Nimos) ha-gardi is presented in texts c and f as a friend of Rabbi Meir of Tiberias, one of the great doctors of the Mishna, who lived under the reign of Hadrian around 132. In g he's in conversation with Gamaliel II, who lived from 80 to 116, knew Greek, encouraged its study, and had contacts with Greeks. The discussions in which Abnimos takes part in these passages, as well as the questions he poses to his interlocutors, reflect a good acquaintance on his part with the problems of Judaism, with the Bible, and even with rabbinical homiletics, but at the same time an outlook in harmony with Cynicism, though in all of these anecdotes Abnimos is never depicted with any specifically Cynic traits. Here are the similarities that may be noted: criticism of the idea of a homeland (c); importance given to education (a and d); affirmation of the value of peace (g); and, generally, the practice of frankness. Except for one text (f) in which he's presented as a weaver, Abnimos appears as one of the leading philosophers among the gentiles (a, d, and e).[72] If Abnimos actually was not Oenomaus, we would have to conclude that during the time of Rabbi Meir, there was a Greek philosopher by that name who was well known in Gadara, but who is otherwise unknown in the Greek literature that has come down to us.

Should we then consider that Abnimos ha-gardi, because of the similarity of names, is a literary reproduction of Oenomaus, pure and simple, and that through him we could recover something of the personality and ideas of Oenomaus? Luz suggests that the character of Abnimos is based not on any individual Greek philosopher but rather on a type corresponding to the Cynic tradition in Gadara; Oenomaus's name would have been borrowed for this character.[73] But even if Oenomaus lent him nothing more than his

70. In a, b, and c, the reading is Abnomos; in d, e, and g, Abnimos; and in f, Nimos.

71. See Menahem Luz, "Abnimos, Nimos and Oenomaus: A Note," *JQR* 77 (1986–1987): 191–95.

72. For the content of these anecdotes, see Hammerstaedt, "Der Kyniker Oenomaus von Gadara," 2837–39; Goulet-Cazé, "Oinomaos de Gadara," *DPhA* 4:753–54.

73. Menahem Luz, "Oenomaus and Talmudic Anecdote," *JSJ* 23 (1992): 42–80, esp. 80: "In none of these traditions, do we find the Abnomos-figure based upon any particular Greek philosopher, but rather on a type. . . . Although Oenomaus may have given his name to Abnomos in this tradition in as much as he exemplifies a type, his own peculiar philosophy cannot

name, his identification with Abnimos certainly marks a notable stage in Jewish-Cynic relations. There are, nevertheless, some gray areas: it remains puzzling that a Cynic who wrote an entire work denouncing the fraudulent character of oracles would have felt sympathy for Judaism, which attached such great importance to prophecies, and it's just as puzzling that the Jews would have borrowed the name of the author of such a work to designate a character who represented the Greek philosopher. But even if there are some curious details like these, they're not enough to discredit the hypothesis that the character of Abnimos either is the same person as Oenomaus or else was inspired by him.

The κυνικός in the Talmud

In the Midrashim and the Talmuds, one frequently witnesses rabbis having encounters with figures who are presented as "philosophers." However, the rabbis don't mention Plato or Aristotle or any of the famous Stoics; rather, they speak of Epicurus, whom they use as a symbol of heresy, and of the *kynikos*. We may well imagine that rabbis did have personal contacts with Cynics. For example, those who lived in Gadara would have met Oenomaus, and others would have met itinerant Cynics. The rabbis may also have encountered Cynics on the journeys they took themselves, for example, to Alexandria, where, in the second century of our era, Agathobulus practiced a rigorous asceticism and received visits from other Cynics, such as Demonax and Peregrinus, who were eager to benefit from his model of asceticism.[74]

The Talmud in fact presents a discussion that makes unambiguous allusion to the Cynic philosopher.[75] Two versions of it are found in the Jerusalem

---

be identified here; this is, however, not to deny that this general Gadarene Cynic tradition of ethical and social criticism does not overlay certain aspects of what is ascribed to Abnomos in nearly all the anecdotes both early and late. As an anecdotal figure, this Gadarene takes a life of its own." See also Jürgen Hammerstaedt, "Le cynisme littéraire à l'époque impériale," in Goulet-Cazé and Goulet, *Le cynisme ancien et ses prolongements*, 399–418, esp. 412: "Les mots d'Abnimos qui apparaissent dans ces anecdotes sont probablement inventés, mais ces narrations se sont formées au plus tôt sous l'impression efficace de la personnalité d'un philosophe de la secte cynique." ("The words of Abnimos that appear in these anecdotes are probably invented, but these narratives were created under the immediate strong impression of the personality of a philosopher from the Cynic sect.")

74. Cf. Lucian, *Demonax* 3; *The Passing of Peregrinus* 17.

75. The three references are noted by Luz, "Description of the Greek Cynic."

Talmud (third to fifth century), in the passages y. Giṭṭin 7, 1, 2 (48c)[76] and y. Terumot 1, 1, 11 (40b),[77] which refer to the figure of the "qeniṭrofos" (commonly understood as "kantropos" for κυνάνθρωπος, "dog-man," along the lines of λυκάνθρωπος, "wolf-man"), as well as to the figure of the "qiniqos/qinoqos" (i.e., "kinukos" [sic]). A third version of the discussion is found in the Babylonian Talmud (fifth century), b. Ḥagigah 3b–4a.[78] It's somewhat different, and the word "kinukos" is lacking, but the definition of the Cynic is nevertheless clearly present. These texts transmit, independently of one another, a discussion specifically of the characteristic signs of a person who's afflicted with madness. It's within this context that the figure of the Hellenistic Cynic is mentioned, confirming that Jewish sages genuinely were acquainted with Cynics.

In the foundational text, that of y. Giṭṭin, the redactor first describes in his preface the characteristic behavior of a madman: "The symptoms of an insane person: one who goes out in the night, stays overnight in a graveyard, tears his clothing and destroys what one gives to him." We then find three reactions to this description, those of the Babylonian Rabbi Ḥuna (middle of the third century), Rabbi Joḥanan (John of Tiberias, beginning of the third century), and Rabbi Avin, a student of Rabbi Ḥuna (end of the third century). Only the reaction of the Babylonian Rabbi Ḥuna introduces the two figures of the "qeniṭrofos" and the "kinukos" (sic), when he explains that one may speak of a person as mad "only if all of that is in him, since otherwise I say that one who goes out in the night is a man-dog [scil. "qeniṭrofos"]; he who stays overnight in a graveyard burns incense to spirits; he who tears up his clothing is (a choleric person [scil. cholikos])[79] and he who destroys what one gives to him is a Cynic [scil. kinukos]." This interpretation, which distinguishes between four behaviors (being a "qeniṭrofos," burning incense to spirits, being a "cholikos," and being a "kinukos"), and which is confirmed

---

76. Heinrich W. Guggenheimer, ed., *The Jerusalem Talmud: Third Order Našim, Tractates Gittin and Nazir*, SJ 39 (Berlin: de Gruyter, 2007), 286. English quotations within the body of the text are taken from this edition.

77. Gerd A. Wewers, *Terumot*, 7–8.

78. Joseph Rabbinowitz, *Hebrew-English Edition of the Babylonian Talmud*, vol. 9 (London: Soncino, 1984), unpaginated.

79. Guggenheimer supplies "a choleric person" and accounts for the addition this way: "from the text in Terumot, missing here." Specifically, in the two witnesses to y. Gittin— namely, the Leiden manuscript and the Venice *editio princeps*—no equivalent for "cholikos" is present. In the Constantinople edition, the word "solikos" appears, which that edition may have taken over from y. Terumot.

by the parallel version in y. Terumot, finds its justification in the repetition of the article *ha-* (which Guggenheimer renders as "one who" or "he who," and which Gerd Wewers, in his translation of y. Terumot, renders as "wenn einer"). If this interpretation is followed, then only the last behavior belongs to the Cynic: "He who destroys what one gives to him is a Cynic." Luz, however, interprets and translates the text differently: "R. Huna said that all of these signs must be present except when the one who goes abroad at night is a *kantropos*—and the one who sleeps in the graveyard, burns incense to the demons, rends his clothing and destroys what people give him, is a *kinukos*."[80] Thus for Luz the *kinukos* is not simply the one who "destroys what people give him" but also "the one who sleeps in the graveyard, burns incense to the demons and rends his clothing." It will be the Talmud specialists who will have to determine how the original text should appropriately be translated and whether it's justified to supply the term *cholikos* in y. Giṭṭin on the basis of the presence of that word in y. Terumot. However, with the exception of the Constantinople edition, all the copyists and editors—including Luz in his reconstitution of the text[81]—separate the groups of words with a point. This is a good indication that for them the "kinukos" relates only to the phrase that follows the last point, and not to the preceding phrases. This reading of the passage certainly seems to be the most accurate and reliable.

These witnesses in the Talmud are of double interest to us. First, the term "qiniqos/qinoqos" is a reference to the Cynic, which proves that the rabbis knew of a category of persons whose characteristics were distinct enough for them to be classified under that name. This information is of primary interest for our purposes. Second, the attitude that's described as specific to the Cynic (he destroys whatever he's given) is well attested by the representatives of that philosophy, at least in the overall sense of the idea, which is to get rid of one's possessions in the interests of αὐτάρκεια, as Luz emphasizes.[82] Diogenes got rid of his cup and his bowl,[83] and Crates threw his goods into the sea.[84] The rabbis were well aware of this fundamental characteristic of Cynicism, which was at the same time an essential component of the asceticism that it advocated—specifically, the rejection of property and possessions. Should we then conclude that Jewish savants in the third cen-

---

80. Luz, "Description of the Greek Cynic," 52–53.

81. Luz, "Description of the Greek Cynic," 51.

82. Luz, "Description of the Greek Cynic," 58 and n. 38.

83. Diogenes Laertius, *Lives* 6.37.

84. Diogenes Laertius, *Lives* 6.87. In Lucian, *Philosophies for Sale* 9, Diogenes also advises throwing one's wealth into the sea.

tury, thanks to the numerous Cynic chreias in circulation, were familiar with the episodes connected with this theme in the lives of Diogenes and Crates, and that the readers and listeners they were addressing would have been able to understand, through a definition of Cynicism provided by the rabbis, the allusions they could have been making to these episodes? That would probably be taking things too far, but these savants, their listeners, and their readers nevertheless had an image of the Cynic sage that was dominated by an essential trait of the asceticism that characterized this movement.

Even though the examples of the "qeniṭrofos" and the "kinukos" are attributed in these witnesses uniquely to Rabbi Ḥuna, Luz thinks the original discussion, along with, as a result, these two examples, goes back to John of Tiberias, who was older than Ḥuna and, unlike him, had mastered Greek and could have had contacts with Cynicism in Gadara. Ḥuna, the Babylonian, might only have reviewed these examples or learned about them through contacts with the Academy at Tiberias. Consequently, according to Luz, these witnesses are describing the Syro-Palestinian type of Cynic, as it was known to the sages of the Tiberias school, and not the Babylonian type, as Rabbi Ḥuna and his student Rabbi Avin knew it.

The City of Gadara and Its Central Role in the Relationship between Cynicism and Judaism

It's now appropriate to note the central role that the city of Gadara played in the relationship between Cynicism and Judaism. This city, known as Umm Qeis today and renowned in antiquity for its hot baths,[85] was built atop a hill 1,194 feet high and surrounded by a perimeter wall with gates, giving it an excellent strategic position in the northwest of the Decapolis, four miles southeast of Lake Tiberias, east of the Jordan.[86] Archaeological excavations

85. Cf. Eunapius, *Lives of the Philosophers and Sophists* 5.17 (Goulet 14.17–22), who describes the disciples of the Neoplatonist Jamblichus going to the baths at Gadara and witnessing their master perform a miracle there; Antoninus Placentinus, *Itinerarium* 7 (Gildemeister 6).

86. See Emil Schürer, *The History of the Jewish People in the Age of Jesus Christ (175 B.C.–A.D. 135)*, new English rev. ed. by Geza Vermes, Fergus Millar, and Matthew Black (Edinburgh: T&T Clark, 1979), 2:49–50, 132–36; Siegfried Mittmann, *Beiträge zur Siedlungs- und Territorialgeschichte des nördlichen Ostjordanlandes*, ADPV (Wiesbaden: Harrassowitz, 1970), 135–37; Victor Tcherikover, *Hellenistic Civilization and the Jews*, 3rd ed., trans. S. Applebaum (Philadelphia: Jewish Publication Society of America, 1966), 98 and 448n65;

have unearthed two theaters, two temples, a fortified acropolis, a monu-
mental gate, a necropolis, a nymphaeum, two mausoleums, a stadium, and
two public baths.[87] After the death of Herod in 4 BCE, Gadara became an
independent city, though still under the control of Rome. The population of
Gadara consisted of Jews and pagans living side by side. The ancestral tradition of the region was actually Jewish, as the name Gadara testifies; it probably comes from the Hebrew *gader*, meaning "border." But the inscriptions
at Hammat-Gader (the hot springs of Gadara) feature Greco-Roman names
that in many cases translate Aramaic names, testifying to the city's complete
integration into the Roman Empire.[88] As we've just seen, rabbinic literature
depicts Abnimos ha-gardi (Oenomaus?) visiting with Rabbi Meir, who lived
in the second century in Tiberias, near Gadara. The city was clearly a major intellectual center in antiquity, if we may judge by the eminent figures
who came from it. It was the hometown not only of the Cynics Menippus
(third century BCE), Meleager (first century BCE), and Oenomaus (second
century of our era), but also of the Epicurean Philodemus (first half of the
first century BCE); the sophist Theodorus, who taught the future emperor
Tiberius;[89] the mathematician Philo (active just before 100 CE);[90] and the
rhetor Apsines, who taught in Athens around 235.[91]

The fact that three prominent Cynics who all came from Gadara may be
mentioned from different time periods does not necessarily imply that they
each developed as writers and philosophers in that city, nor that Gadara was

---

Carsten Peter Thiede, *The Cosmopolitan World of Jesus: New Findings from Archaeology* (London: SPCK, 2004), 41–47. On the necessity of distinguishing this city of the Decapolis,
situated near Lake Tiberias, from the Gadara of Lower Perea and from Gazara (biblical
Gezer), halfway between Jerusalem and Jaffa, see Tiziano Dorandi, "La patria di Filodemo,"
Philologus 131 (1987): 254–56.

87. See Adnan Hadidi, "Umm Qeis (ancient Gadara)," *OEANE* 5:280–82; Thomas M.
Weber, *Gadara-Umm Qēs, Gadara Decapolitana: Untersuchungen zur Topographie, Geschichte, Architektur und der bildenden Kunst einer "Polis Hellenis" im Ostjordanland*, ADPV
30 (Wiesbaden: Harrassowitz, 2002).

88. See Leah Di Segni, "The Greek Inscriptions of Hammat-Gader," in *The Roman
Baths of Hammat Gader: Final Report*, ed. Yizhar Hirschfeld (Jerusalem: Israel Exploration
Society, 1997), 228–33.

89. Cf. Suetonius, *Tiberius* 57.1.

90. Cf. Kurt Orinsky, "Philon, no. 50," *PW* 20.1:55.

91. Cf. Philostratus, *Lives of the Sophists* 2.33 (Olearius 628 = Kayser 127.4–5); *Suda*, s.v.
Ἀψίνης Γαδαρεύς, Α 4735 (Ada Adler, ed., *Suidae Lexicon* [Leipzig: Teubner, 1928–1938],
1:443.21–24). On these figures generally, see Moses Hadas, "Gadarenes in Pagan Literature,"
CW 25 (1931): 25–30, esp. 26–28, where Menippus, Meleager, and Philodemus are discussed;
Weber, *Gadara-Umm Qēs*, 61, 63, 66, 272–74.

a center of Cynic philosophy.[92] We know that Menippus, a Phoenician slave who became a disciple of Crates of Thebes, and who wrote a *Descent into Hell* and a *Sale of Diogenes*, among other works, lived in the region of Pontus and was also a citizen of Thebes (Diogenes Laertius, *Lives* 6.99), where he "ended his days by hanging himself" (Diogenes Laertius, *Lives* 6.100). While Meleager was born in "the famous city of Gadara" (*Palatine Anthology* 7.418.1),[93] he was actually raised in Tyre (*Palatine Anthology* 7.417.1, 7.419.5), and at the end of his life he retired to Cos, where he died. As for Oenomaus, we know nothing of his life other than that he went to Asia Minor three times to consult the oracle at Claros, whose ambiguous and obscure responses left him highly dissatisfied. In light of these things, prudence is advised: the fact that these Cynic philosophers came from Gadara doesn't necessarily indicate that there was a Cynic philosophical school there, as one often hears—particularly considering that the Cynics didn't have schools. But we can at least say that there was an active and longstanding Cynic tradition in Gadara, though a variety of other philosophical movements were certainly represented there as well. However, the fact that the rabbis would cast Oenomaus as the type of the Greek philosopher shows how prominent a place Cynicism did hold in the city. This presence of Cynicism in Gadara illustrates the philosophical and literary interaction that took place between Judaism and Greco-Roman civilization, which at times could amount to a fusion of the two cultures.

It's certainly not unrealistic to portray Gadara as a major cultural center under the Roman Empire, where diverse populations mingled, where there were schools of rhetoric, mathematics, and philosophy (as well as independent philosophers), and where Jews could easily meet Cynics and interact with them.

Literary Connections?

Rudolf Bultmann, in his *History of the Synoptic Tradition*, called attention to the "general historical analogy" that existed between the Greek tradition that preserved the sayings of sages such as Socrates and Diogenes—

---

92. See the persuasive comments by Klaus Döring, *Die Kyniker*, Faszination Philosophie (Bamberg: Buchner, 2006), 103.

93. Cf. *Palatine Anthology* 7.417.2, which says that the country of his birth was the new "Attica situated in Syrian Gadara" (Ἀτθὶς ἐν Ἀσσυρίοις ναιομένα Γαδάροις).

who were remembered for "their personal way of life" rather than for their knowledge—and rabbinic literature and the sayings of Jesus in the primitive community.[94]

Henry Albert Fischel has endeavored to demonstrate that the Greek chreia, which had been the ideal vehicle for teaching the Cynics' nonconformist ideas, came to be adopted in Judea.[95] This was possible because Jews had become familiar with Hellenistic rhetoric, which was encountered everywhere in both written and oral form. And so, Fischel argues, within Jewish Tannaitic literature, Hebraic chreias may be found that have the same structural aspects and literary form, and the identical function, as the Greek chreias that inspired them. Fischel draws a comparison between the variants of an anecdote transmitted by nine Greek sources (in which Socrates invites guests over for dinner, but Xanthippe, the prototype of the cantankerous shrew, spoils the meal) and one Hebraic source (a minor tractate of the Talmud, *Derek Eretz Rabbah*) on an equivalent theme. After studying fifteen aspects of these variants (376–404), Fischel concludes that an acculturation of the Greek chreia took place in which the hero became a Jewish sage and events were relocated to Judea, very frequently to the temple (407). But the function of the chreia is the same in both cultures: to propagate or preserve an ideal and some moral values, and at the same time to distance themselves from the '*Am ha-aretz* in Judea and from the πόλλοι in Greece. Fischel notes, "In the Judaic culture the *chria* is, further, halakhized, i.e., seen as a legal-ethical test case, an instance or precedent for a permanent rule (halakhah). . . . More often a *testimonium* or μαρτύριον, i.e., a confirmatory (biblical) quotation is adduced that affects the sense of shift towards Jewish values" (409). And so, Fischel finds, there are actually significant differences between Greek chreias and Hebrew ones. In the latter, a much greater humanity is evident: the victims are not treated mercilessly with sarcasm, as happens to beggars, for example, in the Greek chreia. And unlike the way Greek chreias express resistance and protest (against tyranny, for example), the Hebrew chreias are apolitical and serve solely socio-ethical and religious ends.

---

94. Rudolf Bultmann, *Die Geschichte der synoptischen Tradition* [1921], 10th ed. (Göttingen: Vandenhoeck & Ruprecht, 1995), 53; *The History of the Synoptic Tradition*, trans. John Marsh (Oxford: Basil Blackwell, 1963), 51.

95. Henry A. Fischel, "Studies in Cynicism and the Ancient Near East: The Transformation of a Chreia," in *Religions in Antiquity: Essays in Memory of Erwin Ramsdell Goodenough*, ed. Jacob Neusner, Supplements to *Numen* 14 (Leiden: Brill, 1968), 372–411, esp. 375. Hereafter, page references are given in parentheses in the text.

The sage who's celebrated in the Jewish chreia belongs to Jewish Tannaitic culture, and he's almost always Hillel the Elder (fl. ca. 30 BCE–10 CE), to whom more maxims are attributed than to all the other Pharisee teachers combined. Hillel, born in Babylon, was regarded as the supreme authority of the Pharisee movement, and he's presented, to use Fischel's formula, as "an ideal Cynic-chriic sage" (375). Among the maxims attributed to him is one that would have an auspicious future career: "What is hateful to yourself, do not do to your neighbor. That is the entire Torah. All the rest is commentary. Now go forth and learn."[96] Hillel's memory began to be perpetuated after 70, but as is the case with Socrates, Diogenes, and Jesus, it goes without saying that reports of his acts and sayings do not necessarily correspond to historical reality. As Neusner puts it, "Hillel *exists*: he endures. He never dies. He is the teacher, he is the paradigm."[97]

More recently, Catherine Hezser has also investigated the question of the connection between Hellenistic chreias and Jewish and Christian ones.[98] The small number of chreias found in intertestamental Jewish literature and in Philo and Flavius Josephus is understandable, she says, because there was little interest then in contemporary individual personalities; rather, the interest was in Judaism as a collective phenomenon. On the other hand, if chreias are to be found in the canonical Gospels and in the *Gospel of Thomas,* this is not because of a process of Hellenization within Palestinian Judaism, but rather because of the interest the writers of the Gospels showed in the individual person of Jesus. The rabbinic chreias in the Mishnah, the Talmud and the Midrashim, the ones about Jesus in the canonical Gospels, and the patristic apothegms are all adaptations, independent of one another, of the Hellenistic literary genre of the chreia. A comparison between these different types of chreia reveals both the common elements of the genre and the ways in which it could be varied, and this, Hezser says, allows us to account for both the similarities that the different forms share and the things that are "spezifisch Christlich," "spezifisch Rabbinisch," and "spezifisch Philosophisch" (i.e., specifically Christian, rabbinic, or philosophical)

96. On Hillel the Elder, see Jacob Neusner, *Judaism in the Beginning of Christianity* (Philadelphia: Fortress, 1984), chap. 4, "The Figure of Hillel," 63–88; the maxim is cited on 50. See also Albrecht Dihle, *Die Goldene Regel: Eine Einführung in die Geschichte der antiken und frühchristlichen Vulgärethik,* Studienhefte zur Altertumswissenschaft 7 (Göttingen: Vandenhoeck & Ruprecht, 1962), 8.

97. Neusner, *Judaism in the Beginning of Christianity,* 88.

98. Catherine Hezser, "Die Verwendung der hellenistischen Gattung Chrie im frühen Christentum und Judentum," *JSJ* 27 (1996): 371–439.

in each of them.[99] Even if the different types all had a common origin, this didn't prevent the very form of the chreia from evolving over time: while the classic chreias were more succinct, the Jewish and Christian ones generally became more expansive. Some, like those in the *Gospel of Thomas*, remained relatively short and concise, while those in Mark, because they have a more developed opening section that often features dialogue, already have a more complicated structure than similar chreias in their Greco-Roman form.[100] However, the words of Jesus themselves most often retain the conciseness that's characteristic of the classic Hellenistic form. The Tannaitic literature, for its part, presents chreias that surpass both the Greco-Roman and New Testament ones in length and in abundance of detail. An introductory section is built up out of dialogues, intercalated narrative remarks, and scriptural quotations. These are full anecdotes that can only be recognized as chreias by the point they make.[101]

There would have been, then, an acculturation of the Hellenistic Greek chreia through contact with Jewish culture. The rabbinic chreias, those in the gospels, and those of the fathers would have been adaptations, independent of one another, of the Hellenistic Greek chreia, which developed when interest began to be shown in contemporary individual personalities such as Jesus and Hillel. It's likely that the Cynic chreia, which quickly became a literary genre with its own rules in the fourth century BCE, starting in the era of the first Cynic philosophers, was disseminated widely through the collections of chreias that we have described and through oral recitation by the itinerant philosophers who wandered the countries of the Mediterranean basin, and that it then took on specific properties based on the milieus in which it was developed further. It's clear that the Cynics and Stoics weren't the only ones to make use of the genre—we need only cite Plutarch—and that, as a result, the chreias that the authors of Q knew about, and those found in rabbinic literature, even if they were Greek, were not exclusively Cynic. Nevertheless, anyone who wants to explore the connections between Cynicism, Judaism, and Christianity clearly must recognize the influence of this literary genre that was born in the Cynic milieu and centered on the figure of the sage.

---

99. Hezser, "Die Verwendung der hellenistischen Gattung Chrie," 379.

100. Hezser, "Die Verwendung der hellenistischen Gattung Chrie," 405, who cites as examples Mark 10:35–40; 11:28–33; 12:14–17.

101. Hezser, "Die Verwendung der hellenistischen Gattung Chrie," 405–6.

Conclusion

A Cynic presence in Gadara is attested as early as the third century BCE, in the person of the philosopher Menippus. We have identified a number of contacts taking place between Cynicism and Judaism in subsequent centuries under various forms. Personal contact was possible between Cynics and Jews who lived in the same city, as was the case for Meleager, who speaks of the Sabbath. There were literary connections for Jews such as Philo of Alexandria, who was steeped in Greek culture, and Flavius Josephus, who learned about the nature of Cynic asceticism through his reading. Some of these contacts led to a symbolic identification: Oenomaus/Abnimos ha-gardi seems to have become the prototype of the pagan philosopher in the Midrash Rabbah. And finally, there was also contact through the chreias about Antisthenes, Diogenes, and Crates that must have begun to circulate rather early throughout the Mediterranean basin.

3. Cynicism and the Jesus Movement

Galilee in the Time of Jesus: "Greek Hypothesis" or "Aramaic Hypothesis"?

Before getting into our main topic, we must extend the investigation we have already begun into the knowledge and use of Greek in Palestine (cf. "How Strongly Hellenized Was the Jewish World in the Hellenistic and Roman Eras?" on p. 108) by asking specifically about Galilee in the time of Jesus. Could he have learned Greek in the Galilee of the first century CE? If this question must be answered negatively, then it would be difficult to imagine a possible connection between Jesus and Cynicism.

Among the disciples of Jesus there were some who had Greek names, such as Andrew and Philip, and others who had names that had originally been Greek but had been Aramaized, such as Bartholomew, which comes from bar-Ptolemaios, and Thaddeus, which could be a short form of Theodotus.[1] But alongside this relatively objective evidence is some further evidence whose value can be more difficult to appreciate. Since the Gospels are written in Greek, they can only portray Jesus as speaking Greek with his followers and his opponents (the Pharisees, for example). But this is no proof that he actually spoke Greek. After all, there are places where the Gospels report words that Jesus spoke in Aramaic and they provide a Greek translation (Mark 5:41; 15:34; Matt. 27:46). Doesn't this indicate that Jesus himself was actually fluent in Aramaic, and that the evangelists, though they spoke Greek themselves and were writing for people who understood Greek, found it appropriate, in the case of certain strong sayings, to present the Aramaic

---

1. Cf. Martin Hengel, in collaboration with Christoph Markschies, *The "Hellenization" of Judaea in the First Century after Christ* (London: SCM, 1989), 16.

and its Greek translation? In the first half of the second century, Papias, the bishop of Hierapolis, affirmed, according to Eusebius, that "Matthew wrote the *logia* of Jesus in the Hebrew language [i.e., in Aramaic], and every one translated (ἡρμήνευσεν) them as he was able."[2] Eusebius also says that when Pantaenus arrived in India, he discovered that the apostle Bartholomew had already preached there and that he had left the inhabitants a copy of the Gospel of Matthew "in the Hebrew language."[3] (Exegetes, however, are not entirely sure what connection these texts have with the canonical Gospels.) Along the same lines, Jerome alludes to an Aramaic version of the Lord's Prayer in an apocryphal gospel: *In Evangelio quod appellatur secundum Hebraeos, pro supersubstantiali pane maar repperi, quod dicitur crastinum* ("In the gospel called 'According to the Hebrews,' for 'supersubstantial' bread I found *mahar*, which means 'tomorrow': it would mean 'give us today our bread for tomorrow'")[4] It's therefore likely that Jesus taught in Aramaic and that some of the apocryphal gospels were originally written in Aramaic before being translated into Greek. But does that mean that Jesus didn't know Greek?

One of the leading proponents of the "Greek hypothesis," Stanley E. Porter, has inquired about the languages Jesus might have spoken.[5] He has concluded that Jesus knew "Aramaic ostensibly because he was Jewish, Hebrew possibly because he was Jewish, perhaps Greek because he lived in Roman-controlled Palestine, and Latin because of Roman occupation."[6]

2. Eusebius, *Ecclesiastical History* 3.39.16 (author's translation). For an interpretation of this text by Papias connected with the hypothesis that the author or compiler of the Q source was Matthew, one of the Twelve, see Marco Frenschkowski, "Welche biographischen Kenntnisse von Jesus setzt die Logienquelle voraus? Beobachtungen zur Gattung von Q im Kontext antiker Spruchsammlungen," in *From Quest to Q: Festschrift James M. Robinson*, ed. Jon Ma Asgeirsson, Kristin de Troyer, and Martin W. Meyer, BETL 156 (Leuven: Leuven University Press, 2000), 3–42, esp. 37–39.

3. Eusebius, *Ecclesiastical History* 5.10.3.

4. Jerome, *Commentary on Matthew,* book I on Matt. 6:11 (CCSL 77:37). In his *Commentary on Matthew*, book II on Matt. 12:13 (CCSL 77:90), Jerome explains that he has recently translated this gospel, in use among the Nazarenes and the Ebionites, from Hebrew (i.e., Aramaic) into Greek and that this gospel was generally identified with the Gospel of Matthew.

5. See, e.g., Stanley E. Porter, *The Criteria for Authenticity in Historical-Jesus Research: Previous Discussion and New Proposals*, JSNTSup 191 (Sheffield: Sheffield Academic Press, 2000).

6. Stanley E. Porter, "The Language(s) Jesus Spoke," in *The Historical Jesus*, vol. 3 of *Handbook for the Study of the Historical Jesus*, ed. Tom Holmén and Stanley E. Porter (Leiden: Brill, 2011), 2455–71, esp. 2458.

Relying on the fact that Greek was the *lingua franca* of the Greco-Roman world and that, in the multilingual environment of Palestine, Koine Greek was a prestige language relative to the Semitic ones, Porter offers a number of arguments that we must consider seriously as we assess the "Greek hypothesis" regarding Palestine in the time of Jesus. Here are some of his arguments. Greek was spoken even in Jerusalem, as may be seen from *The Jewish War* by Flavius Josephus and the New Testament. The crowds that heard Jesus came from different countries and spoke different languages;[7] the Jews who gathered in Jerusalem for Pentecost came from "every nation" (Acts 2:5-11). The only language that could have united all these peoples was Greek. Judea under the Roman Empire was multilingual, and even if the influence of Aramaic was extensive, there's every reason to believe that the influence of Greek must have been just as great. Nearby were entities such as the Decapolis, a confederation of ten cities founded on Greek principles and following Greek practices, including the use of the language. Across the Jordan, the kingdom of Nabatea, under Roman domination since the start of the first century, used Greek, while to the north in Tyre and Sidon, which had been Hellenized since the third century BCE, Greek was the language of government administration and commercial communication. But what about in Galilee? Porter refuses to connect any conclusion about the usage of Greek in Galilee with its degree of Hellenization; he considers that Greek usage was a general linguistic phenomenon of Jewish life, Greek being the only language that could have united the Jews at Pentecost. Hence he concludes that Jesus, if he wanted to be understood by everyone, could only have spoken Greek to the people he met who came from different countries. Porter specifically lists a number of situations in which people who addressed Jesus must have spoken to him in Greek, inviting him to respond to them in Greek as well.[8] As examples he cites the cases of the Roman centurion at Capernaum in Galilee; of Pilate, who interrogated Jesus without using a translator (none is mentioned, at least); of the Syrophoenician woman whose daughter Jesus healed; and of the Samaritan woman. To all appearances, Jesus was led to speak Greek on these occasions; but is it possible to be more certain of this? Porter analyzes these situations and distinguishes between those in which Jesus used Greek with "reasonably high probability," "reasonable

---

7. Stanley E. Porter, "The Role of Greek Language Criteria in Historical Jesus Research," in *How to Study the Historical Jesus*, vol. 1 of Holmén and Porter, *Handbook for the Study of the Historical Jesus*, 361–404, esp. 393–95.

8. Porter, "Role of Greek Language Criteria," 380.

probability," and "some probability."[9] In his interpretation of the Sermon on the Mount, he seeks to prove that this passage constitutes a unity distinct from the rest of the narrative in Matthew, and that it must originally have been a discourse delivered by Jesus in Greek in a context where Greek was the language in use.[10] Porter prefers to conceive of Judaism within Hellenism, rather than thinking in terms of Judaism versus Hellenism, and he may be right: "Hellenism is seen to constitute the larger world in which Judaism was a part. . . . Hellenism provides the overarching cultural, linguistic, educational and socio-economic framework in which Judaism existed, whether inside or outside of Palestine."[11] And so the "Greek hypothesis" for Galilee, so long as it acknowledges the preponderant usage of Aramaic, is a working hypothesis that deserves to be taken seriously.[12]

But once again, it's a matter of proportion. The proponents of the "Aramaic hypothesis"[13] present arguments of their own to defend the idea that we must not dismiss the Aramaic background to the teaching of Jesus, which, they say, is evident from the Semitisms that abound in the Synoptics. Thus P. Maurice Casey criticizes Porter for what he considers to be two major errors.[14] First, Casey says, Porter does not take sufficiently into account the fact that Jesus spoke and certainly taught in Aramaic in an environment where the language of communication between Jews was Aramaic. If the Gospels were written in Greek, that was done in order to proclaim the good news to people who spoke Greek, but that's no reason to think that Jesus gave the essentials of his teaching in Greek. The Aramaic words found in the Synoptics are only explicable if the authors of the Gospels could have expected their readers to know that the ministry of Jesus took place in an Aramaic environment. Casey's second criticism is that Porter exaggerates the extent to which the Greek language was used in Israel, allowing him to hold that Jesus taught in Greek as well as in Aramaic. In actual fact, the Greek inscriptions that Porter cites, spe-

9. Porter, "Role of Greek Language Criteria," 382.

10. Porter, "Role of Greek Language Criteria," 393-404.

11. Stanley E. Porter, "The Context of Jesus: Jewish and/or Hellenistic?," in *The Study of Jesus*, vol. 2 of Holmén and Porter, *Handbook for the Study of the Historical Jesus*, 1441-63, esp. 1461.

12. Archaeological excavations also invite us to envision the possibility that Greek was spoken in Galilee at this time. Cf. Eric M. Meyers and James E. Strange, *Archaeology, the Rabbis and Early Christianity* (Nashville: Abingdon, 1981), 77-117.

13. E.g., P. Maurice Casey, "The Role of Aramaic in Reconstructing the Teaching of Jesus," in *The Study of Jesus*, vol. 2 of Holmén and Porter, *Handbook for the Study of the Historical Jesus*, 1343-75. Casey and Porter debate the problem in opposing essays (see 1361n92).

14. Casey, "Role of Aramaic," 1361-62.

cifically funerary inscriptions from Beth She'arim in lower Galilee, constitute no proof that Greek was used in the first century in that geographical area, since the small number of tombs that date to the first century actually bear no inscriptions.[15] Beyond this, Casey endeavors to reconstruct the Aramaic sources of certain passages in the Gospel of Mark in order to prove that Jesus taught in Aramaic. He also advances other arguments. We know that the Jews needed to have the Torah translated from Hebrew into Aramaic relatively early so that they could understand it. There are numerous Aramaic documents in existence from the period prior to Jesus, including the Aramaic Dead Sea Scrolls,[16] which exhibit an interference from Hebrew rather than from Greek. Casey also cites significant details such as the Aramaic inscriptions on the trumpets in the temple, and Gamaliel's use of Aramaic for a letter to the Jews of Galilee. He concludes, "These points form a massive argument of cumulative weight, showing that Jesus would be brought up with Aramaic as his native tongue, and that he had to teach in Aramaic in order to be understood by normal Jews."[17]

We may conclude that both the "Greek hypothesis" and the "Aramaic hypothesis" no doubt each express some part of the truth. They can't both be right at the same time, but it does make good sense to consider it likely that Jesus spoke Aramaic and that he did most of his teaching in Aramaic, but that at the same time it's possible he knew Greek and that he made use

15. Casey, "Role of Aramaic," 1363 and n. 99. Relying on Nahman Avigad, *Catacombs 12–23*, vol. 3 of *Beth She'arim: Report on the Excavations during 1953–1958* (New Brunswick, NJ: Rutgers University Press on behalf of the Israel Exploration Society and the Institute of Archaeology, Hebrew University, 1976), 124–25 and 261, Casey emphasizes that catacomb 21, which possibly dates to the Herodian period, but which could also come from a later period, is the oldest, and it has no inscriptions. However, it's well known that the dating of tombs is itself subject to controversy. Cf. Sean Freyne, "Galilee in the Hellenistic through Byzantine Periods," *OEANE* 2:370–76, esp. 375: "Some have suggested that chambers 6 and 11 where only Greek is found should be dated to the first century CE (Lifshitz, 1965)."

16. We should note, however, that Greek texts were also found at Qumran. See James C. Vanderkam, "Greek at Qumran," in *Hellenism in the Land of Israel*, ed. John J. Collins and Gregory E. Sterling, CJA 13 (Notre Dame, IN: University of Notre Dame Press, 2001), 175–81. Of the 850 manuscripts, more than 700 were written in Hebrew and 100 others in Aramaic, and 27 Greek texts have been identified dating to the second and first centuries BCE and to the first century CE, of which a good number are copies of texts from the Greek Bible. Thus, even in a literate Jewish community like the one at Qumran, highly loyal to ancient traditions of the Scriptures, there were some who had the habit of reading them in Greek.

17. Casey, "Role of Aramaic," 1365.

of it in certain circumstances—for example, when speaking to crowds that came from different nations (assuming that those accounts are historical).

If Jesus could have known Greek, then we cannot dismiss out of hand the hypothesis that he may have been in contact, in one form or another, with Cynicism. But solid arguments must be advanced in order to substantiate such a hypothesis. It has been argued that since Nazareth wasn't far from the large city of Sepphoris, Jesus could have had contact there with Hellenism and maybe even with Cynicism, since that city was so close. But this is a matter of pure speculation, since the excavations led by Eric M. Meyers in Galilee, particularly in Sepphoris, don't provide any information about the possibility of significant urban influences on Jesus. Moreover, the Jewish population of Sepphoris in the first century seems to have been a "Torah-true population," as if the traditions had been reinforced there in response to the pagan presence. So it's not evident that a young Jew from Nazareth could have had contact with pagans, and specifically with Cynics, in Sepphoris, if he went to that city.[18]

Are There Connections between the Gospel Source Q and Cynicism?

It must be acknowledged that in the end we have no evidence that definitively proves a knowledge of Greek on the part of Jesus. But in recent decades there have been some exegetes who, as they have worked to re-create the literary and sociological background of the canonical Gospels, have raised the question, surprising at first glance, of a possible influence of Cynicism on the message of Jesus and on the organization of the movement of his first disciples. Their research is based on an analysis of the much discussed Gospel source Q. The hypothesis that there are two different sources behind the Synoptic Gospels was formulated for the first time in 1838 by Christian Hermann Weisse.[19] He held that Matthew and Luke were based partly on the Gospel of Mark and partly on a separate source he called "Q" (for *Quelle*), a collection of Jesus's sayings assembled after his death. This lost source was not transmitted intact, but it can be reconstituted from Matthew and Luke. The discovery in 1945 of the Nag Hammadi texts, especially the *Gospel of Thomas*, which

18. These remarks about Sepphoris are taken from Paul R. Eddy, "Jesus as Diogenes? Reflections on the Cynic Jesus Thesis," *JBL* 115 (1996): 449–69.

19. Christian Hermann Weisse, *Die evangelische Geschichte, kritisch und philosophisch bearbeitet*, 2 vols. (Leipzig: Breitkopf & Hartel, 1838).

proves that before the canonical Gospels were written, there was a type of nonnarrative gospel inspired by Jewish wisdom literature,[20] confirmed in one sense the two-source hypothesis. We shall now examine the connections that certain contemporary exegetes have drawn between the Q source and Cynic literary genres, and then we shall analyze whether, from a sociological point of view, we may indeed see Jesus and the "people of Q" as parallel to the Cynics (or even assimilate them, as some of these exegetes do).

The Q source, reconstituted following a new approach by J. M. Robinson, P. Hoffmann, and J. S. Kloppenborg,[21] presents a collection of the sayings of Jesus and John the Baptist. Even though it doesn't offer a continuous narrative thread, it's considered a genuine composition today and not the result of simple literary sedimentation. Besides the collection of sayings, it contains two miracle stories and the episode of Jesus's temptation; however, the account of the passion and the resurrection is absent, and Jesus is never called Messiah or Christ. (He's designated as the Son of Man or the Son of God.)

Are There Literary Connections between Q, the Collections of Cynic Chreias, and the Hellenistic Cynic Bios?

Much research has been conducted on the genre of Q, and the results have been the subject of lively debate, especially during the past thirty years as the ideas have gradually taken root that the meaning of a text is bound up with its literary genre and that the Gospels did not result merely from the sedimentation of primitive oral traditions, as Martin Dibelius and Rudolf Bultmann supposed.[22] Only the major outlines of

20. This text, transmitted in Coptic and posterior to Q by at least some sixty years, consists of 114 *logia* that are introduced as "the secret sayings which the living Jesus spoke and which Didymos Judas Thomas wrote down" (trans. Thomas O. Lambdin).

21. James M. Robinson, Paul Hoffmann, and John S. Kloppenborg, *The Critical Edition of Q: Synopsis Including the Gospel of Matthew and Luke, Mark and Thomas with English, German, and French Translations of Q and Thomas* (Minneapolis: Fortress; Leuven: Peeters, 2000); see also Frédéric Amsler, *L'évangile inconnu: La source des paroles de Jésus*, Essais bibliques 30 (Geneva: Labor et Fides, 2001); Paul Hoffmann and Christoph Heil, eds., *Die Spruchquelle Q: Studienausgabe Griechisch und Deutsch*, 4th ed. (Leuven: Peeters; Darmstadt: Wissenschaftliche Buchgesellschaft, 2013). The translations of Q will be taken from the critical edition of Q by Robinson, Hoffmann, and Kloppenborg.

22. See Howard Clark Kee, "Synoptic Studies," in *The New Testament and Its Modern Interpreters*, ed. Eldon J. Epp and George W. MacRae (Atlanta: Scholars Press, 1989), 245-62, with bibliography, 262-69.

the debate may be given here, through a summary of some representative publications.[23]

Q as a Collection of Isolated Sayings

When, following Martin Dibelius,[24] Rudolf Bultmann, in his most important study *Die Geschichte der synoptischen Tradition*,[25] examined the sayings of Jesus, whose *Sitz im Leben* he wanted to recover through the method of *Formgeschichte*,[26] he reached the conclusion that Q was a collection of isolated fragments that had no organic unity and that lent themselves easily, by their very nature, to expansion. He believed they were originally transmitted orally, but that they were then fixed in writing and underwent editing by the primitive community in Palestine. These isolated fragments laid the groundwork for the gospel, but that form of writing had not yet been created.

Rather, the first exemplar of a "gospel" in the true sense was Mark, which was an original creation of the Hellenistic community (369). That community, which included many converted Jews, drew on the Palestinian tradition to create a presentation of the life of Jesus based on the existing tradition of isolated fragments and short compilations of apothegms and miracle stories. The historical and biographical narrative that emerged naturally from this process gave a central place to the passion story and served to complement and illustrate the original Christian kerygma (371). On the other hand, Q—written first in Aramaic and then translated into Greek, according to Bultmann—is an extension of the tradition of sayings, to which were added, in the course of its transmission, proverbs, bits of popular wisdom, prophecies, and laws that had parenetic value.

23. Sayings from Q will be cited with chapter and verse from the Gospel of Luke with the title Q.

24. Martin Dibelius, *Die Formgeschichte des Evangeliums* [1919], 4th ed. (Tübingen: Mohr Siebeck, 1961).

25. Rudolf Bultmann, *Die Geschichte der synoptischen Tradition* [1921], 10th ed. (Göttingen: Vandenhoeck & Ruprecht, 1995) 393–400; *The History of the Synoptic Tradition*, trans. John Marsh, 3rd ed. (Oxford: Basil Blackwell, 1963), 368–74. Hereafter, page references to the English edition are given in parentheses in the text.

26. Bultmann also noted a historical analogy between this tradition and that of the Greek masters and sages, such as Socrates and Diogenes (*History of the Synoptic Tradition*, 51). I have applied the method of *Formgeschichte* to the apothegms of Diogenes in Marie-Odile Goulet-Cazé, "Le livre VI de Diogène Laërce: Analyse de sa structure et réflexions méthodologiques," *ANRW* 2.36.6:3997–4039.

Bultmann did not even address the question of the literary genres of Q and the Synoptic Gospels because he didn't see a distinction between the oral and written forms of the tradition. He believed that when it was first fixed in writing, this had been done in an entirely nonliterary way.[27] As he saw it, the gospel itself, an original creation of Christians, was strictly speaking not a literary genre, because the notion of a literary genre is something that develops over time, and in the Synoptic Gospels the literary form as such did not have the time to take on a life of its own, since the canonization of the four Gospels cut short any further development of the gospel form (452–53).

Today, however, it's customary to consider the Q source a genuine writing (*Schrift*), rather than the result of simple stratification (*Schicht*), to use Dibelius's terminology,[28] and so its genre must be identified if we are to appreciate its meaning.

Λόγοι σοφῶν

To analyze the literary genre of Q, James M. Robinson introduced the dynamic concept of the "trajectory" of literary genres from their origins to their final shaping. He concluded that the collection of sayings in Q belonged to a genre that he called λόγοι σοφῶν ("sayings of the wise"), to which the *Gospel of Thomas* also belonged.[29] According to him, examples of this literary genre are provided by several Jewish collections of sayings of the wise, such as those in the book of Proverbs, the *Testaments of the Twelve Patriarchs*, and *Pirkei Avot*, as well as in Christian texts such as the *Didache*, the Gospels (especially Matthew), and *1 Clement*. The trajectory of this literary genre begins in Proverbs and culminates with the sayings of the gnostic redeemer in the *Gospel of Thomas*. Robinson suggests that, given the association that primitive Christianity made between Jesus and personified Jewish Wisdom (*Sophia*), Jewish wisdom sayings were included from the start among the sayings of Jesus, and this may have then facilitated his sayings being gathered together under the Λόγοι σοφῶν genre. But orthodox Christians preferred

27. Bultmann, *History of the Synoptic Tradition*, 6, 239.

28. Dibelius, *Die Formgeschichte des Evangeliums*, 236.

29. James M. Robinson, "Zur Gattung der Spruchquelle Q," in *Zeit und Geschichte: Dankesgabe an R. Bultmann zum 80. Geburtstag*, ed. Erich Dinkler (Tübingen: J. C. B. Mohr, 1964), 77–96; Robinson, "*LOGOI SOPHON*: On the Gattung of Q," in *Trajectories through Early Christianity*, ed. James M. Robinson and Helmut Koester (Philadelphia: Fortress, 1971), 71–113.

the collection of sayings in the gospel form, and the gnostics preferred the form of a dialogue between the Resurrected and his disciples.

We must appreciate that Robinson's initiative was not limited to proposing a name for the genre of Q, λόγοι σοφῶν, that would define this genre in terms of static generic traits. The use that Robinson makes of the history of genres to analyze Q, which introduces a matrix of internal dynamics and polarities that are expressed in a group of documents belonging to a single class, represents a genuine methodological advance. Robinson uses it to show that the transition of Jesus's sayings from their oral form into their written form was made possible through the mediation of the literary genre "sayings of the wise." The archetype of Q is therefore to be found among the sages of Israel.[30]

John S. Kloppenborg follows Robinson in classifying some of the sayings in Q under the genre of λόγοι σοφῶν. Relying on a formal analysis of the Sermon on the Plain (Luke) or on the Mount (Matthew) (Q 6:20-49),[31] particularly the Beatitudes, he classifies the wisdom sayings in Q, which he says constitute its formative stratum (= Q1), according to the forms attested (macarisms, imperatives buttressed by maxims, rhetorical questions, gnomic sayings and comparisons, examples drawn from common experience); the nature of the argumentation deployed (appeal to common experience, observation of nature, ordinary social transactions and ordinary activities); and the nature of the one speaking (neither a prophet nor a visionary). All of these characteristics connect this stratum to the genre of "instruction," of which Proverbs 6:20-35, for example, provides a good illustration.

Q and the Cynic Chreia

Kloppenborg, however, says that we should consider not only the Jewish wisdom collections but also the collections of Greek chreias, such as those

---

30. Migaku Sato, *Q und Prophetie: Studien zur Gattungs- und Traditionsgeschichte der Quelle Q*, WUNT 2.29 (Tübingen: Mohr Siebeck, 1988), also sees Q as a collection of sayings. But he considers Q not a collection of wisdom sayings but rather a prophetic book arising from a relatively autonomous circle within primitive Christianity that was oriented toward end-times prophecy. This group would have been made up of settled local communities from which itinerant missionaries were sent to preach the word of Christ. These resembled the prophets in their specific ethos (wandering life, without a country, without a family, without possessions, and without protection).

31. John S. Kloppenborg Verbin, *Excavating Q: The History and Setting of the Sayings Gospel* (Minneapolis: Fortress, 2000), 154-59.

by Metrocles and Hecato and the *Life of Demonax* by Lucian.[32] To under-stand how Kloppenborg envisages the role of chreias in Q, it's necessary first to recall that for him the composition of Q depends on the literary choices made by a community that had a specific historical grounding and that was confronted by rhetorical problems that were just as specific. What interests Kloppenborg is not the authenticity of the sayings but rather the genre of Q as a document, which he shows was a written document (he rejects the "oral hypothesis") compiled by a community that spoke Greek, even if certain of its sayings could have circulated first in Aramaic. It's to Kloppenborg that we owe the stratigraphic conception of Q, which many have adopted since, which distinguishes three redactional layers in the document necessitated by different strategies. Q1 consists of wisdom aphorisms whose function is paraenesis, exhortation, and instruction; they make up six blocks of material. Q2 is an apocalyptic expansion comprising the sayings of John the Baptist, the announcement of judgment, and the punishment of "this generation" that has not responded to the announcement of the kingdom; here polemic is juxtaposed with the paraenesis of Q1, and it's this redactional layer, ac-cording to Kloppenborg, that's characterized by the chreia form. Q3 is the account of the temptation, which introduces a protobiography into Q.[33] However, it's important to realize that for Kloppenborg these successive layers do not represent a chronological succession in the compositional his-tory of Q, as Burton Mack, whose position will be considered later, believes. Inquiring into the relationship between the two types of sayings, the sapi-ential ones in Q1 and the prophetic ones in Q2, Kloppenborg suggests the hypothesis that the sapiential sayings could have been absorbed completely into a prophetic genre. The flexibility built into the "collection of chreias" genre would have allowed the instructive sayings of Q1 to be absorbed into this related but distinct genre Q2, which Kloppenborg happens to describe as a collection of chreias.[34] From this perspective, it's the literary choices of the authors of Q, rather than material or theological criteria, that allow us to determine the genre of Q, which Kloppenborg considers to be, in its final form, "an Expanded Instruction."[35]

---

32. Cf. Diogenes Laertius, *Lives* 6.4, 32, 33, 95; 7.26, 172; Lucian, *Demonax* 12–62. See John S. Kloppenborg, *The Formation of Q: Trajectories in Ancient Wisdom Collections*, SAC (Philadelphia: Fortress, 1987); Kloppenborg Verbin, *Excavating Q*, esp. 160–62, 201–2.

33. This thesis of three layers has been criticized by Christopher M. Tuckett, "On the Stratification of Q: A Response," *Semeia* 55 (1992): 213–22.

34. Kloppenborg, *Formation of Q*, 323.

35. Kloppenborg Verbin, *Excavating Q*, 143–53.

If Kloppenborg detects the chreia form ("a saying with a brief setting") in the sayings of Q2, that's because those sayings are confrontational and polemical, and so they are conceived in a historicizing way and given a narrative framework (which can, however, sometimes be reduced to a simple "Jesus said," as in the *Gospel of Thomas*). These framing devices are, for John the Baptist, the reference to his entry into the region of the Jordan in Q 3:3 and the arrival of the crowds who came to be baptized in 3:7; for Jesus, his entry into Capernaum in 7:1, followed by the arrival of John's disciples to question him in 7:18 and, after their departure, Jesus turning to address the crowds in 7:24; another framing device is the astonished response of the crowds to the exorcism in 11:14. It's in this stratum that we encounter for the first time the prophets, wisdom, and epic history of Israel, with the Deuteronomic theme of prophets who are killed, which serves as an instrument of polemic and reproach. It's also here that "this generation" first appears, the opponents of the "people of Q." Among the curses, warnings of judgment, and their prophetic correlates, chreias appear. Kloppenborg cites 7:10 (the episode of the healing of the centurion's servant); 7:18–23, 24–28, and 31–35 (John's question about the identity of Jesus and his response); 11:14–23 (the exorcism); and 11:29–32 (the sign of Jonah).[36] In these sayings, Jesus and John are responding to specific circumstances or to questions, as the philosophers do in the chreias.

Despite the presence of prophetic sayings in Q2, the majority of sayings in this stratum are constructed as chreias. Often an original chreia is expanded by the addition of another chreia or further sayings. Thus, on a literary level, Q, far from being a simple sedimentation of oral sayings, is a carefully constructed composition, highly organized and structured, which, in Q2, employs the same literary techniques as the collections of Greek chreias.[37] By situating Jesus in a position of conflict with Israel and by preparing the missionaries he sent out for rejection and persecution, the sayings of Jesus in Q2 reinforce the ethos of the community, and they function, according to Kloppenborg, in the same way as the Cynic chreias that portray Antisthenes, Diogenes, and Bion responding to the reproaches they suffered.

36. Kloppenborg Verbin, *Excavating Q*, 202.

37. Kloppenborg, *Formation of Q*, 306–16, analyzes the morphology of the collections of Hellenistic *chreiai*, their function, their tonality, and their dual character, which is "biographical and 'historicizing'" on the one hand and "useful" on the other. He concludes (323–24) that the Q source employed the same techniques as these collections and that it served in a similar way to reinforce the ethos of the group against its opponents.

Within Q2, which he considers "the main redaction," Kloppenborg distinguishes five thematic ensembles spread throughout the document that repetitively evoke judgment, the story of Lot and the Deuteronomic conception of history and the persecution of the prophets. In Q1, "the formative stratum," he finds six ensembles of sayings that deliver paraenesis, exhortation, and instruction based on the idea of a providential God who is just as generous to his enemies as to his friends, and which encourage the practice of a particular way of life. The two strata correspond to two types of material that may be distinguished by their specific literary organization and rhetorical posture. However, the complaints one hears in Q2 about Jesus and the people of Q not being acknowledged actually serve an apologetic strategy that's designed to legitimize the way of life advocated in Q1, whether it's being attacked or merely treated with indifference. As for Q3, the story of Jesus's temptation, though it's a later addition, it's not out of place within Q from the point of view of genre. Kloppenborg cites several collections of chreias that actually begin with a test.[38] Nevertheless, he recognizes that Q is not so homogeneous a document as some of these collections of chreias, since it embraces both briefer chreias such as Q 11:14–20 and 11:16, 29–30, and longer discourses such as 6:20–49 and 10:2–16. (In contrast, he cites collections of chreias about Diogenes and Socrates that are contained within single papyri and are more homogeneous.) Finally, Kloppenborg also supports Downing's thesis, which we will examine shortly, that Q, taken as a document, could belong to the Hellenistic genre of βίος. With the addition of the episode of Jesus's temptations, which constitutes Q3, Q begins moving in the direction of that genre, even before being incorporated into the narrative schema of the Gospels.

However, Kloppenborg is careful to specify that literary genre must not be confused with content: even if Q2 is a collection of chreias, that doesn't necessarily mean that they are Cynic chreias.[39] Even though the *Gospel of Thomas*, for example, is a collection of chreias, it's not Cynic in content.

A Hellenistic βίος κυνικός

In 1977, Charles H. Talbert had already called attention to the similarity between the Gospels and Hellenistic-era "lives" of philosophers in which

38. Kloppenborg Verbin, *Excavating Q*, 161.
39. Kloppenborg Verbin, *Excavating Q*, 163.

biography provided a myth of origin for the philosophical community, as the Gospels did for the Christian community. But he didn't extend this analysis of genre to the question of Gospel origins.[40] This was left to F. Gerald Downing, who argued, by appeal to numerous parallels, that Q resembled the Hellenistic genre of βίος, as represented by Diogenes Laertius's *Lives* of Cynic philosophers and Lucian's *Life of Demonax*. This was true both of Q's internal organization (i.e., the forms of its "sayings") and of its thematic content, which, according to Downing, was close to Cynic teaching in its choice of topics.[41]

In terms of thematic content, Downing parallels, for example, Jesus doing the will of God with Musonius, Dio, and Epictetus also saying they were obeying God; the wanderings of Israel in the desert with Heracles, the Cynic hero par excellence, suffering hunger and thirst in the desert; and the difficulty of following Jesus with that of following Diogenes. He also notes the ideal of poverty and simplicity that both Q and Cynic teaching promote, along with cosmopolitanism and the theme of "two ways."

In terms of literary genre, according to Downing, the Cynic "lives" are more important for determining the genre of Q than the *Gospel of Thomas*, the book of Proverbs, or *Pirkei Avot*, as Robinson had thought. The people who produced Q would have used the model of the Cynic βίος to compose their collection of Jesus's sayings, and the readers of Q would have perceived its literary genre as that of a Cynic philosopher's "life."[42] Q, which must have been about the same length as Lucian's *Life of Demonax*, would therefore have been an example of the "*bios*-genre." Various formal elements are advanced. Everything revolves around a person, in this case Jesus, who's allowed to speak for himself. The Cynic philosopher is characterized primarily through sayings that indicate an implicit biographical interest in his teaching and his way of life; in the same way, Jesus is characterized in Q by numerous

40. Charles H. Talbert, *What Is a Gospel? The Genre of the Canonical Gospels* (Philadelphia: Fortress, 1977).

41. F. Gerald Downing, "Quite like Q: A Genre for 'Q', the 'Lives' of the Cynic Philosophers," *Biblica* 69 (1988): 196–225; Downing, *Cynics and Christian Origins* (Edinburgh: T&T Clark, 1992), 115–22; Downing, "A Genre for Q and a Socio-Cultural Context for Q: Comparing Sets of Similarities with Sets of Differences," *JSNT* 55 (1994): 3–26.

42. See also Kloppenborg's presentation of Downing's arguments in *Excavating Q*, 161–63. Downing's views have been criticized notably by Christopher M. Tuckett, "A Cynic Q?," *Biblica* 70 (1989): 349–76, who, while not denying the parallels, disputes whether we may deduce a generic similarity from them, and by Hans Dieter Betz, "Jesus and the Cynics: Survey and Analysis of a Hypothesis," *JR* 74 (1994): 453–75.

sayings that lack narration. In the philosophers' *Lives*, certain stories and sayings are carefully crafted, even if other units are looser; likewise, the discourses in Q express genuine organization. At the beginning of many *Lives*, the philosopher's masters are introduced; Q begins similarly with John the Baptist's announcement of judgment. (Downing acknowledges, however, that the imperatives and maledictions found in Q are absent from the *Lives* of Diogenes Laertius, and that, moreover, there's no mention in Q of the death of the leading figure, though Diogenes does not always follow that practice either.) Downing says that presence of these elements in Q demonstrates that the work resonates as the "*bios*" of a master, in this case a Cynic master, and that this model, among those that have been suggested, is the one that suits Q the best. For him, however, the document's content, ethos, and social context are still the most determinative factors.

A Lost Gospel with Cynic Wisdom Aphorisms

Burton L. Mack envisions another scenario that has drawn strong reactions, but which has coherence and deserves our attention.[43] At this point we will sketch its major outlines, concentrating for the moment on the issue of Q's form and leaving the question of Cynic ethical content to be addressed in the second part of this chapter. According to Mack, it was Jesus's disciples who collected his sayings into Q, and the book served as a manual and guide throughout most of the first century. Q mentions neither Jesus's death on the cross nor his resurrection. Mack hypothesizes that a myth developed around Jesus: his death was embellished and transformed into an event of crucifixion and miraculous resurrection, and this led to a cult of a resurrected Christ who was the Messiah and Son of God. The "sayings-gospel" Q disappeared at the end of the century, while the myth of the resurrected Christ led to the appearance in the last part of the century of the narrative gospels. These won out within the Christian community, even though they had little to do with the historic events of primitive Christianity. If two writers of "narrative gospels," Matthew and Luke, hadn't incorporated sections of Q into their narratives, the sayings collected by Jesus's first disciples in the Ur-Gospel Q would have been completely lost. Hence the title of Mack's work: *The Lost Gospel*.

43. Burton L. Mack, *The Lost Gospel: The Book of Q and Christian Origins* (San Francisco: HarperSanFrancisco, 1993).

Mack follows Kloppenborg in seeing stratigraphy within Q, but he distinguishes five stages within the work, whereas Kloppenborg found only three. According to Mack, Q1, which contains the wisdom material, actually consists of three stages; it's in Q1 that the people of Q are comparable to Cynics, engaged in social critique and holding a countercultural attitude. The first stage corresponds to the moment of the movement's social formation: along with aphorisms, which reflect the discourse of the oral period prior to Q1 ("A disciple is not above the teacher," "No good tree bears bad fruit"), it contains generalizations in the form of maxims ("Where your treasure is, there your heart will be also") as well as injunctions in the imperative that use the second-person plural to address readers—formal characteristics that demonstrate that some kind of association had formed among the people of Q. The second stage shows an awareness of belonging to a movement: the aphoristic-style injunctions of the preceding stage are codified, developed into rules for the group, and supported by arguments. The aphorism remains the kernel of the saying, but figures and comparisons are now added. According to Mack, the passage about the ravens and the lilies, which counsels not worrying about food and clothing, provides a good example of this development of a "Cynic-like injunction" into the form of a thesis that is solidly argued with analogies and examples. The third stage of Q1—the one that separates Q1, the phase of wisdom instruction, from Q2, the announcement of judgment—reveals social conflicts within the Q groups. Mack says that the sayings of Q1 show that Jesus's disciples regarded him as "a Cynic-like sage." The kingdom, at this level, is not envisioned from an apocalyptic perspective; the alternative social vision of Q1 is based on a way of life, and it's that way of life that makes the ethos of the movement a particular manifestation of the kingdom of God.

In Q2, on the other hand, prophetic and apocalyptic material replaces the aphorisms, and Jesus is perceived as a prophet who gives apocalyptic warnings. Exhortation is replaced by declaration, and in Q2 one encounters narratives, dialogues, examples drawn from Israel's epic tradition, descriptive parables, warnings, and apocalyptic announcements. The kingdom of God will be revealed elsewhere and at another moment, probably at the end of time. While the sayings of Q1 are addressed to the disciples, those in Q2 are addressed to a wider audience (the Pharisees, "this generation," the three cities of Q 10:13–15). Conflicts have arisen within families, because Jesus hasn't come to bring peace to the earth, and the missionaries have experienced rejection. Jesus, the "Cynic-like teacher" of Q1, has become in Q2 "an authoritative model" who founds his movement by giving his disciples instructions about the manner of life they should adopt. Q2, with its figures of the Wisdom of God and the Son of Man, as well as the personage of John, represents a myth of origin for the movement.

Q3, the final stage of the document, which contains particularly the stories of the temptation, proves that the people of Q survived the Jewish-Roman War. The three themes characteristic of this final stratum are the mythology of Jesus as the Son of God; the relationship of Jesus, Son of God, to the temple in Jerusalem; and the authority of the Scriptures.

By contrast with Kloppenborg, Mack considers these strata to represent a chronological succession, but, like Kloppenborg, he draws conclusions about the social history of the Jesus movement from the characteristics of the discourse in Q: Q1, with its wisdom aphorisms, constitutes the original book of Q, and the aphoristic character of the discourse in Q1 is that of Cynicism's practical ethics; according to Mack, the devastating humor of the Cynics was suited for Galileans in the era of primitive Christianity. In Q1, Jesus is much closer to a "Cynic-like sage" who criticizes conventional values and hypocrisy than to a savior Christ or a Messiah offering a program to reform Jewish society and religion. As for Jesus's disciples, if we stay with Mack right to the end of his analysis, they are ultimately not even Christians, since Jesus is not presented in Q as the "Christ."[44]

Leaving aside for the moment the ethical content of Q1 (which Mack says is Cynical), let us examine why he believes that on a formal level the sayings in Q1 can be connected with Cynic sayings: "The aphoristic quality of the sayings in Q1 is strikingly reminiscent of speech characteristic of the Greek tradition of Cynic philosophy."[45] He later elaborates on this thought: "The aphoristic style in Q1 was very close to the Cynics' way of making pointed comment on human behavior, and the logic involved in recommending extravagant behavior in Q was very close to the rhetoric of a Cynic's repartee when challenged about his own behavior."[46] Mack offers a list of seventeen aphorisms that he extracts from Q1 and that he believes

44. These views have been criticized notably by Martin Ebner, "Kynische Jesus-interpretation: 'disciplined exaggeration'? Eine Anfrage," *BZ* 40 (1996): 93–100; Ebner, *Jesus—Ein Weisheitslehrer? Synoptische Weisheitslogien im Traditionsprozess*, Herders Biblische Studien 15 (Freiburg: Herder, 1998).

45. Mack, *Lost Gospel*, 45.

46. Mack, *Lost Gospel*, 46. In *A Myth of Innocence: Mark and Christian Origins* (Minneapolis: Fortress, 1984), 68, Mack had already offered a similar point of view: "Jesus' use of parables, aphorisms, and clever rejoinders is very similar to the Cynics' way with words."

belong to the discourse of the pre-Q1 period of the Jesus movement.[47] These aphorisms function in seven "clusters" that Mack lists as the kernels around which the sayings are arranged. They may be formulated as maxims that describe the social world in which Q1 was created. Here are some by way of illustration, taken from among the best-known: "Blessed are you who are poor, for yours is the kingdom of God"; "Can a blind person guide a blind person?"; "Foxes have holes, and birds of the air have nests; but the Son of Man has nowhere to lay his head"; "For where your treasure is, there your heart will be also." But there may also be imperatives, corresponding to the recommended better way of life, that also have an aphoristic character. Thus: "Love your enemies"; "Do not judge, and you will not be judged"; "Follow me, and let the dead bury their own dead"; "Go on your way; see, I am sending you out like lambs into the midst of wolves"; "Carry no purse, no bag, no sandals, and no staff"; "Do not worry about your life."

Conclusion about the Literary Genre of Q

As a whole, specialists in the Q source agree that it was developed within the Palestinian Judeo-Christian community and that it was not the result of a successive aggregation of oral traditions; rather, it belongs to a full-fledged literary genre and reflects an elaborate process of composition. Nevertheless, as our review of their various positions has just shown, there is still disagreement as to the nature of this genre. However, this question of Q's literary genre, and particularly the relationship between wisdom sayings and announcements of judgment in its composition history, is decisive for the interpretation of the Jesus movement's social history. As Kloppenborg puts it, "The determination of the genre of Q is understood as a necessary preliminary to the determination of the social location of Q."[48] If Q's literary genre is the same as one of the Cynic genres, then the hypothesis that Jesus was "a Cynic-like sage" should be entertained. This is a crucial issue, because alongside the Jesus we know from the Gospels—a prophet and apocalyptic figure—we would have to take into account the figure of another Jesus, who was a popular philosopher analogous to Cynic philosophers. Nevertheless, as Kloppenborg insists, the fact that we find, for example, among the chreias of Q2 the same settings as in the chreias that circulated in Cynic milieus, or

47. Mack, *Lost Gospel*, 110.
48. Kloppenborg Verbin, *Excavating Q*, 154.

the fact that these sayings are often confrontational and polemical (Jesus is in conflict with Israel, just as Antisthenes, Diogenes, and Bion of Borysthenes had to face the reproaches of their contemporaries), doesn't mean that the people of Q accepted the Cynic ideology. This is why we chose first to consider Q's formal character, and its ethical content only afterward.

Kloppenborg adopts an integrated position by conceiving of Q as a collection of chreias that absorbed the wisdom sayings of Q1 and that became a sort of proto-*bios* through the addition of Q3. And that is the position we will investigate here.

So, then, could Q truly be a collection of chreias? To answer this question, we should recall first of all what has already been said about the use of Greek in Galilee in the time of Jesus (see section "Galilee in the Time of Jesus: 'Greek Hypothesis' or 'Aramaic Hypothesis?'" on p. 134), about the literary genre of the chreia (see section "Falsifying the Currency" or the Critique of Civilization: On the Literary Level" on p. 38), and about the influence that the Greek chreia could eventually have had on the Jewish chreia (see section "Contacts between Cynicism and Judaism–Literary Connections?" on p. 129). Collections of Greek chreias about celebrated figures circulated throughout the Mediterranean basin. The chreia, a didactic rhetorical form that transmitted a saying attributed to a specific person and that was furnished with a more- or less-developed narrative framework, was an excellent means of characterizing a figure whom one wanted to promote. It had the advantage of addressing practical and ethical questions in a form that was attractive because of the witty spirit it most often displayed. Since the figure of Jesus lent itself well to the formation of chreias, the presence of these in Q could be explained by the influence of Greek chreias. As we've already explained, the chreia genre is certainly of Cynic origin, but it's clear that this genre gradually came to be used by writers who were not Cynics. And when we do encounter chreias that report the sayings of philosophers of that persuasion, we recognize that their specifically Cynic coloration is essentially due to their witty barbs, which contain the chreia's moral lesson and whose tone blends humor with sarcasm. But we can go no farther until we determine whether the authors of Q could have been familiar with Greek chreias, and specifically with Cynic ones.

Gadara, which had a Cynic tradition, was near Tiberias and the three cities mentioned in Q 10:13–15—that is, Chorazin, Bethsaida, and Capernaum. We should recall that Jesus probably passed through Gadara.[49] It

---

49. The city was known for its demoniacs, who lived among the tombs. According to

was the hometown of Menippus, who in the third century BCE wrote *The Sale of Diogenes* (Διογένους πρᾶσις), a work that was responsible for numerous chreias about Diogenes.[50] The fact that Meleager, who also came from Gadara and who lived in Tyre, came under the influence of Menippus's works in his youth[51] proves that the latter's literary production was still in circulation at the end of the second century and in the first century BCE in the region that extended from Gadara to Tyre. It's evident that collections such as those by the Cynic Metrocles and the Stoics Zeno, Persaeus, Aristo, and Hecato helped the Cynics' sayings to become widely known.[52] As a result, we may hypothesize that even Jesus and the redactors of Q may have been familiar with them. Nevertheless, we can't rule out the possibility that the collections of chreias they might have known were not specifically Cynic; these may have reported the sayings of philosophers from other schools, famous people, generals, and writers, like the collections used in schools of rhetoric. But even if that's the case, the literary genre remains the same, and that's what matters. Kloppenborg himself offers this clarification: "While chriae are indeed common in Cynic lives and may even have originated in Cynic circles, the chria was by the early Roman period not the exclusive property of Cynics: it was widely used in elementary rhetorical education in schools and in various non-Cynic literary contexts. The chriae collection was not exclusively cynic, as m.'Abot and the *Sentences of*

Matthew (Matt. 8:28), Jesus drove out the demons who had possessed two demoniacs (or one, according to Mark) and sent them into a herd of pigs, who threw themselves into the sea and perished in its waters. The episode is related in Matt. 8:28–34, Mark 5:1–20, and Luke 8:26–39. According to Matthew, Jesus arrived "in the country of the Gadarenes" (εἰς τὴν χώραν τῶν Γαδαρηνῶν), an expression that refers to Gadara. But according to Mark and Luke, he arrived instead "in the country of the Gerasenes" (τῶν Γερασηνῶν), which refers to the city of Gerasa, also situated in the Decapolis, but much farther south than Gadara. Beyond this, some manuscripts have the reading τῶν Γεργεσηνῶν, an allusion to the city of Gergesa, on the shores of Lake Tiberias. The presence of pigs nearby proves that there were pagans living alongside the Jewish population. See the objection that Porphyry makes in *Contra Christianos* (Harnack frag. 49, in Macarius, *Monogenes* 3.4.11; R. Goulet 81) to the presence of the pigs and the response that Macarius offers (*Monogenes* 3.11.9–11; R. Goulet 104). It may also be the city of Gadara that Jesus is thinking of when he says, in the *Gospel of Thomas* 32, "A city built upon a high mountain and fortified cannot fall, nor can it be hidden" (trans. Stephen J. Patterson and James M. Robinson).

50. This work is cited in Diogenes Laertius, *Lives* 6.29. About the *chreiai* that came from *The Sale of Diogenes*, see Goulet-Cazé, "Le livre VI de Diogène Laërce," 4005–25.

51. Cf. *Palatine Anthology* 7.417.4.

52. Cf. section "'Falsifying the Currency' or the Critique of Civilization: On the Literary Level" on p. 38.

Secundus[53] clearly demonstrate. . . . The genre of chriae collection was quite adaptable to various sorts of contents."[54]

So we may state a preliminary conclusion: the possibility exists that the people of Q could have been familiar with Greek collections of chreias, maybe even with Cynic collections. But can we go beyond that and try to determine to what extent Greek chreias, possibly even Cynic ones, may have influenced the chreias in Q? The problem we encounter is that the chreia embraces a wide variety of forms, from the short sentence with a witticism to the apothegm with a more- or less-developed narrative framework or even to the anecdote endowed with a genuine narrative. In the case of a genre that covers such a broad range, there's a risk of turning it into a sort of catchall. But since the goal of those exegetes who speak of the chreia in connection with Q is to connect Q with Cynicism, we propose to consider the chreia in its narrow sense, that of a simple saying or an apothegm, that is, a saying accompanied by a general spatiotemporal framework, as in Diogenes Laertius's collections of chreias.[55]

Let us consider first the context of chreias. Along with Kloppenborg, we are prepared to admit a similarity between the context of the chreias in Q and those of a good number of Cynic chreias that present Antisthenes or Diogenes facing reproach or reacting to a behavior, statement, or question that has provoked them. For example, in Diogenes Laertius, *Lives*, we read: "Being reproached because his parents were not both free-born, Antisthenes replied, 'Nor were they both wrestlers, but yet I am a wrestler'" (6.4); "Being reproached with begging when Plato did not beg, Diogenes said, 'Oh yes he does, but when he does so, he holds his head down close, that none may hear'" (6.67); "To one who protested that he was ill adapted for the study of philosophy, Diogenes said, 'Why then do you live, if you do not care to live well?'" (6.65). Parallels can be drawn between this context of a confrontation with an interlocutor, usually a hostile one, and similar situations of confrontation and polemic that Jesus experiences, for example, when he's accused of casting out demons by Beelzebul (Q 11:14–15) or when "this generation" demands a sign (Q 11:16, 29–30).

Then what about structure? As one reads through the chreias in book 6 of Diogenes Laertius, one is struck by the fact that the same expressions

---

53. He adds the *Gospel of Thomas* in a footnote (163n102).

54. Kloppenborg Verbin, *Excavating Q*, 162.

55. In "Quite like Q," 197–203, Downing appeals precisely to the formal fluidity of *chreiai* and to the fact that the collection in Q, like those in Diogenes Laertius's *Lives*, has no narrative structure.

keep recurring. This is also true of the other *Lives* in his whole volume, and of other collections of chreias—for example, Lucian's *Life of Demonax*. Some of the most common expressions are ἐρωθητεὶς . . . ἔφη (or equivalent) (e.g., 6.7, 8, 50; *Dem.* 62); ὀνειδιζόμενος . . . ἔφη (e.g., 6.4, 66, 67); πρὸς τὸν εἰπόντα . . . ἔφη (e.g., 6.8); a genitive absolute indicating the circumstances, followed by ἔφη (e.g., 6.8, 41; *Dem.* 15); a participle in apposition to the subject and indicating the circumstances, followed by ἔφη (e.g., 6.4, 42; *Dem.* 28) or by ἠρώτα (*Dem.* 13); ἐπεί + a subordinate clause, ἔφη (*Dem.* 24); definitions: "He said that the . . . is/are" [e.g., 6.50]; simple affirmations: "He said that . . ." (e.g., 6.4, 24, 27); "He was amazed that (ἐθαύμαζε) . . ." (e.g., 6.27); plays on words (e.g., 6.24); syllogisms (e.g., 6.37, 69).

When these chreias are also given a spatiotemporal framework, it's often very succinct: a simple ποτέ or the mention of a place or an event (a city, a banquet, an inn, a temple, a theater, etc.). We read in Diogenes Laertius, *Lives* 6.29: "When Diogenes was captured and put up for sale, he was asked what he could do. He replied, 'Govern men.'" But when this same chreia reappears in *Lives* 6.74, it offers many more details: "On a voyage to Aegina he was captured by pirates under the command of Scirpalus, conveyed to Crete and exposed for sale. When the auctioneer asked in what he was proficient, he replied, 'In ruling men.'"

In Q2 we find formal structures that are basically analogous to those in the Cynic chreias: many times "he said" (εἶπεν, ἔλεγεν, λέγει), but also, although in very small numbers, some more characteristic expressions. These include ἐπερωτηθεὶς δὲ . . . ἀπεκρίθη (Q 17:20); καὶ ἀποκριθεὶς εἶπεν (Q 7:22); τούτων δὲ ἀπελθόντων, ἤρξατο λέγειν (Q 7:24); participle + "he said" (Q 7:20; 11:17). As for the framework, in Q2 it's generally reduced to a simple "he said," unlike in Cynic chreias, which are most often contextualized. However, the saying is sometimes set within a larger and more extended narrative development in which Jesus responds to an interlocutor. The anecdote of the centurion in Q 7:3–9 is typical in this regard: "There came to him a centurion exhorting him and saying . . . And he said to him . . . And in reply the centurion said . . . But Jesus, on hearing was amazed and said . . . ." The accusation about Jesus casting out demons in Q 11:14–15, 17–20, represents a similar case: "He cast out a demon [which made a person] mute . . . the mute person spoke. And the crowds were amazed. But some said . . . But, knowing their thoughts, he said to them . . ." The presence of a similar context and of similar structures, even though the most characteristic ones do not appear frequently, is enough to give some weight to the hypothesis that Q could belong to the same literary genre as the Greek chreias, and perhaps even the Cynic ones.[56] But what arguments are there for thinking that the chreias in Q are more specifically related to the Cynic chreias, as Greek tradition has made them known to us?

Actually, after we've read book 6 of Diogenes Laertius and Lucian's *Demonax*, when we then read Q, we don't get the sense that we have the same type of chreia collection before us. Why? For one thing, the collection in Q, as Kloppenborg has already underscored, isn't homogeneous on the formal level, while the collections in the *Lives* and in *Demonax* are much more so. Beyond this—and we must insist on the fact—we do not find in the Q-sayings the characteristic wittiness of the Cynics, with its humor, joking, and caustic bite. In the chreias in Diogenes Laertius's *Lives* of philosophers, which are generally brief, all the emphasis is put on the barb. A single example, from 6.47: "Of a public bath which was dirty he said, 'When people have bathed here, where are they to go to get clean?'" In the chreias of *Demonax*, the witticism, which is an element of the philosophical chreia's literary genre, is equally present. For example: "Peregrinus Proteus was shocked at his taking things so lightly, and treating mankind as a subject for humour: 'You don't behave like a dog, Demonax.' 'And you, Peregrinus, you don't behave like a man.'"[57] In the sayings of Jesus there can certainly also be a surprising turn of phrase, but this is not intended as a witticism. For example: "The least significant in God's kingdom is more than he [John the Baptist]" (Q 7:28); "The last [circumstances] of that person become worse than the first" (Q 11:26); "For where your treasure is, there will also be your heart" (Q 12:34); "There will be wailing and grinding of teeth" (Q 13:28). There's definitely an interest in phrases that have impact, but Jesus isn't trying to display wit or humor.

56. The formal analysis test that Ron Cameron applies in "'What Have You Come Out to See?' Characterizations of John and Jesus in the Gospels," *Semeia* 49 (1990): 35–69, esp. 18–35, is both very clever and very misleading. Cameron tries to demonstrate, in light of what Pseudo-Hermogenes says about the different states in the elaboration of a chreia as a preparatory exercise for the study of rhetoric (praise of the author, paraphrase of the chreia, reason, contrary, comparison, example, citation, exhortation), that we find the same elaboration in Q 7:18–35. In fact, Cameron's entire demonstration is misleading, because it implicitly suggests the idea that the people of Q were trained in the preparatory exercises of Greek rhetoric and that they were imitating these strictly, which is highly unlikely. Moreover, besides the fact that this demonstration would have to be confirmed by applying the same schema to other cases in Q, which appears to me difficult to accomplish, I am not convinced by the demonstration itself, which seeks at all costs, and not always felicitously, to make Q's phrases conform to the rubrics of Hermogenes.

57. Lucian, *Demonax* 21 (trans. Henry Watson Fowler and Francis George Fowler, modified).

Another difference, closely related to this one, is in the tone of the sayings as a whole. Both the Cynics and Jesus come up against human folly. The Cynics find that their contemporaries have become slaves to social convention and that they've forgotten the law of nature. Jesus reproaches the scribes and Pharisees for not making their actions match their words; Jerusalem kills the prophets, and "this generation" demands a sign, because it doesn't recognize the imminent arrival of the kingdom. In both situations the protagonist can say, "Woe to you!" In both situations something great is at stake: happiness, for those whom the Cynic moralists address, and the recognition of the kingdom of God, for Jesus's interlocutors. But the tone is not the same. Jesus can certainly be severe in what he says—for example, in his imprecations against the three cities of Galilee (Q 10:13–15) and against the Pharisees (Q 11:39–44), or in his brusque words announcing that there will be divisions within families (Q 12:51–53), or in the reproaches that he addresses to "this generation" (Q 7:31; 11:29–32, 49–51). But his words never have the caustic bite of the Cynics, or their sarcasm, or their extreme critical spirit. Jesus's tone is different. He's a Jew speaking to Jews, even while opening up his message to pagans as well. He's a Jew who's able to assume the tone of the great Jewish prophets,[58] but not that of the Greek philosophers, Cynic or otherwise.

Our overall conclusion must therefore be a cautious one. Given the structural similarities, the collection of Jesus's sayings in Q could be considered analogous to a collection of Greek chreias. Since the hypothesis deserves to be considered that the authors of Q could have been familiar with Cynic chreias and thus could have been influenced by them, particularly since in both cases the context is often that of confrontation and polemic, it's tempting to suppose that the chreias in Q are analogous more precisely to a collection of Cynic chreias. But our investigation has not confirmed this. The impact of the chreias in Q isn't designed to be made through humor, and the tone of the sayings is very different. That's why, even if we're willing to regard Q (and more precisely Q2) as a collection that could belong to the same literary genre as the collections of Greek chreias, and even if we also allow that it's completely possible that the people of Q could have been familiar with the collections of Cynic chreias, we must still acknowledge that we do not have the determinative element on the formal level that would allow us to identify the chreias in Q with a collection of chreias that would have a more

---

58. For a synthetic study on Israel's prophets, see Johannes Lindblom, *Prophecy in Ancient Israel* (Oxford: Basil Blackwell, 1962).

specifically Cynic coloration. In this we agree with Kloppenborg's opinion, cited earlier (see section "Q and the Cynic Chreia" on p. 143). He suggests, moreover, that the collection of chreias in Q2 absorbed the wisdom sayings from Q1, a hypothesis that resolves the question of the relationship between Q1 and Q2 in an ingenious manner.

But we should now revisit the character of the sayings in Q1, since Burton Mack emphasizes their aphoristic style and argues that this is a rhetorical trait typical of Cynicism. ("The aphorisms in Q1 set the Cynic-like tone, and the injunctions reveal a strong sense of vocation that corresponds to the Cynic way of life.")[59] The aphoristic character of these sayings may be granted, but must his conclusion be granted as well? It is true that in some Cynic sayings, such as those by Diogenes preserved by Diogenes Laertius, we may occasionally encounter a maxim. For example: "A dog does not eat beetroot" (6.45); "An ignorant rich man he used to call 'the sheep with the golden fleece'" (6.47); "The stomach he called livelihood's Charybdis" (6.51). We may also encounter an imperative: "Men of Myndus, bar your gates, lest the city should run away" (6.57). Nevertheless, this doesn't lead us to perceive maxims and imperatives as characteristics of Cynic language. It's enough to read through the collections of apothegms in book 6 of Diogenes Laertius to be convinced of this. One might object, however, that the two doxographies of Antisthenes, one anonymous (6.10–11) and the other by Diocles of Magnesia (6.12–13), are presented as collections of aphorisms: "Ill repute is a good thing and much the same as pain" (6.11); "A good man deserves to be loved" (6.12); "Esteem an honest man above a kinsman" (6.12); "Good actions are fair and evil actions foul" (6.12). We also encounter some aphorisms in the doxography of Diogenes: "Nothing in life has any chance of succeeding without strenuous practice; and this is capable of overcoming anything" (6.71); "It is impossible for society to exist without law" (6.72); "The only true commonwealth is that which is as wide as the universe" (6.72). However, even though the δόξαι that we encounter in these places doubtlessly express the thought of Antisthenes and Diogenes, their form has been reworked by the doxographer and their present state is actually characteristic of doxographic literature rather than of Cynic writing. The fact that the same type of sentences can be found in other doxographies in Diogenes Laertius's *Lives*, especially in book 2 (which contains Cyrenaic, Hegesiac, and Annicerian doxographies), confirms this view.[60]

59. Mack, *Lost Gospel*, 120.
60. Some examples from Cyrenaic doxography: "Bodily training contributes to the

Finally, we must evaluate the hypothesis that Q is a Hellenistic Cynic βίος. We need to bear in mind, first of all, that there was no Hellenistic Cynic βίος as such. The most we can say is that there was a βίος literary genre that can be found in the lives of philosophers of all the schools that Diogenes Laertius treats. It's important to realize that Diogenes himself gets his essential biographical information from other biographers who came well before him, to whom he refers: Neanthes of Cyzicus, who lived about 200 BCE and who wrote a work titled *Lives of Illustrious Men* that dealt especially with philosophers;[61] Hermippus of Smyrna, a Peripatetic from the end of the third century BCE, who wrote lives of philosophers, legislators, poets, orators, and historians;[62] Satyrus of Callatis, a Peripatetic similarly of the third century, whose *Lives* were abridged by Heraclides Lembus;[63] and Diocles of Magnesia, from the first century BCE, who wrote both *Lives of Philosophers* and a *Philosophers Overview*,[64] which played a decisive role as a source for Diogenes Laertius's book 6.[65] The works of these Hellenistic biographers have unfortunately not come down to us; we only have fragments of them. But as is evident, they were not Cynics, and their lives treat both philosophers connected with Cynicism and those connected with other philosophies. As a result, no one should be left with the impression that there was a literary genre of βίος that was specifically Cynic. But independently of that issue, it must be asked whether Q resembles a βίος in any way.

Three objective elements may be cited right away that argue against this hypothesis: (1) the absence of biographic details other than the baptism of Jesus and the temptations in the desert; (2) the fact that there are no biographic apothegms as such in Q, by contrast with those found in the Cynic lives of Diogenes Laertius—one thinks, for example, of the sale of Diogenes (6.74–75) and the disappearance of his slave Manes (6.55); (3) the fact that the structure of Q doesn't resemble that of Hellenistic biographies.

---

acquisition of virtue" (Diogenes Laertius, *Lives* 2.91); "Wealth is productive of pleasure, though not desirable for its own sake" (*Lives* 2.92). From Hegesiac doxography: "Life and death are each desirable in turn" (*Lives* 2.94); "The wise man will be guided in all he does by his own interests, for there is none other whom he regards as equally deserving" (*Lives* 2.95). From Annicerian doxography: "The happiness of a friend is not in itself desirable, for it is not felt by his neighbor" (*Lives* 2.96).

61. Cf. Pedro Pablo Fuentes González, "Néanthe de Cyzique," *DPhA* 4:587–94.

62. Cf. Jean-Pierre Schneider, "Hermippe de Smyrne," *DPhA* 3:655–58.

63. See Stefan Schorn, "Satyros de Callatis," *DPhA* 6:133–43; Jean-Pierre Schneider, "Héraclide Lembos," *DPhA* 3:568–71.

64. See Richard Goulet, "Dioclès de Magnésie," *DPhA* 2:775–77.

65. See Goulet-Cazé, "Le livre VI de Diogène Laërce," 3936–51.

We get a good idea of this structure from the major biographies in Diogenes Laertius's collection (though not from the minor ones of disciples that can be included within the life of a master). While there's not a fixed order, in general these present the important stages in the life of a philosopher up to his death, then a collection of apothegms, followed by a list of works if available, and, for the founder of a school, a doxography. A life such as that of Demonax, as Lucian relates it, conforms to such a schema. A purely biographical section (par. 4–11) is followed by one dedicated to his sayings (τῶν εὐστόχως τε ἅμα καὶ ἀστείως ὑπ' αὐτοῦ λελεγμένων, par. 12–62), and the work closes with the philosopher's final years and death (par. 63–67). In Q, by contrast, the biographical framework is truly minimal, not to say nonexistent. There's nothing about the origins of Jesus, or the stages of his life, or his death. The conclusion is inescapable: the literary genre of Q, at least of that document in the form in which it can be reconstituted from Luke and Matthew, is not that of a Hellenistic βίος.

Must we therefore also rule out the hypothesis that the authors of Q were moving toward a life of Jesus? We should acknowledge some details that could support that idea. To begin with, there are the two biographical passages of the baptism and the temptation, which constitute stratum Q3 in Kloppenborg's stratigraphy.[66] Beyond this, the statement in Q 7:1 seems to come within the framework of a βίος, in which events succeed one another: "When Jesus ended these sayings . . . , he entered Capernaum." Similarly in Q 7:18–19: "And John, on hearing about all these things, sending through his disciples, said to him: 'Are you the one to come, or are we to expect someone else?'" Jesus answers in Q 7:22 and the narrative sequence continues in 7:24: "And when they [John's messengers] had left, he [Jesus] began to talk to the crowds about John." Similarly also perhaps in Q 11:14, where Jesus casts out a demon that made a person mute, the mute person speaks, and the crowds are amazed. But providing a context for a few sayings falls far short of writing a biography. These details indicate at best that the authors of Q were aware that they should respect narrative sequences. We must conclude that Q is not a βίος, although in light of the presence of the baptism of Jesus and the temptations, this doesn't rule out the hypothesis of a proto-*bios* that Klop-

---

66. The crucifixion and passion are not treated in Q, but the authors know that Jesus died on the cross (cf. Q 14:27; 13:34). Frenschkowski, "Biographischen Kenntnisse," 3–42. We should consider this fact as highly significant, since even if the Jesus of Q isn't presented as the Messiah, he's the very same historical person—persecuted—as the one spoken of in the kerygmatic tradition.

penborg has put forward.[67] Nevertheless, this still does not imply a Cynic influence, since the βίος was not a specifically Cynic genre.

Could Jesus and His Companions Have Been Cynics?

Gerd Theissen's "Wanderradikalismus"

For his part, Gerd Theissen has pursued a brilliant and productive sociohistorical approach in order to determine, without denying the inspired character of Jesus's words, the social, economic, and cultural milieu in which they were spoken, and to highlight the social stratification of the first Christian communities.[68] His approach rests on a theory of conflicts: since the higher level of society—that is, the petty aristocracy of the Herodian royal house— had reserved property and culture for itself, primitive Christianity wanted to transfer power in different form to the common people at the margins of society. This "aristocratic behavior from below," which constituted not a political revolution but a veritable "revolution of values," raised expectations— the poor, the hungry, and the suffering had to obtain justice—even if they were suppressed or could only be maintained as a utopian hope. Theissen's main idea is that primitive Christianity was a *Wanderradikalismus*—that is, an itinerant radicalism practiced by charismatic figures who agreed to go on mission to make Jesus's words known, under extreme conditions where they would be outside the law, homeless, and without protection. These people abandoned their homes, their families, and their goods and made the decision to become homeless, because while "foxes have holes, and birds of the air have nests," "the Son of Man has nowhere to lay his head" (Matt. 8:20). Prepared to "hate father and mother, wife and children, brothers and sisters" in order to become disciples of Jesus (Luke 14:26), they also adopted a highly critical attitude toward riches.[69] Such an anti-familial ethos could only be practiced on the margins of society, by people who were firmly committed

---

67. Cf. Kloppenborg, *Formation of Q*, 325–28.

68. Gerd Theissen, "Wanderradikalismus: Literatursoziologische Aspekte der Überlieferung von Worten Jesu im Urchristentum," *ZTK* 70 (1973): 245–71; Theissen, *Soziologie der Jesusbewegung: Ein Beitrag zur Entstehungsgeschichte des Urchristentums*, Theologische Existenz Heute 194 (Munich: Kaiser, 1977), 9–32 (*Sociology of Early Palestinian Christianity*, trans. John Bowden [Philadelphia: Fortress, 1978], 7–30); Theissen, *Studien zur Soziologie des Urchristentums*, 3rd ed., WUNT 19 (Tübingen: Mohr Siebeck, 1989).

69. Cf. Mark 10:17–25; Matt. 6:19–21, 24–25.

to putting into practice through their actions the content of Jesus's sayings, of which they were the heralds, even after the formation of the Gospels. Jesus was the first charismatic itinerant, and so this *Wanderradikalismus* goes back to Jesus himself. This ethos would later resurface in movements such as Montanism, Syriac itinerant asceticism, the mendicant orders of the Middle Ages, and the left wing of the Reformation.

Theissen notes that similarly there were many itinerant Cynic philosophers in the first and second centuries CE who were themselves on the margins of the society and who had an ethos comparable to that of Jesus's disciples, an ethos of absence from home, family, and possessions. Both movements insisted on a radical transformation of one's way of life and outlook, and they both renounced accepted social values. In other words, they each called for a conversion, but one that was accessible to everybody. These two marginalized groups could appear to be parasites, and they drew mockery. Nevertheless, even though Theissen recognizes that sociologically, at least, the two groups were comparable, and even though he acknowledges the Cynic tradition at Gadara, he never establishes a historical relationship between the two movements. He goes no further than to emphasize their similarity,[70] because he's aware that the spiritual concerns that animated the two groups were different: the intellectual program of the Cynics was based on the opposition they established between nature and law, while the charismatic itinerants of Christianity opposed a new world to the old one, which was condemned to perdition. Even though some reservations have been expressed about his thesis,[71] Theissen opened new perspectives for research and has had a great influence, particularly through his concept of *Wanderradikalismus*. His work demonstrated the interdependence that can exist between a spiritual tradition and a given set of social conditions. Some, however, have retained Theissen's thesis but abandoned the prudence that he personally observed. The Jesus Seminar in California, for example, did

---

70. Cf. Theissen, "Wanderradikalismus," 256: "Da das kynische Ethos von Wanderphilosophen tradiert wurde, dürfen wir per analogiam schließen, daß die Träger der Jesusüberlieferung zu einem vergleichbaren soziologischen Typus gehören. Dieser Analogieschluß basiert auf strukturellen Ähnlichkeiten, nicht auf historischen Beziehungen." ("Given that the Cynic *ethos* was transmitted by itinerant philosophers, we may conclude *per analogiam* that the heralds of the Jesus tradition belonged to a comparable sociological type. This deduction rests on structural similarities, not on historical relationships.")

71. Cf. Richard A. Horsley, *Sociology and the Jesus Movement* (New York: Crossroad, 1989); William E. Arnal, *Jesus and the Village Scribes: Galilean Conflicts and the Setting of Q* (Minneapolis: Fortress, 2001), 23–52.

not hesitate to affirm that Cynicism provides the best explanatory model for making sense of Jesus's sayings and that the historical Jesus was "Cynic-like." This is what's known as the "Cynic hypothesis."

The "Cynic Hypothesis," from F. Gerald Downing to the Jesus Seminar

Before discussing the efforts of this group of American specialists, we must give F. Gerald Downing's numerous works the credit they deserve.[72] He supports the hypothesis, which has become for him a firmly held conviction, of a direct influence of Cynicism on Jesus and the first Christians, and he has contributed much to the development of the "Cynic Jesus thesis." According to Downing, Jesus, who grew up in Nazareth, could have received a Cynic education at the hands of itinerant Cynic preachers who came into Galilee and especially to Sepphoris, the new capital being rebuilt by Herod Antipas during Jesus's childhood. This city was only a few miles from Nazareth and only twenty-two miles from Gadara, a city that produced three Cynic philosophers. Downing holds that Jesus himself deliberately gave his message a Cynic coloration, as he addressed it to everyone without distinction, through the reversal of values expressed in the Beatitudes (Matt. 5:3–12). Jesus was "a Cynic with a Jewish cultural heritage."[73] Downing believes that this reconstruction of his is the only one that makes possible a coherent interpretation of all the data. Without it, one is forced to imagine a chain of coincidences: "Jesus coinciding with popular cynicism, many of his first disciples happening (unlike Paul) to show no unease with such fortuitous resemblances; and later followers happening to understand the tradition as deliberately Cynic in its direction."[74] From Downing's perspective, in the time of Jesus there existed both a non-Christian Cynicism and a Christian Cynicism, as the choice of topics found in Q testifies. Downing rules out

---

72. See, e.g., F. Gerald Downing, *Christ and the Cynics: Jesus and Other Radical Preachers in First Century Tradition* (Sheffield: JSOT Press, 1988), v–xiii; Downing, *Cynics and Christian Origins*, 143–68; Downing, "Cynics and Early Christianity," in *Le cynisme ancien et ses prolongements*, ed. Marie-Odile Goulet-Cazé and Richard Goulet (Paris: Presses Universitaires de France, 1993), 281–304. Downing's views have been criticized notably by Eddy, "Jesus as Diogenes?," 449–69. Downing responded to these criticisms in "Deeper Reflections on the Jewish Cynic Jesus," *JBL* 117 (1998): 97–104.

73. Downing, *Cynics and Christian Origins*, 161.

74. Downing, "Cynics and Early Christianity," 293.

the possibility that the parallels might be pure coincidences. Starting with the principle that the praxis and language of Jesus could not have been born ex nihilo, he insists that their antecedents are to be found in Cynicism. As a result, he imagines that Cynics must have traveled not only through the cities but also through the villages and countryside of Galilee, and that those who learned to read and write studied the works and sayings of Diogenes and Crates in school, in the various *Progymnasmata*.

The Jesus Seminar, founded in 1985 by Robert B. Funk and John Dominic Crossan and composed of about 150 scholars, centered its reflections on the problem of the historical Jesus and assigned itself the mission of speaking the truth about Jesus. Its members attached a high importance to the *Gospel of Thomas*, which, in their eyes, contained even more authentic material than the oldest Gospel, that of Mark. Hence one of their works is titled *The Five Gospels*. According to the studies of several of their members, which rely on the history and analysis of Palestinian society in the first century, Jesus was an itinerant Cynical Jew who had no apocalyptic eschatology. This is a profile of Jesus that, as may well be imagined, did not sit well with American fundamentalist Christians. Hence the passionate reactions that the thesis of the Jesus Seminar provoked! It must be admitted that the group's methods lent themselves easily to critique, especially their collective voting using four different colors of beads for different types of sayings: red, "Jesus undoubtedly said this or something very like it"; pink, "Jesus probably said something like this"; gray, "Jesus did not say this, but the ideas contained in it are close to his own"; and black, "Jesus did not say this; it represents the perspective or content of a later or different tradition." According to this procedure, Jesus actually never spoke 82 percent of the sayings attributed to him! The members of the Jesus Seminar and, more broadly, the partisans of the "Cynic hypothesis" have written many works, collectively[75] and individually. Several of the most representative will be mentioned here. The suggestion that Jesus and his first companions could have been Cynics, or similar to Cynics, raises many concerns. But we will offer no judgment on the overall interpretation of the Cynic hypothesis and its theological con-

---

75. E.g., Robert W. Funk, Roy W. Hoover, and the Jesus Seminar, *The Five Gospels: What Did Jesus Really Say? The Search for the Authentic Words of Jesus; New Translation and Commentary* (Sonoma, CA: Polebridge, 1993); Robert W. Funk and the Jesus Seminar, *The Acts of Jesus: What Did Jesus Really Do? The Search for the Authentic Deeds of Jesus; Translation and Commentary* (San Francisco: HarperSanFrancisco, 1998); R. W. Funk and the Jesus Seminar, *The Gospel of Jesus: According to the Jesus Seminar* (Santa Rosa, CA: Polebridge, 1999).

sequences. We wish only to examine, as objectively as possible, the idea that Jesus and his disciples could have been influenced, in some fashion or another, by Cynicism in the Galilee of the first century.

John Dominic Crossan's "Peasant Jewish Cynic"

John Dominic Crossan, on the basis of social anthropology, history, and textual analysis, offers a reconstruction of the historical Jesus.[76] He defines him as "a Peasant Jewish Cynic" who must be understood within the context of a Judaism that was confronting Greco-Roman culture, and who emerges directly from the society in which he lived. Jesus and his disciples adopted the same way of life, appearance, clothing, and food as the Cynics. Since his village was located so close to the great city of Sepphoris, it's not at all improbable that Jesus could have been familiar with the countercultural phenomenon of Cynicism. Crossan, however, doesn't affirm that Jesus had any formal knowledge of the Cynic movement; rather, he envisages this as a possibility, even though he knows that it's impossible to prove. But Cynicism at least provides Crossan with a point of comparison in the construction he develops, because the Cynics themselves were also engaged in a radical critique of the social hierarchies, as these were embodied both in the system of patronage and clientelism and in the civilization in general.

Jesus, gifted with good judgment and much courage, was a radical revolutionary, an itinerant always on the move among the farms and villages of lower Galilee. He worked out a social program designed to promote an economic, political, and religious egalitarianism capable of subverting the hierarchical norms of Jewish religion and Roman power. The Cynicism of Jesus was Jewish and rural rather than Greco-Roman and urban. Crossan declares that Jesus and his disciples were "hippies in a world of Augustan yuppies." Regarding the Beatitudes,[77] he notes that the Greek word employed in the expression "blessed are the poor" is πτωχοί, beggars, and not πένητες, poor people. The poor must work to earn a living, but they may acquire some goods, even a farm and a few slaves; beggars, on the other hand, are the marginalized, recognized as such by everybody and scandalous to the people

76. John Dominic Crossan, *The Historical Jesus: The Life of a Mediterranean Jewish Peasant* (San Francisco: HarperSanFrancisco, 1991).

77. Crossan, *Historical Jesus*, 272–73.

of the society in which they live. The term πτωχός actually did form part of the vocabulary of ancient and imperial Cynicism.[78]

According to Crossan, the strategy that Jesus applied implicitly to himself and explicitly to his disciples—the heart of his program, as it were—combined two activities, "magic" and "meal": the freely offered healings by which Jesus was able to identify himself as a magician (if Christian theologians described him as a miracle-worker, this was to protect the religion and its miracles from magic and its effects),[79] and the shared meals at which people of all classes, ranks, sexes, and grades mixed together.[80] The missionary disciples didn't beg; they shared a kingdom, and in exchange they received a table and a house. Although the disciples could have begged in the fashion of Cynics, eating together was a strategy of Jesus to rebuild the peasant community on principles that were radically different from those of clientelism and that would lead to an egalitarianism that was both spiritual and material.

The kingdom of God, rather than being an apocalyptic event in an imminent future, was a way of life in the immediate present. It was a sapiential kingdom that envisioned how one might live here and now, which one entered by means of wisdom, virtue, and justice. In a sense, such a kingdom would be just as eschatological as an apocalyptic kingdom, but its eschatology would be an ethical one that would be realized in the present and mark the end of hierarchical social systems.

Burton L. Mack's "Lost Gospel"

Burton L. Mack argues in *The Lost Gospel* that if, when we read Q, we strip away the patina deposited by its long contact with the four narrative gospels and take into account the sociocultural context in Galilee where it was composed, we will realize that the social role that the historical Jesus plays in Q1 distances him from his traditional image as a Jewish eschatological prophet.

---

78. We may mention, for example, that a work of Diogenes cited by Sotion (Diogenes Laertius, *Lives* 6.80) had the title πτωχός; cf. also Teles, *Diatribe* 4b (Hense 45.3; Pedro Pablo Fuentes González, *Les diatribes de Télès*, Histoire des doctrines de l'Antiquité classique 23 [Paris: Librairie Philosophique J. Vrin, 1998], 426); Plutarch, *Table Talk* 2.1, 7 (632e); Dio Chrysostom, *Discourse 9* (*Diogenes, or the Isthmian Discourse*), 8; Pseudo-Lucian, *The Cynic* 2; Pseudo-Diogenes, *Letter 28*, 5.

79. Crossan, *Historical Jesus*, 304–10.

80. Crossan, *Historical Jesus*, 341–44.

We will recognize him instead to have been a Cynic popular philosopher who, in the social environment of Hellenistic Galilee, gave precepts to his disciples using the same language processes and the same themes as the Cynics did in their ethical practice. (We have already noted the connection that Mack draws between Cynic discourse and the aphorisms of Q1.) From this perspective, the kingdom of God that Jesus announced could well be interpreted in Cynic terms rather than in apocalyptic ones.

Mack explains that Galilee in the first century was a crossroads where peoples and cultures mixed, thanks to the many travel routes that traversed it, which provided access to Damascus, Tyre, Ptolemais in Phoenicia, Caesarea, Samaria, Jerusalem, the Transjordan, and the Decapolis. These routes were joined to major thoroughfares so that Galilee was connected to the Levant, Egypt, Syria, and the Tigris and Euphrates valleys, as well as to some very busy ports on the Mediterranean. Galilee had been under Hellenistic influence for three hundred years. Some of the surrounding cities, such as Scythopolis and Gadara, had been designed along Hellenistic lines; this was also the case for cities within Galilee such as Tiberias. Sepphoris, also within the province, was strongly Hellenized. Given the circumstances that prevailed in Galilee, Mack believes that it would have been propitious for a philosophy such as Cynicism to get a hearing there, and that before the Jewish-Roman War the Jesus movement behind Q developed a discourse inspired by the Cynic spirit.

If this was indeed the case, then Jesus's first followers actually didn't regard him as a Jewish messiah who came to reform Jewish religion, or as a savior Christ who died and rose again. Far from it; they saw him as a Cynic teacher. It's rather to the "narrative gospels," written much later, that we owe the myth of the savior Christ. As a result Mack concludes, "The people of Q were Jesus people, not Christians."[81]

He offers the following arguments for identifying the Jesus of Q and the partisans of Jesus in Q as Cynics. In Q1, Jesus and his followers adopt a nonconventional attitude and a critical posture toward society, practicing παρρησία and challenging any pretension to superior status based on accidental criteria such as wealth, knowledge, rank, or power. It's clear that the sympathy of the people of Q1 lies with the poor, the humble, and the underprivileged. Mack offers a list of themes found in Q1, and among them are some that clearly have a Cynic resonance: "voluntary poverty, critique of riches, etiquette for begging, renunciation of needs, call for

81. Mack, *Lost Gospel*, 5.

authenticity, critique of hypocrisy, fearless and carefree attitude."[82] From this he concludes, "Q1 enjoins a practical ethic of the times widely known as cynic,"[83] though he is careful to specify that the modern caricature of ancient Cynics, which plays up their sarcastic barkings and obscenities, is inaccurate, just as it's unfair to apply the term "cynic" in its modern sense to the Cynics of antiquity. A more balanced view, he believes, would be to see ancient Cynics as the Greek equivalent of the Jewish prophets. Mack hears "a Cynic-like tone" in the aphorisms of Q1 and senses in the imperatives of this strata a strong sense of vocation that corresponds with the Cynic way of life: "The Jesus movement began as a house-grown variety of Cynicism in the rough and ready circumstances of Galilee before the war."[84] For the Jesus movement, as for the Cynics, what mattered was one's conduct, demonstrated through actions that were to be performed in the public arena. The goal was not to fight against Roman power or to reform Jewish religion, but to pursue individual reform by choosing to change the rules of one's life.

Mack notes the fact that the expression "kingdom of God" appears seven times in Q1 without ever expressing an apocalyptic vision of the world. He connects this expression with the political and governmental discussions that Greek philosophy had about the difference between νόμος and φύσις and between a king and a tyrant. The language of royalty was used as a metaphor for self-control; the term "king" was applied to a human being who had reached the most elevated level of ethical excellence; "kingdom" served as a metaphor for the liberty and self-control that this superior individual possessed. Mack recalls in this regard the famous Stoic paradox according to which "the only true king is the sage" and the text in Epictetus that affirms that the Cynic's staff is a scepter, his mission is to represent Zeus, and his sovereignty is to show others how they should live.[85] Mack therefore interprets the allusions to the kingdom in Q1 in Cynic terms rather than religious ones; the ethos of the movement in Q1 is already a particular manifestation of the kingdom of God, and the reign it embodies is the reign of God. Since God is presented five times in Q1 as "father," Mack argues, on the grounds that the idea of a Father God had become widespread by this time, that this Father God is not the specific God of any

82. Mack, *Lost Gospel*, 113.
83. Mack, *Lost Gospel*, 114.
84. Mack, *Lost Gospel*, 120.
85. Mack, *Lost Gospel*, 126.

race or cultural tradition. From his radically secularized perspective, the people of Q did not belong to any particular religious tradition and they were not introducing a new theology.

Jesus, who is a Cynic sage in Q1, becomes in Q2 a prophet who appeals to the familiar epic history of the Hebrew Scriptures. Aphoristic imperatives are replaced by apocalyptic announcements and warnings. New figures appear such as John the Baptist, the Wisdom of God, the Son of Man, and the Holy Spirit. Q2 is no longer addressed just to the people of Q; it also speaks to people who might be outside the movement, such as the Pharisees and "this generation." Jesus, a "Cynic-like teacher," decides what his movement, wracked by tensions, needs to become. The kingdom will be revealed, but probably only at the end of time. By making Jesus the son of the Wisdom of God, Q2 succeeds in reconciling wisdom teachings with apocalyptic ones and in reconceptualizing the kingdom of God in epic and apocalyptic terms.

In Q3, which is very different from the previous two strata, the people of Q have survived the Jewish-Roman War, but a sort of resignation appears; Jewish piety, previously opposed, is now accommodated; Jesus quotes the Scriptures even though he's now seen as the Son of God whose kingdom will only be revealed at the end of time. Q3 is the final witness that has come down to us about the people of Q. In this overall reconstruction of the literary genesis of Q, Mack assigns Cynicism an essential role in the aphoristic stratum Q1.

Leif E. Vaage's "Social Gadfly"

In his own research, Leif E. Vaage has also explored the formation of the social group that's present in the background of Q.[86] Overall he accepts Kloppenborg's stratigraphy. But while Kloppenborg primarily saw a connection between Cynicism and the chreias in Q2, Vaage, like Mack, establishes his comparison with the "Q formative stratum"—in other words, Q1.

---

86. Leif E. Vaage, "Q: The Ethos and Ethics of an Itinerant Radicalism" (PhD diss., Claremont Graduate School, 1987); Vaage, "Q1 and the Historical Jesus: Some Peculiar Sayings (7:33–34; 9:57–58, 59–60; 14:26–27)," *Forum* 5, no. 2 (1989): 159–76; Vaage, *Galilean Upstarts: Jesus' First Followers according to Q* (Valley Forge, PA: Trinity Press International, 1994); Vaage, "Q and Cynicism: On Comparison and Social Identity," in *The Gospel Behind the Gospels: Current Studies on Q*, ed. Roland A. Piper, NovTSup 75 (Leiden: Brill, 1995), 199–229. In this article Vaage responds to Tuckett, "Cynic Q?"

In *Galilean Upstarts*, Vaage relies on social anthropology and the concept of "social identity,"[87] as well as on the "scientific mythology" of the origins of Christianity employed by New Testament specialists, to argue that the social profile of Jesus's disciples corresponds perfectly with that of the Cynic philosophers, those countercultural dissidents who opposed the dominant values of the society in which they lived. For each text in the "Q formative stratum," he presents an impressive number of parallels drawn from Cynicism in various eras, though he's careful to specify that he's not asserting a genealogical derivation of the former from the latter. Vaage believes that the best way to characterize the people of Q is by appeal to Cynicism, its resistance to conformity and its specific style of social life. Q's people shared not only figures of speech and rhetorical forms with the Cynics but also similar social mannerisms. The fact, for example, that when Jesus sent people out on mission, he forbade them to wear sandals may be recognized to have special significance in light of the connection with Cynicism: "In the case of prohibition of sandals, it has already become clear that this particular trait belonged with the Cynics to a much broader strategy of cultural confrontation and resistance. Its specific 'sense' would thus be derivative of that larger logic."[88] Vaage equates the behavior of Jesus's envoys, who entered homes and ate and drank what was given to them (Q 10:5-6), with Cynics begging; he sees in both cases a strategy of social engagement that he calls "a militant mendicancy."[89] He connects the fact that the Cynics were selective about from whom they would beg, preferring to ask of those who'd been initiated into their philosophy (Pseudo-Crates, *Letter 2*), with the fact that Jesus's envoys might encounter a "son of peace" in a house that they entered (Q 10:6). For Vaage, in the memory of the people of Q, John the Baptist was "a serious Cynic," a critic of those around him and their cultural habits. Jesus also appears as a Cynic, but a more convivial one, though no less demanding, a "social gadfly," "an irritant on the skin of conventional mores and values," a marginal figure in the context of provincial Galilee in the first century who urged his listeners to leave the normal path and follow a different one.[90]

87. Vaage, *Galilean Upstarts*, 1: "By 'social identity' or profile I mean simply a coordinated (albeit partial) discussion of the original ethos of the persons whom Q's formative stratum represents (chapter one), their correlative elaboration of this ethos in the form of an ethics (chapter two), the production of an ideology (chapter three) and social critique (chapter four), as well as the developing memory tradition of the group's 'founding fathers' (chapter five)."

88. Vaage, *Galilean Upstarts*, 30.

89. Vaage, *Galilean Upstarts*, 32.

90. Vaage, *Galilean Upstarts*, 102.

Vaage is convinced that in terms of their ethos, ethics, ideology, and critique, the people of Q entirely resembled Cynics. In their actions as in their words, they led a form of popular resistance against the official verities and virtues of their epoch, speaking "a decisive 'no'" to the habits and aspirations of their immediate cultural context, all the while persuaded that they would attain a superior form of happiness.[91]

Vaage argues his case even more strongly in the essay "Q and Cynicism," in which he affirms that the specific character of the community of Q makes the analogy between Q and Cynicism not only possible but inevitable. The parallels that he draws allow us to appreciate how the "Cynic hypothesis" operates, and so we will cite several of them. Among the many passages in Q that he connects with Cynicism, one of the most significant is the passage that's crucial for the social formation of the Q group—that is, Q 10:2–16, where Jesus gives his instructions to those he's sending out on mission, telling them not to bring a purse, bag, sandals, or staff and not to greet anyone on the road (10:4).[92] From the church fathers onward, this text was commonly interpreted as trying deliberately to differentiate the Christian missionaries from Cynics by showing that they practiced an even greater severity in their asceticism.[93] But Vaage challenges the idea that Cynics, as Cynics, always dressed in the same way and that the people of Q were trying deliberately to differentiate themselves from them.[94] He attempts to show, on the contrary, that the Q missionaries actually resembled Cynic preachers.

Even though the prohibition of the staff and sack constitutes a difference with respect to Cynics, some other details suggest a similarity. Not bringing a purse or wearing sandals and not exchanging greetings with anyone along the way correspond with the typical Cynic practice, according to Vaage.

91. Vaage, *Galilean Upstarts*, 106.

92. Vaage, "Q and Cynicism," 208–12.

93. Cf. Jerome, *Commentary on Matthew* 10:9–10 (CCSL 77) 1.66: "Ex hoc praecepto arguit philosophos qui vulgo appellantur bactroperitae quod contemptores saeculi et omnia pro nihilo ducentes cellarium secum vehebant." According to Jerome, by commanding his disciples not to carry a bag, Jesus was denouncing the *bactroperitae*, those who carried a staff and a sack—that is, the Cynic philosophers, who brought their provisions with them; cf. also Salvian, *To the Church* 2.39–40 (Georges Lagarrigue, *Salvien de Marseille: Œuvres*, SC 176 [Paris: Éditions du Cerf], 214–17). See Pierre Courcelle, "La figure du philosophe d'après les écrivains latins de l'antiquité," *JS* (1980): 85–101, esp. 94n53. For a contemporary interpretation along these same lines, see Tuckett, "Cynic Q?," 367: "Thus even at the level of visible outward appearance to others, the Q missionaries must have looked rather un-like Cynic preachers."

94. Vaage, "Q and Cynicism," 208.

And even for the sack and staff, he tries to show that doing without these, though not typical of the Cynics' practice and not widely attested, would certainly be coherent with the logic of their asceticism. He cites Cynic texts to demonstrate that one must beware of too hasty generalizations about the Cynics' traditional clothing and appearance. To show, for example, that a staff was not indispensable, he appeals to Diogenes Laertius, *Lives* 6.23, a passage that explains that Diogenes "did not lean upon a staff until he grew infirm," and that only after that he used it to carry his sack. He also cites Diogenes Laertius, *Lives* 6.102, where the nontraditional outfit that Menedemus[95] wore is described: a tunic, a purple belt, an Arcadian hat, buskins of tragedy, and a staff. With the same passage in Q (10:2–16) still in view, Vaage proceeds to other comparisons: between the abandonment of the purse and Diogenes Laertius, *Lives* 6.87, where Diogenes persuades Crates to throw all the money he has into the sea; between the fact of going barefoot and Pseudo-Lucian, *The Cynic* 17; and between the fact of the envoys not greeting the people they meet on the road and *Philosophies for Sale* 10, where the Cynic, alone in a crowd, does not greet anyone, whether friend or stranger.[96] As for other passages, Vaage sees a structural similarity between the commissioning formula in Q 10:3, "Be on your way! Look, I send you like sheep in the midst of wolves," and the saying of Crates in Diogenes Laertius, *Lives* 6.92, "Those who live with flatterers are as defenseless as calves in the midst of wolves." More generally, he considers that being sent out on mission was common to both groups; the passages in Epictetus 3.22, 23–24, 34, 56, 59, 69, 95 all present the Cynic as someone sent by Zeus into the world. From this same perspective, Vaage connects Q 10:16, "whoever takes you in takes me in, and whoever takes me in takes in the one who sent me," a passage that explains that receiving the people of Q amounts to being visited by God himself, with Dio, *Discourse* 34.4, where Dio presents himself

---

95. Actually, this is the outfit that Menippus, not Menedemus, wore; there appears to be some confusion in the text of Diogenes Laertius, *Lives* 6.102, because the abbreviation Μεν has been wrongly interpreted; cf. Marie-Odile Goulet-Cazé, ed., *Diogène Laërce: Vies et doctrines des philosophes illustres*, 2nd ed. (Paris: Livre de Poche, 1999), 765n1.

96. This comparison, we may say right away, is unfounded. If the people of Q did not exchange greetings, this was so as not to lose time, because their mission was to proclaim the kingdom as quickly as possible. If the Cynic in *Philosophies for Sale* 10, who is entirely bestial and savage, as Lucian says, doesn't greet anyone, it's for an entirely different reason: "Frequent the most crowded place, and in those very places desire to be solitary and uncommunicative, greeting nor friend nor stranger; for to do so is abdication of the empire." The Cynic refuses to greet people because he doesn't want to lose his self-mastery and mastery of others—that is, his prestige.

as a man who is unrelated to the people of Tarsus but who has come among them, directed by God (κατὰ τὸ δαιμόνιον ἥκειν), to speak with them and advise them, and with *Letter 7* of Pseudo-Diogenes, where the philosopher is treated as a "heavenly dog."[97]

We may cite two more examples of passages that Vaage considers significant: the one in the Beatitudes in Q 6:20 that incorporates adversity into experience, which amounts to being content with one's fate, an attitude that Vaage compares with the Cynic reversal of values,[98] and the passage about the ravens and the lilies in Q 12:22b–31, which contrasts the animal kingdom, the kingdom of nature, and the reign of God, on the one hand, with the orders that human civilization gives, on the other hand; this opposition is analogous to the one between law and nature that was fundamental to Cynicism.[99] Vaage acknowledges that the author of Q makes no argument for following nature, but he feels that nature itself nevertheless provides the best analogy for how the kingdom of God functions. He concludes, as he did in *Galilean Upstarts*, that a comparison between Q and Cynicism may be drawn on the levels of social ethos, ethics, ideology, and critique, which are all fundamental aspects for the existence of a group. As he sees it, "the formative stratum of Q was for all intents and purposes a 'Cynic document'"; he sees "the same basic socio-rhetorical strategy" in Q as in Cynicism, and concludes from this that while Jesus's first disciples in Galilee may not have been "'just' Cynics," we should acknowledge that, at the very least, they were "very much like them."

To those who object that the use of Scripture by the authors of Q provides sufficient grounds to hold that they don't actually resemble the Cynics in any way, Vaage responds, in his article "Jewish Scripture,"[100] that the use of Scripture in Q could be termed "a Cynic way with the word." He argues that the authors of Q treated the epic tradition of Israel similarly to the way the Cynics treated their textual traditions (by which he means Homer): as they made literary allusions, they "twisted" the "official" texts to such an extent that the conventional understanding of them was modified by their reading.

---

97. Vaage, "Q and Cynicism," 215.

98. Vaage, "Q and Cynicism," 220–21.

99. Vaage, "Q and Cynicism," 223.

100. Leif E. Vaage, "Jewish Scripture, Q and the Historical Jesus: A Cynic Way with the Word?," in *The Sayings Source Q and the Historical Jesus*, ed. Andreas Lindemann (Leuven: Leuven University Press, 2001), 479–95.

John S. Kloppenborg's Clarification

In *Excavating Q,* John S. Kloppenborg provides a sensible clarification regarding the relationship between Q and Cynicism. While he's aware of the
analogies that can be detected between the two, he recognizes that the Cynics' παρρησία and ἀναίδεια are foreign to Q. He in no way asserts that the
group in the background of Q accepted Cynic ideology, nor that the Jesus
of Q was a paradigm of the Cynic philosopher. He's careful to specify the
conditions of the "Cynic hypothesis" and the issues that it raises in a very
useful way.

> The cynic hypothesis does not require that Cynics be attested in large
> numbers in the early first century CE. It does not require that there were
> any contemporary high-profile Cynics such as Diogenes or Demetrius. It
> only requires one of two assumptions: either there were still some Cyn-
> ics or persons who would be identified as cynic-like on the basis of their
> dress, behavior, or teaching; or that the literary figure of the Cynic and the
> basic profile of Cynic behavior and teaching were sufficiently well known
> to be recognized when they were encountered in a literary presentation
> of Jesus—which is, after all, precisely what Q is. It is clear from the data
> . . . that both of these assumptions are reasonable.[101]

Within these limits, the "Cynic hypothesis" could be reasonable. Kloppenborg gathers and considers the objections that have been made to this
hypothesis, and he concludes that it is intellectually valid, since it helps to
clarify the interface between historiography and theology. He's astonished,
in fact (and I share his astonishment), by the outsized nature of the reaction
against it: "It has touched a very deep nerve" (422). This reaction, he feels,
has been driven not by historiography but rather by theology. He reasserts
that the Jesus movement must be contextualized, that we must take into account its cultural and social environment, including its pagan environment,
where specifically the influence of Cynicism would have been felt. He also
insists that comparing the people of Q with Cynicism doesn't amount to
denying their Jewish identity at all. "A cynic Q" doesn't imply "a non-Jewish
Q," because the people of Q were Jews of Israel and the God of Jesus was
still the God of Israel: "Part of the anxiety expressed toward a cynic-like Q

---

101. Kloppenborg Verbin, *Excavating Q,* 425–26. Hereafter, page references are given
in parentheses in the text.

thus seems to rest on a fundamental misunderstanding of what is claimed. Nothing in the cynic hypothesis entails a non- or anti-Jewish posture. It only *sounds* anti-Semitic if one makes the false collateral assumption that Judaism and Cynicism are polar opposites, and the equally false assumption that the culture of Jewish Palestine was monolithic" (436).

In addition, when some insist on the fact that the Q source is Jewish, too often they're suggesting implicitly that "Jew" means "religious," and that "religion" was a distinct domain, separate from the social and political structures in Galilee. But one assumption of the "Cynic hypothesis" is that we cannot separate religion from other cultural and social forms. Seen in that light, Q's critique of Galilean and Judean institutions is "*analogous to* Cynic criticism of Greek urban culture" (437, italics original). Kloppenborg responds to reservations about the assertion that the people of Q were not just radicals but "deviants" by asserting that the people of Q were indeed deviant compared with pious Christians; one reason why some today may be threatened by the Cynic hypothesis is that it places the possibility of serious social deviance too close to the historical Jesus and the canonical Gospels. The Jesus movement actually did adopt deviant postures that clearly conflict with its portrayal by Luke, the author of 1 Peter, and later apologists as nondeviant, at least as far as the political culture of the Roman Empire was concerned. But if Q2 felt obliged to defend the novelty of Q1 by aligning the figures of Jesus, John, and the people of Q with eminent figures of Israel's past, specifically the prophets, this only indicates, Kloppenborg observes, that the prophets themselves were remembered as deviant persons, even though later piety set about to efface their deviance.

He perceives the Jesus movement as tied to the countryside in Galilee and opposed to the city, to Jerusalem, to Herod's dynasty, to the Pharisees and the teachers of the law. Q, which he defines as "a typically scribal genre," could have been born in the milieu of the scribes, that of the minor cities— not in Jerusalem. These cities would nevertheless have been large enough to have marketplaces where people from lower Galilee could meet city folk, and they would have been close enough to the great centers of Tiberias and Sepphoris to allow periodic contact with Pharisees. Rather than envisioning itinerant missionaries, as Theissen does, Kloppenborg assumes a network of groups with local leaders, perhaps heads of households, on which mobile workers depended. He also insists on the fact that Palestine, far from being isolated, was at the confluence of many different Jewish, Hellenistic, and Roman currents because of the routes that linked the cities of Tiberias, Sepphoris, Bethsaida, and Capernaum and also joined the coast at Ptolemais and Tyre. Those who lived along these routes could have had contact with all sorts of people, possibly even Cynics. However, as to whether there actually were any Cynics present in Galilee, Kloppenborg admits, "I simply do not know" (429). Nevertheless, he insists that this possibility can only be excluded through ignorance of physical geography or a priori ideas about the Galileans and whom they could have encountered. Recognizing the importance of analogies, Kloppenborg concludes that the hypothesis deserves serious investigation that Q, if not Cynic, was at least "perhaps cynic-like" (432).

Critical Reflections

The debate raised by the "Cynic hypothesis" has major theological consequences. If the Jesus Seminar is correct, then traditional Christian faith rests on a distortion of who Jesus really was, which can only be recovered through Q, and institutional Christianity represents a profound alteration of the movement launched by Jesus.

As may well be imagined, this hypothesis has drawn many reactions. We may mention, for example, the works of Christopher M. Tuckett (1989), Hans Dieter Betz (1994), Martin Ebner (1996, 1998), Paul R. Eddy (1996), Luke T. Johnson (1996), David E. Aune (1997), William E. Arnal (2001), and Klaus Döring (2006).[102] Some responses, often methodological in nature, have been very serious scientifically, while others have been purely ideological or faith-based, and even quite violent. Each of these works, in turn, has drawn responses from the partisans of the "Cynic hypothesis." In a 2006 article, John Moles, a specialist in Cynicism, expresses a point of view generally in agreement with the "Cynic hypothesis." While the article is nuanced and careful, it discerns a Cynic influence on Jesus's way of life, his social and political attitudes, and his manner of teaching.[103]

---

102. Tuckett, "Cynic Q?," 349–76; Betz, "Jesus and the Cynics," 453–75; Ebner, "Kynische Jesusinterpretation," 93–100; Ebner, *Jesus—Ein Weisheitslehrer?*; Eddy, "Jesus as Diogenes?," 449–69; Luke Timothy Johnson, *The Real Jesus: The Misguided Quest for the Historical Jesus and the Truth of the Traditional Gospels* (San Francisco: HarperSanFrancisco, 1996; David E. Aune, "Jesus and Cynics in First Century Palestine: Some Critical Considerations," in *Hillel and Jesus: Comparisons of Two Major Religious Leaders*, ed. John H. Charlesworth and Loren L. Johns (Minneapolis: Fortress, 1997), 176–93; Arnal, *Jesus and the Village Scribes*; Klaus Döring, *Die Kyniker*, Faszination Philosophie (Bamberg: Buchner, 2006), 102–5.

103. John Moles, "Cynic Influence upon First-Century Judaism and Early Christianity,"

To illustrate the truth of Kloppenborg's comment, quoted earlier, "It has touched a very deep nerve," we need only describe what is probably the most aggressive critique yet formulated, the one that Luke Timothy Johnson offers from a traditional perspective in *The Real Jesus*. He condemns the Jesus Seminar's sensationalist use of media, its "deliberately provocative style" (e.g., voting with colored beads), and its preference for apocryphal texts such as the *Gospel of Thomas* over canonical texts. As he sees it, the Jesus Seminar wanted to liberate Jesus from the Gospels, and the public from its submission to dogmas, by demonstrating that the historical Jesus was different from the Jesus whom Christians worship and that the Bible was the product of its culture. An author such as Crossan, with his "Peasant Jewish Cynic," was trying to promote his own idea of what Christianity should be—not a church structured around leaders, worship, and symbols of faith, but an informal association of Cynic philosophers. More generally, Johnson criticizes all of these works about the historical Jesus for trying to explain his mission and the movement he inspired through the tools of cultural and social criticism, rather than acknowledging them as religious and spiritual enterprises.[104] For a more carefully considered assessment of what's at stake theologically in the quest for the historical Jesus, Daniel Marguerat's analysis may profitably be consulted.[105]

The Advantages and Difficulties of the "Cynic Hypothesis"

Historians of philosophy don't always give the study of Cynicism the place it deserves, and so the historian of Cynic philosophy can only rejoice over the fact that in recent decades there has been an upsurge of interest in it, and that in an outside field, on the part of New Testament exegetes. But what are we to decide about this "Cynic hypothesis," if we don't want to draw conclusions about the debate over the historical Jesus, a question that lies outside our field of research, if we are eager to keep our assessment free of all influence of a priori theological assumptions and confessional loyalties, and especially if we want to approach the question reasonably? We should

---

in *The Limits of Ancient Biography*, ed. Brian McGing and Judith Mossman (Swansea: Classical Press of Wales, 2006), 89–116: "Jesus must have seen and heard Cynics; he knew what they looked like, he knew some of their characteristic stories and narrative patterns" (103).

104. Johnson, *Real Jesus*, 167–77.

105. Daniel Marguerat, "La 'troisième quête' du Jésus de l'histoire," *RSR* 87 (1999): 397–421.

not attempt here to examine in detail all of the arguments for or against the "Cynic hypothesis"; that has been done at length by the scholars cited above. We may, however, offer some reasonable reflections that, even as they acknowledge the proposed hypothesis to be intellectually interesting, will encourage us to be careful about it.

Anyone who works on ancient texts and wants to be objective must take into account, before offering any interpretation, what those sources say. It must be observed, therefore, that neither Q nor the Synoptics nor the book of Acts mentions Cynicism and its traditions, although these sources do refer to Jewish tradition, and Luke describes the Stoic and Epicurean philosophers who engaged Paul in the agora (Acts 17:18). Moreover, as we established in our chapter on Judaism, there is no evidence of a link between Cynicism and Judaism in the time of Jesus. (The most we can say is that a century before Jesus—though not in Galilee, but in Gadara—the young Meleager, a Cynic poet who spoke Greek, alluded in one of his poets to the Sabbath.) An argument *a silentio* is rarely conclusive, but it nevertheless has a certain weight that should not be dismissed, particularly since archaeological excavations are just as silent as the texts. We do not know to what extent the inhabitants of Galilee might have been influenced by Hellenism. Excavations in Galilee do not permit us to conclude that a young man in Nazareth such as Jesus could have had contacts with Sepphoris, the major city nearby where Galileans could have interacted with Greeks; in any event, Sepphoris is never mentioned in Q or in the Synoptics. Finally, while the thesis that the people of Q were itinerants opens up the possibility of contacts, this thesis has been challenged.

In terms of methodology, it's helpful to remind ourselves, even though this should be self-evident, that surface similarities, especially on the level of vocabulary, don't necessarily imply deeper similarities. For example, it's not clear that the meaning of the word βασιλεία, which is applied in Q to the kingdom of God, is analogous to the word as it's used in the treatises on ideal kingship that schools of philosophy produced.[106] Kingship, for the Cynic, is a demand for the complete autonomy of the individual; the kingdom of God implies submission to the will of God on the part of those who are awaiting it (cf. Q 11:2b, "Let your reign come"). Even when a text is apparently clear, such as the commissioning in Q 10:4, and a link with Cynics is conceivable—"Carry no purse, nor knapsack, nor sandals, nor stick, and greet no one on the road"—the significance of the parallel itself is not

106. Cf. Mack, *Lost Gospel*, 126–27.

necessarily clear. Jesus certainly wanted to tell his missionaries that they needed to make good time and not delay by preparing for their departure or having conversations along the way, because the coming of the kingdom was imminent and there was a risk of not having enough time to proclaim it to all the Jews.[107] But since there was an analogy to the Cynic outfit, this might also have been a means of distinguishing Jesus's missionaries from itinerant Cynic preachers, or of showing that while there was a certain resemblance between the two, the people of Q practiced an asceticism that went beyond that of the Cynics, who didn't bring purses or wear sandals, but who did carry a staff and sack. In any event, this passage does seem to indicate that the Cynic philosophers' outfit was a reality that the people of Q felt the need to take a position on.

There's also the problem of whether sources are reliable. Some witnesses about Cynicism must be handled carefully because they either rest on idealization or else are satire. Beyond this, they may come from the period after Jesus, which is already a problem, but on top of that they don't reflect authentic Cynicism as it was practiced concretely in the streets under the Roman Empire. When Epictetus expounds his conception of the Cynic as a divine messenger (3.22), he's fabricating a theoretical construction, offering a highly personal interpretation of Cynicism in light of his own Stoicism.[108] In *The Fugitives*, when Lucian vehemently attacks those Cynics who've swapped their small trades for the outfit of a so-called philosopher so they won't have to work anymore, he's expressing his personal disgust for people who pass themselves off as philosophers even though they haven't had any access to παιδεία. When someone appeals to such authors to try to establish parallels with Q, we need to be aware that the Cynicism of Epictetus was certainly not the Cynicism of the streets and that the Cynics of the streets were not all charlatans as Lucian would have us believe.

There's a genuine risk of overinterpreting texts, because it's tempting, when one is in search of analogies between Cynicism and Christianity, to make texts mean more than they actually say. As a general rule, one must be very careful about the use of parallels: one text can't necessarily be clarified by another that comes from a completely different milieu. It's imprudent, for example, to create an amalgam of Cynicism and Stoicism and then draw

---

107. We find this idea of urgency, which is not explicit in Q, in Matt. 10:23: "When they persecute you in one town, flee to the next; for truly I tell you, you will not have gone through all the towns of Israel before the Son of Man comes."

108. Cf. Döring, *Die Kyniker*, 104.

conclusions from it, as if the two movements could be treated as one, which we've already shown is definitely not the case. It would be equally imprudent to conclude that since an author such as Dio encountered Cynics at crossroads, street corners, and temple gates in Alexandria at the beginning of the second century (*Discourse* 32.9), the situation must have been the same in Galilee in the first half of the first century. In the same way, it's dangerous to try to "derive" the Zealots from Cynicism on the grounds that they, too, challenged civilized society, not only because Flavius Josephus makes no mention of Cynics, but also because the Zealots' political radicalism had a religious foundation. Finally, whether one supports or opposes the "Cynic hypothesis," it's important to guard against inconsistency. For example, it is actually not valid, as certain opponents of the hypothesis do, to interpret Q 10:4, "Carry no purse, nor knapsack, nor sandals, nor stick," as a rejection of Cynicism on the part of Q's authors, while claiming at the same time that they couldn't have had any contact with Cynics!

So it's absolutely essential to be objective. Nevertheless, evaluating to what extent a similarity of behavior or situation also implies a similarity of motivation and objective remains highly subjective. When the adherents of two subversive belief systems both advocate a reversal of values, what can we legitimately conclude from this similarity? Jesus and the Cynics both rejected wealth; but while the Cynic believed that riches made man a slave and prevented him from obeying his reason, Jesus saw them as something that prevented man from deciding immediately for God and his kingdom: "Blessed are you poor, for God's reign is for you" (Q 6:20). The spirit is so different that the comparison is meaningless.

Similarly, do we really have any right to draw the slightest conclusion from the presence of wolves both in Q 10:3, "Be on your way! Look, I send you like sheep in the midst of wolves," and in Diogenes Laertius, *Lives* 6.92, "Those who live with flatterers are as defenseless as calves in the midst of wolves"? Jesus sent his disciples out on mission, but he knew that they wouldn't be received well everywhere, because the announcement of the kingdom implied a radical change in values; therefore, they needed to be prepared for rejection. Crates, for his part, devoted himself to urging his contemporaries to attain the self-knowledge that was indispensable for his ethical program; to that end, he warned them to beware of flatterers who didn't speak the truth (in fact, he advised them to listen instead to what their enemies said about them). The presence of wolves in both sayings doesn't appear to us to be enough to establish a legitimate parallel between them. We may also cite the passage about the lilies and ravens in Q 12:22b–31, in which

Jesus advises his disciples, perhaps in a context of economic anxiety, not to worry about their food or clothing, because their Father knows what they need. This passage has frequently been compared with Dio, *Discourse* 10.16, "Consider the beasts yonder and the birds, how much freer from trouble they live than men, and how much more happily also. . . . They have one very great blessing—they own no property" (trans. James Wilfried Cohoon). The comparison is similar: ravens and lilies, beasts and birds. But Jesus uses it to invite his disciples to have an appropriate absolute confidence in the Father, while Dio appeals to it to emphasize all the advantages that follow from a natural life and poverty. The two messages have nothing like the same tenor.

Without a doubt, the most striking similarity between the two movements lies in the reversal of conventional values and hierarchical relationships they advocated and the privileged position they accorded to the poorest and most deprived. Diogenes proclaimed that the king of Persia was the most miserable man alive in spite of all his gold (Dio, *Discourse* 6.35); Jesus proclaimed that those who were last—that is, the poor and indigent—were blessed (Q 13:30, "The last will be first, and the first last"; Q 14:11, "Everyone exalting oneself will be humbled, and the one humbling oneself will be exalted").

Nevertheless, despite these similarities, the glaring differences between Q and Cynicism must also be acknowledged; the partisans of the "Cynic hypothesis" are themselves generally aware of these.

In the behavior: The immodesty of the Cynics and their taste for biting sarcasm are totally foreign to Jesus and the first Christians. These characteristic behaviors of Cynicism, far from being a modern caricature of the philosophy,[109] are constitutive of the most authentically Cynic way of life. In the same way, the unbounded arrogance of the Cynic, a champion of asceticism who was indifferent to δόξα, and his feeling that he was superior because he was taking the short, rough road to virtue, are difficult to reconcile with the spirit of the Beatitudes.

In actions: Jesus performed healings and exorcisms, which none of the Cynics did.[110] His missionaries, unlike the Cynics, did not beg; they were

---

109. Cf. Mack, *Lost Gospel*, 114.

110. The case of Peregrinus healing people of the quartan fever after his death, besides being unique within Cynicism and thus of little significance, can also hardly be counted, because it's pure supposition on the part of Lucian and he attributes it to popular credulity: "By Zeus, it would be nothing unnatural if, among all the dolts that there are, some should be found to assert that they were relieved of quartan fevers by him" (*The Passing of Peregrinus* 28).

welcomed and entertained in the cities where they stopped to announce Jesus's message, because "the worker deserves his wages." The asceticism that the people of Q practiced by giving up all material security in order to follow Jesus was of a different spirit from the physical asceticism with a moral goal that Diogenes and his companions practiced: the Cynics depended on the force of their own wills, while the Christian missionaries relied on the will of God.

In the relationships with others: Even though Jesus was sometimes stern with his listeners, and even though he sometimes spoke frankly, he didn't use biting sarcasm like the Cynics, nor did he have their taste for the devastating riposte, nor did he employ the stinging humor of σπουδογέλοιον, a particularly effective weapon for the Cynics against those who took themselves too seriously.

In the perspectives: Behind Cynic humor was a background of despair and pessimism. The Cynic felt that, as the only one who saw clearly, he had to fight desperately to save man, who is captive to the whims of Fortune, and that in this lies his greatness. Jesus himself also battles to save man; however, he calls man not to fight against Fortune but to seek the kingdom of God, which is immediately present (in Q1), or to await the kingdom of God that was to come (in Q2).

In the goals: The Cynic, observing the absurdity of the world and resigning himself to it, nevertheless envisioned that individual happiness was within his grasp. He could reach that happiness–which he identified with life according to virtue–by cultivating self-sufficiency, impassivity, and complete liberty through the practice of asceticism. But the Greek notion of virtue is nowhere to be found in Q. The people of Q1 knew that they would be building their house on the rock (Q 6:47–49) if they put into practice the words of Jesus that invited them to change the image they had of themselves by opposing the social and religious practices of the society in which they lived. They knew that they could ask God directly for anything and their Father would provide it (Q 11:9–13).

Once we have taken these similarities and differences into account, must we find a place for Cynicism in our reading of Q, and if so, what place? And is Cynicism also to provide an explanatory model for the ideology of social critique that the people of Q pursued? We must bear in mind that a person's beliefs about possible connections between Q and Cynicism will differ depending on whether they are Jewish, Christian, agnostic, or atheist and whether they hold conservative or progressive views on theology. What points of agreement can we find between them all? It would be useless, first of all, as Kloppenborg has well shown, to argue about whether Jesus was a Jewish sage or a Cynic one. The fact that Jesus was Jewish doesn't mean that he couldn't also have been a Cynic. But whatever opinion one might have about Jesus as a Cynic, it's essential to recognize the importance of the Jewish background of Q and the relevance of its affinities with the prophetic tradition. Jesus's disciples were victims of suffering and hostility, and their experience takes place against the backdrop of the violence for which the prophets of Israel were destined.

Next, it must be acknowledged that the "Cynic hypothesis," whether one agrees with its conclusions or not, has the value of raising questions not only about Cynicism itself, whose connection with Christianity may not have been limited to relationships with the church fathers that we shall scrutinize later on, but also about the very origins of Christianity. The hypothesis has, among its most significant contributions, brought to light many interesting similarities between the two movements, including radicalism; the abandonment of all security; a concern for authenticity and rejection of hypocrisy; a willing acceptance of suffering and denigration; the sense of having a mission to fulfill toward other people; and reversing social, moral, political, and religious values, but without attempting a political revolution.[111]

The role played by personal decision in both cases is another similarity that should be emphasized. Anxious to live according to reason, the Cynic resolves to make his actions match his words; to accomplish this, he practices asceticism and "falsifies the currency." Jesus demands that his disciples put his words into practice here and now: they must decide, through willing consent and not out of pure legalism, to obey God and love others unconditionally, without expectation of reward, and be prepared to lose their lives in order to save them. But an unbridgeable gulf appears between the two approaches on the level of their deepest meaning. Cynicism was a philosophy that was accessible to everybody, which aimed at human happiness and which stopped with man; the people of Q, under the guidance of Jesus, who said he was sent by God (Q 10:16), were in relationship with God as their Father, who had hidden these mysteries from the wise and learned, and revealed them to little children (Q 10:21). In one sense, Cynicism and Christianity were both "shortcuts" to the goals they set: the former demanded that its followers decide in the present whether they would opt for civilization

---

111. Nevertheless, some of Christianity's moral principles are foreign to Cynicism: "Love your enemies" in Q 6:27-28; "Be full of pity" in Q 6:36; "Do not pass judgment, so you are not judged" in Q 6:37-38.

or for nature; the second whether they would opt for Mammon or for God, because "nobody can serve two masters" (Q 16:13). But at the end of the road? Human happiness after a hard-fought struggle in the first case; a life given by God in the second (Q 17:33, "The one who finds one's life will lose it, and the one who loses one's life for my sake will find it").

In the end, it's not a matter of denying the similarities but a matter of recognizing that they're never conclusive. Why aren't they? The underlying culture isn't the same, the spirit isn't the same, and the content of the message isn't the same either. Jesus lived in a world that had meaning, even if the coming of the kingdom would profoundly modify that meaning or rather fulfill it; Diogenes and the Cynics lived in a world devoid of meaning, dominated by Fortune, in which the Greek gods no longer inspired devotion and man had to rely on his own means to find happiness against all odds. Consequently, it would be an error of judgment, as I see it, to identify the people of Q as Cynics and to make Jesus a Cynic teacher (something that most of the scholars who support the "Cynic hypothesis" aren't asking us to do, in fact).

But even if we don't see the people of Q as Cynics, should we grant that they could have been acquainted with Cynicism? What we've said regarding the literary genre of Q, particularly if it's envisioned as a collection of chreias, leaves this possibility legitimately open. The hypothesis cannot be ruled out that the writings of Cynic philosophers and collections of Greek chreias, possibly Cynic ones, were in circulation. If this was indeed the case, this would not only explain, at least partially, the literary genre of Q as a collection of sayings; it would also account for certain thematic similarities. But should we go beyond hypothesizing that the people of Q were familiar with Cynic chreias and imagine that there were actually contacts in Galilee between the members of these two movements? Such a hypothesis would be purely theoretical, and even if it were verified by some new archaeological excavation, it still wouldn't allow us to identify Jesus and his missionaries as Cynics or as "Cynic-like figures." Rather, in our view, it would invite us to see the two movements as groups that were concurrently delivering a radical message aimed at the common people. This would be an illustrative case of two historical groups having many thematic similarities that cumulatively would suggest some historical link without being sufficient to prove it. In the expectation that new elements will be introduced to fuel the debate, the enterprise of comparing Q and Cynicism appears to be both legitimate and intellectually fertile. It invites us to imagine, through the conceptual framework that Cynicism offers, what the people of Q were thinking and what motivated their actions and attitudes. It's just a matter of being clear about whether we are approaching the problem from a comparatist perspective, as is done in the *Corpus Hellenisticum Novi Testamenti*, or whether we are looking for direct influences or even trying to identify the groups with each another.

The Problems with Bernhard Lang's Position

In light of these conclusions, it should be clear that Bernhard Lang's book, which appeared in 2010 with the provocative title and subtitle *Jesus der Hund: Leben und Lehre eines jüdischen Kynikers* (Jesus the Dog: the life and teaching of a Jewish Cynic), illustrates the excesses that a too-vague understanding of Cynicism and a lack of rigor in the use of sources may lead to. The chapter we have devoted to Judaism suffices to show what difficulties the historian encounters in seeking to rely on trustworthy texts, interpret them without too much subjectivity, and draw plausible conclusions. But this work abruptly appears and informs us that a broad current of Cynicism washed across ancient Judaism and that the evidence of it has been right before our eyes, but we have unfairly ignored it! Even though the author, unlike the studies discussed above, begins not with Q but with the canonical Gospels, his conclusion is similar to theirs: Jesus was a Jewish Cynic, his message was a compendium of Cynical and Jewish ethics, and the Jesus movement was neither a religion nor a Jewish reform group but rather a philosophical movement. While Lang's presentation of Greek Cynicism is well documented and generally accurate, he also affirms without hesitation that there was a Jewish Cynicism, whose origins he traces back to Elijah around the year 800 BCE. He sees Qohelet as another representative of this Jewish Cynicism in the Old Testament. In the New Testament, he cites John the Baptist and Jesus, who took Elijah as their example and emulated him. Lang also sees this Jewish Cynicism in a certain Bannus, an ascetic with whom Flavius Josephus spent three years in training and of whom he gives us a brief description,[112] as well as in Jesus the son of Ananus, whom Josephus presents as a prophet.[113] According to Lang, Cynicism had two branches, one Greek and the other Jewish, which Jesus united in his person, because he'd had the benefit of two kinds of training: Jewish, in the tradition

112. Josephus, *Life* 11–12.
113. Josephus, *Jewish War* 6.300–309.

of the prophet Elijah, and Hellenistic, in the tradition of Diogenes! Lang also draws a distinction, as if one were evident, between an Aristippean Cynicism, to which he assigns Jesus, and a Spartan Cynicism, which he says fits the figure of John the Baptist! His interpretation, brilliant and intelligent overall, is certainly based on a great number of parallels, but the theses he supports with these are not justified. If he'd been content to present a comparatist study of concepts or situations that have interesting similarities (for example, the theme of two ways; the royalty of the philosopher and that of Jesus; the sharing of goods in the earliest Christian communities and in Diogenes's *Republic*; the analogy between Heracles and Elijah), he would have performed a useful service. His work would have been of benefit to anyone interested in the origins of Christianity and the development of philosophy in the countries of the Mediterranean basin at the same time. But by trying at all costs to turn Jesus into a Cynic, without any proof beyond some parallels that some will find convincing and others will not (along the lines of the glass being half full or half empty), he leaves the reader perplexed, seduced by his intellectual construction but at the same time skeptical in the face of arbitrary conclusions that Lang wants us to accept without proof, based simply on gratuitous affirmations. A few examples, briefly sketched, will suffice to justify our concerns.

The first issue is the presence of the word "dog" as an implicit reference to Cynicism. Ecclesiastes 9:4 says, "Whoever is joined with all the living has hope, for a living dog is better than a dead lion." Lang's commentary: "The royal condition is represented by the lion, however this lion as a corpse is anything but a symbol of power. The self-comparison of the philosopher [i.e., Qohelet] with a dog can be understood as a reference to Cynicism."[114] The parable in Luke 16:19–31 of the rich man and the pauper Lazarus says that Lazarus "longed to satisfy his hunger with what fell from the rich man's table; . . . even the dogs would come and lick his sores." Commentary: "The dogs mentioned in the parable should probably be interpreted as a Cynic reference that was grasped by the ancient reader" (126).

Another issue has to do with figures assumed to be Cynics on a completely arbitrary basis. Lang sees a direct influence of Monimus on Qohelet's recurrent theme, "All is vanity" (*Alles ist Windhauch*). In Diogenes Laertius, *Lives* 6.83, for example, Monimus is quoted as saying, "Wholly vain (τῦφος) all man's supposings" (*Alles ist Dunst*). Commentary: "We know too little

---

114. Bernhard Lang, *Jesus der Hund: Leben und Lehre eines jüdischen Kynikers* (Munich: Beck, 2010), 64. Hereafter, page references are given in parentheses in the text.

about Monimus's work to be able to scrutinize Qohelet's connection to this Cynic. Nevertheless one is tempted to see in Monimus a direct source of Qohelet" (65). But if we simply understand the sense that the Cynics had of fighting against τῦφος, which they understood to be both pride and self-delusion,[115] we realize that this has nothing to do with the τὰ πάντα ματαιότης καὶ προαίρεσις πνεύματος ("all is vanity and a chasing after wind," Eccl. 2:17) of Qohelet. And it's enough just to read Ecclesiastes to recognize that Qohelet's psychological and intellectual profile, steeped in discouragement and dissatisfaction, is foreign to the bracing courage of the Cynics and their defiant attitude toward life and its sufferings. For Qohelet, the "virtue" of the Cynic sage would be just as vain as the stupidity of the fool. He puts the fool and the wise on the same plane (Eccl. 2:12–23), which is a total contradiction of the contrast that Diogenes constantly draws between the two.[116]

Flavius Josephus, after becoming acquainted with the three Jewish sects—the Pharisees, Sadducees, and Essenes—became a disciple (ζηλωτής) for three years of a Jewish ascetic named Bannus, who "lived in the desert and used no other clothing than grew upon trees, and had no other food than what grew of its own accord, and bathed himself in cold water frequently, both by night and by day, in order to preserve his chastity."[117] Commentary: "The endurance mentioned, which Josephus connects to cultic purity, is a general characteristic of Cynicism" (68). Lang cites as a parallel the anecdotes in Diogenes Laertius, *Lives* 6.23 and 34, from which we learn that Diogenes, "using every means of inuring himself to hardship," would roll around in the hot sand in summer and walk barefoot in the snow and embrace snow-covered statues in winter. However, all we learn from the passage in Josephus is that Bannus was a Jewish ascetic who lived in the desert; there's absolutely nothing to indicate that he was a Cynic. Besides, Josephus goes on to say that he himself returned to the city, where he joined "the sect of the Pharisees, which is of kin to the sect of the Stoics, as the Greeks call them." Given this precision about the Pharisees, we have every reason to expect that if Bannus had been a Cynic, the author would have mentioned this.

Josephus also tells us in his *Jewish War* that around 63 CE Jesus the son of Ananus would cry out all day long, "Woe, woe to Jerusalem!" Exasperated

---

115. Cf. Marie-Odile Goulet-Cazé, *L'ascèse cynique: Un commentaire de Diogène Laërce VI 70–71* [1986], 2nd ed., Histoire des doctrines de l'antiquité classique 10 (Paris: Librarie Philosophique J. Vrin, 2001), 17n2, 34.

116. See the numerous references to this contrast in Goulet-Cazé, *L'ascèse cynique,* 17–22, 142n12, 150.

117. Josephus, *Life* 11–12 (trans. William Whiston).

by these lamentations, the people beat him, and they brought him before the Roman governor, who scourged him, but nothing stopped him. In 6.307 Josephus makes this remark: "Nor did he give ill words to any of those that beat him every day, nor good words to those that gave him food." Commentary: "These traits combine to form the portrait of a Jew who is both a Cynic and a prophet. We are not able to say whether he loved his enemies, but he has—following in Cynic manner—renounced any action of vengeance or thanks" (134). It is well attested that the Cynics never thanked those who gave them anything, especially when they begged; they believed that everything belonged to the gods, that they were friends of the gods, and that as a result, since friends held everything in common, they were simply being given back what was already theirs.[118] Diogenes, "being short of money, told his friends that he applied to them not for alms, but for repayment of his due" (Diogenes Laertius, *Lives* 6.46). It's more problematic, however, that Lang also presents "Feindesliebe" as part of the Cynic ethos—that is, not cursing one's enemies and not seeking revenge against them, but rather loving them. Epictetus, in the portrait he gives of the idealized Cynic, seems to assume such a love for one's enemies: "For this is a very pretty thread that is woven into the Cynic way of life, that he must be thrashed like a donkey, and that while being thrashed, he must love those who beat him as though he were the father or brother of them all."[119] We may also cite a statement that comes shortly afterward, though it has less to do with love for enemies than with the Cynic's complete absence of desire for vengeance: "No one can insult him, no one can strike him, no one can assault him; as for his poor body, he himself has handed that over for anyone to deal with as he thinks fit."[120] Lang also appeals to Musonius Rufus, Seneca, and Marcus Aurelius. But all those authors are Stoics, and love for enemies appears to have been much more a Stoic theme than a Cynic one. Rather, when it comes to the Cynics, one might be tempted instead to cite a saying attributed to Diogenes: "Being asked how one might defend himself against his adversary, he said, 'By proving honourable and upright himself [καλὸς καὶ ἀγαθός].'"[121] The emphasis is certainly not the same: Diogenes means that the moral quality of a man is the best response to any attacks he might suffer. We might also recall the

118. Cf. Diogenes Laertius, *Lives* 6.37, 72.

119. Epictetus, *Discourse* 3.22.54 (trans. Robin Hard).

120. Epictetus, *Discourse* 3.22.100.

121. Plutarch, *How a Young Man Should Study Poetry* 4 (21f) (trans. Frank Cole Babbitt, LCL); see also *How to Profit by One's Enemies* 4 (88b); *Gnomologium Vaticanum*, no. 187 (Sternbach 76).

two anecdotes in Diogenes Laertius, *Lives* 6.33 and 89, where Diogenes and Crates, after being struck, went about bearing the names of those who had struck them, the one writing them on a tablet hung around his neck and the other on a plaster on his forehead. It's specified in the case of Diogenes that by doing this, he hoped to bring blame and even blows upon his attackers, an attitude that seems to have very little in common with the attitude of Jesus the son of Ananus!

When Lang connects (126–27) the episode of the rich man and the pauper Lazarus in Luke 16:19–31 with that of Megapenthes and the cobbler Micyllus in Lucian's *The Downward Journey or the Tyrant*, this is comparatism, and interesting comparatism at that. In both cases a rich man is condemned to suffer thirst—the former amidst the flames of hell and the latter in fetters next to Tantalus—while the poor man is happy in the afterlife. But why should Jesus's parable be considered "Cynic"? Commentary: "No reader of the parable of Jesus aware of this Hellenistic tradition can doubt its Cynic character. The Shoemaker (of Lucian) and the Beggar (of Jesus) embody— like the great cynical figures Heracles and Elijah—the poor philosopher who waits in the afterlife for a happy destiny" (127). In other words, no sooner does Judaism or Christianity mention one of Cynicism's main emphases, such as poverty, asceticism, or the critique of riches, than Lang hears an echo of this philosophy. This happens to such an extent that the word "Cynicism" begins to take on vague outlines and ceases to mean very much. If Lang hopes in the end to persuade a careful reader that Jesus was a Cynic, this is not the way to go about it!

The Case of Paul

About fifteen years after Jesus's death, a Pharisee was converted to faith in him. To promote that faith, he took to the roads, and there he encountered Cynicism—not merely the Cynic cultural legacy but quite likely flesh-and-blood Cynics themselves. He had to distinguish himself intentionally from them.

This was Paul, who was born in Tarsus of Cilicia to Jewish parents in an Aramaic-speaking community. As a Pharisee, he was greatly devoted to Jewish traditions and was trained in Jerusalem by Gamaliel the Elder (Acts 22:3). But he was equally familiar with Greek culture and was a citizen of both Tarsus and Rome (Acts 21:39; 22:28). Though he proclaimed himself an apostle to the gentiles, he challenged Greek ethics just as much as Jewish legalism. He spoke to pagans, Jews, and "God-fearers" (that is, those who hesitated to take the final step of complete conversion to Judaism because they didn't want to lose their social status or give up some of their activities, as Jewish religious prescriptions would have required).

From Theissen's perspective,[122] Paul belongs not to the original "Wanderradikalismus" phase of Christianity but to the next one, which he calls, following Ernst Troeltsch,[123] "Liebespatriarchalismus." This was a new model of social organization. Within it, to resolve social problems, inequalities would be voluntarily accepted between Jews and pagans, Greeks and barbarians, slave and free, men and women, but these would be attenuated by the love of neighbor (Gal. 3:28; 1 Cor. 12:13; Rom. 1:14). Paul's world was no longer the rural milieu of Q, but that of urban Hellenistic communities. Times had changed, and the Christian faith was now focused on a confession of the crucified and risen Christ. While the Q missionaries appear not to have left Palestine, Paul, who spoke Greek, roamed the entire Mediterranean basin and went notably to Antioch, Cyprus, Corinth, Athens, Ephesus, Philippi, Thessalonica, and Rome.

Cynicism could have had an influence on Paul, though more on his way of expressing himself than on his mode of life. However, Ronald F. Hock has emphasized the similarities between Paul, who worked as an artisan in a workshop, where he cut and sewed leather to make tents (that's how Hock interprets σκηνοποιοί in Acts 18:3), and the Cynics, who were the only philosophers other than Socrates who ever worked as artisans in workshops.[124] Hock also recalls how Simon the cobbler, admired by Antisthenes, represents the Cynic ideal of αὐτάρκεια in the *Socratic Letters*.[125] Appealing to 1 Thessalonians 2:9 ("you remember our labor and toil, brothers and sisters; we worked night and day, so that we might not burden any of you while we proclaimed to you the gospel of God"), and on the assumption that Cynics could have had philosophical discussions in their workshops, Hock concludes that Paul could have done his missionary preaching from the workshop where he was employed. It's true that while he was in Corinth, Paul earned his own living rather than ask the Corinthians for support. But

122. Theissen, *Soziologie der Jesusbewegung*, 106–11, esp. 107; *Sociology of Early Palestinian Christianity*, 111–19, esp. 115.

123. Ernst Troeltsch, *Die Soziallehren der christlichen Kirchen und Gruppen*, vol. 1 of *Gesammelte Schriften* (Tübingen: Mohr Siebeck, 1912), 67.

124. Ronald F. Hock, *The Social Context of Paul's Ministry: Tentmaking and Apostleship* (Philadelphia: Fortress, 1980), 66–68.

125. *Socratic Letters* 9.4, 13.1 (Malherbe 246 and 250).

the texts that Hock cites (1 Cor. 9:1–19; 2 Cor. 11:7; 12:13–16) don't allow us to determine how Paul viewed manual labor or in what social class this work was situated. The most we can conclude is that working allowed Paul not to depend on anyone and so to offer the gospel free of charge. And we should not make too much of the comparison to Cynics in the workshops. The conversation that Teles reports Crates having with the shoemaker Philiscos demonstrates that Cynics certainly could speak with others in those settings,[126] but they didn't work there themselves. The witness of Lucian, who claims in *The Fugitives* that artisans were leaving their shops in order to become philosophers, does attest that there were contacts between Cynic philosophers and artisans,[127] but it tends to prove, on the contrary, that manual labor and philosophy didn't go together, because the artisans abandoned their work when they became philosophers.

The works of Abraham J. Malherbe have no doubt shed the most light on Paul's relationship with popular philosophies, particularly with Cynicism.[128] Paul was not a Cynic; he was a founder of communities, and so he didn't share the Cynics' individualism. But he did borrow certain themes from Cynicism and use them in his preaching, though he adapted them to his own faith perspective. This is the case, for example, with the language and imagery of Spartan moral armament, such as Antisthenes employed when he compared the soul of the sage to a city fortified against a siege, or when he compared Ulysses's clothing to a soldier's armor.[129] In 2 Corinthians 10:3–6 Paul uses this imagery, but as Malherbe shows, he applies it to himself in an entirely different manner: unlike the Cynics, he puts his confidence not in himself but in the power of God ("the weapons of our warfare are not merely human, but they have divine power to destroy strongholds," v. 4).[130] As for why Paul would speak in the tradition of Antisthenes, Malherbe suggests that his opponents may have described him in terms reminiscent of the negative description of Ulysses (duplicitous behavior, making use of expe-

---

126. Teles, *Diatribe* 4b (Hense 46; Fuentes González, *Les diatribes de Télès*, 426): Crates reads Aristotle's *Protrepticus* in the shop of the shoemaker Philiscos.

127. Lucian, *The Fugitives* 12, 17, 28, 33; *The Double Indictment* 6: Lucian presents the Cynics as former artisans who prefer to become philosophers.

128. Particularly Abraham J. Malherbe, *Paul and the Popular Philosophers* (Minneapolis: Fortress, 1986); Malherbe, *Paul and the Thessalonians: The Philosophical Tradition of Pastoral Care* (Philadelphia: Fortress, 1987), 99–101.

129. Abraham J. Malherbe, "Antisthenes and Odysseus and Paul at War," in *Paul and the Popular Philosophers*, 91–119.

130. Malherbe, "Antisthenes and Odysseus and Paul at War," 117.

dients), and he may have answered them by appropriating the tradition for his own purposes. His use of military imagery was quite apt, since he was addressing people in Corinth, a city that was renowned for its fortifications, particularly the Acrocorinth, and could withstand a direct attack, though it was vulnerable to a furtive one.

In 1 Corinthians 15:32 Paul says that he "fought with wild animals at Ephesus" (ἐθηριομάχησα ἐν Ἐφέσῳ). Malherbe demonstrates that here Paul is using the diatribe style and that the wild animals implicitly mentioned in the verb he employs represent human passions.[131] The fight against the passions is associated particularly with two Cynic heroes, Diogenes and Heracles, the Cynics' patron. Malherbe recalls that Lucian, in *Lexiphanes* 19, uses the word θηριόμαχος to describe Heracles; that Dio Chrysostom describes how Heracles was able to free himself from lusts (*Discourse* 5.22–23); and that Diogenes himself, taking Heracles as his model, also fought against desires (*Philosophies for Sale* 8). So Malherbe concludes that Paul employed this verb against the background of its use by moralists to describe the sage's battle against pleasures. The implicit allusion to the two Cynic heroes is worth noting. We might also hear an echo of the πόνοι that Heracles had to face in Paul's descriptions of the difficult conditions he endured—in 2 Corinthians 6:4–5 and 11:20–27, for example.

In 1 Thessalonians, Paul is addressing the community in Thessalonica, the cosmopolitan capital of the Roman province of Macedonia. He uses the methods, vocabulary, and *topoi* of the Greek hortatory tradition, but he adapts them in order to describe himself as the bearer of a divine message ("you accepted it [the word of God that Paul brought to the Thessalonians] not as a human word but as what it really is, God's word," 2:13). Cynics of the time, by contrast, boasted of the confidence they had in themselves, comparing themselves to Heracles and declaring themselves victorious over πόνοι.[132]

In this same letter (chap. 2), Paul draws on Cynic traditions about the ideal philosopher to describe his initial ministry in Thessalonica. What he says about himself is very similar to Dio Chrysostom's description of the ideal (Cynic) philosopher: he expresses himself frankly, clearly, and guilelessly (1 Thess. 2:2–3, ἐπαρρησιασάμεθα . . . ἡ γὰρ παράκλησις ἡμῶν οὐκ

131. Abraham J. Malherbe, "The Beasts at Ephesus," in *Paul and the Popular Philosophers*, 79–89.

132. Abraham J. Malherbe, "Exhortation in 1 Thessalonians," in *Paul and the Popular Philosophers*, 49–66.

ἐκ πλάνης οὐδὲ ἐξ ἀκαθαρσίας οὐδὲ ἐν δόλῳ; *Discourse* 32.11, καθαρῶς καὶ ἀδόλως παρρησιαζόμενον).[133] However, despite these formal parallels, since the παρρησία that Paul demonstrates in his speech doesn't come from his reason or from his own will, but comes from God—which is nothing like Cynicism—Malherbe himself concludes prudently that the verbal similarities don't mean that Paul and Dio understood the same words in the same way.[134] We mustn't let the commonalities in method, expression, and even behavior mask these differences. The philosophers appealed to reason, while Paul always referred to the will of God and the action of the Holy Spirit. The philosophers highlighted results that they claimed they'd achieved, while Paul, even though he presents the (Cynic) sage as a moral paradigm, emphasizes the initiative and power of God. Many Cynics (for example, those Lucian speaks of in *The Fugitives* 17) tried to escape their work as artisans by becoming philosophers, while Paul counseled the Thessalonians to work with their own hands (1 Thess. 4:11). The Cynics advocated scandalous behavior, while Paul warned his disciples to "give no offense" (1 Cor. 10:32). Finally, the Cynics invited people to experience virtue and happiness as something they could achieve through their own natural potential; Paul wanted the people he was addressing to "discern what is the will of God" (Rom. 12:1-2). The differences between Paul and Cynicism are therefore considerable, even though the methods he employed were those of popular philosophy. According to Malherbe, because Paul was well aware of the similarities that could be recognized between Cynicism and Christianity, he worked to prevent his converts from adopting the Cynic way of life; he would have made the differences abundantly clear, so that there would have been no confusion between his message and Cynicism.

F. Gerald Downing has devoted a work specifically to *Cynics, Paul and the Pauline Churches*.[135] He insists that Paul, "hungry and thirsty, poorly clothed and beaten and homeless," weary from the work of his own hands and exposed to various torments such as insults and persecution (1 Cor. 4:11), though not a Cynic, must nevertheless have been perceived as one by the pagans of the time, and he must have been aware of this perception. When Paul says that the law makes a person a slave and that it has no le-

133. See Abraham J. Malherbe, "'Gentle as a Nurse': The Cynic Background to 1 Thessalonians 2," in *Paul and the Popular Philosophers*, 35–48, esp. 45–48.

134. Malherbe, "Gentle as a Nurse," 48.

135. F. Gerald Downing, *Cynics, Paul and the Pauline Churches* [1988], 2nd ed. (London: Routledge, 1998). A list of parallels between Paul's epistles and Cynic texts may also be found in his work *Christ and the Cynics*, 187–91.

gitimacy, his discourse is identical to that of the Cynics. So Downing can't see how Paul, given his ascetic practice, could have been seen as anything but a renegade Jewish Cynic. As a result, he doesn't hesitate to speak of a Cynicism that was Christian and Jewish, and to use the expression "a Cynic Jewish-Christian Paul" to define him. Nevertheless, he recognizes that even if Cynicism plays an important role in Paul, it's not dominant, because a major part of Paul's formation came from his Hellenistic Jewish education and there are certain evident differences—for example, Paul's attitude toward wealth (1 Cor. 13:3; 2 Cor. 8:13; 9:8), which is more nuanced than the Cynics' radical rejection of riches.[136] Downing has also attempted to highlight how, in his message to the Galatians, Paul is inspired by Cynicism in what he says and in the way he says it.[137] In Galatians 3:28 ("there is no longer Jew or Greek, slave or free, male and female; for all of you are one in Christ Jesus"), we may indeed recognize an echo both of Cynic cosmopolitanism—Paul was no doubt aware of this, and the cities of first-century Galatia would have perceived it as well—and of the idea that it's not a human being's social status, ethnic origin, or sex that determines his value, but rather each person's ability to attain, for the Cynics, virtue and happiness, and for Paul, the will of God.

While we are speaking of Paul and Cynicism, we shouldn't fail to mention the connection that has been drawn between his preaching and what is customarily called the Cynico-Stoic diatribe. Following Rudolf Bultmann,[138] but working from a new perspective, Stanley K. Stowers[139] and Thomas Schmeller[140] have taken up the problem of what influence the diatribe may have had on Paul. Stowers abandons the rigid conception that was held in the nineteenth century of the diatribe as a literary genre, but he still maintains the concept of the diatribe as a genre, along with that name. However, he reserves it for works that depict the kind of communication that was

---

136. Downing, *Cynics, Paul and the Pauline Churches*, 154.

137. F. Gerald Downing, "A Cynic Preparation for Paul's Gospel for Jew and Greek, Slave and Free, Male and Female," *NTS* 42 (1996): 454–62.

138. Rudolf Bultmann, *Der Stil der paulinischen Predigt und die kynisch-stoische Diatribe*, FRLANT 13 (Göttingen: Vandenhoeck & Ruprecht, 1910).

139. Stanley K. Stowers, *The Diatribe and Paul's Letter to the Romans*, SBLDS 57 (Chico, CA: Scholars Press, 1981).

140. Thomas Schmeller, *Paulus und die "Diatribe": Eine vergleichende Stilinterpretation*, NTAbh NF 19 (Münster in Westfalen: Aschendorff, 1987). See also Abraham J. Malherbe, "Hellenistic Moralists and the New Testament," *ANRW* 2.26.1:267–330, esp. chap. 4, devoted to the diatribe, 313–20; Fuentes González, *Les diatribes de Télès*, 44–78.

typical of a school of philosophy, understood in a broad sense, where there was a master and an audience, or where such a situation was reproduced as a "rhetorical strategy." He applies this concept to Paul because in his letters he's addressing churches that he wants to instruct and exhort, rather than crowds in the streets or marketplaces whom he wants to convert. Stowers considers the use that Paul makes in his Epistle to the Romans of the "address," of objections, and of false conclusions to be analogous to parallel phenomena in the diatribe. But Paul was able to make the diatribe style his own by adapting it to the communication of Christian beliefs and traditions and by using it within the framework of the Greek epistolary form. Thus, according to Stowers, Paul presents himself in this letter as a master dispensing his teaching to the Romans, and he consciously and deliberately uses the dialogical style of the diatribe to communicate his message. But Stowers recognizes that this letter represents a special case, since the dialogical element of the diatribe is central to the expression of its message, which is not true of Paul's other epistles.

Schmeller, for his part, believes that the use of the term διατριβή since the end of the nineteenth century to designate a literary genre of popular philosophy that conveyed moral content through a precise form is pure terminological fiction. He does grant, however, that what moderns have in mind when they use the term actually does correspond to real content (practical ethics) and a real form (dialogue with rhetorical devices) that were originally associated with oral delivery. Even though, unlike Stowers, he refuses to see the "diatribe" as a literary genre and he doesn't place it within the framework of instruction in a school, he nevertheless believes that a common structural principle ("the transformation of intellectual content into existential encouragement with an ethical message")[141] allows us to gather a certain number of ancient texts together under this name. This is why he's always careful to use the word within quotation marks. In the case of Paul, he suggests that we should distinguish between three groups of epistles: 1 Corinthians and Romans are closest to being "diatribes"; 2 Corinthians and Galatians represent a middle group; 1 Thessalonians, Philemon, and Philippians are only faintly influenced by the diatribic style.[142] However, even though he considers 1 Corinthians and Romans to be infused with this style, he acknowledges that the Pauline texts belong to theology and deal with problems connected with the working out of Christian faith, while the

---

141. Schmeller, *Paulus und die "Diatribe,"* 434.
142. Schmeller, *Paulus und die "Diatribe,"* 408.

"diatribe" proper belongs to philosophy and deals with problems of every-day life. "The 'Diatribe' refers to a general praxis that is different from that of Paul."[143] The "diatribe" is also more clearly popular; it relegates theory completely to the background, it aims to help each and every person in daily life, and it provides stereotyped solutions, which anyone can use and which are made available to everyone for whenever they're needed—for example, a reversal of values, or independence from external things. This is not the case with Paul; we can almost always recognize that a theological or controversial concern is fundamental in his letters. Even though Schmeller acknowledges that his formula is somewhat simplified, he expresses the essential difference between those passages in Paul's letters that can be associated with the dia-tribe and the diatribic texts themselves by drawing the following contrast: "In the case of Paul, it's more a matter of instruction ["Belehrung"] than of conversion ["Bekehrung"]."[144]

So, on the one hand, Paul's words have a Cynic feel to them; he bor-rowed approaches, indeed themes, from popular philosophy. But on the other hand, he was not a Cynic, and in fact he did everything he could to distinguish himself from Cynicism and to get his converts to do the same. From this we may conclude that there was a common sociocultural legacy, influenced by Cynicism but also by Stoicism, and that many people consid-ered it legitimate to draw on this legacy to express their ideas and convic-tions, especially their religious ones, though they did not actually embrace these philosophies.

143. Schmeller, *Paulus und die "Diatribe,"* 432.
144. Schmeller, *Paulus und die "Diatribe,"* 436.

4. The Relationship between Cynicism and Christianity under the Roman Empire

While much uncertainty still remains regarding the relationship between the Jesus movement and Cynicism in the first century of our era, close contacts between Cynicism and Christianity are well attested from the second century through at least the fifth. These contacts were no doubt facilitated by the fact that Christianity was no longer limited to Galilee, where it began, but had rather expanded widely throughout the countries of the Mediterranean basin. The ambivalence of the relationship is striking: in some cases Christians and Cynics regarded one another with open and mutual hostility, while in other cases they were sympathetic to one another, to the point where a person could be both a Christian and a Cynic.[1] Pagan observers, who were looking on from a distance and didn't appreciate the underlying motivations of the two movements, could even assimilate them, most often for purposes of denigration.

Cynics and Christians Compared and Assimilated

By Pagans

Pagans who weren't careful about fine distinctions could lump Christians together with Cynics and make the very same accusations against Christians

1. Cf. Marie-Odile Goulet-Cazé, "Le cynisme à l'époque impériale," *ANRW* 2.36.4:2720–833, esp. 2788–800; Gilles Dorival, "Cyniques et chrétiens au temps des Pères grecs," in *Valeurs dans le stoïcisme: Du Portique à nos jours, Mélanges en l'honneur de M. Le Doyen Spanneut* (Lille: Presses Universitaires de Lille, 1993), 57–88; Dorival, "L'image des Cyniques chez les Pères grecs," in *Le cynisme ancien et ses prolongements*, ed. Marie-Odile Goulet-Cazé and Richard Goulet (Paris: Presses Universitaires de France, 1993), 419–43.

that they used against Cynics. Christians were being accused by pagans of practicing a community of women, incestuous unions, and cannibalism. In the second century, Theophilus, bishop of Antioch, complained about such accusations bitterly in the apologetic works he addressed to Autolycus: "Godless mouths falsely accused us, the godly who are called Christians. They said that our wives are the common property of all and live in promiscuity, that we have intercourse with our own sisters, and—most godless and savage of all—that we partake of human flesh."[2] These charges must have been commonplace, because around the same time Athenagorus of Athens, another Christian apologist, writing to defend Christians against charges of atheism and immorality, mentions three accusations of the same type: atheism, "Thyestean feasts" (that is, cannibalism), and "Œdipodean intercourse."[3]

It's understandable that pagans would have identified Christians with Cynics, since both groups refused to worship the Greek gods and to obey the authorities. The second-century orator Aelius Aristides, a contemporary of Peregrinus (who was born, like him, in Mysia), criticizes certain opponents of Hellenism for such behavior in his discourse *To Plato: In Defense of the Four.*[4] He doesn't name them explicitly, but he likens them in this regard to the "impious men of Palestine":

> They [i.e., the opponents of Hellenism] give the name of sharing [κοινωνεῖν] to stealing [ἀποστερεῖν], the name of philosophy to envy, the scorn of money to want. . . . They scent them [the rich] out right away when they approach, and they take them by the hand and act as their escorts, and they promise that they will bestow virtue upon them. . . . And they hang about at the vestibules, associating more with the doorkeepers than their masters, amending their flattery with their shamelessness. . . . For these are the men who believe that shamelessness [τὴν ἀναισχυντίαν] is freedom [ἐλευθερίαν], that to be obnoxious [τὸ ἀπεχθάνεσθαι] is to speak freely

---

2. Theophilus of Antioch, *To Autolycus* 3.4 (trans. Robert M. Grant). These accusations were the very things that Christians themselves, as we shall see, would customarily accuse the Cynics of practicing, by reference to Diogenes's *Republic*. Theophilus himself accuses the Cynics of cannibalism in 3.5.

3. Athenagoras, *Embassy for the Christians* 3.1, 31.1, 32.1.

4. Charles Allison Behr, ed., *P. Aelii Aristidis: Opera quae exstant omnia* (Leiden: Brill, 1978), 1:513–16 (*Oration* 3.666–73 = Dindorf, *Discourse* 46 [2:399–406]). Behr's translation modified (*P. Aelius Aristides: The Complete Works* [Leiden: Brill, 1986], 1:274–75). Aelius Aristides defends Miltiades, Cimon, Themistocles, and Pericles against Plato, who, in the *Gorgias*, accused them of corrupting the Athenians.

[παρρησιάζεσθαι], and that to receive is a mark of philanthropy.... But now some, as I hear, have also reached this decision: to accept what is given, but to become abusive when they receive [λαμβάνοντες δὲ λοιδορεῖν]. These men alone should be classed neither among flatterers nor free men. For they deceive like flatterers, but they are insolent as if they were of higher rank [ὡς κρείττονες], since they are involved in the two most extreme and opposite evils, baseness [ταπεινότης] and willfulness [αὐθάδεια], *behaving like those impious men of Palestine* [emphasis added]. For the proof of the impiety of those people is that they do not believe in the higher powers [τοὺς κρείττους]. And these men [i.e., the opponents of Hellenism] in a certain fashion have defected from the Greek race, or rather from all that is higher [πάντων τῶν κρειττόνων].[5] ... They [i.e., the opponents of Hellenism] are the most useless of all in helping to accomplish anything which is necessary. But they are cleverest of all at housebreaking, in upsetting those within and bringing them into conflict with one another, and in claiming that they can take care of everything ... They seem to me to speak badly of everyone, not without reason, since they take great advantage of that; and even if they mention no one, they speak badly whatever they speak.... If one should take away their falsehood and malice, he has removed, as it were, the strong points of their life. (666–73)

Even though the text of Aelius Aristides isn't perfectly explicit as to the identity of the two groups he is comparing, violently condemning both for reprehensible practices, it's not difficult to recognize whom he has in mind.[6] Given the behaviors he emphasizes, the opponents of Hellenism are no doubt Cynics, as André Boulanger,[7] Pierre de Labriolle,[8] and Donald R.

5. Πάντων τῶν κρειττόνων could be either masculine or neuter. As a masculine, the expression could designate superior men (cf., e.g., Lucian, *Demonax* 11) or even superior beings—that is, the gods. It was used in that sense in the preceding lines (κρείττονες ... τοὺς κρείττους). As a neuter, it would be referring to superior values. According to Behr, *P. Aelius Aristides*, 1:477n746, οἱ κρείττονες, "an expression frequently used by Aristides," designates the gods, while τὰ κρείττονα means "the better things of life."

6. See Goulet-Cazé, "Le cynisme à l'époque impériale," 2788–89, as well as Dorival's in-depth analysis of this text in "Cyniques et chrétiens," 75–79.

7. André Boulanger, *Aelius Aristide et la sophistique dans la province d'Asie au IIe siècle de notre ère*, Bibliothèque des Écoles françaises d'Athènes et de Rome 126 (Paris: de Boccard, 1923), 250–65, esp. 262. But besides the Cynics, Boulanger also mentions the possibility that these might be Epicureans or Neopythagoreans.

8. Pierre de Labriolle, *La Réaction païenne: Étude sur la polémique antichrétienne du Ier au VIe siècle* (Paris: L'Artisan du livre, 1934), 79–87.

Dudley[9] have argued. As for the "impious men of Palestine," the expression apparently refers to Christians (Labriolle, Charles A. Behr).[10]

The testimony of Aelius Aristides is valuable because of the traits he uses to characterize the Cynics, because these traits correspond to the perception that pagans of the second century would have had of Cynicism: poverty, disregard for wealth, and begging; insulting others under the guise of frankness; impudence, baseness, arrogance, falsehood, malice. Aelius Aristides's view is perfectly in line with the one that emerges from Lucian's *Fugitives* (12, 21). As we have seen, the Cynics justified begging from the rich by appeal to the following reasoning: everything belongs to the gods; the sages are friends of the gods; since friends hold everything in common, everything also belongs to the sages; and so in the end, the Cynic who begs is simply reclaiming his due. Aelius Aristides, on the other hand, saw this as outright theft. However, the comparison his testimony draws to the "impious men of Palestine" is actually based on another aspect of Cynic behavior. Because the expression πάντων τῶν κρειττόνων is grammatically ambiguous, some doubt exists regarding the exact nature of this comparison. If the expression is masculine, then it means that, just like the Christians, who were "impious" because they didn't recognize superior *beings* (that is, the Greek gods, and perhaps also the emperors, whom they refused to worship), the Cynics also declined to show deference to superiors, meaning not just the Greek gods but also the duly constituted authorities. If the expression is neuter, the meaning would be slightly different: just as the Christians did not recognize the *values* of Greek religion and didn't respect the cult of emperor-worship, so the Cynics rejected the "superior" values of Hellenism. However, since the term is unambiguously masculine in the other two of the three cases where it's used in this passage, and since its first use (par. 671) can only be a reference to men who are considered superior, probably because of their rank, it seems preferable to understand it to be masculine in the context we are considering as well. Aelius Aristides's reaction, therefore, is that of a pagan who finds that these two groups, Cynics and Christians, are undermining Hellenism by their impiety toward the Greek gods, and no doubt also through their disrespect for the authorities—and this was objectively true of Cynics just as it was of Christians.

9. Donald R. Dudley, *A History of Cynicism: From Diogenes to the 6th Century A.D.* (London: Bloomsbury, 1937), 174.

10. Behr, *P. Aelius Aristides*, 1:477n745, refers to Lucian, *The Passing of Peregrinus* 11 and *The Lover of Lies* 16, as well as to Julian, *Discourse 7* (*Against the Cynic Heracleios*), 18 (224a). Boulanger, *Aelius Aristide*, 253n2 and 259n2–3, however, believes the reference is to Jews.

In the fourth century, the emperor Julian, though he was highly critical of the Cynics of his own day, offered high praise for their noble ancestors Diogenes and Crates, possibly to show that there was a pagan asceticism that was just as valid as Christian asceticism. He stigmatizes contemporary Cynics by calling them "Apotactites," which was "a name applied to certain [Christian] persons by the impious Galileans."[11] He accuses these of trying to "gain . . . everything from all sources," which they do by "levying tribute on specious pretexts . . . which they call 'alms'" (ἐλεημοσύνη). But besides these alms, which Julian judges to be specific to Christians, he considers that, in all other respects, the habits of the Cynics and the Apotactites are very much alike; for example, both abandon their countries, and both cause trouble in the military camp.[12] The fact that this comparison came so readily to Julian shows that the similarities in behavior between the two groups could lead people to confuse one with the other. But the links between Cynics and Christians seem to have gone well beyond such similarities. In his discourse *To the Uneducated Cynics,* Julian says disparagingly to the anonymous Cynic he's addressing, "You admire and emulate the life of wretched women"—a reference, to all appearances, to Christian nuns living in a monastery in Egypt.[13] As Julian addresses this Cynic, he uses an expression from Genesis 9:3 and adds, "You recognize, I suppose, the words of the Galileans."[14] This leads us to believe that the Cynic in question was a Christian. There are good grounds to believe, as I have argued, that this anonymous Cynic may be identified as the Christian Cynic Maximus Hero of Alexandria,[15] to whom we shall return shortly. Julian doesn't consider his interlocutor worthy of the authentic Cynicism of the past, that of Diogenes and Crates, two figures for whom he has tremendous respect and whom he discusses at length in his seventh and ninth discourses. This Cynic, moreover, had the temerity to ridicule Diogenes for eating a raw octopus, saying that when he died from it, he "paid a sufficient penalty for his folly and vanity."[16] Julian responds ironically, "It becomes you well to ridicule such

11. Julian, *Discourse 7* (*Against the Cynic Heracleios*), 18 (224a–b [trans. Wright, LCL]). This was an extremist Christian sect whose members Cassian calls *renuntiantes* (*Institutions* 4) and *abrenuntiantes* (*Conferences* 3).

12. Julian, *Discourse 7* (*Against the Cynic Heracleios*), 18 (224c).

13. Julian, *Discourse 9* (*Against the Uneducated Cynics*), 20 (203c).

14. Julian, *Discourse 9* (*Against the Uneducated Cynics*), 12 (192d).

15. Cf. Marie-Odile Goulet-Cazé, "Qui était le philosophe anonyme attaqué par Julien dans son *Discours* IX?," *Hermes* 136 (2008): 97–118.

16. Julian, *Discourse 9* (*Against the Uneducated Cynics*), 1 (180d–181a).

a man."[17] Rather than staying faithful to the Greek gods, this man was sympathetic toward the new religion, like other Cynics of the same time. This was something Julian couldn't accept. And so, as he saw it, there were two Cynicisms: one was authentic, that of Diogenes and Crates; the other had strayed from its origins and was freely consorting with Christianity.

By Christians

It wasn't only pagans who compared and assimilated Cynicism and Christianity. Among the Christians themselves, there were those who considered pagan philosophers responsible—after the fact, of course—for certain Christian heresies. This is the case, for example, with Pseudo-Hippolytus, author of the *Elenchos*, who sees in the Encratites, an extremist ascetic Christian sect founded by Tatian (a disciple of Justin), a Cynic perversion of orthodox Christianity: "Others . . . call themselves Encratites. . . . They abstain from animal foods and drink only water. They forbid their people to marry. For the rest of their lives, they devote themselves to ascetic practices. But persons of this description should be considered Cynics rather than Christians."[18] Pseudo-Hippolytus also criticizes Tatian, who "habituates himself to a very Cynical mode of life,"[19] and Marcion, the founder of another sect, for leading his disciples toward this way of life.[20] Along the same lines, Irenaeus argued that the Valentinians, a heretical sect of gnostic inspiration, had inherited certain of their views from the Cynics—for example, the indifferent character of foods and certain actions, and the belief that "they can in no degree at all contract pollution, whatever they eat or perform."[21]

But alongside these entirely abstract reconstructions by the heresiologists, it appears that a Christian could appeal to the Cynics to defend a Christian behavior against a pagan who was attacking it. In the second century, Celsus criticized Christians not only for displaying "their trickery in the market-places," and "going about begging," but also, when doing this, for "never entering a gathering of intelligent men," but rather addressing "ado-

---

17. Julian, *Discourse 9* (*Against the Uneducated Cynics*), 20 (203b).

18. Pseudo-Hippolytus, *Elenchos* 8.20.1. (The quotations in the text are from NPNF 5. J. H. MacMahon.)

19. Pseudo-Hippolytus, *Elenchos* 10.18.1 (κυνικωτέρῳ δὲ βίῳ ἀσκεῖται).

20. Pseudo-Hippolytus, *Elenchos* 7.29.2 (σχολὴν ἐσκεύασεν ἀπονοίας γέμουσαν καὶ κυνικοῦ βίου); 10.9.4 (κυνικωτέρῳ δὲ βίῳ προσάγων τοὺς μαθητάς).

21. Irenaeus, *Against Heresies* 2.14.5 (trans. Alexander Roberts and William Rambaut).

lescent boys and a crowd of slaves and a company of fools." In response, Origen cites the positive example of the Cynics, whom he praises for "conversing publicly with any whom they meet," even with "the common people."[22]

So pagans as well as Christians were capable of hasty assimilations, of amalgams, but at the same time, a Christian could appeal to a Cynic behavior in order to justify a Christian one. Concretely, what relationship did the two groups have with each another?

A Relationship of Mutual Opposition

In Actual Fact

The Martyrdom of Justin in 165

Justin received a solid philosophical foundation from his training with a Stoic, a Peripatetic, a Pythagorean, and a Platonist,[23] but he abandoned paganism after meeting an old man who told him that only the prophets had announced the truth.[24] He decided then that he would defend the Christian faith but continue to wear the mantle of a philosopher. At first he became an itinerant teacher, but he later founded a school in Rome. (Among his students was Tatian, mentioned earlier in connection with the Encratites.) Then an opponent challenged him, the Cynic Crescens, whom he regarded as a "lover of bravado [φιλόψοφος] and boasting [φιλόκομπος]," someone who spoke about Christianity without understanding it and who didn't hesitate to accuse Christians publicly of atheism and impiety in order to "win favor with the deluded mob."[25] Even though he was perfectly aware of the dangers he faced, Justin didn't pull any punches in his criticisms of Crescens. As far as he was concerned, a Cynic obviously couldn't understand any of Christ's teachings: "It is impossible for a Cynic, who makes indifference his end, to know any good but indifference."[26] When the prefect of Rome condemned three Christians to death, Justin wrote, "I too, therefore, expect to

22. Origen, *Against Celsus* 3.50 (trans. Henry Chadwick).

23. Justin, *Dialogue with Trypho*, Prologue 2.3–6. Trans. from Ante-Nicene Fathers, vol. 1.

24. Justin, *Dialogue with Trypho* 3.1 and 7.1

25. Justin, *Second Apology* 3.1 (trans. Marcus Dods and George Reith in Ante-Nicene Fathers, vol. 1).

26. Justin, *Second Apology* 3.7.

be plotted against [ἐπιβουλευθῆναι] and fixed to the stake, by some of those I have named, or perhaps by Crescens, that lover of bravado and boasting; for the man is not worthy of the name of philosopher who publicly bears witness against us in matters which he does not understand, saying that the Christians are atheists and impious, and doing so to win favor with the deluded mob, and to please them."[27]

Justin would continue to oppose Crescens in public discussions on many occasions over the course of a dozen years, and it's possible that Crescens, through his machinations, was the direct cause of Justin's martyrdom with six of his students, probably in Rome in 165 under the reign of Marcus Aurelius. This, at least, is what Tatian claimed around 171;[28] Eusebius made the same claim around the start of the fourth century.[29] What motive might have driven Crescens? Justin himself, as he envisions several scenarios that might explain this Cynic philosopher's hostile attitude toward him and toward Christianity, suggests the possibility that Crescens might fear being suspected of Christianity himself.

> For if he assails us without having read the teachings of Christ, he is thoroughly depraved, and far worse than the illiterate, who often refrain from discussing or bearing false witness about matters they do not understand. Or, if he has read them and does not understand the majesty that is in them, or, understanding it, acts thus that he may not be suspected of being such [a Christian], he is far more base and thoroughly depraved, being conquered by illiberal and unreasonable opinion and fear. For I would have you to know that I proposed to him certain questions on this subject, and interrogated him, and found most convincingly that he, in truth, knows nothing.[30]

In light of this, Stephen Benko has concluded that Crescens could have been a Christian who later became a Cynic, and that his machinations against Justin were designed to make the authorities overlook his earlier

---

27. Justin, *Second Apology* 3.1.
28. Tatian, *Address to the Greeks* 19.1.
29. Jerome, *Eusebius' Chronicle* (for the year 154) (Helm 203.13–18), and Eusebius, *Ecclesiastical History* 4.16.1 and 7, where the author presents Crescens as a man "who emulated the life and manners of the Cynics." The idea that Crescens was responsible for Justin's martyrdom is found in Photius, *Bibliotheca*, 125 (Bekker 95a.10–16), and in the *Suda*, s.v. Ἰουστῖνος, I.448 (Ada Adler, ed., *Suidae Lexicon* [Leipzig: Teubner, 1928–1938], 2:646.1–5).
30. Justin, *Second Apology* 3.3–4.

beliefs.[31] It is quite clear that the two men had several discussions and that these persuaded Justin either that Crescens knew nothing of Christian doctrine or else that, if he was familiar with it, he didn't dare admit this for fear of those who were listening.[32] Eusebius confirms that Justin frequently refuted Crescens in discussions while others were listening (ἐν διαλόγοις ἀκροατῶν παρόντων).[33] Justin began by assuming that Crescens could have had some understanding of Christian doctrine, which leads us to believe that a Christian in the middle of the second century could reasonably expect a Cynic to be familiar with Christianity. Be that as it may, was Crescens responsible for Justin's death? Since *The Acts of Martyrdom of St. Justin and His Companions* doesn't mention Crescens participating in any way in the accusation or the trial, some have expressed reservations about this theory, suggesting that Eusebius may have advanced it not on the basis of historical evidence but out of apologetic aims. Independently of their Christianity as such, Justin and his students seem to have been regarded as enemies of Marcus Aurelius because of their critical attitude toward cultural practices and the state religion. This would suffice to explain a legal proceeding whose goal was actually to destroy Justin's school.[34]

Justin's disciple Tatian not only showed unrestrained hostility toward Crescens, accusing him of pederasty and greed;[35] he also adopted a highly critical attitude toward Cynics who claimed to be self-sufficient but who, like Peregrinus Proteus, "need a currier for their wallet, and a weaver for their mantle, and a wood-cutter for their staff, and the rich [to beg from], and a cook also for their gluttony." He accuses Crescens in particular of trying to outdo a dog: "Because he does not know God, he stoops so low as to imitate an animal that's devoid of reason."[36] Even worse, Crescens, who claimed to despise death, was actually afraid of death himself.[37] (Ironically, half a century later, a Christian, Pseudo-Hippolytus, would consider Tatian himself a Cynic!)[38]

31. See Stephen Benko, *Pagan Rome and the Early Christians* (Bloomington: University of Indiana Press, 1986), 46–47.

32. Justin, *Second Apology* 3.6

33. Cf. Eusebius, *Ecclesiastical History* 4.16.1.

34. This is the view of Jakob Speigl, *Der Römische Staat und die Christen: Staat und Kirche von Domitian bis Commodus* (Amsterdam: A. M. Hakkert, 1970), 164–66.

35. Tatian, *Address to the Greeks* 19.1 (trans. Alexander Roberts and James Donaldson, Ante-Nicene Fathers, vol. 2).

36. Tatian, *Address to the Greeks* 25.1.

37. Tatian, *Address to the Greeks* 19.1.

38. Pseudo-Hippolytus, *Elenchos* 10.18.1. Cf. Speigl, *Der Römische Staat und die Christen*, 159–60, who appeals to Hippolytus in order to see in Tatian the radical Christianity of a

The Martyrdom of Apollo(nio)s Sakkeas in 180–185

During the reign of Commodus, at some point between 180 and 185, the martyr Apollos Sakkeas (whom Eusebius calls Apollonios) was put on trial before Tigidius Perennius, the prefect of the Praetorian Guard. The fact that Eusebius emphasizes his παιδεία and φιλοσοφία leaves open the possibility that he was a philosopher.[39] We know that a Cynic took part in his trial along with other sages and that this Cynic expressed his hostility toward the accused during the proceedings.[40] When Apollos reproached Perennius for being ignorant of the beauties of grace, since "the word of the Lord belongs to the heart that sees, just as light belongs to the eyes that see," the Cynic said Apollos should reproach himself, rather than Perennius, since despite all his subtlety of speech, he was the one who had gone astray. Apollos retorted that the Cynic should have learned how to pray rather than how to insult, and that his hypocrisy—something of which the Cynics were frequently accused[41]—was in keeping with the blindness of his heart.[42] We have no idea what prior relationship Apollos may have had with this Cynic, but it's legitimate to ask whether the latter may have played the same role in this trial as Crescens may have played some twenty years earlier in Justin's trial. Both proceedings ended in martyrdom, showing that the relationship between Cynics and Christians could be openly hostile.

A Cynic Persecuted by Christians in 359?

An episode took place in 359 under the reign of the Christian emperor Constantius II, whose suspicious nature made him fearful of political divination. He launched an inquiry against the devotees of the god Besa, who had an oracle at Abydum, a town in a remote part of the Thebaid in Egypt, and who was worshiped in a local cult that went back to ancient times.[43] Scythopolis in Palestine, about nineteen miles south of Lake Tiberias, was chosen

---

Cynic philosopher, but who nevertheless acknowledges, "There is, of course, no connection with the Cynic philosophy" (160n8).

39. Eusebius, *Ecclesiastical History* 5.21.1.

40. *The Acts of the Christian Martyrs* 7.33, trans. Herbert Musurillo (Oxford: Clarendon, 1972), 98.22.

41. Cf., e.g., Julian, *Discourse 9* (*To the Uneducated Cynics*), 16 (198b–c).

42. *The Acts of the Christian Martyrs* 7.32–34 (Musurillo, 98.17–27).

43. Cf. Ammianus Marcellinus, *History* 19.12.3.

as a torture center because it was isolated and because it was halfway between Antioch and Alexandria, the cities from which the accused would be brought.[44] According to Ammianus Marcellinus,[45] Demetrius, a philosopher who was surnamed Cythras, and who, though aged, was "hardy of body and mind" (*corpore durus et animo*), was tortured because he had offered sacrifices to this god Besa on several occasions. Not only didn't he deny this; he specified that he'd done so from the time he was quite young, but only to propitiate the deity. He was kept on the rack for a long time, but he never changed his story, and finally he was declared innocent and allowed to return to Alexandria, his native city. Modern scholars have surmised that this Demetrius may have been a Cynic, citing a passage in Julian's *Discourse 7: To the Cynic Heracleios* (18, 224d), where Julian mentions, among other Cynics, a certain Chytron.[46] But does the relative resemblance of the names Cythras and Chytron (Χύτρων) really allow us to equate the two men and conclude that Christians could have persecuted Cynics? Gilles Dorival disputes this hypothesis by additionally raising the issue of age: Could Demetrius, who was already aged in Alexandria in 359, really have appeared, even older, in Constantinople in 362 among those around Julian?[47] We might add further that Cynics did not customarily engage in acts of worship like this (even if the case of Asclepiades that follows provides something of a counterexample).

Christians as Scapegoats in 362?

The temple of Apollo at Daphne, a suburb of Antioch on the Orontes, burned down in October 362. The emperor Julian suspected that Christians had started the fire, on the basis that the temple had just been enclosed by a magnificent colonnade and that Christians would have resented this. But word spread that the cause of the fire was actually accidental. Apparently it was started by a certain Asclepiades, who may be identified, to all appearances, with the Cynic philosopher of the same name that Julian mentions in one of his discourses.[48] Ammianus Marcellinus relates that Asclepiades, who'd come to Daphne to visit Julian, placed a statue of the mother of the gods at

44. Cf. Ammianus Marcellinus, *History* 19.12.8.
45. Cf. Ammianus Marcellinus, *History* 19.12.12.
46. Cf. O. Seeck, "Demetrius, no. 63," *PW* 4.2:2804.
47. Dorival, "Cyniques et chrétiens," 65.
48. Julian, *Discourse 7* (*To the Cynic Heracleios*), 18 (224d).

the feet of the colossal statue of Apollo and lit some tapers. After he'd gone, in the middle of the night, some sparks from the tapers set the dry woodwork on fire, and the whole temple burned down.[49] Julian inquired into whether it had been an accident, negligence, or the work of a sacrilegious hand. He became convinced that the Christians had been responsible for the fire, and as a reprisal he ordered the Great Church of Antioch, which Constantius II had dedicated not long before, to be closed.[50] Properly speaking, these events do not illustrate a conflict between Cynics and Christians, but it is possible that, without intending to, a Cynic became the cause of retaliatory measures that the emperor Julian took against Christians.

Were Cynics and Monks Rivals in Antioch in 387?

John Chrysostom, in the last quarter of the fourth century, responds in his *Homilies* to an event that reflects a rivalry between Cynics and monks in Antioch. In 387 the Antiochenes rebelled in protest against an increase in taxes. During a riot, the statues of the emperor Theodosius and the empress Flacilla were overturned. This provided the occasion for Chrysostom to write his twenty-one homilies *On the Statues*. In *Homily 17* he lets it be known that the Cynic philosophers—he actually speaks of "Cynic garbage" (τὰ κυνικὰ καθάρματα)—fled the city and hid in caves to escape the inquest that Theodosius launched. The monks who lived in the mountains and the deserts, on the other hand, came back into the city to answer to the inquest.[51] Chrysostom's testimony doesn't establish that the Cynics were guilty; their flight might simply have been a prudent measure, since they probably realized that they could easily be used as scapegoats. Returning to them in *Homily 19*, Chrysostom contrasts these Cynics, who have "nothing to show" for their philosophy besides a "threadbare cloak" and a beard, with Christians who adorn their souls with the doctrines of the true philosophy and especially with their worthy acts. Chrysostom pursues the contrast with a particularly interesting remark about how the peasants of the countryside have been won to Christianity, the vain words of the

---

49. Ammianus Marcellinus, *History* 22.13.3.

50. Ammianus Marcellinus, *History* 22.13.1–2; Julian, *Misopogon* 15 (346b); 33 (361bc). See J. Bidez and F. Cumont, *Imp. Caesaris Flavii Claudii Iuliani Epistulae, leges, poematia, fragmenta varia* (Paris, 1922), 163–64 (no. 105).

51. John Chrysostom, *Homily 17 on the Statues*, 2 (PG 49:173d–174a).

Cynics having failed to win them over to their propaganda. According to Dorival's analysis of these passages, Cynics and Christians, not content to divide up the space (the city for the former, the desert and the mountains for the latter), competed to conquer the countryside, and it was the latter who were more successful: "Christian doctrine is in the process of spreading and replacing Hellenism. . . . There's a genuine rivalry between Cynics and Christians, a competition to convince people, and the Christians are beginning to get the advantage."[52]

We will give the last word about this opposition between Cynics and Christians—which, as we've seen, could be fierce—to the Arian Eunomius, who lived in this same time period. In a context in which he contrasts Diogenes, who answered a question with his staff, and Paul, who taught that one should "correct opponents with gentleness," Eunomius makes this observation, which basically agrees with our analysis of the preceding episodes: "The philosophy of a Cynic is vastly remote from Christianity."[53]

In Representations

The Christian Critique of Cynicism

Christians customarily made all kinds of accusations against Cynics. Their accusations became more and more stereotyped until a caricature of the Cynic philosopher emerged as hypocritical, shameless, and eager for vainglory.[54] But the Cynic trait that aroused the greatest virulence on their part was "indifference" (ἀδιαφορία). We may legitimately ask, however, why no one spoke of "Cynic indifference" until the second century of our era. In fact, the concept of indifference, though it was widely used within Stoicism in light of Zeno's and Aristo's theories of indifferents, was not part of the conceptual legacy of ancient Cynicism, even though Diogenes and his disciples practiced an actual indifference to the opinion of others. Beyond this, curiously, the majority of witnesses to this Cynic indifference that have

---

52. Dorival, "Cyniques et chrétiens," 64–65.

53. Eunomius, *Apology* 19 (trans. William Whiston).

54. For the Cynics, vain glory (κενὴ δόξα) was a glory based on vain things, those without value—for example, glorying in one's riches. But when Christians reproached the Cynics for their concern for vain glory, they were certainly also thinking of a glory that was itself vain, that was meaningless and ultimately an evidence of pride.

come down to us, both pagan and Christian,[55] associate it with breaches of modesty that flouted the judgment of society, while these were not the implications of the concept within Stoicism. The Cynics were strongly criticized for things they did in public without feeling any shame, on the grounds that they were only trying to do what was good according to nature and mocking what was good by convention (τὸ θέσει καλόν).[56] Christians hardly bore Cynics taking no account of δόξα—that is, both the opinion of others and the good or bad reputation that society confers on its members as a result of their actions. To explain the connotation of immodesty that was linked with Cynic indifference, we have advanced the hypothesis that, in the second century of our era, people must have made an association in their minds between the provocative behavior of the earliest Cynics, which was accompanied by a total indifference to the judgments of others, to the point where they didn't hesitate to go head-on against the modesty of their contemporaries, and the theory of fully undifferentiated indifferents inherited from Aristo of Chios, according to which δόξα was certainly one of those indifferents.[57]

Disapproval mounted on all sides against these "Dogs" who were spreading an indecency that actually reflected the most authentic tradition of Diogenes. The Cynic in Lucian's *Philosophies for Sale* gives the following advice: "Do boldly in full view of all what another would not do in secret."[58] Christians envisioned definite content behind this concept of Cynic indifference, specifically all the scandalous acts that Diogenes described in his *Republic*, especially incest, parricide, cannibalism, and nonburial. Christians' bad faith in this regard reached its height when, under their pens, Cynics, along with Stoics, were transformed into actual cannibals. If these critics are to be believed, Cynics and Stoics even committed murder! Along these lines, Theophilus of Antioch refers to "the ideas of Zeno or Diogenes and Cleanthes as contained in their books, which advocate canibalism and the cooking and eating of fathers by their own children, and teach that if anyone refuses to eat or rejects some part of the abominable food, he who does not eat is to be eaten. In addition to these, a more godless voice is heard, that of Diogenes, who teaches that children should lead their own parents to the

55. These witnesses are collected in Marie-Odile Goulet-Cazé, *Les "Kynika" du stoïcisme*, Hermes Einzelschriften 89 (Stuttgart: Steiner, 2003), 112–19.

56. These two concepts are used by Olympiodorus in a passage in which he explains how Cynic philosophers got that name: *In Aristotelis Categorias Prolegomena*, CAG 12.1 (Busse 3.21–28).

57. Goulet-Cazé, *Les "Kynika" du stoïcisme*, 129–32.

58. Lucian, *Philosophies for Sale* 10.

slaughter and eat them."[59] Theophilus declares that such "indifferent" Cynic behaviors as illicit sexual unions and the practice of cannibalism are incompatible with Christian teaching.[60] The way certain Christians told it, Cynics reenacted the tragedy of Atreus and Thyestes in daily life. Two centuries later, John Chrysostom accused philosophers who "wore a long beard and assumed the grave cloak" of practicing a community of women and children,[61] while Theodoret of Cyrus paints a portrait of Diogenes as a slave of pleasure who consorted with prostitutes, and he recalls the "dog's marriage" that Crates consummated in public.[62] In the same way, Augustine devotes a chapter to the Cynics in *The City of God* (book 14, chap. 20) with the evocative title *De vanissima turpitudine Cynicorum* ("On the Utterly Absurd Indecency of the Cynics"). Deeply disturbed and shocked by the Cynics' assault on modesty (*verecundia*), he saw their doctrine as an *inmunda inpudensque sententia* ("base and shameless" opinion),[63] although he also noted that a "natural sense of shame" had ultimately restrained them so that in his day no Cynic would perform the matrimonial act in public.[64]

Many other Cynic traits also drew sharp criticism from Christians.[65] Tatian reproaches them for their boastfulness (ἀλαζονεία) and for their wild and pompous speech (τὴν ἔντυφον . . . γλωσσομανίαν), which is a paradoxical claim to make about people who had always opposed the deceptions

---

59. Theophilus of Antioch, *To Autolycus* 3.5 (trans. Robert M. Grant). See also 3.4.

60. Theophilus of Antioch, *To Autolycus* 3.15.

61. John Chrysostom, *Homily 5 on the Epistle to Titus*, 4 (PG 62:694, trans. *NPNF*, vol. 13).

62. Theodoret of Cyrus, *Therapeutic for Hellenic Maladies* 12.48–49.

63. Augustine, *City of God* 14.20 (trans. Philip Levine, LCL). Augustine is arguing that Cynic doctrine is base and shameless because the ancient Cynics went so far as to claim that "since the act is lawful when it is done with a wife, no one should feel ashamed to do it openly and engage in marital intercourse on any street or square." He actually attenuates the effrontery of these philosophers somewhat by speculating that the people who witnessed them supposedly copulating beneath a cloak didn't see what was actually happening: "I prefer to think that Diogenes and others who reputedly did such a thing rather acted out the motions of lying together before the eyes of men who really did not know what was done under the cloak, I do not believe that there could have been any achievement of such pleasure under the glare of human gaze" (*City of God* 14.20). In the case of Crates and Hipparchia, we may think that the interpretation of Augustine is too prudish.

64. Augustine, *City of God* 14.20: "Yet none of them dares to behave so, for it would bring down upon any who had dared a shower, if not of stones, at any rate of spittle from the outraged public."

65. On all these themes, see Dorival, "L'image des Cyniques," 420–30.

of pride and illusions of all sorts.[66] Cynics were also accused of hypocrisy by Tatian[67] as well as by Apollos, as he responded to the anonymous Cynic who reproached him during his trial.[68] John Chrysostom also suggests that these philosophers, sheltered behind their outfits, could be hypocrites,[69] and Lactantius similarly suggests that their long hair and cloaks concealed their vices.[70] Other Christian authors go so far as to deny that Cynic asceticism has any value, so long as it's not accompanied by Christian virtues. Thus Palladius speaks of an overflow of vainglory (κουφοδοξία) on the part of Pythagoras, Diogenes, and Plato because they drank only water,[71] and Nilus of Ancyra accuses the Cynics of practicing their asceticism, in the absence of Christian hope, out of nothing more than ostentation and love for glory (χάριν ἐπιδείξεως καὶ φιλοδοξίας).[72] Isn't it the height of insanity, he asks, to keep silent, eat only vegetables, cover the body with worn-out rags, and spend one's life enclosed in a barrel, but then not receive any reward for it after death? Without Christian faith, such asceticism is simply meaningless; all these efforts produce nothing but sweat. Eager to discredit these philosophers who were sometimes able to compete with them in the moral field, various Christians from the second century through the fourth declared that Cynicism itself was completely useless.[73]

But Christians didn't just criticize the Cynic philosophers; they also mocked them for being "hairy as goats" (*hircosus Cynicus*)[74] and for carrying a "Herculean club" (*Herculea clava*).[75] In the fifth century, an author such as

66. Tatian, *Address to the Greeks* 2.1 and 3.3.

67. Tatian, *Address to the Greeks* 19.1 (Crescens taught that we should despise death, but he was afraid of it himself); 25.1 (Peregrinus Proteus claimed not to need anything but in fact he satisfied a great number of needs in his manner of dressing and living).

68. *The Acts of the Christian Martyrs* 7.34 (Musurillo, 98.25–26).

69. John Chrysostom, *On Virginity* 7.1.

70. Lactantius, *Divine Institutes* 5.2–3.

71. Palladius, *Lausiac History*, Prologue 11.

72. Nilus of Ancyra, *Ascetic Discourse* 2 (PG 79:720b–721a). Cf. Theodoret of Cyrus, *Therapeutic for Hellenic Maladies* 12.31–32.

73. Theophilus of Antioch, *To Autolycus* 3.2; John Chrysostom, *Homily 10 on Matthew*, 4 (PG 57:188); *Homily 35 on 1 Corinthians*, 4 (PG 61:302); and *On Babylas* 45–49, where, to draw a contrast with Babylas, he chooses Diogenes as his target and accuses him of seeking vainglory through his frank speech, of being indifferent to cannibalism, and of being licentious and irresponsible. Cf. Derek Krueger, "Diogenes the Cynic among the Fourth Century Fathers," *VC* 47 (1993): 29–49, esp. 39; on the Father's criticisms of Diogenes, see Horst Kusch, "Diogenes von Sinope," *RAC* 3:1063–75, esp. 1072–74.

74. Prudence, *Apotheosis*, 201.

75. Prudence, *Hamartigenia*, 401.

Sidonius Apollinaris could explain, in a letter addressed to Pope Faustus, that the Cynics, along with the Stoics and Peripatetics, would be "shattered with their own arms and their own engines," because the "barbed syllogisms" that Faustus would use himself would "hook the glib tongues of the casuists."[76] He foresaw their defeat as imminent, but at the same time he recognized that they were resisting.[77]

Were These Severe Judgments Justified?

Such a caricaturized picture rests on misrepresentation and polemical malice, but also, and perhaps primarily, on the awareness of a genuine danger. Might the misrepresentations of certain Christians not have been intentional? Were they the result of ignorance, or of an intentional desire to deceive? Since we know that second-century writers such as Theophilus of Antioch[78] and Clement of Alexandria[79] did read Diogenes, it's legitimate to wonder whether some Christians didn't decide deliberately to leave out the Cynics' philosophical perspective, which was the only thing that could account for why they expressed ideas that seemed so scandalous at first glance. Diogenes allowed in his *Republic*, at least on a theoretical basis, all the acts that could be performed in a state of nature that was assumed to be prior to civilization. And once it was accepted that nothing that was natural could really be shameful, then modesty was a sentiment that Diogenes didn't need to take into account.[80] He was a libertarian anarchist who was eager to dismantle the mechanisms of a society that required individuals to judge certain behaviors reprehensible on the basis of its own categories of good and evil. And so he sought his examples in the behaviors of animals,[81] barbarian peoples,[82] and children[83]—in other words, in places where civilization with its traditions and conventions hadn't been able to carry out its work of enslavement. Diogenes wasn't asking man to regress to an animal state, but rather to recover his own unique nature—which was close to that of animals

---

76. Sidonius Apollinaris, *Letters* 9.9.15 (trans. William B. Anderson, LCL).
77. Sidonius Apollinaris, *Carmen* 15.124–25.
78. Theophilus of Antioch, *To Autolycus* 3.5.
79. Clement of Alexandria, *Miscellanies* 2.20.119.5–6.
80. See above, pp. 34–35.
81. E.g., Diogenes Laertius, *Lives* 6.22; Dio Chrysostom, *Discourse* 6.13, 16, 18.
82. Cf. Diogenes Laertius, *Lives* 6.73.
83. Cf. Diogenes Laertius, *Lives* 6.37.

but at the same time very different because of the presence of the *logos*—a nature that man had perverted by inventing civilization with its assortment of irrational conventions.[84] While Diogenes's attitude was perfectly coherent intellectually, it remained theoretical to a certain extent. While he refused to condemn incest and cannibalism, he certainly never practiced such acts himself, nor did he encourage others to do so. This could be the essence of the misunderstanding. On the one hand, Philodemus and Christian writers present such acts as being proscribed or prohibited by Diogenes. Describing the views of Diogenes's *Republic*, Philodemus writes, "People *have to* kill their parents [i.e., in order to eat them],"[85] and Theophilus claims that the books of Zeno, Diogenes, and Cleanthes all advocate cannibalism.[86] But on the other hand, we read in Diogenes Laertius and Sextus that it was *not improper* (οὐκ ἄτοπον) to eat human flesh.[87] It wasn't improper, because it was "according to nature" (κατὰ φύσιν), and the criteria of social morality shouldn't be applied to nature. In all likelihood, Philodemus and Theophilus are advancing a slanderous interpretation of Diogenes's writings. In two ways they are falsely describing these acts that were not improper from a theoretical point of view: first, by connecting them with murder, which was totally incompatible with the respect that Cynics had for the liberty of others; and second, by describing them as obligatory. Theophilus and certain other Christians are therefore misrepresenting Diogenes's meaning, no doubt intentionally. Diogenes succeeded in regrounding morality by ridding it of all opinions and conventions that had nothing to do with virtue; in order to do this, he was obliged, at least on a theoretical level, as is the case in his *Republic*, to accept nature—all of nature. By refusing to understand this perspective, or at least to take it into account, Christians turned Cynics into cannibals, parricides, and degenerates of the worst kind.

This misrepresentation was accompanied by open polemical malice, comparable to the type that could be expressed toward Cynics by pagan writers such as Lucian in *The Fugitives* and his treatise *The Passing of Peregrinus*, Porphyry in his treatise *On Abstinence*,[88] and Julian.[89] To say that Cynic philosophy was useless, that Diogenes's disciples were hypocrites, that their actions deliberately contradicted their doctrines, and that they were only

---

84. Diogenes Laertius, *Lives* 6.44.
85. Philodemus, *On the Stoics* 7 (col. 20.3) (Dorandi, "Filodemo, Gli Stoici," 103).
86. Theophilus of Antioch, *To Autolycus* 3.5.
87. Diogenes Laertius, *Lives* 6.73; Sextus, *Outlines of Pyrrhonism* 3.207.
88. Porphyry, *On Abstinence* 1.42.5.
89. Julian, *Discourse 9* (*To the Uneducated Cynics*), 16 (198b–c).

after vainglory—this was the most traditional kind of polemic (since pagans said the same things) and the most unfair. It was the same polemic that the Christians mounted against the Epicureans, whom they readily associated with the Cynics.[90] As Dorival has aptly observed,[91] the one way in which the church fathers were original in their polemic against the Cynics, compared with the pagans, was to turn them into representatives par excellence of Hellenism, and so an ideal foil.

Why did the fathers react in this way? No doubt they were aware of the danger that the Cynics represented. They saw them as potential rivals, and often they were actual ones. From the outside, it was easy to confuse the two groups. Cynic asceticism, in its particular forms, had much in common with Christian asceticism of the first centuries, even if the goal was not the same. Cynics and Christians both denounced society and its false values—riches, glory, and so on. The two groups had the same insistence on authenticity and radicalism, and both believed that they'd been sent on a mission to their contemporaries. Even though the two movements were completely different in spirit, pagans could nevertheless confuse them, and such confusions appear to have been frequent, especially in the case of ascetic Christian sects, as we've already seen with the Encratites and Apotactites. As a result, it was important for Christians to distinguish themselves clearly from these cumbersome rivals who were causing such a stir in the great cities of the Roman Empire. This was all the more true because Cynicism—and this may have been the greatest danger—was attractive to Christians themselves, causing embarrassment but also inspiring admiration, to the point where some declared themselves to be both Cynics and Christians.

Ambivalent Attitudes

A Certain Admiration

Since a number of Cynic values converged with Christian ones, independently of any telos, it is not all that surprising that we find some Christians expressing an admiration for Cynicism. However, it's important to

90. Cf. Sidonius Apollinaris, *Carmen* 2.164–68: "the company of Cynics . . . copying the disciples of Epicurus" (trans. William B. Anderson); Claudianus Mamertus, *De statu animae* 2.9 (Engelbrecht 113.15).
91. Dorival, "L'image des Cyniques," 432.

note that this admiration was for the earlier Cynics, Diogenes and Crates, and in particular for their physical asceticism with a moral goal. The case of Clement of Alexandria illustrates this positive disposition. He appeals to Diogenes, for example, in his denunciation of effeminacy, recalling that this philosopher, when he was being sold as a slave, said to one of those who was thinking of buying him, "Come youngster, buy for yourself a man!"[92] But Clement especially recognizes in Cynicism certain values with which he is in agreement himself. In his *Miscellanies*, for example, he says that he agrees with Antisthenes's condemnation of Aphrodite, of the kind of lust and pleasure that this philosopher calls a "vice of nature."[93] He notes a similarity of thought between the prophetic word of Isaiah, "To whom have you likened me? says the Lord," and Antisthenes's statement that "God is like no one; wherefore no one can come to the knowledge of Him from an image."[94] (Clement specifies, however, that in this case it's the disciple of Socrates, rather than the Cynic, who's speaking.)

But the qualities that Cynics demonstrated that Christians valued most highly were no doubt poverty and self-control. In *Against Celsus*, Origen goes so far as to make a very complimentary allusion to a Cynic philosopher: "Some time ago the Greek philosopher who loved poverty and set an example of a happy life to show that he was not prevented from being happy by being entirely without possessions, called himself a Cynic."[95] Is he speaking of Diogenes, or of Crates? The mention of εὐτέλεια, "frugality," has led some to think of the hymn that Crates composed specifically to frugality,[96] but since Origen also associates Diogenes with frugality in another passage in this work,[97] that argument is not definitive. Specifically in that other passage, Origen is seeking to refute an educated Jew to whom Celsus is appealing, who claims that "Jesus did not show himself to be pure from all evils." In response, Origen defines what evil is, envisioning the hypothesis that it might consist in "poverty and the cross . . . and conspiracy of wicked men." He observes that in the last case, Socrates himself wouldn't be able to prove that he was pure from all evil. As for poverty, he appeals to the host of philosophers who chose it voluntarily: Socrates and Democritus, but also Crates, who sold

92. Clement of Alexandria, *Christ the Educator* 3.3.16.1 (trans. William Wilson).

93. Clement of Alexandria, *Miscellanies* 2.20.107.2–3; see also 2.20.121.1.

94. Clement of Alexandria, *Miscellanies* 5.14.108.4. Similarly *Exhortation to the Greeks* 6.71.2.

95. Origen, *Against Celsus* 6.28 (trans. Henry Chadwick).

96. Julian, *Discourse 9 (To the Uneducated Cynics)*, 16 (198d).

97. Origen, *Against Celsus* 2.41.

everything he had and distributed the money among the Thebans, as well as Diogenes, who "used to live in a tub on account of his abject poverty." He concludes that "yet no person even of mean intelligence thinks that on this account Diogenes was subject to evils."[98] Origen therefore doesn't hesitate to refer to pagan philosophers, and notably Cynics, to defend Jesus against the attacks of Celsus's Jew. This is a clear indication that in his time Cynic heroes continued to be admired, even in Christian circles. Nevertheless, when it comes to comparing the "firm" (literally, "well-tight," εὔτονος) life of the prophets with the firmness of Antisthenes, Diogenes, and Crates, it's quite evident that Origen considers the former to have held the advantage.[99] Another example is highly illustrative because it has to do with providing examples of virtuous philosophers to help young Christians of the fourth century in their formation: Basil of Caesarea, in his *Address to Young Men on Reading Greek Literature*, says that he admires "the scorn of Diogenes for all human goods without exception,"[100] and he also appeals to the Cynic philosopher when he wants to stigmatize spending excessive time "on the care of the hair or on dress."[101] Under the pen of Jerome, Diogenes appears as "the conqueror of human nature," whose death demonstrated his courage and self-mastery,[102] and even Theodoret, who, as we saw earlier, could be very severe with regard to Diogenes,[103] recognizes Antisthenes, Diogenes, and Crates as "athletes of virtue"—even though he considers Christian "athletes" superior to them, since they strive for the good in and of itself, and not, like the Cynics, for vainglory.[104] In his *Discourse on Providence*, written shortly after 435, he cites Socrates, Diogenes, and Anaxarchus as examples of people who renounced riches and led a life of poverty.[105] Nilus of Ancyra, the author of a treatise *On Voluntary Poverty*, expresses the same kind of admiration for those Greek philosophers who practiced poverty, living outdoors the way dogs do and eating whatever they could find. To illustrate his point, he cites

98. Origen, *Against Celsus* 2.41.

99. Origen, *Against Celsus* 7.7.

100. Basil, *Address to Young Men on Reading Greek Literature* 9.112–15 (trans. Roy J. Deferrari, LCL).

101. Basil, *Address to Young Men on Reading Greek Literature* 9.15–17. Krueger, "Diogenes the Cynic," 35–36, emphasizes the major influence that this work had; it was translated into Syriac several times, both in late antiquity and in the Byzantine epoch.

102. Jerome, *Against Jovinianus* 2.14.

103. Theodoret, *Therapeutic for Hellenic Maladies* 12.48.

104. Theodoret, *Therapeutic for Hellenic Maladies* 12.32.

105. Theodoret, *Discourse on Providence* 6 (PG 83:649.43).

the famous anecdote, though without mentioning Diogenes by name, of the philosopher casting away the cup he had been using for eating and drinking after he saw young shepherds drinking water from their cupped hands.[106] And so it wasn't shocking—instead, it was actually rather natural—to recommend as models for Christians those Cynic philosophers whose moral stature allowed them to be considered "athletes of virtue."

Eusebius of Caesarea's Appeal to Oenomaus of Gadara

The only major work that Cynicism produced under the Roman Empire was by Oenomaus of Gadara (second century or start of the third). This was *Charlatans Exposed* (Γοήτων φώρα), a highly virulent work against divination. In order to fight Hellenism, Eusebius of Caesarea appeals to this work,[107] citing long extracts from it in his *Preparation for the Gospel*, written between 312 and 322.[108] Eusebius skillfully draws from the Cynic an entire stock of arguments designed to fortify his own polemic against the pagans. Oenomaus launches an all-out attack against the Delphic oracles, which he says aim only at deceiving the crowds;[109] against the guardians of the temples, whom he reproaches for their fraudulent activities, since they practice a divination that deceives people and incites their consultants to go to war against one another, rather than being arbiters of peace;[110] against the gods, whom he criticizes directly[111] (Apollo is called a "sophist"[112]); and against the people who believe in divination.[113] Oenomaus also takes on the philosophical schools, attacking determinists like Democritus and fatalists like Chrysippus, convinced that human freedom must be defended against Fate. Since Oenomaus is serving his cause, though indirectly and from the

---

106. Nilus of Ancyra, *On Voluntary Poverty* 39 (PG 79:1017a–b). Dorival, "L'image des cyniques," 436, appeals to the contradiction between this passage and the one from *Ascetic Discourse* cited above (p. 212) to formulate the hypothesis that this treatise may actually be from a Pseudo-Nilus.

107. The fragments have been edited, with commentary, by Jürgen Hammerstaedt, *Die Orakelkritik des Kynikers Oenomaus*, Beiträge zur klassischen Philologie 188 (Frankfurt am Main: Athenäum, 1988).

108. Eusebius, *Preparation for the Gospel* 5.18.6–36.5 and 6.7.1–42.

109. Eusebius, *Preparation for the Gospel* 5.21.6.

110. Eusebius, *Preparation for the Gospel* 5.26.5.

111. Eusebius, *Preparation for the Gospel* 5.19.3.

112. Eusebius, *Preparation for the Gospel* 5.26.3.

113. Eusebius, *Preparation for the Gospel* 5.26.2–3.

distance of two centuries, Eusebius doesn't fail to highlight his qualities: he cites his "vigorous argument,"[114] his "fine vigorous spirit,"[115] his "plain speaking," and his "Cynical bitterness."[116] This work by Oenomaus was well known among Christians. It's actually possible that Clement of Alexandria read it and at different times drew various themes from it that are found in several of his works.[117] Origen, the author of *Contra Celsus*, no doubt also read it, and he was possibly the one who subsequently brought the volume to Caesarea, where Eusebius was later able to read it in the library of his master Pamphilus.[118] Theodoret quotes extracts from Oenomaus, which he draws from Eusebius's *Preparation for the Gospel*.[119] Cyril of Alexandria, in his work against Julian,[120] and John Chrysostom, in his discourse *On Babylas* against Julian,[121] demonstrate that they're aware of the work. It's certainly the Cynic work produced under the Roman Empire that had the greatest influence on Christianity. But by contrast, the emperor Julian severely denounced Oenomaus as a man without modesty or shame, who scorned everything human or divine, and whom he considered dangerous for his project of restoring Hellenism.[122]

The Sometimes-Ambivalent Attitude of Christians

Curiously, some Christian writers didn't manage to adopt a coherent attitude toward Cynicism, so that we witness the same person taking contradictory positions. This ambivalence is explained by the coexistence of two sentiments that were impossible to reconcile: on the one hand, the attraction that Christians felt toward the authentic asceticism of the Cynics, and on the other hand, the repulsion that the Cynics provoked through their immodesty, their impudence, and what Christians considered to be their

---

114. Eusebius, *Preparation for the Gospel* 5.18.6 (trans. Edwin Hamilton Gifford).

115. Eusebius, *Preparation for the Gospel* 6.6.74.

116. Eusebius, *Preparation for the Gospel* 5.21.6.

117. Cf. Hammerstaedt, *Die Orakelkritik des Kynikers Oenomaus*, 22–24.

118. Cf. Andrew Carriker, *The Library of Eusebius of Caesarea*, VCSup 67 (Leiden: Brill, 2003), 96.

119. Theodoret, *Therapeutic for Hellenic Maladies* 6.8–11 and 10.41–42.

120. Cyril of Alexandria, *Against Julian* 6.204 (PG 76:812d).

121. John Chrysostom, *On Babylas* 2.80, 88.

122. Cf. Julian, *Discourse 9* (*To the Uneducated Cynics*), 17 (199a); *Discourse 7* (*Against the Cynic Heracleios*), 5 (209b).

false wisdom. We may cite two significant examples. John Chrysostom, who spoke in his *Homily 17* of the Cynics as "garbage" and criticized their uselessness, presents Diogenes in another of his writings as an example of freely assumed poverty, declares him to be richer than the kings of the earth, and offers him as an example of the ascetic life![123] Origen, for his part, is capable both of comparing the fourth plague of Egypt, the "dog-fly" (also known as the horsefly), to "the sect of Cynics who, in addition to other depravities of their deception, proclaim pleasure and lust as the highest good,"[124] and of admiring the extreme poverty of Diogenes as well as the freedom Crates demonstrated when he distributed all of his money among the Thebans.[125]

Despite this ambivalence, which must have been quite widespread, there were some who claimed to be both Christians and Cynics without this situation appearing contradictory in their eyes or in the eyes of those around them. There were not many such cases, but the fact that they existed at all is proof enough that some people were able to find a balance and belong to both groups.

Cynic and Christian at the Same Time

Justin suggests that the Cynic Crescens could have been a Christian and that he could conspire against him and provoke his martyrdom out of opportunism, in order to get the authorities to overlook his Christian past. Whether things actually happened the way Justin feared remains a hypothesis. By contrast, in the two cases we are about to examine, we're no longer dealing with a hypothesis; it's clearly attested that Peregrinus and Maximus were Cynics and Christians at the same time, the former at a certain period in his life and the latter for his whole life.

The Troubling Case of Peregrinus Proteus

Peregrinus is certainly an exceptional figure; his colorful life, full of adventures, which ended in a voluntary death on a pyre near Olympia, was defi-

---

123. John Chrysostom, *Against the Opponents of the Monastic Life* 2.4 and 2.5 (PG 47:337 and 339).

124. Origen, *Homily 4 on Exodus*, 6(PG12:322b) (trans. Ronald E. Heine).

125. Origen, *Against Celsus* 2.41.

nitely lived outside normal bounds.[126] But he had the misfortune to have a biographer who despised Christianity and, moreover, wanted to ridicule Cynicism at his expense. Lucian was completely hostile to Peregrinus and, probably quite unfairly, left a most unflattering portrait of him to posterity. His treatise *The Passing of Peregrinus* is actually a work motivated by bad faith; fortunately, it can be corrected from the countertestimony of Aulus Gellius. It reveals how exasperated Lucian was by this complex individual who took the surnames Proteus and Phoenix, and who, at the end of a troubled childhood (if Lucian can be believed), chose to become a Christian, then appeared as a Christian Cynic, and finally renounced Christianity to follow Cynicism exclusively. Even though Lucian had only a partial understanding of Christianity, and even though we have to ignore all the slanderous insinuations his text contains, it remains a witness of primary interest regarding Palestinian Christianity in the second century.

The Christian Phase and the Break with Christianity

Lucian insists that Peregrinus played a leading role within the Christian community in Palestine, where he not only held several positions at once but also worked as an exegete and wrote many works of his own on Christian themes (*The Passing of Peregrinus* 11). When he was imprisoned in Palestine because of his faith, the Christians there made every possible effort to get him freed. When they found that this was no use, they showered him zealously with all kinds of attention. From the break of day, aged widows and orphan children could be seen waiting near the prison, while Christian dignitaries, after bribing the guards, slept inside the building with him, brought in elaborate meals, and read their sacred books out loud to him. The Christians called Peregrinus "the new Socrates" (12), probably by allusion to Socrates's own imprisonment. The mobilization on his behalf was impressive. People came without hesitation from cities in Asia, sent by the Christian communities there to help, defend, and encourage him. Because of his imprisonment, Peregrinus received many monetary gifts from them, from which "he procured not a little revenue," Lucian claims maliciously,

---

126. See Peter Pilhofer et al., eds., *Lukian, Der Tod des Peregrinos: Ein Scharlatan auf dem Scheiterhaufen*, Sapere 9 (Darmstadt: Wissenschaftliche Buchgesellschaft, 2005); Heinz-Günther Nesselrath, "Lukian von Samosata," *RAC* 23:676–702, esp. 692–93; Marie-Odile Goulet-Cazé, "Pérégrinus surnommé Proteus," *DPhA* 5a:199–230.

using the occasion to mock the gullibility of the Christians who gave Peregrinus their goods: "The poor wretches [οἱ κακοδαίμονες] have convinced themselves, first and foremost, that they are going to be immortal and live for all time, in consequence of which they despise death and even willingly give themselves into custody." Lucian doesn't hesitate to present Peregrinus as a "charlatan and trickster, able to profit by occasions" (γόης καὶ τεχνίτης ἄνθρωπος καὶ πράγμασιν χρῆσθαι δυνάμενος) and to exploit the credulity of these "simple folk" (ἰδιῶται) whose "first lawgiver"—probably Christ, though possibly Paul—"persuaded them that they are all brothers of one another, so that they despise all things indiscriminately and consider them common property, receiving such doctrines traditionally without any definite evidence" (13).[127]

Once Peregrinus had been set free by the governor of Syria (who did this, according to Lucian, to thwart his plans to "gladly die in order to leave behind a glorious reputation"), he returned to his home in Parium. It was there, before the assembly of the Parians, that he appeared for the first time dressed as a Cynic: long hair, dirty mantle, sack and staff. Just as Crates had distributed his goods, Peregrinus there renounced everything his father had left him as an inheritance, making it a gift to the city, which led to him being acclaimed by the poor as "The one and only philosopher! The one and only patriot! The one and only disciple of Diogenes and Crates!" (15)—in other words, the Cynic par excellence.

He left Parium for a second time and resumed an itinerant life, but the Christians made sure that he lacked nothing. "He fattened himself thus for a time" (χρόνον μέν τινα), Lucian specifies. But shortly after his second departure from Parium, he broke with the Christian community. Lucian suggests an explanation, without insisting that it's the real one: "Then, after he had transgressed in some way even against them—he was seen, *I think*, eating some of the food that is forbidden them—they no longer accepted him" (16, emphasis added).

Before we seek to determine the value of Lucian's testimony, we should pause to consider the titles he attributes to Peregrinus within the Christian community in Palestine.

127. English translations are by Austin M. Harmon, LCL. Cf. Acts 2:44–45, "All who believed were together and had all things in common; they would sell their possessions and goods and distribute the proceeds to all, as any had need"; cf. Acts 4:32.

Peregrinus's Titles and Functions

The main problem posed by the pages that Lucian devotes to the Christianity of Peregrinus arises from the vocabulary he uses to designate both the people who held positions of responsibility in the Palestinian community (priests and scribes) and the functions that Peregrinus fulfilled within that same community (prophet, cult leader, head of synagogue, lawgiver, and protector). At first these seem to be precise terms, but to what functions do they actually correspond?

> It was then that he learned the remarkable wisdom of the Christians [τὴν θαυμαστὴν σοφίαν τῶν χριστιανῶν], by associating in Palestine with their priests and scribes [τοῖς ἱερεῦσιν καὶ γραμματεῦσιν]. And how else could it be? In a trice he made them all look like children, for all by himself he was prophet, cult-leader and head of the synagogue [προφήτης καὶ θιασάρχης καὶ ξυναγωγεύς]. He interpreted and explained some of their books and even composed many himself. They revered him as a god [θεόν], made use of him as a lawgiver [νομοθέτῃ] and set him down as a protector [προστάτην], next after that other whom they still worship, the man who was crucified in Palestine because he introduced this new cult into the world.[128]

When Peregrinus decided to embrace Christian doctrines and he entered the Palestinian community, he associated with ἱερεῖς and with γραμματεῖς, two categories that must therefore correspond to two important functions within the community. In actuality, by the time of Peregrinus there were no longer any priests within Judaism—the priests had officiated in the temple in Jerusalem, but that was in a long bygone era, before its destruction in 70 CE—and there were none within Christianity, either: not ἱερεῖς but πρεσβύτεροι are recognized in the New Testament era.[129] By contrast, we need to be more nuanced regarding the function of the scribe.[130] Well attested in the Old Testament, the scribe also features in Jesus's commission-

128. Lucian, *The Passing of Peregrinus* 11.

129. In Rev. 20:6, ἱερεύς doesn't designate a function. Contrary to that of the πρεσβύτερος (Titus 1:5; James 5:14), the function of a ἱερεύς didn't exist in the primitive church.

130. The primary function of the scribe within Judaism was to write and copy documents; scribes therefore played an important role in the villages as well as in the cities, in the temple as well as at the court. The scribe was also an expert in the Scriptures.

ing of his followers, when he envisions very positively the case of a Jewish scribe who might become a disciple of the kingdom ("every scribe who has been trained for the kingdom of heaven is like the master of a household who brings out of his treasure what is new and what is old," Matt. 13:52) and when he declares to the hypocritical scribes and Pharisees that he will send them "prophets, sages, and scribes" (Matt. 23:34). At the time of the earliest Christian communities, some Jewish scribes left Judaism to follow Christ, and they were able thereby to make Jewish wisdom and Christian faith flourish together. Could Peregrinus have met such Christian scribes? Two unknowns keep us from answering. First, we don't know whether what Matthew says during the 70s CE would still apply during the years 120–130, when Peregrinus was in Palestine. Beyond this, even if there still were scribes within the Christian communities (ones that had converted to Christianity in earlier decades), we don't know whether they would have continued to fulfill their former function as scribes.

An examination of the trilogy προφήτης καὶ θιασάρχης καὶ ξυναγωγεύς also raises more questions than it answers. We may justifiably ask whether these titles correspond to specific functions that Peregrinus may have fulfilled with the Christian community of Palestine. We've just seen that the term προφήτης is used in Matthew 23:34 in the context of sending forth in mission. It's also used in Matthew 10:41 in that same context. It's found again in the *Didache*, a work produced between 100 and 150 within a community of converted Jews in Syria, where we hear of prophets who go from community to community and who have the right to celebrate the Eucharist (10). So the prophet was a familiar reality within the earliest Christian communities, and also within those of the early second century.

The word θιασάρχης, a hapax, clearly designates someone who directs a θίασος. The term *thiasos* is found frequently in pagan literature, where it designates a procession made up of satyrs and maenads who accompany Dionysius.[131] But it can also be applied to other cultic groups,[132] and in fact to any group without having a specifically religious connotation.[133]

---

131. Cf. Dio Chrysostom, *Discourse 4* (*On Kingship*), 83: "the wicked and wanton troop [πονηρὸς καὶ ἀσελγὴς θίασος] of revelers that follows the wicked and frenzied fool who leads them," a phrase that probably refers to a Dionysian procession.

132. Cf. Harpocration, *Lexicon of Ten Attic Orators* (Dindorf 156): Θίασος. Δημοσθένης ἐν τῷ κατ'Αἰσχίνου. θίασός ἐστι τὸ ἀθροιζόμενον πλῆθος ἐπὶ τελετῇ καὶ τιμῇ θεῶν ("Thiase. Demosthenes, in his *Against Aeschines*: A thiase is the gathering of many people in order to perform the mystery rites and honor the gods").

133. Cf. Julius Pollux, *Onomasticon* 9.143, where the word *thiasos* appears as a syn-

Since the terms "prophet" and *thiasos* are used in the *Bacchae* of Euripides (vv. 551 and 558), it has been suggested that the term θιασάρχης could refer to groups of actors performing during the festivals of Dionysus, and that here it suggests that there was an actor's side to Peregrinus.[134] The term θίασος occurs frequently in Philo, where it can designate a group in general,[135] a group of philosophers,[136] or even a group of abstract realities.[137] It's only natural, therefore, that Philo would also use the word to designate brotherhoods within the Jewish context.[138] It's the word he chooses when he's talking about the Essenes, to explain that they live together in *thiases*.[139] So the word θίασος in Philo isn't a technical term that he uses to designate a specifically Jewish social reality. Rather, he's applying a term that was well known in Greek and that would be easily comprehensible to his readers to realities that were not necessarily Greek and that probably had other names. The word also appears in a Christian context in Eusebius, where it refers to the whole community of Christians (θιασῶται designating the disciples of Christ),[140] but as in Philo, it's borrowed from the vocabulary of Greek religious associations, and so we shouldn't find any particular significance in it. We should also note two inscriptions from the imperial era, one coming from the north coast of the Black Sea (mid-second century to third century)[141] and the other also coming from the region of Pontus, specifically

---

onym of συναγωγή, συλλογή, and χορός, and where we find it applied to those who teach (παιδευόντων θίασος).

134. Cf. Thomas Schirren, "Lukian über die ΚΑΙΝΗ ΤΕΛΕΤΗ der Christen (*De morte Peregrini* 11)," *Philologus* 149 (2005): 354–59, esp. 355: "Θιασάρχης verweist auf die Technitenvereine insbesondere der Dionysosfeste, was zur Charakterisierung des Peregrinus als eines Schauspielers in 11 passt. [vgl. Poland in *RE* 5 A 2 (1934) 2473–2558, bes. 2514 ff. 2521 ff. *s.v.* Technitai]."

135. Cf. Philo, *On the Migration of Abraham* 90; *On the Special Laws* 2.44, 2.193, 4.47.

136. Cf. *On the Posterity of Cain* 101; *Every Good Man Is Free* 2.

137. Cf. *On the Life of Moses* 2.185.

138. Cf. *On Drunkenness* 94 and *On Flight and Finding* 89, referring to the brotherhood of Levites; *On Flight and Finding* 10 ("Of this company Jacob is a votary," trans. Francis Henry Colson, LCL). By contrast, the reference in *On Dreams* 2.127 refers to Philo's own time: "And will you sit in your conventicles and assemble your regular company and read in security your holy books?" (trans. Francis Henry Colson, LCL).

139. Cf. *Every Good Man Is Free* 85; *Hypothetica* 11.5 (Eusebius, *Preparation for the Gospel* 8.11.5).

140. Cf. Eusebius, *Ecclesiastical History* 10.1.8. The word θιασῶται is also used in 1.3.13 and 19.

141. *IosPE* I² 425.11.

from Sebastopolis.[142] They both testify to the use of the verb θιασαρχεῖν to designate, it would appear, the exercise of a magistracy consisting of directing, in a pagan context, a brotherhood of religious character. Still, it must be acknowledged that we have no indication suggesting that the word Lucian uses designates a specific function that Peregrinus might have been fulfilling within the Christian community.[143]

The last word is ξυναγωγεύς, "head of assembly." The term συναγωγή is not the usual Greek designation for the synagogue—that is, the location where the gathering for prayer meets. Philo most often uses the term προσευχή. However, he does speak of συναγωγαί in *Quod omnis probus* 81 and of συναγώγια in *Legatio ad Gaium* 311. In James 2:2, συναγωγή designates a Christian or Jewish-Christian assembly (ἐὰν γὰρ εἰσέλθῃ εἰς συναγωγὴν ὑμῶν ἀνήρ, "If a person comes into your assembly"). But it would not be reasonable to conclude that the συναγωγαί—Christian prayer gatherings of the primitive church—necessarily took place in locations that physically were former Jewish synagogues. When Ignatius in the first century, in a letter addressed to Polycarp,[144] expresses the wish that the συναγωγαί would be better attended, or when the *Didache* requires confession of sins within the assembly (10), the term συναγωγή designates a gathering of the faithful, without necessarily implying that it takes place within a synagogue building. However, contrary to all expectations, the term ξυναγωγεύς isn't used within the context of the synagogue: the president of the synagogue council was called a *gerousiarch*, or less often a προστάτης,[145] while the person who officiated over the Sabbath ceremonies in the synagogue was called an Ἀρχισυνάγωγος.[146] It has been suggested

142. *IGR* 3.115.5. On this latter inscription, see Brigitte Le Guen and Bernard Rémy, "La cité de Sébastopolis du Pont," *Anatolia antiqua* 18 (2010): 97–107, esp. 102.

143. We are not considering the fact that the orientalists use the expression "head of *thiasos*" to translate the Semitic term *rbmrzḥ*. See, e.g., Javier Teixidor, "Le thiase de Bêlastor et de Beelshamên d'après une inscription récemment découverte à Palmyre," *Comptes rendus de l'Académie des Inscriptions et Belles Lettres* 123 (1981): 306–14. The word *rbmrzḥ* is also found on the tesserae from the first three centuries recovered at Palmyra (see Henri Seyrig, "Les tessères palmyréniennes et le banquet rituel," in *Mémorial Lagrange* [Paris: Gabalda, 1940], 51–58, esp. 54).

144. Ignatius, *Letter to Polycarp* 4.2.

145. Several texts of inscriptions attesting to the functions of the *gerousiarch* and the προστάτης are presented in Margaret H. Williams, *The Jews among the Greeks and Romans: A Diasporan Sourcebook* (Baltimore: Johns Hopkins University Press, 1998), 38.

146. Cf. Acts 13:14–15. See Williams, *Jews among the Greeks and Romans*, where the witnesses to the Ἀρχισυνάγωγος are presented in Section II, 56–63.

that the title ξυναγωγεύς was a technical term applied to the founder of an association.[147] But the word is actually rarely attested; it's known essentially from inscriptions. One, from the Augustan era in the first century, refers to Aithibelios, president of the college of Sabbatists in Elaeusa (Cilicia Tracheia), a community that worshiped the Sabbath god Sabbatistes, and in whose worship Jewish Christians may have participated.[148] Other attestations are found in inscriptions from Istros, a Greek city near the mouth of the Danube in Lower Scythia. In one of these inscriptions, dated to 138 CE, the term is used to describe several people on a list of generous benefactors,[149] while in another, from the end of the first century or beginning of the second century, along with the word συναγωγεύς, after a lacuna, the term προστάτης is used.[150] We also find συναγωγεύς in an inscription from Delos (after 65 CE).[151] These inscriptions prove that in the first and second centuries the term had a meaning in Greek that designated people who played a role in an association that was not necessarily religious. In any event, once more we have nothing to suggest that the word indicated a precise function within Christian communities.

Beyond this trilogy, Lucian says that the Christians made Peregrinus a lawgiver (νομοθέτης) and that they claimed him as a προστάτης. It's not surprising that we find no reference to the function of a νομοθέτης in the earliest Christian communities, since Matthew 5:17–18 presents Christ as having come to fulfill the law. Beyond this, in Origen's *Against Celsus* 3.8, Celsus applies the term to Christ.[152] It seems natural, therefore, that no Christian would have assumed such a function.

---

147. See, e.g., Schirren, "Lukian," 355: "ξυναγωγεύς ist ein Vereinstitel, der als *terminus technicus* den Gründer einer Vereinigung bezeichnet, vielleicht unter jüdischem Einfluß . . . unter solcher Bezeichnung erscheint Peregrinus auch als ein Religionsstifter des Christentums."

148. *OGIS* 2 no. 573, cited by Williams, *Jews among the Greeks and Romans*, 176, who specifies (202n62) that the name is Syrian ("Protos proposes that the συναγωγεύς (A)i(th)ibelios be crowned"). See Schürer, *History of the Jewish People*, 2:624–26; H. Gressman, "Sabbatistai," *PW* 1A2:1560–65.

149. *IScM* 1.193.8–10 = *SEG* 1.330.

150. *IScM* 2.19.4 = *SEG* 24.1055.

151. *ID* 1641; the term is also found in two inscriptions from Perga in Pamphylia, from the third century CE (*IK Perge* 294 and 321.3).

152. Similarly, the Syrian Stoic Mara Bar Serapion makes an allusion, in a letter written to his son in Syriac and dated by the majority of scholars to the end of the first century or the beginning of the second, to the "wise king of the Jews"—that is, to Jesus, and to the laws that he promulgated (Cureton 73–74).

As for the last term, προστάτης, it could be used to designate any person carrying out a commission. Consequently, an officer, a steward, a person responsible for a particular task, or a presiding officer could be called a προστάτης. The term appears in several places in the Septuagint.[153] The president of the synagogue council, who was most often called a *gerousiarch*, could also be designated as a προστάτης, as five different inscriptions testify.[154] In Christian writings, the term is attested, for example, in Justin, where it refers to leaders of the Jewish people such as Enoch, Noah, Abraham, and Moses.[155] It's also found in Basil's writings, in the fourth century.[156]

Different opinions have been formulated regarding these appellations, especially the trilogy "prophet, cult-leader and head of synagogue." H. D. Betz believes that these were cultic titles characteristic of Hellenistic paganism, and that the same applies to νομοθέτης and προστάτης, which he considers to be customary Hellenistic notions that have been transposed.[157] For J. Schwartz, who appeals to the *Bacchae* of Euripides and to the inscription that mentions the president of the college of Sabbatists, the three functions, as well as that of a προστάτης, are consistent with the notion of a religious college, in this case a religious community of Bacchic inspiration.[158] P. Pilhofer challenges the idea that the three terms employed by Lucian refer to any kind of hierarchy—Christian, Jewish, or otherwise:[159] "Such a hierarchy has not existed anywhere, neither among Christians, nor among Jews, nor anywhere else. It is designed by Lucian to ridicule the Christian career of Peregrinus."[160]

---

153. In 1 Chron. 27:31 it designates the stewards of King David's property; in 1 Chron. 29:6, the "officers over the king's work"; in 2 Chron. 8:10, the two hundred fifty chief officers of King Solomon "who exercised authority over the people"; in 2 Chron. 24:11, the "officer of the chief priest" within the Levites; in 1 Esdras 2:8 (LXX), Sheshbazzar, governor of Judea; in 2 Macc. 3:4, Simon, "captain of the temple."

154. See Williams, *Jews among the Greeks and Romans*, 26, 38, and 165.

155. Justin, *Dialogue with Trypho* 92.2.

156. Basil, *Letters* 214.4 (the *prostatēs* of the churches); 190.1 (the *prostatēs* of the city); 28.2 (the *prostatēs* of the people).

157. Hans Dieter Betz, "Lukian von Samosata und das Christentum," *NovT* 3 (1959): 226–37, esp. 230n1 and 3, which refers to Walter Bauer, *Wörterbuch zum Neuen Testament*, 5th ed. (Berlin: de Gruyter, 1958), s.v. "νομοθέτης" and "προστάτης," and to F. Poland, "Συναγωγεύς," *PW* 4A2:1316–22.

158. Jacques Schwartz, ed., *Lucien de Samosate, Philopseudès et De morte Peregrini*, Publications de la Faculté des Lettres de l'Université de Strasbourg: Textes d'étude 12 (1951; repr., Paris: Les Belles Lettres, 1963), 93–94.

159. See Pilhofer et al., *Lukian, Der Tod des Peregrinos*, 58–62 (nn. 37, 39, 40).

160. Pilhofer et al., *Lukian, Der Tod des Peregrinos*, 102n16.

Although I have suggested, in an earlier work, the hypothesis that these terms could refer to connections that Peregrinus had with the Jewish-Christian community in Palestine,[161] further research into ancient witnesses has convinced me that Lucian uses terms that seem to designate functions but which are actually not specifically Christian or Jewish-Christian; rather, he borrows these terms from Greek culture and applies them to Peregrinus. It seems to me that the explanation for all these terms, which appear to have a precise meaning but are actually quite vague, is found in the sentence in chapter 11 where the trilogy appears: "In a trice he made them [i.e., the Christians] all look like children, for all by himself he was prophet, cult-leader and head of the synagogue. . . . They revered him as a god [θεόν], made use of him as a lawgiver [νομοθέτῃ] and set him down as a protector [προστάτην]."

Lucian wants to characterize Peregrinus as a charlatan who was able to take advantage of everyone by making them think he was the most important figure in the Christian community, "next after that other whom they still worship, the man who was crucified in Palestine," and at the same time ridicule him by piling up all the Greek terms he knew that designated functions of authority. He even adds "god," without taking into account the fact that he was describing a monotheistic religion. It's therefore useless to try to draw conclusions from these different terms in order to understand how the earliest Christian communities functioned. We certainly can't rule out the possibility that Lucian may have confused some Jewish realities with Christian ones, but such a hypothesis is not essential. What Lucian was really trying to do was denounce what he considered to be an imposture on the part of Peregrinus, and he succeeded in doing so. Nevertheless, even if an investigation into these terms doesn't teach us much about the specific role that Peregrinus played within the Christian milieu, the details that Lucian provides are of primary interest regarding life in the Christian communities.

---

161. Goulet-Cazé, "Pérégrinus surnommé Proteus," *DPhA* 5a:224–25.

The Value of Lucian's Testimony to Life
in the Christian Communities

Several details deserve our intention, because they confirm what we know
from other sources.[162] As Hans Dieter Betz observes,[163] what Lucian says
about Christians providing aid to their imprisoned fellow believers finds
confirmation in Ignatius's *Letter to the Smyrnaeans* 6, while Lucian's remark
θεραπεία πᾶσα οὐ παρέργως ἀλλὰ σὺν σπουδῇ ἐγίγνετο ("every form of attention . . . not in any casual way but zealously," *The Passing of Peregrinus* 12)
echoes a theme of early Christian paraenesis.[164] Similarly, the lines of people
waiting near the prison to help, with others sleeping inside the building,
testifies to a practice of primitive Christianity, as do the presence of widows[165] and the meals and religious services that took place in the prison.[166]
Peregrinus received money; people came to help him from cities in Asia
Minor.[167] The members of the community were united by brotherly love,
but also by their belief in the immortality of the soul and their disdain for
death. We must therefore admit that the vision that emerges from Lucian's
text is reasonably fair and that it corresponds to the reality that a pagan
could perceive from the outside. Lucian had certainly not read any Christians' books, and clearly he was completely ignorant of their theology, but
he knew their behavior and the stereotypes that were in circulation about
them. What shocks him the most is their credulity, their gullibility, their lack
of any critical spirit, and their naïveté regarding Peregrinus, whom Lucian
sees as a hypocritical impostor.

Peregrinus's break with the Christians poses further problems. Lucian
offers an explanation that can be interpreted in various ways: Peregrinus ate
forbidden food. "Then, after he had transgressed in some way even against
them—he was seen, *I think* [ὡς οἶμαι], eating some of the food that is forbidden them—they no longer accepted him" (*The Passing of Peregrinus* 16).
The expression Lucian uses indicates that he's not personally aware of exactly
what happened, but he offers a hypothesis based on the fact that he knows

162. On the image of the Christian communities that Lucian's treatise presents, see
Peter Pilhofer, "Das Bild der christlichen Gemeinden in Lukians *Peregrinos*," in Pilhofer et
al., *Lukian, Der Tod des Peregrinos*, 97–110.
163. Cf. Betz, "Lukian von Samosata," 230–31.
164. Cf., e.g., Rom. 12:8, 11; 2 Cor. 7:11–12; Heb. 6:11.
165. Cf. 1 Tim. 5.
166. Cf. Acts 16:25, 34.
167. Cf. Acts 11:29; 24:17; Rom. 15:25–27; 1 Cor. 16:1–4; 2 Cor. 8–9; Gal. 2:10.

Christians observed certain food taboos. Was it a matter of *idolothuta*—that is, meat offered in sacrifice to idols and therefore forbidden to Christians (cf. Acts 15:29; 1 Cor. 8)? This is the most likely explanation.[168] However, Gilbert Bagnani proposes another interpretation: Peregrinus was an Essene Ebionite who followed the Mosaic dietary laws.[169] "If he was, as his career would seem to indicate, an Essene Ebionite, he will have strictly observed the Mosaic Law and its prohibition of pork, and the real reason for his conflict with orthodox Christianity will have been not on his partaking of forbidden food, but on his refusal to partake of lawly food, that is to say he was excommunicated as an Ebionite."[170] As an Ebionite, Peregrinus would have observed the law of Moses, which forbade eating pork. This would have put him in conflict with orthodox Christianity, which considered pork to be licit food. His dietary regimen would have identified him as an Ebionite, and according to Bagnani, this was what provoked his excommunication. There's a major problem with this interpretation, however: Lucian's text says that Peregrinus ate some kind of food that was forbidden to Christians, while Bagnani's interpretation says just the opposite, that Peregrinus refused to eat food that was permitted to Christians!

Peregrinus: Christian and Cynic, Then Just a Cynic

According to Lucian, Peregrinus ceased to be a Christian from the moment this break occurred. We may imagine that he then practiced Cynicism until the end of his life. After the break, he went to Egypt to consult Agathobulus, the great master of Cynic asceticism. There, if Lucian can be believed, he practiced the "act of indifference" by masturbating in public, beating others on the buttocks, and being beaten similarly himself. Afterward he sailed for Italy, but he was banished by the emperor, apparently Antoninus the Pious

---

168. This is the interpretation of Betz in "Lukian von Samosata," 226–37, esp. 232n8, and of Mark J. Edwards in "Satire and Verisimilitude: Christianity in Lucian's 'Peregrinus,'" *Historia* 38 (1989): 89–98. Schwartz, *Lucien de Samosate*, 99, identifies this forbidden food with the sacrificial meats displayed and sold at crossroads—in other words, with the meats from "Hecate's supper," forbidden to Christians but enjoyed by Cynics (Lucian, *Dialogues of the Dead* 1.1, 22.3; *The Downward Journey, or The Tyrant* 7).

169. The Ebionites followed the law of Moses and recognized Jesus as the Christ, the Messiah whom Israel was expecting, but they didn't identify him as the Son of God.

170. Gilbert Bagnani, "Peregrinus Proteus and the Christians," *Historia* 4 (1955): 107–12, esp. 111.

(*The Passing of Peregrinus* 17–18). Peregrinus, imitating the Indian Brahmins, especially Calanus, who self-immolated near Susa in 324 BCE, decided to arrange for his own death by fire. He announced this project at the end of the Olympic Games of 161 CE (20), and he carried it out, surrounded by leaders of the Cynic movement, at the Olympic Games of 165.[171] Lucian specifies that he was dressed in the characteristic Cynic outfit: "the knapsack, the cloak, and that notable Heracles-club" (36). Through this spectacular death, he was trying to save men by teaching them to despise death and endure difficulties (23)—requirements consistent with those of Cynic philosophy—but Lucian claims that he was motivated instead, as in all his other acts, by a love of glory. It may be tempting to see a Christian influence in the apparition of Peregrinus, "dressed in white raiment" and "wearing a garland of wild olive," to an old man after the immolation (40). But this is not the generally accepted interpretation.[172] After his death, Peregrinus became a hero alongside Heracles and Hephaestus (29), and a cult was established in his honor, something he and his disciple Theagenes had helped significantly to arrange in advance, sending ambassadors well before his death to carry letters, testamentary dispositions, exhortations, and prescriptions to all the major cities (41). In the end, Peregrinus may represent a new kind of Cynicism, a mystic and syncretistic type quite different from the original Cynicism, which was agnostic.

So Peregrinus appears to have been both Christian and Cynic only for a limited period of time, five or six years, between his return to Parium after his release from prison and his second departure from Parium. What are we to make of his membership in both movements? In order to see him from the most objective view possible, we need to take into account the countertestimony of Aulus Gellius, which dates from the years when Peregrinus was in Greece, after 153. Peregrinus is lucky enough that another text

171. On the matter of these dates, see Goulet-Cazé, "Pérégrinus surnommé Proteus," *DPhA* 5a:209.

172. We may think of Matt. 17:2 (the episode of Jesus's transfiguration, when his garments became dazzlingly white); Matt. 28:3 (the angel who rolled back the stone from the empty tomb); Luke 24:4 (the two men in dazzling clothes who appeared to the women near the empty tomb); and the twenty-four elders in Rev. 4:4 (dressed in white robes with golden crowns on their heads). But Christopher P. Jones, "Le cas de Pérégrinus Proteus," in Goulet-Cazé and Goulet, *Le cynisme ancien et ses prolongements*, 305–17, esp. 314–15, believes that interpreting this apparition as an echo of the transfiguration of Jesus or the twenty-four elders of Revelation would be succumbing to an optical illusion. He sees no Cynic/Christian syncretism in Peregrinus's death, only a tradition of piety that's purely Greek.

has fortuitously been transmitted to us that challenges Lucian's version of the story and counterbalances the dubious traits in the portrait we would otherwise have.[173] Gellius had the opportunity to visit on several occasions with Peregrinus, a man he found to be *gravis atque constans*, who was then living in a hut outside Athens and holding forth on moral problems. One day, for example, Peregrinus explained that sages must not commit sins even if neither the gods nor men would ever know that they had sinned, because it shouldn't be fear of punishment or of a bad reputation that keeps us from sinning, but love for justice, honesty, and a sense of duty. The content of this reflection is highly compatible with Christian views. Since Lucian was attacking both Christianity and Cynicism, while Gellius had no a priori interest in the matter, we should have more confidence in the latter's judgment.

The figure of Peregrinus struck the imagination of the moderns, who identified him with Ignatius of Antioch, Marcion, a Montanist, and so on.[174] His example remains troubling because he was a notorious Christian in Palestine and then, after his Christian phase, a leader of the Cynic movement in both Rome and Greece. The Sibylline oracle celebrated him as "the noblest of Cynics" (*The Passing of Peregrinus* 29), while his disciple Theagenes felt that neither Diogenes nor Antisthenes nor even Socrates was worthy of being compared to him, but only Zeus (5). Perhaps we should draw a distinction between his years of dual allegiance, when Peregrinus lived out his Christianity in the garb of a Cynic—thus illustrating one of Varron's classifications—and the Cynic phase that followed, when he adopted not only the Cynic outfit and way of life but no doubt also the τέλος and δόγματα of that philosophy. We may deduce this from the visit he paid in Alexandria to Agathobulus, the great master of Cynic asceticism (17), and from the motivations that led him to take his own life by fire (23). According to such an interpretation, there were a few years in Peregrinus's life when he lived out his Christianity as a Cynic, and a much longer phase when, after abandoning Christianity, he became one of the leaders of the Cynic movement. But Lucian, as a pagan, was just as exasperated by the Cynicism as by the Christianity of a person in whom he could only see a love of glory.

---

173. Aulus Gellius, *Attic Nights* 12.11.
174. See Goulet-Cazé, "Pérégrinus surnommé Proteus," *DPhA* 5a:226–27.

The Cynic Christian Maximus Hero of Alexandria

Our main source on Maximus Hero, the Cynic philosopher of Egyptian origin who championed a militant Christianity that conformed to the orthodoxy of Nicaea, is Gregory of Nazianzus. But the value of his testimony remains doubtful, because after a personal rivalry with Maximus to obtain the bishopric of Constantinople, he moved from the most unrestrained praise to the most virulent attacks, to such an extent that it's very difficult to come to an opinion about the person of Maximus.[175]

Basil of Caesarea, in a letter to Maximus written in 361 or 362 (*Letter 9*), praises him for his "zeal for the knowledge of the divine" (1) and describes him as a man who's closely interested in theological questions—he invites him to come and visit so that they can discuss consubstantiality (3)—and who's clearly eager to read theological works. A letter to him from Athanasius, written in 371, attests that at that time Maximus was actively writing against pagans and heretics.[176] We have every indication, therefore, that Maximus had a genuine intellectual dimension and that he hardly resembled Cynics of the ignorant, unrefined type. Gregory himself had sympathies for Cynicism, and he didn't object to having a Cynic for a friend. In fact, he was very pleased to see a Cynic prefer Christ to Heracles, saying of Maximus in his poem *De vita sua* that "it was a great thing for [him] that this dog should patter through [his] hall and worship Christ instead of Heracles."[177] Gregory further salutes him as a victorious champion of the faith.[178] He invited him to his table and considered him a friend, especially appreciating his support in defense of orthodoxy. As late as the early months of 379, he composed an oration in his praise and delivered it in his presence before the faithful, in which he commended Maximus just as much for his Cynicism as for his Christianity. Gregory presents him as a "most authentic defender of the truth, a champion of the Trinity to the death,"[179] and at the same time as an ideal philosopher, one who disdains luxury, fortune, and power.[180]

---

175. See above, pp. 24–26. On the life of Maximus and the "Maximus affair," see Marie-Odile Goulet-Cazé, "Maxime Héron d'Alexandrie," *DPhA* 4:348–63.

176. Athanasius, *Letter to Maximus* (PG 26:1085–90).

177. Gregory of Nazianzus, *Concerning His Own Life*, vv. 974–75 (Carolinne White, ed. and trans., *Gregory of Nazianzus: Autobiographical Poems*, Cambridge Medieval Classics 6 [Cambridge: Cambridge University Press, 1996]).

178. Gregory of Nazianzus, *Concerning His Own Life*, v. 978.

179. Gregory of Nazianzus, *Discourse* 25.3.3 (Mossay, SC 284:160).

180. Gregory of Nazianzus, *Discourse* 25.4.5–6 (Mossay 164).

While Gregory does mention his cosmopolitanism,[181] it's noticeable how, as he's praising Maximus as a Cynic, he's careful to contrast his personal characteristics with those one would ordinarily find in a Cynic, as if Maximus were actually an exception within the movement: "You are a 'dog' not out of impudence, but frankness; not out of gluttony, but by taking no care for the future; not by barking, but by guarding what is good—through spiritual vigilance; and also by demonstrating your attachment to everything that accords with virtue, and only barking against things that are foreign to it."[182]

Because Gregory knows that Cynics have a well-established reputation for atheism, he's careful to ensure that no doubt remains about the faith of his friend. The major difference between Maximus and other Cynics, at least in his eyes, is that he doesn't share their atheism; in other words, the Maximus whom Gregory appreciates is above all a Christian, but one who also holds to a selective Cynicism, identifiable especially by the outfit: "He repudiates the atheism of Cynic philosophy, but adopts its frugality: this is what we now see before our very eyes; as a 'dog' hostile to those who actually are 'dogs,' and as a philosopher hostile to those who are not truly philosophers, and above all as a Christian, he undercuts the haughtiness of the other Cynics by wearing the same robe that they did, and the complacency of some who may be found among us by the distinctiveness of his clothing."[183] So Maximus is a Cynic, to a certain extent, but by his outfit, not by being an atheist. And he's also a Christian, one who stands out against other Christians precisely by that same outfit. So Maximus is a genuine Cynic, but of another order, superior not only to contemporary Cynics but even to their great ancestors. Everything Maximus does is superior to "Antisthenes' insolence, Diogenes's consumption of raw flesh and Crates' public marriage."[184]

But then, in the first half of the year 380, Maximus's attempted "usurpation" suddenly took place. Bishop Peter of Alexandria, even though he had previously sent Gregory a letter recognizing him to be bishop of Constantinople,[185] decided, for reasons of ecclesiastical politics that are still not entirely clear, to have the Egyptian bishops secretly consecrate Maximus as

181. Gregory of Nazianzus, *Discourse* 25.3.19 (Mossay 162).

182. Gregory of Nazianzus, *Discourse* 25.2.14–18 (Mossay 158 and 160).

183. Gregory of Nazianzus, *Discourse* 25.6.5–10 (Mossay 168).

184. Gregory of Nazianzus, *Discourse* 25.7.18–20 (Mossay 172). I have corrected ὀψοφαγία, gluttony, which makes little sense here, to ὠμοφαγία, the act of eating raw flesh. As for the term κοινογαμία, it seems to refer to the union of Crates and Hipparchia that took place in public and which was intended to be a κυνογαμία, a "dog's marriage."

185. Gregory of Nazianzus, *Concerning His Own Life*, vv. 858–63.

bishop of that city instead. This was the beginning of the "Maximus affair," which is difficult to understand completely. Starting with *Discourse 26*, Gregory changes his tone completely and launches vehement attacks: "I also fear the dogs who have been accepted so improbably as pastors, even though, paradoxically, they have not demonstrated any qualifications to be pastors beyond tonsuring their hair, to which they disingenuously devote all their attention. Such people don't remain the dogs they once were, and they don't truly become pastors, either, except to rip apart, scatter and overturn the efforts of others—it's always easier to destroy than to preserve."[186] But it's in the *De vita sua* that the attacks become the most strident. Maximus is called an "effeminate creature" (v. 750), a "phantom from Egypt" and a "pestilential fanatic" (v. 751), who dyed his hair blond and curled it—a fact that came out during his tonsure for his secret consecration as a bishop (v. 754–55, 764, 915–19). He then becomes "that most vile dog" (v. 1004), and as a result, Antisthenes, Diogenes, and Crates are suddenly rehabilitated in comparison to Maximus and contemporary Cynics (v. 1030–33). Wounded to the quick, Gregory is incapable of impartiality under the circumstances. But if we look closely, we see that he doesn't bring any specific charges against Maximus. His innuendo, combined with his complete imprecision, gives the impression that he has only rumors to support his accusations: "Numerous were the wicked ways, so we hear, along which this man had passed—but let others concern themselves with that, for I have not the time to search it all out, the police records can reveal what they were—before he finally settled in this city."[187]

Was Gregory truly naive, the victim of an ambitious schemer who wanted to usurp the episcopal seat of Constantinople? We may legitimately have our doubts. But what motives might have led Maximus to accept this secret ordination? We must admit that there are still many gray areas.

I have shown in a recent study[188] that the anonymous Cynic philosopher from Egypt whom Julian attacks in 362 in Constantinople in his *Discourse 9: To the Uneducated Cynics* could well be Maximus Hero, who, in 380, still in Constantinople, then drew the wrath of Gregory of Nazianzus. The Christianity of this anonymous Cynic is hardly in doubt. Indeed, Julian suggests, after quoting an expression from Genesis 9:3, that his interlocutor is capa-

---

186. Gregory of Nazianzus, *Discourse* 26.3.15–20 (Mossay 230).

187. Gregory of Nazianzus, *Concerning His Own Life*, vv. 773–77.

188. Marie-Odile Goulet-Cazé, "Qui était le philosophe cynique anonyme attaqué par Julien dans son Discours IX?," *Hermes* 136 (2008): 97–118.

ble of recognizing "the words of the Galileans," meaning that he has read the Scriptures, meaning that he's a Christian. Beyond this, Julian ends his discourse with the reproach, "You admire and emulate the life of wretched women."[189] The exact meaning of the phrase is unclear, but it could be referring to a group of nuns living in a monastery in or near Alexandria in Egypt, or to women leading a solitary ascetic life in Alexandria or in the Egyptian desert.[190] Maximus, as a Cynic Christian, might therefore have succeeded in arousing the hostility of both a pagan emperor and a Christian bishop, eighteen years apart.

But what can we learn from the relationship between Gregory and Maximus, independently of the "Maximus affair"? It appears that Gregory considered Maximus to be something of an exception within the landscape of Cynicism, a philosophy that, in his eyes, remained fundamentally foreign to Christian faith. Nevertheless, in the final years of his life, he continued to hold that virtuous pagans, particularly Diogenes, had something to offer to Christians, even if they hadn't been animated by the love of God.[191] As for Maximus, nothing indicates that his dual allegiance was difficult for him. He seems to illustrate Varro's theory, which Augustine reprised and extended to Christianity, of a Cynicism that was reduced to a way of living—asceticism—and dressing (cloak, sack, and staff), which would be compatible with philosophies whose telos was different, and even with Christianity. However, Maximus's case doesn't strike us as at all identical with that of Peregrinus. The latter apparently wasn't born into a Christian family; rather, he became a Christian and was already one when he adopted the Cynic outfit, so that his Cynic Christian phase may well correspond with what Varro was envisioning. He then abandoned Christianity but became a true Cynic, adopting the Cynic philosophy with its telos, and not shrinking back from indecency, as he would have done if he had continued to practice Christianity. He remained a Cynic right up through his suicide by fire. Maximus, for his part, was born into a family of Christian martyrs; while we don't know at what point he adopted the Cynic outfit, it's likely that he remained a member of both movements for the rest of his life, though we have no actual proof of this. His Cynicism was thus identical with the superficial Cynicism that

189. Julian, *Discourse 9* (*To the Uneducated Cynics*), 20 (203b).

190. In *Concerning His Own Life*, vv. 933–37, Gregory, after the Maximus affair, describes the women whom Maximus had in the past trained in godliness, and with whom he'd lived in community, as "Corinthians"—that is, as courtesans.

191. Gregory of Nazianzus, *Carmina Theologica* 1.2.10.218–27 (PG 37:696).

Peregrinus practiced during his dual-allegiance phase. It's probably to such a Cynicism, envisioned only as a way of life and compatible with Christianity, that Gregory of Nazianzus is alluding to when he speaks of a "middle way," which derives its appearance and setting (τὸ σχῆμα καὶ ἡ σκηνή) from the Greeks but embraces the truth and exaltedness (ἡ ἀλήθεια καὶ τὸ ὕψος) of Christianity.[192] According to this view of Cynicism, which makes it compatible with any telos, someone who was following the Cynic way of life could easily adopt the telos of Christianity.

It's clear that the two movements shared a certain number of common values, such as a concern for authenticity and the rejection of vainglory, and that they also had a certain number of behaviors in common, such as asceticism, frankness of speech, and the practice of poverty. And so, as Augustine put it, Cynics could become Christians without a problem, provided, however, that they gave up their false doctrines—he was thinking no doubt primarily of atheism—and their indecency. On the other hand, the Cynic who remained faithful to Diogenes's precepts, who had ἀτυφία and ἀπάθεια for his telos, who practiced asceticism in order to achieve happiness but who didn't renounce "indifference," would find it difficult to feel an affinity with the Christian who sought salvation through the imitation of Christ and who respected modesty. The cases of Peregrinus and Maximus Hero lead us to conclude that a simultaneous allegiance could only accommodate a superficial Cynicism.

Cynicism and Monasticism

Within Christianity, monasticism requires particular attention. Monks often wore the same clothing as Cynics, the pallium that was the equivalent of the τρίβων, and they practiced just as rigorous an asceticism as the Cynics, even if the monks didn't mortify their bodies in the same spirit as the Cynics did in their ascetic training. Weren't the monks, in some way, the Cynics of Christianity? Monasticism emerged in the third century and developed over the centuries that followed; monks and anchorites eventually settled in the Egyptian desert, especially in the Thebaid and around Alexandria, but also in Palestine, Syria, Asia Minor, Mesopotamia, Rome, Constantinople, and Gaul. While Cynics lived primarily in cities, monks often preferred the solitude of the desert, mountains, and countryside. We've already seen, in the episode

192. Gregory, *Discourse* 25.5.18–20 (Mossay 168).

of the statues in Antioch in 387, that there could be a rivalry for influence in the countryside between Cynics and monks, with the latter coming more and more to displace the former. Objectively, the two groups had many points in common: they both refused to follow the norms of civilization, they rejected the pagan gods, and they practiced an ascetic life.

Christian monks often adopted the philosopher's cloak.[193] Sulpicius Severus attests that Martin of Tours, in the fourth century, wore the pallium,[194] as did the monks who came to pay him their last respects.[195] John Cassian describes the monks in Egypt outfitted in a *palliolum* (narrow cape), *melotis* or *pera* (goatskin),[196] and *baculus* (staff).[197] The *melotis* was a goatskin or sheepskin garment, like the one John the Baptist wore centuries earlier. However, there could also have been monks who didn't wear a specific outfit. The fifth-century bishop Palladius presents Sarapion, an Egyptian monk, as having "no purse, no sheep-skin coat" when he went to Athens and spoke there with the "wearers of the philosopher's cloak" (τριβωνοφόροι).[198]

But can we therefore speak of a direct influence of Cynicism on monasticism? We have no explicit and definitive proof of this, and we must take into account that there was also an ascetic tradition within Judaism, as evidenced by John the Baptist as well as the Essenes and the Therapeutae, whom Philo describes. It's therefore wiser to speak of a similarity between behaviors, rather than of an influence. The anchorites' way of life—for example, that of the desert fathers—resembles the Cynics' asceticism in many ways. They lived in caves and tombs, had long hair and beards, wore sandals or went barefoot, were clothed in goatskins, lived on fruits and vegetables,[199] and

193. In fact, even before the emergence of monasticism, some Christians had already adopted the Cynics' cloak. Tertullian, for example, who believed that nothing was more practical than Crates's double pallium, had already decided, when he wrote his treatise *On the Mantle* in 209, to exchange the toga of a Roman citizen for the Greek philosopher's pallium, for which he offered high praise (*On the Mantle* 5.3.26).

194. Sulpicius Severus, *Dialogues* 2.3.2 (CSEL 1:183).

195. Sulpicius Severus, *Letter to Bassula* 3.19.

196. According to Pierre Courcelle ("La figure du philosophe d'après les écrivains latins de l'antiquité," *JS* [1980]: 101), the word signifies here a goatskin garment and not a sack. Indeed, that's what John Cassian's use of *melotis* and *pera* as equivalent terms suggests.

197. John Cassian, *Institutions* 1.6–7 (trans. Edgar Charles Summer Gibson).

198. Palladius, *Lausiac History* 37.5–6 (trans. William Kemp Lowther Clark).

199. The anchorites adopted the Cynics' favorite dish: lentils. Cf. A. J. Festugière, *Antioche païenne et chrétienne: Libanius, Chrysostome et les moines de Syrie* (Paris: de Boccard, 1959), who cites the Syriac monk Simeon the Stylite (325 and 496), as well as John Chrysostom, describing lentils as the food that the monks ate (329).

endured the cold of winter and the heat of summer. In *A History of the Monks of Syria*, Theodoret describes the monk Zeno, who lived for forty years as an ascetic, in terms that would be perfectly suitable for a Cynic ascetic: "For this reason he had neither bed nor lamp nor hearth nor jar nor flask nor chest nor book nor anything else, but he used to wear old rags and likewise shoes that needed straps, since the pieces of leather had come apart."[200]

The anchorites' resemblance to Cynics was sometimes cited in their favor, but sometimes it was held against them. Christians themselves were actually not unanimous regarding these Christian ascetics whose appearance was so reminiscent of the Cynics'. Some defended them. John Chrysostom, who recognized that Christian elites were not very favorable toward this monastic asceticism because it required its adherents to make a radical break with upper-class life in order to renounce the world, appealed to Diogenes to defend and justify monasticism. He wanted to make the elites realize that if they felt admiration for Diogenes's asceticism, then Christian asceticism was even more deserving of their respect![201] But others accused these Christian ascetics on the grounds of their appearance. Jerome, for example, warns the virgin Eustochium against men with long hair, black cloaks, and goat-like beards.[202] He's probably talking about Christian ascetics in Rome, monks whose appearance was much like the Cynics'. But pagans such as Libanius and Eunapius[203] also opposed these Christian ascetics dressed in black, whom they probably regarded as a new species of Cynic.[204]

It seems valid to draw a parallel between the pagan philosophers and Cynics, on the one hand, and the fathers and monks, on the other. The monks were, in a certain sense, the Cynics of the early church.[205] They were

---

200. Theodoret, *A History of the Monks of Syria* 12.2.10–14 (SC 234). English translations are from Theodoret of Cyrrhus, *A History of the Monks of Syria*, trans. Richard M. Price (Kalamazoo, MI: Cistercian Publications, 2008).

201. John Chrysostom, *Against the Opponents of the Monastic Life* 2.4 and 2.6 (PG 47:337 and 339). See the study by Krueger, "Diogenes the Cynic," 37–39.

202. Jerome, *Letter 22 to Eustochium* 28 (CSEL 54:185.1–4).

203. Cf. Libanius, *Discourse 30* (*In Favor of the Temples*), 8; Eunapius, *Chronicle*, Blockley, frag. 56; *Lives of Philosophers and Sophists* 6.112–15 (Goulet 40.22–41.16). On the attitudes of Christians and pagans toward monks, see Heinz-Günther Nesselrath, "Libanios und die Mönche," in *Von Homer bis Landino: Beiträge zur Antike und Spätantike sowie zu deren Rezeptions und Wirkungsgeschichte. Festgabe für Antonie Wlosok zum 80. Geburtstag*, ed. Beate Regina Suchla (Berlin: Pro Business GmbH, 2011), 243.

204. Cf. Courcelle, "La figure du philosophe," 95–96.

205. The Cynic spirit resurfaced in the church, many centuries later, with the Capuchins, whom Justus Lipsius compared to the Cynics (*Manuductio ad Stoicam philosophiam* 1.13).

not accepted unanimously by the church—far from it, just as the Cynics didn't please everybody among the pagan philosophers. The two groups had in common an asceticism of a specific character: while it worked through the body (it was, above all, a physical asceticism), it had another goal, beyond the body—a moral goal, in the case of the Cynics, and a spiritual goal in the case of Christian ascetics. Neither group was devoted to the Greek παιδεία: the Syrian monks were often simple, uneducated peasants, just as the Cynics about whom Lucian complains in *The Fugitives* weren't educated. We may also note that each of the communities had its charlatans. We've already met, among the Cynics, people who wore the outfit without practicing any asceticism and who behaved like parasites. Similarly, a monk such as Nilus of Ancyra could reproach other monks for using a monastic appearance to get great wealth[206] and for behaving like parasites at the doors of the rich.[207]

However, Cynicism may have had a literary influence on monasticism. The Coptic apothegms of the Egyptian Fathers depict a meeting between the emperor Theodosius and a monk that could tacitly have been inspired by the meeting between Alexander the Great and Diogenes, the account of which was still in circulation at the time when these apothegms were collected, that is, most likely a little after 450.[208]

Perhaps we should also regard the life of Symeon the Fool, a Syrian monk of the sixth century whose biography Leontius, the Cypriot bishop of Neapolis, wrote in the seventh century, from the angle of a possible literary influence. This Symeon, after living for twenty-nine years as a hermit, returned to Emesa, where he began to behave in a way that broke social codes, in many respects reminiscent of the behavior of Diogenes of Sinope. He ate raw meat and lupins, defecated in public, consorted with prostitutes, and pretended to be mad. If we accept the interpretation of Lennart Rydén,[209] who notes the parallels between Symeon's behavior and that of Diogenes, but who rules out any influence of Cynicism on the monk because Symeon's

206. Nilus of Ancyra, *Ascetic Discourse* 9 (PG 79:729a–b).

207. Nilus of Ancyra, *Ascetic Discourse* 8 (PG 79:728c–d).

208. Cf. Siegfried Morenz, "Ein koptischer Diogenes: Griechischer Novellenstoff in ägyptischer Mönchserzählung," ZÄSA 77 (1941): 52–54; for a different interpretation, see Jean Doresse, "À propos d'un apophtegme copte: Diogène et les moines égyptiens," *RHR* 128 (1944): 84–93.

209. Lennart Rydén, *Das Leben des heiligen Narren Symeon von Leontios von Neapolis*, Studia Graeca Upsaliensia 4 (Uppsala: Almqvist & Wiksell, 1963); Rydén, *Bemerkungen zum Leben des heiligen Narren Symeon von Leontios von Neapolis*, Studia Graeca Upsaliensia 6 (Uppsala: Almqvist & Wiksell, 1970), 17–18.

Syriac culture would hardly have been open to the Hellenistic figure of the philosopher, we will conclude that the historical figure of Symeon illustrates a non-Greek type of asceticism that has nothing to do with the Cynics but only represents a parallel phenomenon. However, if we follow instead the stimulating proposal of Derek Krueger,[210] this *Life* tells us less about Symeon as a historical person than about the literary endeavors of the bishop Leontius a century later. Thanks to his education, Leontius was able to depict and comment on the actions of Symeon by using the figure of Diogenes as it had been transmitted in the schools of rhetoric through the Cynic chreias. Symeon would thus have been both an *alter Christos* and an *alter Diogenes*. We therefore need to recognize in this *Life*, not a concrete influence of Cynicism on the life of a sixth-century monk, but a seventh-century use of Cynic chreias and their message criticizing the categories of social morality (polite/impolite, public/private, appropriate/inappropriate, pure/impure) with a view toward Christian moral exhortation. Krueger recognizes that Symeon is not a Cynic and that Leontius isn't presenting a Cynic interpretation of Jesus. Nevertheless (and we share his opinion here), the *Life of Symeon the Fool* illustrates an implicit—neither Diogenes nor the Cynics are mentioned—but nevertheless real literary use of Cynic chreias and anecdotes as a means of Christian instruction. To this point it has appeared that Christians could follow the Cynic way of life, so long as they renounced immodesty. But if we interpret the life of Symeon as that of a historical person, his case would certainly be an exception, because Symeon engaged in every kind of immodesty. But if we take Krueger's perspective, Symeon is a literary fiction who goes well beyond Cynicism, because while the Cynics tried to respond only to the needs of their bodies, Symeon actually succeeded in transcending his body—that is, in living as if he did not have a body. Thus, in his spiritual perfection, he surpassed the Cynics' life "according to nature" by living a life "according to virtue" and "according to God."

And so we come full circle: the Cynic chreias that could have influenced the authors of the Q source were also at work behind the work that a seventh-century Cypriot bishop wrote about the life of a Syrian monk of the previous century who was unlikely historically to have had any encounter with Diogenean Cynicism. But it would certainly be a mistake to try to turn the actual Symeon of history into a Cynic monk.

210. Derek Krueger, *Symeon the Holy Fool: Leontius's Life and the Late Antique City*, Transformations of the Classical Heritage 25 (Berkeley: University of California Press, 1996), esp. chap. 6, "Symeon and the Cynics," 90–107.

It seems in the end that Christians in general and monastics in particular were fascinated by these Cynic "athletes of virtue," these "tonics of Hellenism" (to use Father Festugière's phrase),[211] who demonstrated the worth and dignity of asceticism. But at the same time, they felt repulsion for the Cynics because of their immodesty, impudence, and agnosticism (or even, their atheism). In fact, even when it came to asceticism, the practice had a different meaning for the two groups. On the one hand, the Cynic trained his body to face πόνοι so that he could affirm that he was stronger than nature, stronger than Fate; accordingly, Cynic asceticism may be understood as a manifestation of hubris on the part of man. On the other hand, the Christian, especially the anchorite, practiced asceticism to annihilate himself through mortification, to turn toward God and do his will, in full imitation of Christ. If Christians turned Cynics into the quintessence of Hellenism, it's probably because they perceived in them this extraordinary pride, which Diogenes, for example, expressed when he was struggling with Fortune: "Really, Fortune, you do well to stand up to me in as virile a way as possible." This was the source of the accusations of "vainglory" that Christians made against Cynics. The Syrian monk James, described in Theodoret's *History of the Monks of Syria*, contrasted vainglory with true glory. When one of his servants suggested that he hide the cup from which he drank his gruel so that his asceticism would appear even more perfect, he told this servant, "Clear off, boy, do not hide from men what is manifest to the God of the universe. Wishing to live for him alone, I have paid no thought to my reputation with men; for what benefit is it, if the latter think more of my asceticism but God thinks less? For they are not the givers of reward for labors, but God is the bestower." Theodoret adds this commentary: "In this way he has expelled from his mind the passion of vainglory [τῆς κενῆς δόξης τὸ πάθος], together with the others."[212] The same type of asceticism resulted, in the case of the Cynic, in the affirmation of self, but in the case of the monk, in submission to the will of God. Rather than speak of a genuine influence of Cynicism on monasticism, it seems much better to see in both movements two manifestations, sometimes rival ones, of ancient asceticism, having certain points in common but also differences that ultimately are more important than these commonalities.

---

211. André Jean Festugière, "Antisthenica," *RSPT* 3 (1932): 345–76, repr. in André-Jean Festugière, *Études de philosophie grecque* (Paris: Librairie philosophique J. Vrin, 1971), 283–314, esp. 314.

212. Theodoret, *A History of the Monks of Syria* 21.11.27–32 and 21.12.17–18.

CONCLUSION

Despite all the questions that still remain, a comparison of Cynicism and Christianity has proven to be extremely informative. On the one hand, we've encountered a philosophical movement of antiquity that, by practicing asceticism and challenging social values, pushed the affirmation of the autonomy of the human will to what were no doubt its most extreme limits. On the other hand, we've met a religion that, from its origins, with the sending forth of its disciples on mission, had a role for asceticism—this became determinative within monasticism—and distanced itself from the usual criteria of social success. A comparison between the two movements is justified even more by their well-attested contacts under the Christian Empire, which went so far as acknowledging the possibility of dual membership.

In this study, we have taken great care to avoid unwarranted schematizations in our approach to Cynicism. This philosophy, despite its doctrinal simplicity and its constantly reaffirmed insistence on practicing a rigorous physical asceticism toward a moral goal, actually displayed great diversity over its nearly ten centuries of existence. We have found it necessary to challenge the contrast drawn within the academic tradition between a "soft" Cynicism and an "austere" Cynicism, which we see as connected much more with the personalities of Cynic philosophers than to the actual existence of two Cynicisms. However, we have quite seriously taken into account the contrast, well attested in Diogenes Laertius, between Cynicism as a "school of thought" and Cynicism simply as a "way of life"; this allows us to envision two possible ways of being a Cynic. We have also considered a further contrast, this one found in texts from the imperial era, between an educated Cynicism and a popular version of the philosophy. Under the Roman Empire, the situation became even more complicated because of two distortions of Cynicism. There was an idealized version, nostalgic for Diogenes and Crates, illustrated by philosophers such as Dio Chrysostom, Epictetus, and Julian. And there was a caricatured Cynicism, sketched by the pen of a satirist such as Lucian and depicted in the hostile claims of certain church fathers. Finally, we have tried to show how the complex relationship between Cynics and Stoics, who could feel admiration for Cynicism but at the same time be embarrassed by it, and who could do anything from rejecting Cynicism to wishing for the two movements to be assimilated, keeps us from treating Cynicism as a vague concept with poorly defined boundaries and from confusing Cynics with Stoics.

In addition to this complexity, the historian of philosophy must face another difficulty inherent in a certain component of Cynicism that makes it similar to primitive Christianity. Because Cynicism didn't require its followers to have benefited from παιδεία, it was the sole philosophy in antiquity that gave a positive answer to the question "Can a person be both uneducated and a philosopher?" In fact, under the Roman Empire, a great number of Cynics, even though they were uneducated, practiced an authentic Cynicism that was faithful to Diogenes's dissenting attitudes and consistent with the idea, unpopular among elites, that each and every person, even the most humble, could have access to philosophy because it wasn't a matter of knowledge but of moral training. But how can we be sure that all these uneducated people who claimed to be Cynics weren't actually charlatans who wore the τρίβων but didn't practice asceticism? Frauds are even harder to distinguish from genuine Cynics because other intellectuals, Lucian to be sure, but also philosophers such as Epictetus and Dio Chrysostom, were sympathetic to the Cynicism of Diogenes and Crates but pointedly wanted to make their readers believe that the shaggy, uneducated Cynics they met in the streets were all charlatans who were usurping the philosopher's cloak. So how can we enable these voiceless but genuine imperial Cynics to be heard, since we only meet them through their detractors, because they didn't receive the same education as the elites and so weren't able to write? Because there certainly were some charlatans, and because the credentialed contemporary philosophers did everything they could to denigrate these voiceless Cynics who roamed the streets of the Roman Empire, it's up to the historian of philosophy to rehabilitate them. We have no reason to believe that the asceticism they practiced was inauthentic. The pseudepigraphal *Letters of Diogenes* and *Letters of Crates* acknowledge a genuine risk of counterfeits in that they emphasize that it's not the cloak that makes the Cynic but rather the Cynic who makes the cloak. Nevertheless, the advice regarding the ascetic life that's sprinkled throughout this popular literature expresses an aspiration for a genuine asceticism.

Once this complexity of Cynicism had been demonstrated—and it was vital to highlight this—it was then of interest to analyze to what extent, and in what forms, Cynicism and Christianity may have had contacts in antiquity. This question has taken on considerable significance in recent years because some have tried to derive the image of a Jesus with Cynic traits from a study of the Gospel source Q. It was therefore important to verify whether such a comparison was valid. To do this, it was prudent first of all to ask whether contacts between Cynicism and Judaism were attested in antiquity. The indications are few, but they may nevertheless be found from the Septuagint through the Talmud. From the affection that a young Meleager of Gadara felt for Demo in competition with a Jewish rival, to the admiration that Philo of Alexandria showed in his works for Diogenes, from the character of Abnimos ha-gardi, a friend of Rabbi Meir, whom rabbinic literature likely created from the Cynic philosopher Oenomaus of Gadara, to the figure of the "kynikos" who illustrated a certain madness in the eyes of the Talmud authors, Judaism certainly was aware that Cynicism existed. The city of Gadara, a renowned intellectual center where the Cynic tradition was active, may have played an important role in this. Still, we had to face the evidence: Cynicism isn't mentioned anywhere in the Scriptures where Jesus is described, and archaeological excavations in Galilee offer no decisive help in settling the question of any possible contacts between local Galileans like Jesus and the Cynics. Despite all this, the "Cynic hypothesis" doesn't hesitate to recommend that the Gospel source Q be read in light of Cynic philosophy.

It's always very stimulating to see a hypothesis emerge from new work on ancient texts that have already been thoroughly and frequently examined. This interpretive hypothesis struck us as attractive and promising because of the questions it raised, but in the absence of clear literary or archaeological proofs, all it could do was to suggest numerous parallels that unfortunately were never completely decisive. The "Cynic hypothesis" is based on a stratigraphic analysis of the Gospel source Q, and it appeals to arguments connected with both the literary genre of Q and its content. The hypothesis that the authors of Q may have been familiar with the collections of Greek chreias, possibly Cynic ones, which played a decisive role in the diffusion of Cynicism, seems like a reasonable possibility. However, the numerous parallels that supposedly reveal similarities of behavior and moral attitude between the Q community and Cynic philosophers are not convincing. An examination of the Q source revealed persuasively that the appeals proponents of the "Cynic hypothesis" made to such parallels were clearly overdone. Such a methodological tool must be handled delicately, because describing surface similarities is far from establishing analogous intentions or identical realities. Even if the Cynics and the people of Q had in common a desire to overturn conventions and hierarchies, they were on very different paths, as the ends each envisioned testify. For the Cynics, the goal was to liberate man from all social constraints by means of a difficult but freely chosen training. For the people of Q—except for Burton Mack, who postulates a radically secular stratum within Q1 not easy to conceive in Palestine of the time of Jesus—the goal was to accomplish the will of a Father-God. Because the spirit of the sayings in Q is so different from that of Cynicism, it's not legitimate to speak of Jesus as a "Cynic-like teacher," as if one were trying at all costs to find a message with Cynic content in the text of Q. However, if one still wished to advance the hypothesis that the people of Q had some connection with the Cynics, it would be interesting to suggest that the two groups might be related by concurrence, as was sometimes the case afterward with Christianity and monasticism in the early centuries, because both wanted to deliver a radical message to their contemporaries that needed to be put into practice immediately.

It's actually well attested that over the course of the early centuries, Cynicism and Christianity maintained a lively relationship, often a conflicted one, with Christians divided between fascination, admiration, embarrassment, and even revulsion for Cynics (the last provoked notably by their immodesty). Both groups advocated for the equality of all people, praised poverty, and stressed the imperative of making one's actions match one's words. But while the Cynic pushed the affirmation of self to the utmost limit, eliminated any dependence on others through asceticism, and defied Fortune by the arrogant assertion of his freedom, the Christian humbly searched for and awaited the kingdom of God that Christ had come to introduce. Both groups were prepared to give up everything they had—all material security—but despite such surface similarities, the spirit of Cynicism was ultimately incompatible with the spirit of the Beatitudes.

Monasticism deserved special attention within our comparison of the two movements because the τρίβων, Cynic in origin, would become—and the fact itself remains astonishing—the characteristic garment not only of the philosopher but also of the monk, and the practice of asceticism would furnish monastic life with one of its principal components. It must be acknowledged that the Cynic way of life, with its austerity and demands, must have seemed, to Christians who were eager to renounce the world and live radically, to be the greatest model of wisdom and heroism that Hellenism had bequeathed. Monks adopted this way of life with its outfit, but they gave each a new significance within their walk of faith. As Augustine suggested, as he took up from a Christian perspective the distinction that Varro had established between the goals of the various philosophical schools, one could wear the Cynic outfit without becoming entirely a Cynic, provided specifically that one rejected immodesty, which was considered absolutely incompatible with Christianity. The τρίβων had value as a symbol, the symbol of a radical way of life that was able to eliminate through asceticism everything that wasn't essential. It was this symbol, long in use by the Cynics, and then adopted by other philosophers, that the monks decided to adopt. But beyond the symbol, the goals of the two movements were profoundly different. The Cynic challenged everything that belonged to civilization, which was seen as opposed to nature; the monk challenged everything that belonged to the world, which was seen as opposed to the will of God. The Cynic relied arrogantly on his own will; the monk humbly relied on God as an act of faith. Over the course of the early centuries, monks and Cynics probably related to one another as members of concurrent and rival movements, each trying to convince those around them to join in with them.

This work has hardly exhausted the study of the relationship between Cynicism and Christianity. However, I hope that I have at least helped advance it, if only methodologically, by warning against invalid appeals to surface similarities and against ideological bias of any kind.

BIBLIOGRAPHY

Amsler, Frédéric. *L'évangile inconnu: La source des paroles de Jésus (Q)*. Essais bibliques 30. Geneva: Labor et Fides, 2001.

Arnal, William E. *Jesus and the Village Scribes: Galilean Conflicts and the Setting of Q*. Minneapolis: Fortress, 2001.

Asmus, Rudolf. "Gregorius von Nazianz und sein Verhältnis zum Kynismus." *TSK* 67 (1894): 314–39. Reprint, pages 185–205 in Billerbeck, *Die Kyniker in der modernen Forschung*.

Attridge, Harold W. *First-Century Cynicism in the Epistles of Heraclitus*. HTS 29. Missoula, MT: Scholars Press, 1976.

Aune, David E. "Jesus and Cynics in First Century Palestine: Some Critical Considerations." Pages 176–93 in *Hillel and Jesus: Comparisons of Two Major Religious Leaders*, edited by James H. Charlesworth and Loren L. Johns. Minneapolis: Fortress, 1997.

Avi-Yonah, Michael. *Geschichte der Juden im Zeitalter des Talmud in den Tagen von Rom und Byzanz*. SJ 2. Berlin: de Gruyter, 1962.

Bagnani, Gilbert. "Peregrinus Proteus and the Christians." *Historia* 4 (1955): 107–12.

Bastomsky, Saul J. "Abnimos and Oenomaus: A Question of Identity." *Apeiron* 8 (1974): 57–61.

Bees, Robert. *Zenons Politeia*. Studies on the Interaction of Art, Thought and Power 4. Leiden: Brill, 2011.

Benko, Stephen. *Pagan Rome and the Early Christians*. Bloomington: Indiana University Press, 1986.

Betz, Hans Dieter. "Jesus and the Cynics: Survey and Analysis of a Hypothesis." *JR* 74 (1994): 453–75.

———. "Lukian von Samosata und das Christentum." *NovT* 3 (1959): 226–37.

Billerbeck, Margarethe, ed. *Der Kyniker Demetrius: Ein Beitrag zur Geschichte der frühkaiserzeitlichen Popularphilosophie.* PhA 36. Leiden: Brill, 1979.

————. *Die Kyniker in der modernen Forschung: Aufsätze mit Einführung und Bibliographie.* Bochumer Studien zur Philosophie 15. Amsterdam: Grüner, 1991.

————. "Greek Cynicism in Imperial Rome?," AC 51 (1982): 151–73. Reprint, pages 147–66 in Billerbeck, *Die Kyniker in der modernen Forschung.*

Bouffartigue, Jean. "Le cynisme dans le cursus philosophique au IVᵉ siècle." Pages 339–58 in Goulet-Cazé and Goulet, *Le cynisme ancien et ses prolongements.*

Boulanger, André. *Aelius Aristide et la sophistique dans la province d'Asie au IIᵉ siècle de notre ère.* Bibliothèque des Écoles françaises d'Athènes et de Rome 126. Paris: de Boccard, 1923.

Brancacci, Aldo. *Antisthène: Le discours propre.* Translated by Sophie Aubert. Tradition de la pensée classique. Paris: Librairie Philosophique J. Vrin, 2005.

————. "La théologie d'Antisthène." *Philosophia* 15–16 (1985–1986): 218–30.

————. "Libertà e fato in Enomao di Gadara." Pages 37–67 in *La filosofia in età imperiale: Le scuole e le tradizioni filosofiche. Atti del colloquio, Roma, 17–19 giugno 1999*, edited by Aldo Brancacci. Elenchos 31. Naples: Bibliopolis, 2000.

Branham, Robert Bracht, and Marie-Odile Goulet-Cazé, eds. *The Cynics: The Cynic Movement in Antiquity and Its Legacy.* HCS 23. Berkeley: University of California Press, 1996.

Bultmann, Rudolf. *Der Stil der paulinischen Predigt und die kynisch-stoische Diatribe.* FRLANT 13. Göttingen: Vandenhoeck & Ruprecht, 1910.

————. *Die Geschichte der synoptischen Tradition* [1921]. 10th ed. Göttingen: Vandenhoeck & Ruprecht, 1995.

————. *The History of the Synoptic Tradition.* Translated by John Marsh. Oxford: Basil Blackwell, 1963.

Cameron, Ron. "'What Have You Come Out to See?' Characterizations of John and Jesus in the Gospels." *Semeia* 49 (1990): 35–69.

Casey, Philip Maurice. "The Role of Aramaic in Reconstructing the Teaching of Jesus." Pages 1343–75 in *The Study of Jesus*, vol. 2 of Holmén and Porter, *Handbook for the Study of the Historical Jesus.*

Collins, John J. *Jewish Cult and Hellenistic Culture: Essays on the Jewish Encounter with Hellenism and Roman Rule.* JSJSup 100. Leiden: Brill, 2005.

Collins, John J., and Gregory E. Sterling, eds. *Hellenism in the Land of Israel.* CJA 13. Notre Dame, IN: University of Notre Dame Press, 2001.

Courcelle, Pierre. "La figure du philosophe d'après les écrivains latins de l'antiquité." *JS* (1980): 85–101.

Crossan, John Dominic. *The Historical Jesus: The Life of a Mediterranean Jewish Peasant*. San Francisco: HarperSanFrancisco, 1991.

Delia, Diana. "The Population of Roman Alexandria." *TAPA* 118 (1988): 275–92.

Desmond, William D. *Cynics*. Ancient Philosophies 3. Berkeley: University of California Press, 2008.

Dibelius, Martin. *Formgeschichte des Evangeliums*. Tübingen: Mohr Siebeck, 1919. 4th ed., 1961.

Di Segni, Leah. "The Greek Inscriptions of Hammat-Gader." Pages 185–266 in *The Roman Baths of Hammat Gader: Final Report*, edited by Yizhar Hirschfeld. Jerusalem: Israel Exploration Society, 1997.

Dobbin, Robert. *The Cynic Philosophers from Diogenes to Julian*. London: Penguin Classics, 2013.

Dorandi, Tiziano, ed. *Diogenes Laertius: Lives of Eminent Philosophers*. CCTC 50. Cambridge: Cambridge University Press, 2013.

———. "Filodemo, Gli Stoici (PHerc. 155 e 339)." *CErc* 12 (1982): 91–133.

———. "La patria di Filodemo." *Philologus* 131 (1987): 254–56.

———. "La *Politeia* de Diogène de Sinope et quelques remarques sur sa pensée politique." Pages 57–68 in Goulet-Cazé and Goulet, *Le cynisme ancien et ses prolongements*.

Döring, Klaus. *Die Kyniker*. Faszination Philosophie. Bamberg: Buchner, 2006.

———. "Sokrates, die Sokratiker und die von ihnen begründeten Traditionen." Pages 139–364 in *Sophistik, Sokrates, Sokratik, Mathematik, Medizin*, vol. 2.1 of *Die Philosophie der Antike*, edited by Hellmut Flashar. Grundriß der Geschichte der Philosophie. Basle: Schwabe, 1998.

———. "'Spielereien mit verdecktem Ernst vermischt': Unterhaltsame Formen literarischer Wissensvermittlung bei Diogenes von Sinope und den frühen Kynikern." Pages 337–52 in *Vermittlung und Tradierung von Wissen in der griechischen Kultur*, edited by Wolfgang Kullmann and Jochen Althoff. Script Oralia 61. Tübingen: Narr, 1993.

Dorival, Gilles. "Cyniques et chrétiens au temps des Pères grecs." Pages 57–88 in *Valeurs dans le stoïcisme: Du Portique à nos jours. Mélanges en l'honneur de M. Le Doyen Spanneut*. Lille: Presses Universitaires de Lille, 1993.

———. "L'image des Cyniques chez les Pères grecs." Pages 419–43 in Goulet-Cazé and Goulet, *Le cynisme ancien et ses prolongements*.

Downing, F. Gerald. *Christ and the Cynics: Jesus and Other Radical Preachers in First Century Tradition*. Sheffield: JSOT Press, 1988.

———. "Contemporary Analogies to the Gospels and Acts: 'Genres' or 'Motifs'?" Pages 51–65 in *Synoptic Studies: The Ampleforth Conferences of 1982 and 1983*, edited by Christopher M. Tuckett. Sheffield: Sheffield Academic Press, 1984.

———. "A Cynic Preparation for Paul's Gospel for Jew and Greek, Slave and Free, Male and Female." *NTS* 42 (1996): 454–62.

———. *Cynics and Christian Origins*. Edinburgh: T&T Clark, 1992.

———. "Cynics and Early Christianity." Pages 281–304 in Goulet-Cazé and Goulet, *Le cynisme ancien et ses prolongements*.

———. *Cynics, Paul and the Pauline Churches: Cynics and Christian Origins II*. London: Routledge, 1988. 2nd ed., London: Routledge, 1998.

———. "Deeper Reflections on the Jewish Cynic Jesus." *JBL* 117 (1998): 97–104.

———. "A Genre for Q and a Socio-Cultural Context for Q: Comparing Sets of Similarities with Sets of Differences." *JSNT* 55 (1994): 3–26.

———. *Jesus and the Threat of Freedom*. London: SCM, 1987.

———. "Quite like Q. A Genre for 'Q': The 'Lives of the Cynic Philosophers.'" *Bib* 69 (1988): 196–225.

———. "The Social Contexts of Jesus the Teacher: Construction and Reconstruction." *NTS* 33 (1987): 439–51.

Dudley, Donald R. *A History of Cynicism: From Diogenes to the 6th Century A.D.* London: Bloomsbury, 1937.

Ebner, Martin. *Jesus—Ein Weisheitslehrer? Synoptische Weisheitslogien im Traditionsprozess*. Herders Biblische Studien 15. Freiburg im Breisgau, 1998.

———. "Kynische Jesusinterpretation: 'disciplined exaggeration'? Eine Anfrage." *BZ* 40 (1996): 93–100.

Eddy, Paul Rhodes. "Jesus as Diogenes? Reflections on the Cynic Jesus Thesis." *JBL* 115 (1996): 449–69.

Edwards, Mark J. "Satire and Verisimilitude: Christianity in Lucian's 'Peregrinus.'" *Historia* 38 (1989): 89–98.

Epp, Eldon J., and George W. MacRae, eds. *The New Testament and Its Modern Interpreters*. Bible and Its Modern Interpreters 3. Atlanta: Scholars Press, 1989.

Feldman, Louis H. "How Much Hellenism in the Land of Israel?" *JSJ* 33 (2002): 290–313.

Festugière, André Jean. *Antioche païenne et chrétienne: Libanius, Chrysostome et les moines de Syrie*. Paris: de Boccard, 1959.

Fischel, Henry A. "Studies in Cynicism and the Ancient Near East: The Transformation of a Chreia." Pages 372–411 in *Religions in Antiquity: Essays in*

Memory of Edwin Ramsdell Goodenough, edited by Jacob Neusner. Supplements to *Numen* 14. Leiden: Brill, 1968.

Follet, Simone. "Les cyniques dans la poésie épigrammatique à l'époque impériale." Pages 359–80 in Goulet-Cazé and Goulet, *Le cynisme ancien et ses prolongements*.

Foucault, Michel. *Le courage de la vérité: Le gouvernement de soi et des autres II; Cours au Collège de France, 1983-1984*. Edited by Frédéric Gros. Hautes études. Paris: Gallimard, 2009.

Frenschkowski, Marco. "Welche biographischen Kenntnisse von Jesus setzt die Logienquelle voraus? Beobachtungen zur Gattung von Q im Kontext antiker Spruchsammlungen." Pages 3–42 in *From Quest to Q: Festschrift James M. Robinson*, edited by Jon Ma Asgeirsson, Kristin de Troyer, and Marvin W. Meyer. BETL 156. Leuven: Leuven University Press, 2000.

Freyne, Sean. "Galilee in the Hellenistic through Byzantine Periods." *OEANE* 2:370–76.

Fritz, Kurt von. *Quellenuntersuchungen zu Leben und Philosophie des Diogenes von Sinope*. Philologus Supplement 18.2. Leipzig: Dieterich, 1926.

Fuentes González, Pedro Pablo. "En defensa del encuentro entre dos Perros, Antístenes y Diógenes: historia de una tensa amistad." *Cuadernos de Filología Clásica: Estudios griegos e indoeuropeos* 23 (2013): 225–67.

———. "Le *Démonax* de Lucien entre réalité et fiction." *Prometheus* 35 (2009): 139–58.

———. *Les diatribes de Télès*. Histoire des doctrines de l'antiquité classique 23. Paris: Librairie Philosophique J. Vrin, 1998.

———. "Néanthe de Cyzique." *DPhA* (2005) 4:587–94.

Funk, Robert B., Roy W. Hoover, and the Jesus Seminar. *The Five Gospels: What Did Jesus Really Say? The Search for the Authentic Words of Jesus; New Translation and Commentary*. Sonoma, CA: Polebridge, 1993.

Funk, Robert B., and the Jesus Seminar. *The Acts of Jesus: What Did Jesus Really Do? The Search for the Authentic Deeds of Jesus; Translation and Commentary*. San Francisco: HarperSanFrancisco, 1998.

———. *The Gospel of Jesus: According to the Jesus Seminar*. Santa Rosa, CA: Polebridge, 1999.

Gerhard, Gustav Adolf. "Zur Legende vom Kyniker Diogenes." *AR* 15 (1912): 388–408.

Giannantoni, Gabriele. *Socratis et Socraticorum Reliquiae*. 4 vols. Elenchos 18. Naples: Bibliopolis, 1990.

Goulet-Cazé, Marie-Odile. "A Comprehensive Catalogue of Known Cynic Philosophers." Pages 389–413 in Branham and Goulet-Cazé, *The Cynics*.

————. "Cratès de Thèbes." *DPhA* (1994) 2:496–500.

————, ed. *Diogène Laërce: Vies et doctrines des philosophes illustres* [1998]. 2nd ed. Paris: Le Livre de Poche, 1999.

————. "Diogène Laërce, Livre VI: Introduction, traduction et notes." Pages 655–772 in Goulet-Cazé, *Diogène Laërce*.

————. "Kynismus." *RAC* (2008) 22:631–87.

————. "La contestation de la loi dans le cynisme ancien." Pages 405–33 in "Actes du Colloque international: Les doctrines de la loi dans la philoso-phie de langue arabe et leurs contextes grecs et musulmans, Villejuif, 12–13 Juin 2007," edited by Maroun Aouad, *MUSJ* 61 (2008).

————. *L'ascèse cynique: un commentaire de Diogène Laërce VI 70–71* [1986]. Histoire des doctrines de l'antiquité classique 10. 2nd ed. Paris: Librairie Philosophique J. Vrin, 2001.

————. "Le cynisme à l'époque impériale." *ANRW* 2.36.4 (1990):2720–833.

————. "Le cynisme est-il une philosophie?" Pages 273–313 in *L'antiplatonisme dévoilé*, vol. 1 of *Contre Platon*, edited by Monique Dixsaut. Tradition de la pensée classique. Paris: Librairie Philosophique J. Vrin, 1993.

————. *Le cynisme, une philosophie antique.* Textes et Traditions 29. Paris: Librairie Philosophique J. Vrin, 2017.

————. "Le livre VI de Diogène Laërce: Analyse de sa structure et réflexions méthodologiques." *ANRW* 2.36.6:3881–4048.

————. "Les cyniques et la falsification de la monnaie: Avant-propos." Pages 5–29 in Paquet, *Les cyniques grecs*, 1992.

————. "Les cyniques et la religion." Pages 116–58 in Goulet-Cazé and Goulet, *Le cynisme ancien et ses prolongements*.

————. *Les Kynika du stoïcisme.* Hermes Einzelschriften 89. Stuttgart, 2003.

————. "Les premiers cyniques et la religion." Pages 117–58 in Goulet-Cazé and Goulet, *Le cynisme ancien et ses prolongements*.

————. "Maxime Héron d'Alexandrie." *DPhA* 4 (2005):348–63.

————. "Ménippe de Gadara." *DPhA* 4 (2005):467–75.

————. "Michel Foucault et sa vision du cynisme dans *Le courage de la vérité*." Pages 105–24 in *Michel Foucault: éthique et vérité, 1980–1984*, edited by Daniele Lorenzini, Ariane Revel, and Arianna Sforzini. Problèmes et con-troverses. Paris: Librairie Philosophique J. Vrin, 2013.

————. "Oinomaos de Gadara." *DPhA* 4 (2005):751–61.

————. "Pérégrinus surnommé Proteus." *DPhA* 5a (2012):199–230.

————. "Qui était le philosophe anonyme attaqué par Julien dans son *Discours* IX?" *Hermes* 136 (2008): 97–118.

————. "Religion and the Early Cynics." Pages 47–80 in Branham and Goulet-Cazé, *The Cynics*.

————. "Un syllogisme stoïcien sur la loi dans la doxographie de Diogène le Cynique: A propos de Diogène Laërce VI 72." *RhM* 125 (1982): 214–40.

————. "Une liste de disciples de Cratès le Cynique en Diogène Laërce 6, 95." *Hermes* 114 (1986): 247–52.

————. "Who Was the First Dog?" Pages 414–15 in Branham and Goulet-Cazé, *The Cynics*.

Goulet-Cazé, Marie-Odile, and Richard Goulet, eds. *Le cynisme ancien et ses prolongements.* Paris: Presses Universitaires de France, 1993.

Griffin, M. T. "Le mouvement cynique et les Romains: attraction et répulsion." Pages 241–58 in Goulet-Cazé and Goulet, *Le cynisme ancien et ses prolongements.*

Hadas, Moses. "Gadarenes in Pagan Literature." *CW* 25 (1931): 25–30.

Hadidi, Adnan. "Umm Qeis (ancient Gadara)." *OEANE* 5:281–82.

Hammerstaedt, Jürgen. "Der Kyniker Oenomaus von Gadara." *ANRW* 2.36.4 (1990):2834–65.

————. *Die Orakelkritik des Kynikers Oenomaus.* Beiträge zur klassischen Philologie 188. Frankfurt am Main: Athenäum, 1988.

————. "Le cynisme littéraire à l'époque impériale." Pages 399–418 in Goulet-Cazé and Goulet, *Le cynisme ancien et ses prolongements.*

Heinemann, Isaak. *Philons griechische und jüdische Bildung: Kulturvergleichende Untersuchungen zu Philons Darstellung der jüdischen Gesetze.* Breslau: M. & H. Marcus, 1932.

Hengel, Martin. *Die Zeloten: Untersuchungen zur jüdischen Freiheitsbewegung in der Zeit von Herodes I bis 70 n. Chr.* Leiden: Brill, 1976.

————. *Jews, Greeks and Barbarians: Aspects of the Hellenization of Judaism in the Pre-Christian Period.* Translated by John Bowden. Philadelphia: Fortress 1980.

————. *Judaism and Hellenism: Studies in Their Encounter in Palestine during the Early Hellenistic Period.* Translated by John Bowden. Philadelphia: Fortress, 1974.

————. *Juden, Griechen und Barbaren: Aspekte der Hellenisierung des Judentums in vorchristlicher Zeit.* SBS 76. Stuttgart: Katholisches Bibelwerk, 1976.

————. *Judentum und Hellenismus.* WUNT 10. Tübingen: Mohr Siebeck, 1969.

Hengel, Martin, in collaboration with Christoph Markschies. *The "Hellenization" of Judaea in the First Century after Christ.* London: SCM, 1989.

Hezser, Catherine. "Die Verwendung der hellenistischen Gattung Chrie im frühen Christentum und Judentum." *JSJ* 27 (1996): 371–439.

Hicks, Robert D. *Diogenes Laertius*. 2 vols. LCL. Cambridge, MA: Harvard University Press, 1925.

Hock, Ronald F. "Simon the Shoemaker as an Ideal Cynic." *GRBS* 17 (1976): 41–53. Reprint, pages 259–71 in Billerbeck, *Die Kyniker in der modernen Forschung*.

———. *The Social Context of Paul's Ministry: Tentmaking and Apostleship*. Philadelphia: Fortress, 1980.

Hock, Ronald F., and Edward N. O'Neil. *The Progymnasmata*. Vol. 1 of *The Chreia in Ancient Rhetoric I*. SBLTT 27. Atlanta: Scholars Press, 1986.

Hoffmann, Paul, and Christoph Heil. *Die Spruchquelle Q: Studienausgabe Griechisch und Deutsch* [2002]. 4th ed. Darmstadt: Wissenschaftliche Buchgesellschaft, 2013.

Höistad, Ragnar. "Cynic Hero and Cynic King: Studies in the Cynic Conception of Man." PhD diss., University of Uppsala, 1948.

Holmén, Tom, and Stanley E. Porter. *Handbook for the Study of the Historical Jesus*. 4 vols. Leiden: Brill, 2011.

Horsley, Richard A. *Sociology and the Jesus Movement*. New York: Crossroad, 1989.

Husson, Suzanne. *La "République" de Diogène: Une cité en quête de la nature*. Histoire des doctrines de l'Antiquité classique 40. Paris: Librairie Philosophique J. Vrin, 2011.

Johnson, Luke Timothy. *The Real Jesus: The Misguided Quest for the Historical Jesus and the Truth of the Traditional Gospels*. San Francisco: HarperSanFrancisco, 1996.

Jones, Christopher P. "Le cas de Pérégrinus Proteus." Pages 305–17 in Goulet-Cazé and Goulet, *Le cynisme ancien et ses prolongements*.

Jouan, Francis. "Le Diogène de Dion Chrysostome." Pages 381–97 in Goulet-Cazé and Goulet, *Le cynisme ancien et ses prolongements*.

Kee, Howard Clark. "Synoptic Studies." Pages 245–69 in Epp and MacRae, *New Testament and Its Modern Interpreters*.

Kindstrand, Jan Fredrik, ed. *Bion of Borysthenes: A Collection of the Fragments with Introduction and Commentary*. Acta Universitatis Upsaliensis, Studia Graeca Upsaliensia 11. Uppsala: Almqvist & Wiksell, 1976.

———. "Diogenes Laertius and the Chreia Tradition." *Elenchos* 7 (1986): 217–43.

Kloppenborg, John S. *Excavating Q: The History and Setting of the Sayings Gospel*. Minneapolis: Fortress, 2000.

———. *The Formation of Q: Trajectories in Ancient Wisdom Collections*. SAC. Philadelphia: Fortress, 1987.

Krueger, Derek. "The Bawdy and Society: The Shamelessness of Diogenes in Roman Imperial Culture." Pages 222–39 in Branham and Goulet-Cazé, *The Cynics*.

———. "Diogenes the Cynic among the Fourth Century Fathers." *VC* 47 (1993): 29–49.

———. *Symeon the Holy Fool: Leontius's Life and the Late Antique City*. Transformations of the Classical Heritage 25. Berkeley: University of California Press, 1996.

Kusch, Horst. "Diogenes von Sinope." *RAC* 3 (1957):1063–75.

Labriolle, Pierre de. *La Réaction païenne: Étude sur la polémique antichrétienne du Ier au VIe siècle*. Paris: L'Artisan du livre, 1934.

Lang, Bernhard. *Jesus der Hund: Leben und Lehre eines jüdischen Kynikers*. Munich: Beck, 2010.

Lieberman, Saul. *Greek in Jewish Palestine; Hellenism in Jewish Palestine*. With a new introduction by Dov Zlotnick. New York: Jewish Theological Seminary of America, 1994.

———. *Greek in Jewish Palestine: Studies in the Life and Manners of Jewish Palestine in the II–IV Centuries CE*. New York: Jewish Theological Seminary of America, 1942.

———. *Hellenism in Jewish Palestine*. New York: Jewish Theological Seminary of America, 1950.

———. "How Much Greek in Jewish Palestine?" Pages 123–41 in *Biblical and Other Studies*, edited by Alexander Altmann. Cambridge, MA: Harvard University Press, 1963.

Lifshitz, Baruch. "L'hellénisation des Juifs de Palestine: A propos des inscriptions de Besara (Beth-Shearim)." *RB* 72 (1965): 520–38.

Livrea, Enrico. *Studi Cercidei (P. Oxy. 1082)*. Papyrologische Texte und Abhandlungen 37. Bonn: R. Habelt, 1986.

Lomiento, Liana, ed. *Cercidas, testimonia et fragmenta*. Lyricorum Graecorum quae exstant 10. Roma: Gruppo Editoriale Internazionale, 1993.

López Cruces, Juan L. *Les Méliambes de Cercidas de Mégalopolis: Politique et tradition littéraire*. Classical and Byzantine Monographs 32. Amsterdam: A. M. Hakkert, 1995.

———. "Une tragédie perdue: l'*Héraclès* de Diogène le cynique." *Les études classiques* 78 (2010): 3–24.

Luck, Georg. *Die Weisheit der Hunde: Texte der antiken Kyniker in deutscher Übersetzung*. Stuttgart: Alfred Kröner, 1997.

Luz, Menahem. "Abnimos, Nimos and Oenomaus: A Note." *JQR* 77 (1986–1987): 191–95.

———. "A Description of the Greek Cynic in the Jerusalem Talmud." *JSJ* 20 (1989): 49–60.

———. "Oenomaus and Talmudic Anecdote." *JSJ* 23 (1992): 42–80.

Mack, Burton L. *The Lost Gospel: The Book of Q and Christian Origins*. San Francisco: HarperSanFrancisco, 1993.

———. *A Myth of Innocence: Mark and Christian Origins*. Minneapolis: Fortress, 1984.

Malherbe, Abraham J. "Antisthenes and Odysseus and Paul at War." *HTR* 76, no. 2 (1983): 143–73. Reprint, pages 91–119 in Malherbe, *Paul and the Popular Philosophers*.

———. "The Beasts at Ephesus." *JBL* 87 (1968): 71–80. Reprint, pages 79–89 in Malherbe, *Paul and the Popular Philosophers*.

———. *The Cynic Epistles*. SBLSBS 12. Missoula, MT: Scholars Press, 1977.

———. "Exhortation in 1 Thessalonians." *NovT* 25 (1983): 238–56. Reprint, pages 49–66 in Malherbe, *Paul and the Popular Philosophers*.

———. "'Gentle as a Nurse': The Cynic Background to 1 Thessalonians 2." *NovT* 12, no. 2 (1970): 203–17. Reprint, pages 35–48 in Malherbe, *Paul and the Popular Philosophers*.

———. "Hellenistic Moralists and the New Testament." *ANRW* 2.26.1 (1992):267–333.

———. *Paul and the Popular Philosophers*. Minneapolis: Fortress, 1986.

———. *Paul and the Thessalonians: The Philosophical Tradition of Pastoral Care*. Philadelphia: Fortress, 1987.

Marguerat, Daniel. "La 'troisième quête' du Jésus de l'histoire." *RSR* 87 (1999): 397–421.

Meyers, Eric M., and James F. Strange. *Archaeology, the Rabbis, and Early Christianity*. Nashville: Abingdon, 1981.

Mittmann, Siegfried. *Beiträge zur Siedlungs- und Territorialgeschichte des nördlichen Ostjordanlandes*. ADPV. Wiesbaden: Harrassowitz, 1970.

Moles, John. "Cynic Influence upon First-Century Judaism and Early Christianity." Pages 89–116 in *The Limits of Ancient Biography*, edited by Brian McGing and Judith Mossman. Swansea: Classical Press of Wales, 2006.

———. "'Honestius quam ambitiosius'? An Exploration of the Cynic's Attitude to Moral Corruption in His Fellow Men." *JHS* 103 (1983): 103–23.

———. "Le cosmopolitisme cynique." Pages 259–80 in Goulet-Cazé and Goulet, *Le cynisme ancien et ses prolongements*. English version: "Cynic Cosmopolitanism." Pages 105–20 in Branham and Goulet-Cazé, *The Cynics*.

Morenz, Siegfried. "Ein koptischer Diogenes: Griechischer Novellenstoff in ägyptischer Mönchserzählung." ZÄSA 77 (1941): 52–54.

Morgan, Teresa. *Popular Morality in the Early Roman Empire*. Cambridge: Cambridge University Press, 2007.

Müseler, Eike, ed. *Die Kynikerbriefe: Kritische Ausgabe mit deutscher Übersetzung*. Studien zur Geschichte und Kultur des Altertums 1.7. Paderborn: F. Schöningh, 1994.

Nesselrath, Heinz-Günther. "Libanios und die Mönche." Pages 243–67 in *Von Homer bis Landino: Beiträge zur Antike und Spätantike sowie zu deren Rezeptions-und Wirkungsgeschichte. Festgabe für Antonie Wlosok zum 80. Geburtstag*, edited by Beate Regina Suchla. Berlin: Pro Business GmbH, 2011.

———. "Lucien et le cynisme." *AC* 67 (1998): 121–35.

———. "Lukian von Samosata." *RAC* 23:676–702.

Neusner, Jacob. *Judaism in the Beginning of Christianity*. Philadelphia: Fortress, 1984.

———. *Le judaïsme à l'aube du christianisme*. Translated by J.-P. Bagot. Paris: Cerf, 1986.

Niehues-Pröbsting, Heinrich. *Der Kynismus des Diogenes und der Begriff des Zynismus*. München: Fink, 1979.

Overwien, Oliver. "Das Gnomologium, das Gnomologium Vaticanum und die Tradition." *GFA* 4 (2001): 99–131. https://gfa.gbv.de/dr,gfa,004,2001,a,05.pdf.

———. *Die Sprüche des Kynikers Diogenes in der griechischen und arabischen Überlieferung*. Hermes Einzelschriften 92. Stuttgart: Franz Steiner Verlag, 2005.

Paquet, Léonce. *Les cyniques grecs: Fragments et témoignages* [1975]. 2nd ed. Philosophica 35. Ottawa: Presses de l'Université d'Ottawa, 1988.

———. *Les cyniques grecs: Fragments et témoignages*. Choix, traduction, introduction et notes par Léonce Paquet. Les Classiques de la Philosophie. Paris: Le Livre de Poche, 1992.

Patzer, Andreas. *Antisthenes der Sokratiker: Das literarische Werk und die Philosophie, dargestellt am Katalog der Schriften*. PhD diss. [Teildruck], Heidelberg University, 1970.

Pilhofer, Peter. "Das Bild der christlichen Gemeinden in Lukians *Peregrinos*." Pages 97–110 in Pilhofer, Baumbach, Gerlach, and Hansen, *Lukian, Der Tod des Peregrinos*.

Pilhofer, Peter, Manuel Baumbach, Jens Gerlach, and Dirk U. Hansen, eds.

Lukian, Der Tod des Peregrinos: Ein Scharlatan auf dem Scheiterhaufen.
Sapere 9. Darmstadt: Wissenschaftliche Buchgesellschaft, 2005.

Pizzone, A. "Solone, Diogene e la *paracharaxis*: Contributo alla storia di un'immagine e della sua fortuna." *Acme* 55 (2002): 91–116.

Porter, Stanley E. "The Context of Jesus: Jewish and/or Hellenistic?" Pages 1441–63 in *The Study of Jesus*, vol. 2 of Holmén and Porter, *Handbook for the Study of the Historical Jesus.*

—————. *The Criteria for Authenticity in Historical-Jesus Research: Previous Discussion and New Proposals.* JSNTSup 191. Sheffield: Sheffield Academic Press, 2000.

—————. "The Language(s) Jesus Spoke." Pages 2455–71 in *The Historical Jesus*, vol. 3 of Holmén and Porter, *Handbook for the Study of the Historical Jesus.*

—————. "The Role of Greek Language Criteria in Historical Jesus Research." Pages 361–404 in *The Study of Jesus*, vol. 2 of Holmén and Porter, *Handbook for the Study of the Historical Jesus.*

Praechter, Karl. *Die Philosophie des Altertums.* 12th ed. Berlin, 1926 = vol. 1 of *Friedrich Überwegs Grundriß der Geschichte der Philosophie.*

Robinson, James M. "*LOGOI SOPHON*: On the Gattung of Q." Pages 71–113 in *Trajectories through Early Christianity*, edited by James M. Robinson and Helmut Koester. Philadelphia: Fortress, 1971.

—————. "Zur Gattung der Spruchquelle Q." Pages 77–96 in *Zeit und Geschichte: Dankesgabe an Rudolf Bultmann zum 80. Geburtstag*, edited by Erich Dinkler. Tübingen: J. C. B. Mohr, 1964.

Robinson, James M., Paul Hoffmann, and John S. Kloppenborg. *The Critical Edition of Q: Synopsis Including the Gospel of Matthew and Luke, Mark and Thomas with English, German, and French Translations of Q and Thomas.* Minneapolis: Fortress; Leuven: Peeters, 2000.

Sato, Migaku. *Q und Prophetie: Studien zur Gattungs- und Traditionsgeschichte der Quelle Q.* WUNT 2.29. Tübingen: Mohr Siebeck, 1988.

Schirren, Thomas. "Lukian über die ΚΑΙΝΗ ΤΕΛΕΤΗ der Christen (De morte Peregrini 11)." *Philologus* 149 (2005): 354–59.

Schmeller, Thomas. *Paulus und die "Diatribe": Eine vergleichende Stilinterpretation.* NTAbh NF 19. Münster in Westfalen: Aschendorff, 1987.

Schürer, Emil. *The History of the Jewish People in the Age of Jesus Christ (175 B.C.–A.D. 135).* New English rev. ed. by Geza Vermes, Fergus Millar, Matthew Black. Vol. 2. Edinburgh: T&T Clark, 1979.

Schwartz, Jacques, ed. *Lucien de Samosate: Philopseudès et De morte Peregrini.* Publications de la Faculté des Lettres de l'Université de Strasbourg. Textes d'étude 12. 1951. 2nd ed. Paris: Belles Lettres, 1963.

Speigl, Jakob. *Der Römische Staat und die Christen: Staat und Kirche von Domitian bis Commodus.* Amsterdam: A. M. Hakkert, 1970.

Stern, Menahem. *Greek and Latin Authors on Jews and Judaism: Edited with Introductions, Translations and Commentary.* Fontes ad res judaicas spectantes. Jerusalem: The Israel Academy of Sciences and Humanities. Vol. 1: From Herodotus to Plutarch, 1974. Vol. 2: From Tacitus to Simpticius, 1980.

Stowers, Stanley K. *The Diatribe and Paul's Letter to the Romans.* SBLDS 57. Chico, CA: Scholars Press, 1981.

Talbert, Charles H. *What Is a Gospel? The Genre of the Canonical Gospels.* Philadelphia: Fortress, 1977.

Tcherikover, Victor. *Hellenistic Civilization and the Jews* [1959]. 3rd ed. Translated by S. Applebaum. Philadelphia: Jewish Publication Society of America, 1966.

Theissen, Gerd. *Sociology of Early Palestinian Christianity.* Translated by John Bowden. Philadelphia: Fortress, 1978.

———. *Soziologie der Jesusbewegung: Ein Beitrag zur Entstehungsgeschichte des Urchristentums.* Theologische Existenz heute 194. Munich: Kaiser, 1977.

———. *Studien zur Soziologie des Urchristentums.* 3rd ed. WUNT 19. Tübingen: Mohr Siebeck, 1989.

———. "Wanderradikalismus: Literatursoziologische Aspekte der Überlieferung von Worten Jesu im Urchristentum." *ZTK* 70 (1973): 245–71.

Thiede, Carsten Peter. *The Cosmopolitan World of Jesus: New Findings from Archaeology.* London: SPCK, 2004.

Troeltsch, Ernst. *Die Soziallehren der christlichen Kirchen und Gruppen.* Vol. 1 of *Gesammelte Schriften.* Tübingen: Mohr Siebeck, 1912.

Tuckett, Christopher. M. "A Cynic Q?" *Biblica* 70 (1989): 349–76.

———. "On the Stratification of Q: A Response." *Semeia* 55 (1992): 213–22.

Vaage, Leif E. *Galilean Upstarts: Jesus' First Followers according to Q.* Valley Forge, PA: Trinity Press International, 1994.

———. "Jewish Scripture, Q and the Historical Jesus: A Cynic Way with the Word?" Pages 479–95 in *The Sayings Source Q and the Historical Jesus,* edited by Andreas Lindemann. Leuven: Leuven University Press, 2001.

———. "Q: The Ethos and Ethics of an Itinerant Radicalism." PhD diss., Claremont Graduate School, 1987.

———. "Q and Cynicism: On Comparison and Social Identity." Pages 199–229 in *The Gospel Behind the Gospels: Current Studies on Q,* edited by Roland A. Piper. NovTSup 75. Leiden: Brill, 1995.

————. "Q1 and the Historical Jesus: Some Peculiar Sayings (7:33–34; 9:57–58, 59–60; 14:26– 27)." *Forum* 5, no. 2 (1989): 159–76.

Vanderkam, James C. "Greek at Qumran." Pages 175–81 in Collins and Sterling, *Hellenism in the Land of Israel.*

Weber, Thomas Maria. *Gadara-Umm Qēs. Gadara Decapolitana: Untersuchungen zur Topographie, Geschichte, Architektur und der bildenden Kunst einer "Polis Hellenis" im Ostjordanland.* ADPV 30. Wiesbaden: Otto Harrassowitz, 2002.

Weisse, Christian Hermann. *Die evangelische Geschichte, kritisch und philosophisch bearbeitet.* 2 vols. Leipzig: Breitkopf & Hartel, 1838.

Williams, Margaret H. *The Jews among the Greeks and Romans: A Diasporan Sourcebook.* Baltimore: Johns Hopkins University Press, 1998.

INDEX OF AUTHORS

INDEX OF SCRIPTURE REFERENCES

INDEX OF OTHER ANCIENT TEXTS